The Complete Mediterranean Diet
Cookbook for Beginners

2000 Days Super Easy & Mouthwatering Recipes for Living and
Eating Well Every Day | No-Stress 30 Day Meal Plans

Gladys F. Cohen

Table of Contents

INTRODUCTION

As a mother of two young children, I am always looking for ways to provide nutritious and delicious meals for my family. When I discovered the Mediterranean diet, I was immediately drawn to its emphasis on whole, nutrient-dense foods and its proven health benefits. Not only has this way of eating transformed my own health, but it has also become a staple in my family's daily routine.

I am thrilled to share with you my collection of Mediterranean-inspired recipes, which includes breakfast options, snacks, desserts, poultry, fish and seafood, salads, and more. Each recipe has been thoughtfully crafted to incorporate the flavors and ingredients of the Mediterranean region, while also being easy to prepare and family-friendly.

One of the things I love most about the Mediterranean diet is that it's not about restriction or deprivation, but rather about celebrating the abundance of fresh, whole foods that are available. In this cookbook, you will find plenty of delicious and satisfying meals that are packed with nutrients and flavor, such as lemon and herb fish packets, citrus-roasted broccoli florets and wheat berry pilaf.

But the Mediterranean diet is not just about the food itself; it's also about the lifestyle that goes along with it. Taking time to savor meals with loved ones, enjoying regular physical activity, and cultivating a sense of community are all integral parts of this way of life. I hope that this cookbook not only provides you with delicious meal ideas, but also inspires you to embrace the Mediterranean way of living and all of its health benefits.

Thank you for joining me on this journey towards vibrant health and delicious eating. I can't wait for you to try these recipes and discover the joys of the Mediterranean diet for yours

Chapter 1 Mediterranean Diet 101

What is Mediterranean Diet?

The Mediterranean diet is a way of eating that is inspired by the traditional cuisine of countries bordering the Mediterranean Sea, such as Greece, Italy, and Spain. This diet has gained popularity over the years due to its numerous health benefits, including reducing the risk of chronic diseases such as heart disease, stroke, and diabetes.

At the core of the Mediterranean diet is an emphasis on whole, plant-based foods such as fruits, vegetables, whole grains, nuts, and legumes. These foods provide a wide range of vitamins, minerals, and fiber, which are essential for maintaining optimal health. In addition to plant-based foods, the Mediterranean diet also includes moderate amounts of lean protein, such as fish, chicken, and eggs.

Healthy fats are a key component of the Mediterranean diet, and olive oil is a staple ingredient. Olive oil is rich in monounsaturated fats, which have been shown to improve cholesterol levels and reduce inflammation. Other healthy sources of fat in the Mediterranean diet include nuts, seeds, and fatty fish like salmon and sardines.

The Mediterranean diet also emphasizes the importance of enjoying meals with family and friends, and savoring the flavors of fresh, locally sourced ingredients. In addition to its health benefits, this way of eating has been shown to promote overall well-being and a positive relationship with food.

Overall, the Mediterranean diet is a flexible and sustainable way of eating that offers numerous health benefits. By focusing on whole, plant-based foods, healthy fats, and moderate amounts of lean protein, individuals can improve their health and enjoy delicious, flavorful meals that promote longevity and vitality.

The Benefits of Mediterranean Diet

◆ Reduced risk of heart disease: Research has consistently shown that following a Mediterranean diet can help lower the risk of heart disease. This is due to the high intake of heart-healthy foods such as fruits, vegetables, whole grains, nuts, and healthy fats.

◆ Improved brain function: The Mediterranean diet has been linked to improved cognitive function and a reduced risk of dementia and Alzheimer's disease.

◆ Lower risk of certain cancers: Studies have suggested that following a Mediterranean diet may help lower the risk of certain cancers, such as breast, colon, and prostate cancer.

◆ Better weight management: The Mediterranean diet emphasizes whole, nutrient-dense foods that are low in calories, making it an effective approach for weight management.

◆ Improved blood sugar control: The Mediterranean diet may help improve blood sugar control in individuals with type 2 diabetes, due to its emphasis on whole grains, fruits, vegetables, and healthy fats.

◆ Reduced inflammation: The high intake of antioxidant-rich foods in the Mediterranean diet may help reduce inflammation in the body, which is a key factor in the development of many chronic diseases.

◆ Longer lifespan: Studies have shown that following a Mediterranean diet is associated with a longer lifespan and a reduced risk of premature death.

The Mediterranean Diet Pyramid

Overall, the Mediterranean diet is a highly nutritious, sustainable way of eating that offers numerous health benefits. By emphasizing whole, nutrient-dense foods and healthy fats, individuals can improve their health, reduce their risk of chronic diseases, and enjoy delicious, flavorful meals.

The Mediterranean Diet Pyramid is a visual representation of the traditional Mediterranean diet, which has been recognized as a healthy and sustainable way of eating by the scientific community. The pyramid is divided into several levels, each representing different food groups and recommended serving sizes.

At the base of the pyramid are whole, minimally processed plant-based foods such as fruits, vegetables, whole grains, and legumes. These foods are rich in fiber, vitamins, minerals, and phytonutrients, and form the foundation of the Mediterranean diet. The pyramid recommends consuming these foods daily in abundance, as they provide the body with essential nutrients and help promote overall health.

The next level of the pyramid includes healthy fats such as olive oil, nuts, and seeds. These foods provide the body with essential fatty acids, which are important for maintaining optimal health. The pyramid recommends consuming these foods in moderation on a daily basis.

The third level of the pyramid includes lean protein sources such as fish, poultry, eggs, and dairy products. These foods are consumed in moderation and provide the body with essential amino acids, which are important for muscle growth and repair.

At the top of the pyramid are foods that should be consumed sparingly, such as red meat, sweets, and processed foods. These foods are high in saturated and trans fats, refined sugars, and sodium, and should be consumed in limited amounts as part of a healthy, balanced diet.

In addition to the food groups, the Mediterranean Diet Pyramid also emphasizes the importance of physical activity and social connections. Regular physical activity is important for maintaining a healthy weight, reducing the risk of chronic diseases, and improving overall well-being. Social connections, such as sharing meals with family and friends, have been shown to promote a positive relationship with food and overall health.

The Mediterranean Diet Pyramid is a flexible and adaptable framework that encourages individuals to make healthy food choices that align with their cultural and personal preferences. By emphasizing whole, nutrient-dense foods and healthy fats, and limiting processed and high-sugar foods, individuals can improve their health, reduce their risk of chronic diseases, and enjoy delicious, flavorful meals that promote longevity and vitality.

Food to Eat and Avoid

Foods to Eat	Foods to Minimize or Avoid
Fruits (e.g. berries, apples, oranges, grapes)	Processed foods (e.g. packaged snacks, frozen meals)
Vegetables (e.g. spinach, broccoli, tomatoes, eggplant)	Refined sugars (e.g. candy, cookies, cake)
Whole grains (e.g. quinoa, brown rice, whole grain bread)	Sweets (e.g. ice cream, chocolate bars)
Legumes (e.g. chickpeas, lentils, black beans)	Sweetened beverages (e.g. soda, juice, energy drinks)
Nuts and seeds (e.g. almonds, cashews, pumpkin seeds)	Red meat (e.g. beef, pork, lamb)
Fish and seafood (e.g. salmon, sardines, shrimp)	Processed meats (e.g. bacon, sausage, deli meats)
Poultry (e.g. chicken, turkey)	High-fat dairy products (e.g. cheese, butter, cream)
Olive oil	Butter and margarine
Herbs and spices (e.g. oregano, basil, garlic, cinnamon)	High-sodium foods (e.g. canned soup, potato chips)

Remember, this is not an exhaustive list, and you can be creative with your meal choices as long as you focus on incorporating more whole, nutrient-dense foods into your diet and limiting your intake of processed and high-sugar foods.

6 Tips to Getting Started with the Mediterranean Diet

Start with the basics: Begin by incorporating more whole, minimally processed plant-based foods into your diet, such as fruits, vegetables, whole grains, and legumes. Aim to fill at least half of your plate with these foods at every meal.

Emphasize healthy fats: Use healthy fats such as olive oil, nuts, and seeds in place of saturated and trans fats such as butter and margarine. Drizzle olive oil over your salads, use it for cooking and roasting vegetables, and snack on nuts and seeds.

Choose lean protein sources: Opt for lean protein sources such as fish, poultry, eggs, and dairy products in moderation. Try incorporating fish into your diet at least twice a week, such as grilled salmon or baked cod.

Reduce your intake of processed and high-sugar foods: Limit your consumption of processed and high-sugar foods such as sweets, pastries, and sugary drinks. Instead, enjoy fresh fruit as a dessert or snack, and satisfy your sweet tooth with a small piece of dark chocolate.

Experiment with Mediterranean flavors: Explore new Mediterranean flavors by incorporating herbs and spices such as oregano, thyme, rosemary, and garlic into your cooking. Try making a homemade hummus dip with chickpeas, tahini, and lemon juice, or a Greek salad with feta cheese, olives, and cucumber.

Stay hydrated: Drink plenty of water throughout the day, and enjoy a glass of red wine in moderation if desired.

Remember, the Mediterranean diet is all about balance and flexibility, so don't be afraid to experiment with new foods and flavors, and make it work for your individual needs and preferences.

30 Days Mediterranean Diet Meal Plan

DAYS	BREAKFAST	LUNCH	DINNER	SNACK/DESSERT
1	Buffalo Egg Cups	Spinach and Paneer Cheese	Zesty Cabbage Soup	Marinated Olives
2	Strawberry Basil Honey Ricotta Toast	Mini Moroccan Pumpkin Cakes	Spicy Wilted Greens with Garlic	Classic Hummus with Tahini
3	Kagianas	Zucchini Pomodoro	Mediterranean Lentil Sloppy Joes	Salmon-Stuffed Cucumbers
4	Homemade Pumpkin Parfait	Roasted Cauliflower and Tomatoes	Rustic Cauliflower and Carrot Hash	Lemon-Pepper Chicken Drumsticks
5	Breakfast Farro with Dried Fruit and Nuts	Coriander-Cumin Roasted Carrots	Crispy Green Beans	Taco-Spiced Chickpeas
6	Savory Cottage Cheese Breakfast Bowl	Puff Pastry Turnover with Roasted Vegetables	Garlic and Herb Roasted Grape Tomatoes	Sardine and Herb Bruschetta
7	Strawberry Collagen Smoothie	Parmesan and Herb Sweet Potatoes	Roasted Broccolini with Garlic and Romano	Red Lentils with Sumac
8	ortobello Eggs Benedict	Chopped Tuna Salad	Herbed Shiitake Mushrooms	Lemon Shrimp with Garlic Olive Oil
9	Honey-Apricot Granola with Greek Yogurt	Citrus Asparagus with Pistachios	Root Vegetable Hash	Sweet Potato Hummus
10	Sunny-Side Up Baked Eggs with Swiss Chard, Feta, and Basil	Toasted Pita Wedges	Green Beans with Pine Nuts and Garlic	Baked Eggplant Baba Ganoush
11	Poached Eggs on Whole Grain Avocado Toast	Stuffed Artichokes	Garlic Zucchini and Red Peppers	Sfougato
12	C+C Overnight Oats	Greek Stewed Zucchini	Baba Ghanoush	Stuffed Fried Mushrooms
13	Red Pepper and Feta Egg Bites	Spanish Green Beans	Corn Croquettes	Savory Mediterranean Popcorn
14	Herb & Cheese Fritters	Brown Rice and Vegetable Pilaf	Broccoli Salad	Quick Garlic Mushrooms
15	Peachy Green Smoothie	Cucumbers with Feta, Mint, and Sumac	Turkish Stuffed Eggplant	Spiced Maple Nuts
16	Almond Date Oatmeal	Caramelized Root Vegetables	Caramelized Eggplant with Harissa Yogurt	Mini Lettuce Wraps
17	Baked Egg and Mushroom Cups	Cheesy Cauliflower Tots	Green Veg & Macadamia Smash	Cretan Cheese Pancakes
18	Crunchy Vanilla Protein Bars	Asparagus Fries	Traditional Greek Salad	Crunchy Sesame Cookies

DAYS	BREAKFAST	LUNCH	DINNER	SNACK/DESSERT
19	Breakfast Quinoa with Figs and Walnuts	Herb Vinaigrette Potato Salad	Lemon and Herb Fish Packets	Crispy Apple Phyllo Tart
20	Grilled Halloumi with Whole-Wheat Pita Bread	Balsamic Beets	Easy Greek Salad	Spanish Cream
21	Mediterranean Muesli and Breakfast Bowl	Hearty Minestrone Soup	Traditional Greek Salad	Almond Cookies
22	Peachy Oatmeal with Pecans	Wild Mushroom Soup	Mediterranean Quinoa and Garbanzo Salad	Banana Cream Pie Parfaits
23	Baklava Hot Porridge	Dill-and-Garlic Beets	Chopped Greek Antipasto Salad	Almond Rice Pudding
24	Jalapeño Popper Egg Cups	Mashed Sweet Potato Tots	Lentil and Spinach Curry	Fruit Compote
25	Spinach and Mushroom Mini Quiche	Paprika Crab Burgers	Sicilian Salad	Tortilla Fried Pies
26	Tortilla Española (Spanish Omelet)	Spicy Creamer Potatoes	Turkish Shepherd'S Salad	Steamed Dessert Bread
27	Oat and Fruit Parfait	Melitzanes Yiahni (Braised Eggplant)	Black Chickpeas	Almond Pistachio Biscotti
28	Ricotta and Fruit Bruschetta	Sweet and Crispy Roasted Pearl Onions	Lemon and Garlic Rice Pilaf	Fresh Figs with Chocolate Sauce
29	Egg Salad with Red Pepper and Dill	Cauliflower Steaks with Creamy Tahini Sauce	Wheat Berry Pilaf	Tahini Baklava Cups
30	Black Olive Toast with Herbed Hummus	Beet and Watercress Salad with Orange and Dill	Fish Tagine	Asiago Shishito Peppers

Chapter 2 Breakfasts

Buffalo Egg Cups

Prep time: 10 minutes | Cook time: 15 minutes | Serves 2

4 large eggs
2 ounces (57 g) full-fat cream cheese

2 tablespoons buffalo sauce
½ cup shredded sharp Cheddar cheese

1. Crack eggs into two ramekins. 2. In a small microwave-safe bowl, mix cream cheese, buffalo sauce, and Cheddar. Microwave for 20 seconds and then stir. Place a spoonful into each ramekin on top of the eggs. 3. Place ramekins into the air fryer basket. 4. Adjust the temperature to 320ºF (160ºC) and bake for 15 minutes. 5. Serve warm.

Per Serving:
calories: 354 | fat: 29g | protein: 21g | carbs: 3g | fiber: 0g | sodium: 343mg

Strawberry Basil Honey Ricotta Toast

Prep time: 10 minutes | Cook time: 0 minutes | Serves 2

4 slices of whole-grain bread
½ cup ricotta cheese (whole milk or low-fat)
1 tablespoon honey

Sea salt
1 cup fresh strawberries, sliced
4 large fresh basil leaves, sliced into thin shreds

1. Toast the bread. 2. In a small bowl, combine the ricotta, honey, and a pinch or two of sea salt. Taste and add additional honey or salt if desired. 3. Spread the mixture evenly over each slice of bread (about 2 tablespoons per slice). 4. Top each piece with sliced strawberries and a few pieces of shredded basil.

Per Serving:
calories: 275 | fat: 8g | protein: 15g | carbs: 41g | fiber: 5g | sodium: 323mg

Kagianas

Prep time: 5 minutes | Cook time: 10 minutes | Serves 2

2 teaspoons extra virgin olive oil
2 tablespoons finely chopped onion (any variety)
¼ teaspoon fine sea salt, divided
1 medium tomato (any variety), chopped

2 eggs
1 ounce (28 g) crumbled feta
½ teaspoon dried oregano
1 teaspoon chopped fresh mint
Pinch of freshly ground black pepper for serving

1. Heat the olive oil in a small pan placed over medium heat. When the oil begins to shimmer, add the onions along with ⅛ teaspoon sea salt. Sauté for about 3 minutes or until the onions are soft. 2. Add the tomatoes, stir, then reduce the heat to low and simmer for 8 minutes or until the mixture thickens. 3. While the tomatoes are cooking, beat the eggs in a small bowl. 4. When the tomatoes have thickened, pour the eggs into the pan and increase the heat to medium. Continue cooking, using a spatula to stir the eggs and tomatoes continuously, for 2–3 minutes or until the eggs are set. Remove the pan from the heat. 5. Add the feta, oregano, and mint, and stir to combine. 6. Transfer to a plate. Top with a pinch of black pepper and the remaining ⅛ teaspoon sea salt. Serve promptly.

Per Serving:
calories: 156 | fat: 12g | protein: 8g | carbs: 4g | fiber: 1g | sodium: 487mg

Breakfast Farro with Dried Fruit and Nuts

Prep time: 10 minutes | Cook time: 20 minutes | Serves 8

16 ounces (454 g) farro, rinsed and drained
4½ cups water
¼ cup maple syrup
¼ teaspoon salt

1 cup dried mixed fruit
½ cup chopped toasted mixed nuts
2 cups almond milk

1. Place farro, water, maple syrup, and salt in the Instant Pot® and stir to combine. Close lid, set steam release to Sealing, press the Multigrain button, and set time to 20 minutes. When the timer beeps, let pressure release naturally, about 30 minutes. 2. Press the Cancel button, open lid, and add dried fruit. Close lid and let stand on the Keep Warm setting for 20 minutes. Serve warm with nuts and almond milk.

Per Serving:
calories: 347 | fat: 7g | protein: 9g | carbs: 65g | fiber: 9g | sodium: 145mg

Savory Cottage Cheese Breakfast Bowl

Prep time: 10 minutes | Cook time: 0 minutes | Serves 4

2 cups low-fat cottage cheese
2 tablespoons chopped mixed fresh herbs, such as basil, dill, flat-leaf parsley, and oregano
½ teaspoon ground black pepper
1 large tomato, chopped

1 small cucumber, peeled and chopped
¼ cup pitted kalamata olives, halved
1 tablespoon extra-virgin olive oil

1. In a medium bowl, combine the cottage cheese, herbs, and pepper. Add the tomato, cucumber, and olives and gently stir to combine. Drizzle with the oil to serve.

Per Serving:
calories: 181 | fat: 10g | protein: 15g | carbs: 8g | fiber: 1g | sodium: 788mg

Strawberry Collagen Smoothie

Prep time: 5 minutes | Cook time: 0 minutes | Serves 1

3 ounces (85 g) fresh or frozen strawberries
¾ cup unsweetened almond milk
¼ cup coconut cream or goat's cream
1 large egg
1 tablespoon chia seeds or flax meal

2 tablespoons grass-fed collagen powder
¼ teaspoon vanilla powder or 1 teaspoon unsweetened vanilla extract
Zest from ½ lemon
1 tablespoon macadamia oil
Optional: ice cubes, to taste

1. Place all of the ingredients in a blender and pulse until smooth and frothy. Serve immediately.

Per Serving:
calories: 515 | fat: 42g | protein: 10g | carbs: 30g | fiber: 4g | sodium: 202mg

Peachy Green Smoothie

Prep time: 10 minutes | Cook time: 0 minutes | Serves 2

1 cup almond milk
3 cups kale or spinach
1 banana, peeled
1 orange, peeled

1 small green apple
1 cup frozen peaches
¼ cup vanilla Greek yogurt

1. Put the ingredients in a blender in the order listed and blend on high until smooth. 2. Serve and enjoy.

Per Serving:
calories: 257 | fat: 5g | protein: 9g | carbs: 50g | fiber: 7g | sodium: 87mg

Poached Eggs on Whole Grain Avocado Toast

Prep time: 5 minutes | Cook time: 7 minutes | Serves 4

Olive oil cooking spray
4 large eggs
Salt
Black pepper

4 pieces whole grain bread
1 avocado
Red pepper flakes (optional)

1. Preheat the air fryer to 320°F(160°C). Lightly coat the inside of four small oven-safe ramekins with olive oil cooking spray. 2. Crack one egg into each ramekin, and season with salt and black pepper. 3. Place the ramekins into the air fryer basket. Close and set the timer to 7 minutes. 4. While the eggs are cooking, toast the bread in a toaster. 5. Slice the avocado in half lengthwise, remove the pit, and scoop the flesh into a small bowl. Season with salt, black pepper, and red pepper flakes, if desired. Using a fork, smash the avocado lightly. 6. Spread a quarter of the smashed avocado evenly over each slice of toast. 7. Remove the eggs from the air fryer, and gently spoon one onto each slice of avocado toast before serving.

Per Serving:
calories: 232 | fat: 14g | protein: 11g | carbs: 18g | fiber: 6g | sodium: 205mg

Honey-Apricot Granola with Greek Yogurt

Prep time: 10 minutes | Cook time: 30 minutes | Serves 6

1 cup rolled oats
¼ cup dried apricots, diced
¼ cup almond slivers
¼ cup walnuts, chopped
¼ cup pumpkin seeds
¼ cup hemp hearts
¼ to ⅓ cup raw honey, plus more for drizzling

1 tablespoon olive oil
1 teaspoon ground cinnamon
¼ teaspoon ground nutmeg
¼ teaspoon salt
2 tablespoons sugar-free dark chocolate chips (optional)
3 cups nonfat plain Greek yogurt

1. Preheat the air fryer to 260°F(127°C). Line the air fryer basket with parchment paper. 2. In a large bowl, combine the oats, apricots, almonds, walnuts, pumpkin seeds, hemp hearts, honey, olive oil, cinnamon, nutmeg, and salt, mixing so that the honey, oil, and spices are well distributed. 3. Pour the mixture onto the parchment paper and spread it into an even layer. 4. Bake for 10 minutes, then shake or stir and spread back out into an even layer. Continue baking for 10 minutes more, then repeat the process of shaking or stirring the mixture. Bake for an additional 10 minutes before removing from the air fryer. 5. Allow the granola to cool completely before stirring in the chocolate chips (if using) and pouring into an airtight container for storage. 6. For each serving, top ½ cup Greek yogurt with ⅓ cup granola and a drizzle of honey, if needed.

Per Serving:
calories: 342 | fat: 16g | protein: 20g | carbs: 31g | fiber: 4g | sodium: 146mg

Sunny-Side Up Baked Eggs with Swiss Chard, Feta, and Basil

Prep time: 15 minutes | Cook time: 10 to 15 minutes | Serves 4

1 tablespoon extra-virgin olive oil, divided
½ red onion, diced
½ teaspoon kosher salt
¼ teaspoon nutmeg
⅛ teaspoon freshly ground

black pepper
4 cups Swiss chard, chopped
¼ cup crumbled feta cheese
4 large eggs
¼ cup fresh basil, chopped or cut into ribbons

1. Preheat the oven to 375°F (190°C). Place 4 ramekins on a half sheet pan or in a baking dish and grease lightly with olive oil. 2. Heat the remaining olive oil in a large skillet or sauté pan over medium heat. Add the onion, salt, nutmeg, and pepper and sauté until translucent, about 3 minutes. Add the chard and cook, stirring, until wilted, about 2 minutes. 3. Split the mixture among the 4 ramekins. Add 1 tablespoon feta cheese to each ramekin. Crack 1 egg on top of the mixture in each ramekin. Bake for 10 to 12 minutes, or until the egg white is set. 4. Allow to cool for 1 to 2 minutes, then carefully transfer the eggs from the ramekins to a plate with a fork or spatula. Garnish with the basil.

Per Serving:
calories: 140 | fat: 10g | protein: 9g | carbs: 4g | fiber: 4g | sodium: 370mg

ortobello Eggs Benedict

Prep time: 10 minutes | Cook time: 10 to 14 minutes | Serves 2

1 tablespoon olive oil	pepper, to taste
2 cloves garlic, minced	2 large eggs
¼ teaspoon dried thyme	2 tablespoons grated Pecorino
2 portobello mushrooms, stems removed and gills scraped out	Romano cheese
2 Roma tomatoes, halved lengthwise	1 tablespoon chopped fresh parsley, for garnish
Salt and freshly ground black	1 teaspoon truffle oil (optional)

1. Preheat the air fryer to 400°F (204°C). 2. In a small bowl, combine the olive oil, garlic, and thyme. Brush the mixture over the mushrooms and tomatoes until thoroughly coated. Season to taste with salt and freshly ground black pepper. 3. Arrange the vegetables, cut side up, in the air fryer basket. Crack an egg into the center of each mushroom and sprinkle with cheese. Air fry for 10 to 14 minutes until the vegetables are tender and the whites are firm. When cool enough to handle, coarsely chop the tomatoes and place on top of the eggs. Scatter parsley on top and drizzle with truffle oil, if desired, just before serving.

Per Serving:
calories: 189 | fat: 13g | protein: 11g | carbs: 7g | fiber: 2g | sodium: 87mg

C+C Overnight Oats

Prep time: 5 minutes | Cook time: 0 minutes | Serves 2

½ cup vanilla, unsweetened almond milk (not Silk brand)	liquid sweetener
½ cup rolled oats	1 teaspoon chia seeds
2 tablespoons sliced almonds	¼ teaspoon ground cardamom
2 tablespoons simple sugar	¼ teaspoon ground cinnamon

1. In a mason jar, combine the almond milk, oats, almonds, liquid sweetener, chia seeds, cardamom, and cinnamon and shake well. Store in the refrigerator for 8 to 24 hours, then serve cold or heated.

Per Serving:
calories: 131 | fat: 6g | protein: 5g | carbs: 17g | fiber: 4g | sodium: 45mg

Herb & Cheese Fritters

Prep time: 10 minutes | Cook time: 15 minutes | Serves 5

3 medium zucchini	coconut flour
8 ounces (227 g) frozen spinach, thawed and squeezed dry (weight excludes water squeezed out)	¼ cup grated Pecorino Romano
	2 cloves garlic, minced
4 large eggs	¼ cup chopped fresh herbs, such as parsley, basil, oregano, mint, chives, and/or thyme
½ teaspoon salt	
¼ teaspoon black pepper	¼ cup extra-virgin avocado oil or ghee
3 tablespoons flax meal or	

1. Grate the zucchini and place in a bowl lined with cheesecloth. Set aside for 5 minutes, then twist the cheesecloth around the zucchini and squeeze out as much liquid as you can. You should end up with about 13 ounces (370 g) of drained zucchini. 2. In a mixing bowl, combine the zucchini, spinach, eggs, salt, and pepper. Add the flax meal and Pecorino and stir again. Add the garlic and herbs and mix through. 3. Heat a large pan greased with 1 tablespoon of ghee over medium heat. Once hot, use a ¼-cup measuring cup to make the fritters (about 57 g/2 ounces each). Place in the hot pan and shape with a spatula. Cook in batches for 3 to 4 minutes per side, until crisp and golden. Grease the pan between each batch until all the ghee has been used. 4. Eat warm or cold, as a breakfast, side, or snack. Store in the fridge for up to 4 days or freeze for up to 3 months.

Per Serving:
calories: 239 | fat: 20g | protein: 10g | carbs: 8g | fiber: 3g | sodium: 426mg

Almond Date Oatmeal

Prep time: 5 minutes | Cook time: 12 minutes | Serves 4

1 cup sliced almonds	oil
4 cups water	¼ teaspoon salt
2 cups rolled oats	½ cup chopped pitted dates
1 tablespoon extra-virgin olive	

1. Press the Sauté button on the Instant Pot® and add almonds. Toast, stirring constantly, until almonds are golden brown, about 8 minutes. Press the Cancel button and add water, oats, oil, salt, and dates to the pot. Stir well. Close lid and set steam release to Sealing. Press the Manual button and set time to 4 minutes. 2. When the timer beeps, quick-release the pressure until the float valve drops, open lid, and stir well. Serve hot.

Per Serving:
calories: 451 | fat: 25g | protein: 14g | carbs: 52g | fiber: 9g | sodium: 320mg

Red Pepper and Feta Egg Bites

Prep time: 5 minutes | Cook time: 8 minutes | Serves 6

1 tablespoon olive oil	6 large eggs, beaten
½ cup crumbled feta cheese	¼ teaspoon ground black
¼ cup chopped roasted red peppers	pepper
	1 cup water

1. Brush silicone muffin or poaching cups with oil. Divide feta and roasted red peppers among prepared cups. In a bowl with a pour spout, beat eggs with black pepper. 2. Place rack in the Instant Pot® and add water. Place cups on rack. Pour egg mixture into cups. Close lid, set steam release to Sealing, press the Manual button, and set time to 8 minutes. 3. When the timer beeps, quick-release the pressure until the float valve drops and open lid. Remove silicone cups carefully and slide eggs from cups onto plates. Serve warm.

Per Serving:
calories: 145 | fat: 11g | protein: 10g | carbs: 3g | fiber: 1g | sodium: 294mg

Grilled Halloumi with Whole-Wheat Pita Bread

Prep time: 5 minutes | Cook time: 10 minutes | Serves 4

2 teaspoons olive oil
8 (½-inch-thick) slices of halloumi cheese
4 whole-wheat pita rounds
1 Persian cucumber, thinly sliced
1 large tomato, sliced
½ cup pitted Kalamata olives

1. Brush a bit of olive oil on a grill pan and heat it over medium-high heat. 2. Brush the cheese slices all over with olive oil. Add the cheese slices in a single layer and cook until grill marks appear on the bottom, about 3 minutes. Flip the slices over and grill until grill marks appear on the second side, about 2 to 3 minutes more. 3. While the cheese is cooking, heat the pita bread, either in a skillet or in a toaster. 4. Serve the cheese inside of the pita pockets with the sliced cucumber, tomato, and olives.

Per Serving:
calories: 358 | fat: 24g | protein: 17g | carbs: 21g | fiber: 4g | sodium: 612mg

Baked Egg and Mushroom Cups

Prep time: 5 minutes | Cook time: 15 minutes | Serves 6

Olive oil cooking spray
6 large eggs
1 garlic clove, minced
½ teaspoon salt
½ teaspoon black pepper
Pinch red pepper flakes
8 ounces (227 g) baby bella mushrooms, sliced
1 cup fresh baby spinach
2 scallions, white parts and green parts, diced

1. Preheat the air fryer to 320°F (160°C). Lightly coat the inside of six silicone muffin cups or a six-cup muffin tin with olive oil cooking spray. 2. In a large bowl, beat the eggs, garlic, salt, pepper, and red pepper flakes for 1 to 2 minutes, or until well combined. 3. Fold in the mushrooms, spinach, and scallions. 4. Divide the mixture evenly among the muffin cups. 5. Place into the air fryer and bake for 12 to 15 minutes, or until the eggs are set. 6. Remove and allow to cool for 5 minutes before serving.

Per Serving:
calories: 83 | fat: 5g | protein: 8g | carbs: 2g | fiber: 1g | sodium: 271mg

Crunchy Vanilla Protein Bars

Prep time: 10 minutes | Cook time: 5 minutes | Serves 8

Topping:
½ cup flaked coconut
2 tablespoons raw cacao nibs
Bars:
1½ cups almond flour
1 cup collagen powder
2 tablespoons ground or whole chia seeds
1 teaspoon vanilla powder or 1
tablespoon unsweetened vanilla extract
¼ cup virgin coconut oil
½ cup coconut milk
1½ teaspoons fresh lemon zest
⅓ cup macadamia nuts, halved
Optional: low-carb sweetener, to taste

1. Preheat the oven to 350°F (180°C) fan assisted or 380°F (193°C)

conventional. 2. To make the topping: Place the coconut flakes on a baking tray and bake for 2 to 3 minutes, until lightly golden. Set aside to cool. 3. To make the bars: In a bowl, combine all of the ingredients for the bars. Line a small baking tray with parchment paper or use a silicone baking tray. A square 8 × 8–inch (20 × 20 cm) or a rectangular tray of similar size will work best. 4. Press the dough into the pan and sprinkle with the cacao nibs, pressing them into the bars with your fingers. Add the toasted coconut and lightly press the flakes into the dough. Refrigerate until set, for about 1 hour. Slice to serve. Store in the refrigerator for up to 1 week.

Per Serving:
calories: 285 | fat: 27g | protein: 5g | carbs: 10g | fiber: 4g | sodium: 19mg

Breakfast Quinoa with Figs and Walnuts

Prep time: 10 minutes | Cook time: 12 minutes | Serves 4

1½ cups quinoa, rinsed and drained
2½ cups water
1 cup almond milk
2 tablespoons honey
1 teaspoon vanilla extract
½ teaspoon ground cinnamon
¼ teaspoon salt
½ cup low-fat plain Greek yogurt
8 fresh figs, quartered
1 cup chopped toasted walnuts

1. Place quinoa, water, almond milk, honey, vanilla, cinnamon, and salt in the Instant Pot®. Stir to combine. Close lid, set steam release to Sealing, press the Rice button, and set time to 12 minutes. When the timer beeps, let pressure release naturally, about 20 minutes. 2. Press the Cancel button, open lid, and fluff quinoa with a fork. Serve warm with yogurt, figs, and walnuts.

Per Serving:
calories: 413 | fat: 25g | protein: 10g | carbs: 52g | fiber: 7g | sodium: 275mg

Mediterranean Muesli and Breakfast Bowl

Prep time: 10 minutes | Cook time: 0 minutes | Serves 12

Muesli:
3 cups old-fashioned rolled oats
1 cup wheat or rye flakes
1 cup pistachios or almonds, coarsely chopped
½ cup oat bran
8 dried apricots, chopped
8 dates, chopped
8 dried figs, chopped
Breakfast Bowl:
½ cup Mediterranean Muesli (above)
1 cup low-fat plain Greek yogurt or milk
2 tablespoons pomegranate seeds (optional)
½ teaspoon black or white sesame seeds

1. To make the muesli: In a medium bowl, combine the oats, wheat or rye flakes, pistachios or almonds, oat bran, apricots, dates, and figs. Transfer to an airtight container and store for up to 1 month. 2. To make the breakfast bowl: In a bowl, combine the muesli with the yogurt or milk. Top with the pomegranate seeds, if using, and the sesame seeds.

Per Serving:
calories: 234 | fat: 6g | protein: 8g | carbs: 40g | fiber: 6g | sodium: 54mg

Spinach Pie

Prep time: 10 minutes | Cook time: 25 minutes | Serves 8

Nonstick cooking spray
2 tablespoons extra-virgin olive oil
1 onion, chopped
1 pound (454 g) frozen spinach, thawed
¼ teaspoon garlic salt
¼ teaspoon freshly ground black pepper
¼ teaspoon ground nutmeg
4 large eggs, divided
1 cup grated Parmesan cheese, divided
2 puff pastry doughs, (organic, if available), at room temperature
4 hard-boiled eggs, halved

1. Preheat the oven to 350°F(180°C). Spray a baking sheet with nonstick cooking spray and set aside. 2. Heat a large sauté pan or skillet over medium-high heat. Put in the oil and onion and cook for about 5 minutes, until translucent. 3. Squeeze the excess water from the spinach, then add to the pan and cook, uncovered, so that any excess water from the spinach can evaporate. Add the garlic salt, pepper, and nutmeg. Remove from heat and set aside to cool. 4. In a small bowl, crack 3 eggs and mix well. Add the eggs and ½ cup Parmesan cheese to the cooled spinach mix. 5. On the prepared baking sheet, roll out the pastry dough. Layer the spinach mix on top of dough, leaving 2 inches around each edge. 6. Once the spinach is spread onto the pastry dough, place hard-boiled egg halves evenly throughout the pie, then cover with the second pastry dough. Pinch the edges closed. 7. Crack the remaining egg in a small bowl and mix well. Brush the egg wash over the pastry dough. 8. Bake for 15 to 20 minutes, until golden brown and warmed through.

Per Serving:
calories: 417 | fat: 28g | protein: 17g | carbs: 25g | fiber: 3g | sodium: 490mg

Whole Wheat Blueberry Muffins

Prep time: 10 minutes | Cook time: 15 minutes | Serves 6

Olive oil cooking spray
½ cup unsweetened applesauce
¼ cup raw honey
½ cup nonfat plain Greek yogurt
1 teaspoon vanilla extract
1 large egg
1½ cups plus 1 tablespoon whole wheat flour, divided
½ teaspoon baking soda
½ teaspoon baking powder
½ teaspoon salt
½ cup blueberries, fresh or frozen

1. Preheat the air fryer to 360°F(182°C). Lightly coat the inside of six silicone muffin cups or a six-cup muffin tin with olive oil cooking spray. 2. In a large bowl, combine the applesauce, honey, yogurt, vanilla, and egg and mix until smooth. 3. Sift in 1½ cups of the flour, the baking soda, baking powder, and salt into the wet mixture, then stir until just combined. 4. In a small bowl, toss the blueberries with the remaining 1 tablespoon flour, then fold the mixture into the muffin batter. 5. Divide the mixture evenly among the prepared muffin cups and place into the basket of the air fryer. Bake for 12 to 15 minutes, or until golden brown on top and a toothpick inserted into the middle of one of the muffins comes out clean. 6. Allow to cool for 5 minutes before serving.

Per Serving:
calories: 186 | fat: 2g | protein: 7g | carbs: 38g | fiber: 4g | sodium: 318mg

Peachy Oatmeal with Pecans

Prep time: 10 minutes | Cook time: 4 minutes | Serves 4

4 cups water
2 cups rolled oats
1 tablespoon light olive oil
1 large peach, peeled, pitted,
and diced
¼ teaspoon salt
½ cup toasted pecans
2 tablespoons maple syrup

1. Place water, oats, oil, peach, and salt in the Instant Pot®. Stir well. Close lid, set steam release to Sealing, press the Manual button, and set time to 4 minutes. 2. When the timer beeps, quick-release the pressure until the float valve drops. Press the Cancel button, open lid, and stir well. Serve oatmeal topped with pecans and maple syrup.

Per Serving:
calories: 399 | fat: 27g | protein: 8g | carbs: 35g | fiber: 7g | sodium: 148mg

Jalapeño Popper Egg Cups

Prep time: 10 minutes | Cook time: 10 minutes | Serves 2

4 large eggs
¼ cup chopped pickled jalapeños
2 ounces (57 g) full-fat cream
cheese
½ cup shredded sharp Cheddar cheese

1. In a medium bowl, beat the eggs, then pour into four silicone muffin cups. 2. In a large microwave-safe bowl, place jalapeños, cream cheese, and Cheddar. Microwave for 30 seconds and stir. Take a spoonful, approximately ¼ of the mixture, and place it in the center of one of the egg cups. Repeat with remaining mixture. 3. Place egg cups into the air fryer basket. 4. Adjust the temperature to 320°F (160°C) and bake for 10 minutes. 5. Serve warm.

Per Serving:
calories: 375 | fat: 30g | protein: 23g | carbs: 3g | fiber: 0g | sodium: 445mg

Homemade Pumpkin Parfait

Prep time: 5 minutes | Cook time: 0 minutes | Serves 4

1 (15-ounce / 425-g) can pure pumpkin purée
4 teaspoons honey, additional to taste
1 teaspoon pumpkin pie spice
¼ teaspoon ground cinnamon
2 cups plain, unsweetened, full-fat Greek yogurt
1 cup honey granola

1. In a large bowl, mix the pumpkin purée, honey, pumpkin pie spice, and cinnamon. Cover and refrigerate for at least 2 hours. 2. To make the parfaits, in each cup, pour ¼ cup pumpkin mix, ¼ cup yogurt and ¼ cup granola. Repeat Greek yogurt and pumpkin layers and top with honey granola.

Per Serving:
calories: 264 | fat: 9g | protein: 15g | carbs: 35g | fiber: 6g | sodium: 90mg

Polenta with Sautéed Chard and Fried Eggs

Prep time: 5 minutes | Cook time: 20 minutes | Serves 4

For the Polenta:
2½ cups water
½ teaspoon kosher salt
¾ cups whole-grain cornmeal
¼ teaspoon freshly ground black pepper
2 tablespoons grated Parmesan cheese
For the Chard:
1 tablespoon extra-virgin olive oil
1 bunch (about 6 ounces / 170

g) Swiss chard, leaves and stems chopped and separated
2 garlic cloves, sliced
¼ teaspoon kosher salt
⅛ teaspoon freshly ground black pepper
Lemon juice (optional)
For the Eggs:
1 tablespoon extra-virgin olive oil
4 large eggs

Make the Polenta: 1. Bring the water and salt to a boil in a medium saucepan over high heat. Slowly add the cornmeal, whisking constantly. 2. Decrease the heat to low, cover, and cook for 10 to 15 minutes, stirring often to avoid lumps. Stir in the pepper and Parmesan, and divide among 4 bowls. Make the Chard: 3. Heat the oil in a large skillet over medium heat. Add the chard stems, garlic, salt, and pepper; sauté for 2 minutes. Add the chard leaves and cook until wilted, about 3 to 5 minutes. 4. Add a spritz of lemon juice (if desired), toss together, and divide evenly on top of the polenta. Make the Eggs: 5. Heat the oil in the same large skillet over medium-high heat. Crack each egg into the skillet, taking care not to crowd the skillet and leaving space between the eggs. Cook until the whites are set and golden around the edges, about 2 to 3 minutes. 6. Serve sunny-side up or flip the eggs over carefully and cook 1 minute longer for over easy. Place one egg on top of the polenta and chard in each bowl.

Per Serving:
calories: 310 | fat: 18g | protein: 17g | carbs: 21g | fiber: 1g | sodium: 500mg

Baked Peach Oatmeal

Prep time: 5 minutes | Cook time: 30 minutes | Serves 6

Olive oil cooking spray
2 cups certified gluten-free rolled oats
2 cups unsweetened almond milk
¼ cup raw honey, plus more for drizzling (optional)

½ cup nonfat plain Greek yogurt
1 teaspoon vanilla extract
½ teaspoon ground cinnamon
¼ teaspoon salt
1½ cups diced peaches, divided, plus more for serving (optional)

1. Preheat the air fryer to 380°F(193ºC). Lightly coat the inside of a 6-inch cake pan with olive oil cooking spray. 2. In a large bowl, mix together the oats, almond milk, honey, yogurt, vanilla, cinnamon, and salt until well combined. 3. Fold in ¾ cup of the peaches and then pour the mixture into the prepared cake pan. 4. Sprinkle the remaining peaches across the top of the oatmeal mixture. Bake in the air fryer for 30 minutes. 5. Allow to set and cool for 5 minutes before serving with additional fresh fruit and honey for drizzling, if desired.

Per Serving:
calories: 197 | fat: 3g | protein: 9g | carbs: 36g | fiber: 4g | sodium: 138mg

Baked Ricotta with Pears

Prep time: 5 minutes |Cook time: 25 minutes| Serves: 4

Nonstick cooking spray
1 (16-ounce / 454-g) container whole-milk ricotta cheese
2 large eggs
¼ cup white whole-wheat flour or whole-wheat pastry flour

1 tablespoon sugar
1 teaspoon vanilla extract
¼ teaspoon ground nutmeg
1 pear, cored and diced
2 tablespoons water
1 tablespoon honey

1. Preheat the oven to 400°F(205ºC). Spray four 6-ounce ramekins with nonstick cooking spray. 2. In a large bowl, beat together the ricotta, eggs, flour, sugar, vanilla, and nutmeg. Spoon into the ramekins. Bake for 22 to 25 minutes, or until the ricotta is just about set. Remove from the oven and cool slightly on racks. 3. While the ricotta is baking, in a small saucepan over medium heat, simmer the pear in the water for 10 minutes, until slightly softened. Remove from the heat, and stir in the honey. 4. Serve the ricotta ramekins topped with the warmed pear.

Per Serving:
calories: 306 | fat: 17g | protein: 17g | carbs: 21g | fiber: 1g | sodium: 131mg

Quinoa Porridge with Apricots

Prep time: 10 minutes | Cook time: 12 minutes | Serves 4

1½ cups quinoa, rinsed and drained
1 cup chopped dried apricots
2½ cups water

1 cup almond milk
1 tablespoon rose water
½ teaspoon cardamom
¼ teaspoon salt

1. Place all ingredients in the Instant Pot®. Stir to combine. Close lid, set steam release to Sealing, press the Rice button, and set time to 12 minutes. When the timer beeps, let pressure release naturally, about 20 minutes. 2. Press the Cancel button, open lid, and fluff quinoa with a fork. Serve warm.

Per Serving:
calories: 197 | fat: 2g | protein: 3g | carbs: 44g | fiber: 4g | sodium: 293mg

Mediterranean-Inspired White Smoothie

Prep time: 5 minutes | Cook time: 0 minutes | Serves

½ medium apple (any variety), peeled, halved, and seeded
5 roasted almonds
½ medium frozen banana, sliced (be sure to peel the

banana before freezing)
¼ cup full-fat Greek yogurt
½ cup low-fat 1% milk
¼ teaspoon ground cinnamon
½ teaspoon honey

1. Combine all the ingredients in a blender. Process until smooth. 2. Pour into a glass and serve promptly. (This recipe is best consumed fresh.)

Per Serving:
calories: 236 | fat: 7g | protein: 8g | carbs: 40g | fiber: 5g | sodium: 84mg

Flax, Date, and Walnut Steel-Cut Oats

Prep time: 5 minutes | Cook time: 5 minutes | Serves 4

1 tablespoon light olive oil
1 cup steel-cut oats
3 cups water
⅓ cup chopped pitted dates
¼ cup ground flax
¼ teaspoon salt
½ cup toasted chopped walnuts

1. Place oil, oats, water, dates, flax, and salt in the Instant Pot® and stir well. Close lid, set steam release to Sealing, press the Manual button, and set time to 5 minutes. 2. When the timer beeps, let pressure release naturally for 10 minutes, then quick-release the remaining pressure until the float valve drops. Press the Cancel button, open lid, and stir in walnuts. Serve hot.

Per Serving:
calories: 322 | fat: 18g | protein: 10g | carbs: 42g | fiber: 8g | sodium: 150mg

Savory Zucchini Muffins

Prep time: 10 minutes | Cook time: 35 minutes | Serves 13

1 tablespoon extra virgin olive oil plus extra for brushing
2 medium zucchini, grated
⅛ teaspoon fine sea salt
1 large egg, lightly beaten
1½ ounces (43 g) crumbled feta
¼ medium onion (any variety), finely chopped
1 tablespoon chopped fresh parsley
1 tablespoon chopped fresh dill
1 tablespoon chopped fresh mint
¼ teaspoon freshly ground black pepper
3 tablespoons unseasoned breadcrumbs
1 tablespoon grated Parmesan cheese

1. Preheat the oven to 400°F (205°C), and line a medium muffin pan with 6 muffin liners. Lightly brush the bottoms of the liners with olive oil. 2. Place the grated zucchini in a colander and sprinkle with the sea salt. Set aside for 10 minutes to allow the salt to penetrate. 3. Remove the zucchini from the colander, and place it on a tea towel. Pull the edges of the towel in and then twist and squeeze the towel to remove as much of the water from the zucchini as possible. (This will prevent the muffins from becoming soggy.) 4. In a large bowl, combine the egg, feta, onions, parsley, dill, mint, pepper, and the remaining tablespoon of olive oil. Mix well, and add the zucchini to the bowl. Mix again, and add the breadcrumbs. Use a fork to mash the ingredients until well combined. 5. Divide the mixture among the prepared muffins liners and then sprinkle ½ teaspoon grated Parmesan over each muffin. Transfer to the oven, and bake for 35 minutes or until the muffins turn golden brown. 6. When the baking time is complete, remove the muffins from the oven and set aside to cool for 5 minutes before removing from the pan. Store in an airtight container in the refrigerator for 3 days, or tightly wrap individual muffins in plastic wrap and freeze for up to 3 months.

Per Serving:
calories: 39 | fat: 2g | protein: 2g | carbs: 3g | fiber: 1g | sodium: 80mg

Berry Baked Oatmeal

Prep time: 10 minutes | Cook time: 45 to 50 minutes | Serves 8

2 cups gluten-free rolled oats
2 cups (10-ounce / 283-g bag) frozen mixed berries (blueberries and raspberries work best)
2 cups plain, unsweetened almond milk
1 cup plain Greek yogurt
¼ cup maple syrup
2 tablespoons extra-virgin olive oil
2 teaspoons ground cinnamon
1 teaspoon baking powder
1 teaspoon vanilla extract
½ teaspoon kosher salt
¼ teaspoon ground nutmeg
⅛ teaspoon ground cloves

1. Preheat the oven to 375°F (190°C). 2. Mix all the ingredients together in a large bowl. Pour into a 9-by-13-inch baking dish. Bake for 45 to 50 minutes, or until golden brown.

Per Serving:
calories: 180 | fat: 6g | protein: 6g | carbs: 28g | fiber: 4g | sodium: 180mg

Black Olive Toast with Herbed Hummus

Prep time: 5 minutes | Cook time: 5 minutes | Serves 2

¼ cup store-bought plain hummus
2 tablespoons finely chopped fresh flat-leaf parsley
1 tablespoon finely chopped fresh dill
1 tablespoon finely chopped fresh mint
1 teaspoon finely grated lemon peel
2 slices (½" thick) black olive bread
1 clove garlic, halved
1 tablespoon extra-virgin olive oil

1. In a small bowl, combine the hummus, herbs, and lemon peel. 2. Toast the bread. Immediately rub the warm bread with the garlic. 3. Spread half the hummus over each slice of bread and drizzle with the oil.

Per Serving:
calories: 197 | fat: 11g | protein: 6g | carbs: 20g | fiber: 4g | sodium: 177mg

Apple and Tahini Toast

Prep time: 10 minutes | Cook time: 0 minutes | Serves 1

2 tablespoons tahini
2 slices whole-wheat bread, toasted
1 small apple of your choice, cored and thinly sliced
1 teaspoon honey

1. Spread the tahini on the toasted bread. 2. Lay the apples on the bread and drizzle with honey. Serve immediately.

Per Serving:
calories: 439 | fat: 19g | protein: 13g | carbs: 60g | fiber: 10g | sodium: 327mg

Smoked Salmon Egg Scramble with Dill and Chives

Prep time: 5 minutes | Cook time: 5 minutes | Serves 2

4 large eggs
1 tablespoon milk
1 tablespoon fresh chives, minced
1 tablespoon fresh dill, minced
¼ teaspoon kosher salt
⅛ teaspoon freshly ground black pepper
2 teaspoons extra-virgin olive oil
2 ounces (57 g) smoked salmon, thinly sliced

1. In a large bowl, whisk together the eggs, milk, chives, dill, salt, and pepper. 2. Heat the olive oil in a medium skillet or sauté pan over medium heat. Add the egg mixture and cook for about 3 minutes, stirring occasionally. 3. Add the salmon and cook until the eggs are set but moist, about 1 minute.

Per Serving:
calories: 325 | fat: 26g | protein: 23g | carbs: 1g | fiber: 0g | sodium: 455mg

Garden Scramble

Prep time: 10 minutes | Cook time: 10 minutes | Serves 4

1 teaspoon extra-virgin olive oil
½ cup diced yellow squash
½ cup diced green bell pepper
¼ cup diced sweet white onion
6 cherry tomatoes, halved
1 tablespoon chopped fresh basil
1 tablespoon chopped fresh parsley
½ teaspoon salt
¼ teaspoon freshly ground black pepper
8 large eggs, beaten

1. In a large nonstick skillet, heat the olive oil over medium heat. Add the squash, pepper, and onion and sauté until the onion is translucent, 3 to 4 minutes. 2. Add the tomatoes, basil, and parsley and season with salt and pepper. Sauté for 1 minute, then pour the beaten eggs over the vegetables. Cover the pan and reduce the heat to low. 3. Cook until the eggs are cooked through, 5 to 6 minutes, making sure that the center is no longer runny. 4. To serve, slide the frittata onto a platter and cut into wedges.

Per Serving:
calories: 165 | fat: 11g | protein: 13g | carbs: 3g | fiber: 1g | sodium: 435mg

Red Pepper and Feta Frittata

Prep time: 10 minutes | Cook time: 20 minutes | Serves 4

Olive oil cooking spray
8 large eggs
1 medium red bell pepper, diced
½ teaspoon salt
½ teaspoon black pepper
1 garlic clove, minced
½ cup feta, divided

1. Preheat the air fryer to 360°F(182°C). Lightly coat the inside of a 6-inch round cake pan with olive oil cooking spray. 2. In a large bowl, beat the eggs for 1 to 2 minutes, or until well combined. 3. Add the bell pepper, salt, black pepper, and garlic to the eggs, and mix together until the bell pepper is distributed throughout. 4. Fold in ¼ cup of the feta cheese. 5. Pour the egg mixture into the prepared cake pan, and sprinkle the remaining ¼ cup of feta over the top. 6. Place into the air fryer and bake for 18 to 20 minutes, or until the eggs are set in the center. 7. Remove from the air fryer and allow to cool for 5 minutes before serving.

Per Serving:
calories: 204 | fat: 14g | protein: 16g | carbs: 4g | fiber: 1g | sodium: 606mg

Baklava Hot Porridge

Prep time: 5 minutes | Cook time: 5 minutes | Serves 2

2 cups riced cauliflower
¾ cup unsweetened almond, flax, or hemp milk
4 tablespoons extra-virgin olive oil, divided
2 teaspoons grated fresh orange peel (from ½ orange)
½ teaspoon ground cinnamon
½ teaspoon almond extract or vanilla extract
⅛ teaspoon salt
4 tablespoons chopped walnuts, divided
1 to 2 teaspoons liquid stevia, monk fruit, or other sweetener of choice (optional)

1. In medium saucepan, combine the riced cauliflower, almond milk, 2 tablespoons olive oil, grated orange peel, cinnamon, almond extract, and salt. Stir to combine and bring just to a boil over medium-high heat, stirring constantly. 2. Remove from heat and stir in 2 tablespoons chopped walnuts and sweetener (if using). Stir to combine. 3. Divide into bowls, topping each with 1 tablespoon of chopped walnuts and 1 tablespoon of the remaining olive oil.

Per Serving:
calories: 414 | fat: 38g | protein: 6g | carbs: 16g | fiber: 4g | sodium: 252mg

Spinach and Mushroom Mini Quiche

Prep time: 10 minutes | Cook time: 15 minutes | Serves 4

1 teaspoon olive oil, plus more for spraying
1 cup coarsely chopped mushrooms
1 cup fresh baby spinach, shredded
4 eggs, beaten
½ cup shredded Cheddar cheese
½ cup shredded Mozzarella cheese
¼ teaspoon salt
¼ teaspoon black pepper

1. Spray 4 silicone baking cups with olive oil and set aside. 2. In a medium sauté pan over medium heat, warm 1 teaspoon of olive oil. Add the mushrooms and sauté until soft, 3 to 4 minutes. 3. Add the spinach and cook until wilted, 1 to 2 minutes. Set aside. 4. In a medium bowl, whisk together the eggs, Cheddar cheese, Mozzarella cheese, salt, and pepper. 5. Gently fold the mushrooms and spinach into the egg mixture. 6. Pour ¼ of the mixture into each silicone baking cup. 7. Place the baking cups into the air fryer basket and air fry at 350°F (177°C) for 5 minutes. Stir the mixture in each ramekin slightly and air fry until the egg has set, an additional 3 to 5 minutes.

Per Serving:
calories: 156 | fat: 10g | protein: 14g | carbs: 2g | fiber: 1g | sodium: 411mg

Tiropita (Greek Cheese Pie)

Prep time: 15 minutes | Cook time: 45 minutes | Serves 12

1 tablespoon extra virgin olive oil plus 3 tablespoons for brushing	2 tablespoons chopped fresh dill, or 1 tablespoon dried dill
1 pound (454 g) crumbled feta	¼ teaspoon freshly ground black pepper
8 ounces (227g) ricotta cheese	3 eggs
2 tablespoons chopped fresh mint, or 1 tablespoon dried mint	12 phyllo sheets, defrosted
	1 tsp white sesame seeds

1. Preheat the oven to 350°F (180 C). Brush a 9 × 13-inch (23 × 33cm) casserole dish with olive oil. 2. Combine the feta and ricotta in a large bowl, using a fork to mash the ingredients together. Add the mint, dill, and black pepper, and mix well. In a small bowl, beat the eggs and then add them to the cheese mixture along with 1 tablespoon olive oil. Mix well. 3. Carefully place 1 phyllo sheet in the bottom of the prepared dish. (Keep the rest of the dough covered with a damp towel.) Brush the sheet with olive oil, then place a second phyllo sheet on top of the first and brush with olive oil. Repeat until you have 6 layers of phyllo. 4. Spread the cheese mixture evenly over the phyllo and then fold the excess phyllo edges in and over the mixture. Cover the mixture with 6 more phyllo sheets, repeating the process by placing a single phyllo sheet in the pan and brushing it with olive oil. Roll the excess phyllo in to form an edge around the pie. 5. Brush the top phyllo layer with olive oil and then use a sharp knife to score it into 12 pieces, being careful to cut only through the first 3–4 layers of the phyllo dough. Sprinkle the sesame seeds and a bit of water over the top of the pie. 6. Place the pie on the middle rack of the oven. Bake for 40 minutes or until the phyllo turns a deep golden color. Carefully lift one side of the pie to ensure the bottom crust is baked. If it's baked, move the pan to the bottom rack and bake for an additional 5 minutes. 7. Remove the pie from the oven and set aside to cool for 15 minutes. Use a sharp knife to cut the pie into 12 pieces. Store covered in the refrigerator for up to 3 days.

Per Serving:
calories: 230 | fat: 15g | protein: 11g | carbs: 13g | fiber: 1g | sodium: 510mg

Chickpea Hash with Eggs

Prep time: 20 minutes | Cook time: 35 minutes | Serves 4

1 cup dried chickpeas	and chopped
4 cups water	1 teaspoon minced garlic
2 tablespoons extra-virgin olive oil, divided	½ teaspoon ground cumin
1 medium onion, peeled and chopped	½ teaspoon ground black pepper
1 medium zucchini, trimmed and sliced	¼ teaspoon salt
	4 large hard-cooked eggs, peeled and halved
1 large red bell pepper, seeded	½ teaspoon smoked paprika

1. Place chickpeas, water, and 1 tablespoon oil in the Instant Pot®. Close lid, set steam release to Sealing, press the Manual button, and set time to 30 minutes. 2. When the timer beeps, quick-release the pressure until the float valve drops, press the Cancel button, and open lid. Drain chickpeas well, transfer to a medium bowl, and set aside. 3. Clean and dry pot. Return to machine, press the Sauté button, and heat remaining 1 tablespoon oil. Add onion, zucchini, and bell pepper. Cook until tender, about 5 minutes. Add garlic, cumin, black pepper, and salt and cook for 30 seconds. Add chickpeas and turn to coat. 4. Transfer chickpea mixture to a serving platter. Top with eggs and paprika and serve immediately.

Per Serving:
calories: 274 | fat: 14g | protein: 15g | carbs: 36g | fiber: 16g | sodium: 242mg

Smoky Sausage Patties

Prep time: 30 minutes | Cook time: 9 minutes | Serves 8

1 pound (454 g) ground pork	½ teaspoon fennel seeds
1 tablespoon coconut aminos	½ teaspoon dried thyme
2 teaspoons liquid smoke	½ teaspoon freshly ground black pepper
1 teaspoon dried sage	
1 teaspoon sea salt	¼ teaspoon cayenne pepper

1. In a large bowl, combine the pork, coconut aminos, liquid smoke, sage, salt, fennel seeds, thyme, black pepper, and cayenne pepper. Work the meat with your hands until the seasonings are fully incorporated. 2. Shape the mixture into 8 equal-size patties. Using your thumb, make a dent in the center of each patty. Place the patties on a plate and cover with plastic wrap. Refrigerate the patties for at least 30 minutes. 3. Working in batches if necessary, place the patties in a single layer in the air fryer, being careful not to overcrowd them. 4. Set the air fryer to 400°F (204ºC) and air fry for 5 minutes. Flip and cook for about 4 minutes more.

Per Serving:
calories: 70 | fat: 2g | protein: 12g | carbs: 0g | fiber: 0g | sodium: 329mg

Oat and Fruit Parfait

Prep time: 5 minutes | Cook time: 12 minutes | Serves 2

½ cup whole-grain rolled or quickcooking oats (not instant)	1 cup sliced fresh strawberries
½ cup walnut pieces	1½ cups vanilla low-fat Greek yogurt
1 teaspoon honey	Fresh mint leaves for garnish

1. Preheat the oven to 300°F(150ºC). 2. Spread the oats and walnuts in a single layer on a baking sheet. 3. Toast the oats and nuts just until you begin to smell the nuts, 10 to 12 minutes. Remove the pan from the oven and set aside. 4. In a small microwave-safe bowl, heat the honey just until warm, about 30 seconds. Add the strawberries and stir to coat. 5. Place 1 tablespoon of the strawberries in the bottom of each of 2 dessert dishes or 8-ounce glasses. Add a portion of yogurt and then a portion of oats and repeat the layers until the containers are full, ending with the berries. Serve immediately or chill until ready to eat.

Per Serving:
calories: 541 | fat: 25g | protein: 21g | carbs: 66g | fiber: 8g | sodium: 124mg

Butternut Squash and Ricotta Frittata

Prep time: 10 minutes | Cook time: 33 minutes | Serves 2 to 3

1 cup cubed (½-inch) butternut squash (5½ ounces / 156 g)
2 tablespoons olive oil
Kosher salt and freshly ground black pepper, to taste
4 fresh sage leaves, thinly sliced
6 large eggs, lightly beaten
½ cup ricotta cheese
Cayenne pepper

1. In a bowl, toss the squash with the olive oil and season with salt and black pepper until evenly coated. Sprinkle the sage on the bottom of a cake pan and place the squash on top. Place the pan in the air fryer and bake at 400°F (204°C) for 10 minutes. Stir to incorporate the sage, then cook until the squash is tender and lightly caramelized at the edges, about 3 minutes more. 2. Pour the eggs over the squash, dollop the ricotta all over, and sprinkle with cayenne. Bake at 300°F (149°C) until the eggs are set and the frittata is golden brown on top, about 20 minutes. Remove the pan from the air fryer and cut the frittata into wedges to serve.

Per Serving:
calories: 289 | fat: 22g | protein: 18g | carbs: 5g | fiber: 1g | sodium: 184mg

Tortilla Española (Spanish Omelet)

Prep time: 10 minutes | Cook time: 40 minutes | Serves 4

1½ pounds (680 g) Yukon gold potatoes, scrubbed and thinly sliced
3 tablespoons olive oil, divided
1 teaspoon kosher salt, divided
1 sweet white onion, thinly sliced
3 cloves garlic, minced
8 eggs
½ teaspoon ground black pepper

1. Preheat the oven to 350°F(180°C). Line 2 baking sheets with parchment paper. 2. In a large bowl, toss the potatoes with 1 tablespoon of the oil and ½ teaspoon of the salt until well coated. Spread over the 2 baking sheets in a single layer. Roast the potatoes, rotating the baking sheets halfway through cooking, until tender but not browned, about 15 minutes. Using a spatula, remove the potatoes from the baking sheets and let cool until warm. 3. Meanwhile, in a medium skillet over medium-low heat, cook the onion in 1 tablespoon of the oil, stirring, until soft and golden, about 10 minutes. Add the garlic and cook until fragrant, about 2 minutes. Transfer the onion and garlic to a plate and let cool until warm. 4. In a large bowl, beat the eggs, pepper, and the remaining ½ teaspoon salt vigorously until the yolks and whites are completely combined and slightly frothy. Stir in the potatoes and onion and garlic and combine well, being careful not to break too many potatoes. 5. In the same skillet over medium-high heat, warm the remaining 1 tablespoon oil until shimmering, swirling to cover the whole surface. Pour in the egg mixture and spread the contents evenly. Cook for 1 minute and reduce the heat to medium-low. Cook until the edges of the egg are set and the center is slightly wet, about 8 minutes. Using a spatula, nudge the omelet to make sure it moves freely in the skillet. 6. Place a rimless plate, the size of the skillet, over the omelet. Place one hand over the plate and, in a swift motion, flip the omelet onto the plate. Slide the omelet back into the skillet, cooked side up. Cook until completely

set, a toothpick inserted into the middle comes out clean, about 6 minutes. 7. Transfer to a serving plate and let cool for 5 minutes. Serve warm or room temperature.

Per Serving:
calories: 376 | fat: 19g | protein: 15g | carbs: 37g | fiber: 5g | sodium: 724mg

Ricotta and Fruit Bruschetta

Prep time: 5 minutes | Cook time: 0 minutes | Serves 2

¼ cup full-fat ricotta cheese
1½ teaspoons honey, divided
3 drops almond extract
2 slices whole-grain bread, toasted
½ medium banana, peeled and
cut into ¼-inch slices
½ medium pear (any variety), thinly sliced
2 teaspoons chopped walnuts
2 pinches of ground cinnamon

1. In a small bowl, combine the ricotta, ¼ teaspoon honey, and the almond extract. Stir well. 2. Spread 1½ tablespoons of the ricotta mixture over each slice of toast. 3. Divide the pear slices and banana slices equally on top of each slice of toast. 4. Drizzle equal amounts of the remaining honey over each slice, and sprinkle 1 teaspoon of the walnuts over each slice. Top each serving with a pinch of cinnamon.

Per Serving:
calories: 207 | fat: 7g | protein: 8g | carbs: 30g | fiber: 4g | sodium: 162mg

Egg Salad with Red Pepper and Dill

Prep time: 5 minutes | Cook time: 10 minutes | Serves 6

6 large eggs
1 cup water
1 tablespoon olive oil
1 medium red bell pepper, seeded and chopped
¼ teaspoon salt
¼ teaspoon ground black pepper
½ cup low-fat plain Greek yogurt
2 tablespoons chopped fresh dill

1. Have ready a large bowl of ice water. Place rack or egg holder into bottom of the Instant Pot®. 2. Arrange eggs on rack or holder and add water to the Instant Pot®. Close lid, set steam release to Sealing, press the Manual button, and set time to 5 minutes. 3. When the timer beeps, let pressure release naturally for 5 minutes, then quick-release the remaining pressure until the float valve drops. Press the Cancel button and open lid. Carefully transfer eggs to the bowl of ice water. Let stand in ice water for 10 minutes, then peel, chop, and add eggs to a medium bowl. 4. Clean out pot, dry well, and return to machine. Press the Sauté button and heat oil. Add bell pepper, salt, and black pepper. Cook, stirring often, until bell pepper is tender, about 5 minutes. Transfer to bowl with eggs. 5. Add yogurt and dill to bowl, and fold to combine. Cover and chill for 1 hour before serving.

Per Serving:
calories: 111 | fat: 8g | protein: 8g | carbs: 3g | fiber: 0g | sodium: 178mg

Blender Cinnamon Pancakes with Cacao Cream Topping

Prep time: 10 minutes | Cook time: 10 minutes | Serves 4

Cinnamon Pancakes:
2 cups pecans
4 large eggs
1 tablespoon cinnamon
½ teaspoon baking soda
1 teaspoon fresh lemon juice or apple cider vinegar
1 tablespoon virgin coconut oil or ghee
Cacao Cream Topping:

1 cup coconut cream
1½ tablespoons raw cacao powder
Optional: low-carb sweetener, to taste
To Serve:
9 medium strawberries, sliced
1 tablespoon unsweetened shredded coconut

1. To make the pancakes: Place the pecans in a blender and process until powdered. Add all of the remaining ingredients apart from the ghee. Blend again until smooth. 2. Place a nonstick pan greased with 1 teaspoon of the coconut oil over low heat. Using a ¼-cup (60 ml) measure per pancake, cook in batches of 2 to 3 small pancakes over low heat until bubbles begin to form on the pancakes. Use a spatula to flip over, then cook for 30 to 40 seconds and place on a plate. Grease the pan with more coconut oil between batches. Transfer the pancakes to a plate. 3. To make the cacao cream topping: Place the coconut cream in a bowl. Add the cacao powder and sweetener, if using. Whisk until well combined and creamy. 4. Serve the pancakes with the cacao cream, sliced strawberries and a sprinkle of shredded coconut. You can enhance the flavor of the shredded coconut by toasting it in a dry pan for about 1 minute.

Per Serving:
calories: 665 | fat: 65g | protein: 14g | carbs: 17g | fiber: 9g | sodium: 232mg

Warm Fava Beans with Whole-Wheat Pita

Prep time: 5 minutes | Cook time: 10 minutes | Serves 4

1½ tablespoons olive oil
1 large onion, diced
1 large tomato, diced
1 clove garlic, crushed
1 (15-ounce / 425-g) can fava beans, not drained
1 teaspoon ground cumin

¼ cup chopped fresh parsley
¼ cup lemon juice
Salt
Freshly ground black pepper
Crushed red pepper flakes
4 whole-grain pita bread pockets

1. Heat the olive oil in a large skillet set over medium-high heat. Add the onion, tomato, and garlic and cook, stirring, for about 3 minutes, until the vegetables soften. 2. Add the fava beans, along with the liquid from the can, and bring to a boil. 3. Lower the heat to medium and stir in the cumin, parsley, and lemon juice. Season with salt, pepper, and crushed red pepper. Simmer over medium heat, stirring occasionally, for 5 minutes. 4. While the beans are simmering, heat the pitas in a toaster oven or in a cast-iron skillet over medium heat. To serve, cut the pitas into triangles for dipping into and scooping the bean mixture, or halve the pitas and fill the pockets up with beans.

Per Serving:
calories: 524 | fat: 8g | protein: 32g | carbs: 86g | fiber: 31g | sodium: 394mg

South of the Coast Sweet Potato Toast

Prep time: 5 minutes | Cook time: 15 minutes | Serves 4

2 plum tomatoes, halved
6 tablespoons extra-virgin olive oil, divided
Salt
Freshly ground black pepper
2 large sweet potatoes, sliced lengthwise
1 cup fresh spinach

8 medium asparagus, trimmed
4 large cooked eggs or egg substitute (poached, scrambled, or fried)
1 cup arugula
4 tablespoons pesto
4 tablespoons shredded Asiago cheese

1. Preheat the oven to 450°F(235°C). 2. On a baking sheet, brush the plum tomato halves with 2 tablespoons of olive oil and season with salt and pepper. Roast the tomatoes in the oven for approximately 15 minutes, then remove from the oven and allow to rest. 3. Put the sweet potato slices on a separate baking sheet and brush about 2 tablespoons of oil on each side and season with salt and pepper. Bake the sweet potato slices for about 15 minutes, flipping once after 5 to 7 minutes, until just tender. Remove from the oven and set aside. 4. In a sauté pan or skillet, heat the remaining 2 tablespoons of olive oil over medium heat and sauté the fresh spinach until just wilted. Remove from the pan and rest on a paper-towel-lined dish. In the same pan, add the asparagus and sauté, turning throughout. Transfer to a paper towel-lined dish. 5. Place the slices of grilled sweet potato on serving plates and divide the spinach and asparagus evenly among the slices. Place a prepared egg on top of the spinach and asparagus. Top this with ¼ cup of arugula. 6. Finish by drizzling with 1 tablespoon of pesto and sprinkle with 1 tablespoon of cheese. Serve with 1 roasted plum tomato.

Per Serving:
calories: 441 | fat: 35g | protein: 13g | carbs: 23g | fiber: 4g | sodium: 481mg

Mediterranean Fruit Bulgur Breakfast Bowl

Prep time: 5 minutes |Cook time: 15 minutes| Serves: 6

1½ cups uncooked bulgur
2 cups 2% milk
1 cup water
½ teaspoon ground cinnamon
2 cups frozen (or fresh, pitted) dark sweet cherries

8 dried (or fresh) figs, chopped
½ cup chopped almonds
¼ cup loosely packed fresh mint, chopped
Warm 2% milk, for serving (optional)

1. In a medium saucepan, combine the bulgur, milk, water, and cinnamon. Stir once, then bring just to a boil. Cover, reduce the heat to medium-low, and simmer for 10 minutes or until the liquid is absorbed. 2. Turn off the heat, but keep the pan on the stove, and stir in the frozen cherries (no need to thaw), figs, and almonds. Stir well, cover for 1 minute, and let the hot bulgur thaw the cherries and partially hydrate the figs. Stir in the mint. 3. Scoop into serving bowls. Serve with warm milk, if desired. You can also serve it chilled.

Per Serving:
calories: 273 | fat: 7g | protein: 10g | carbs: 48g | fiber: 8g | sodium: 46mg

Creamy Cinnamon Porridge

Prep time: 10 minutes | Cook time: 10 minutes | Serves 2

¼ cup coconut milk
¾ cup unsweetened almond milk or water
¼ cup almond butter or hazelnut butter
1 tablespoon virgin coconut oil
2 tablespoons chia seeds
1 tablespoon flax meal
1 teaspoon cinnamon
¼ cup macadamia nuts
¼ cup hazelnuts
4 Brazil nuts
Optional: low-carb sweetener, to taste
¼ cup unsweetened large coconut flakes
1 tablespoon cacao nibs

1. In a small saucepan, mix the coconut milk and almond milk and heat over medium heat. Once hot (not boiling), take off the heat. Add the almond butter and coconut oil. Stir until well combined. If needed, use an immersion blender and process until smooth. 2. Add the chia seeds, flax meal, and cinnamon, and leave to rest for 5 to 10 minutes. Roughly chop the macadamias, hazelnuts, and Brazil nuts and stir in. Add sweetener, if using, and stir. Transfer to serving bowls. In a small skillet, dry-roast the coconut flakes over medium-high heat for 1 to 2 minutes, until lightly toasted and fragrant. Top the porridge with the toasted coconut flakes and cacao nibs (or you can use chopped 100% chocolate). Serve immediately or store in the fridge for up to 3 days.

Per Serving:
calories: 646 | fat: 61g | protein: 13g | carbs: 23g | fiber: 10g | sodium: 40mg

Greek Yogurt Parfait

Prep time: 5 minutes | Cook time: 0 minutes | Serves 1

½ cup plain whole-milk Greek yogurt
2 tablespoons heavy whipping cream
¼ cup frozen berries, thawed with juices
½ teaspoon vanilla or almond
extract (optional)
¼ teaspoon ground cinnamon (optional)
1 tablespoon ground flaxseed
2 tablespoons chopped nuts (walnuts or pecans)

1. In a small bowl or glass, combine the yogurt, heavy whipping cream, thawed berries in their juice, vanilla or almond extract (if using), cinnamon (if using), and flaxseed and stir well until smooth. Top with chopped nuts and enjoy.

Per Serving:
calories: 333 | fat: 27g | protein: 10g | carbs: 15g | fiber: 4g | sodium: 71mg

Crostini with Smoked Trout

Prep time: 10 minutes | Cook time: 5 minutes | Serves 4

½ French baguette, cut into 1-inch-thick slices
1 tablespoon olive oil
¼ teaspoon onion powder
1 (4-ounce / 113-g) can smoked
trout
¼ cup crème fraîche
¼ teaspoon chopped fresh dill, for garnish

1. Drizzle the bread on both sides with the olive oil and sprinkle with the onion powder. 2. Place the bread in a single layer in a large skillet and toast over medium heat until lightly browned on both sides, 3 to 4 minutes total. 3. Transfer the toasted bread to a serving platter and place 1 or 2 pieces of the trout on each slice. Top with the crème fraîche, garnish with the dill, and serve immediately.

Per Serving:
calories: 206 | fat: 10g | protein: 13g | carbs: 15g | fiber: 1g | sodium: 350mg

Mediterranean Omelet

Prep time: 10 minutes | Cook time: 12 minutes | Serves 2

2 teaspoons extra-virgin olive oil, divided
1 garlic clove, minced
½ red bell pepper, thinly sliced
½ yellow bell pepper, thinly sliced
¼ cup thinly sliced red onion
2 tablespoons chopped fresh
basil
2 tablespoons chopped fresh parsley, plus extra for garnish
½ teaspoon salt
½ teaspoon freshly ground black pepper
4 large eggs, beaten

1. In a large, heavy skillet, heat 1 teaspoon of the olive oil over medium heat. Add the garlic, peppers, and onion to the pan and sauté, stirring frequently, for 5 minutes. 2. Add the basil, parsley, salt, and pepper, increase the heat to medium-high, and sauté for 2 minutes. Slide the vegetable mixture onto a plate and return the pan to the heat. 3. Heat the remaining 1 teaspoon olive oil in the same pan and pour in the beaten eggs, tilting the pan to coat evenly. Cook the eggs just until the edges are bubbly and all but the center is dry, 3 to 5 minutes. 4. Either flip the omelet or use a spatula to turn it over. 5. Spoon the vegetable mixture onto one-half of the omelet and use a spatula to fold the empty side over the top. Slide the omelet onto a platter or cutting board. 6. To serve, cut the omelet in half and garnish with fresh parsley.

Per Serving:
calories: 218 | fat: 14g | protein: 14g | carbs: 9g | fiber: 1g | sodium: 728mg

Quinoa and Yogurt Breakfast Bowls

Prep time: 10 minutes | Cook time: 12 minutes | Serves 8

2 cups quinoa, rinsed and drained
4 cups water
1 teaspoon vanilla extract
¼ teaspoon salt
2 cups low-fat plain Greek yogurt
2 cups blueberries
1 cup toasted almonds
½ cup pure maple syrup

1. Place quinoa, water, vanilla, and salt in the Instant Pot®. Close lid and set steam release to Sealing. Press the Rice button and set time to 12 minutes. 2. When the timer beeps, let pressure release naturally, about 20 minutes. Open lid and fluff quinoa with a fork. 3. Stir in yogurt. Serve warm, topped with berries, almonds, and maple syrup.

Per Serving:
calories: 376 | fat: 13g | protein: 16g | carbs: 52g | fiber: 6g | sodium: 105mg

Spinach and Swiss Frittata with Mushrooms

Prep time: 10 minutes | Cook time: 20 minutes | Serves 4

Olive oil cooking spray
8 large eggs
½ teaspoon salt
½ teaspoon black pepper
1 garlic clove, minced

2 cups fresh baby spinach
4 ounces (113 g) baby bella mushrooms, sliced
1 shallot, diced
½ cup shredded Swiss cheese, divided
Hot sauce, for serving (optional)

1. Preheat the air fryer to 360°F(182°C). Lightly coat the inside of a 6-inch round cake pan with olive oil cooking spray. 2. In a large bowl, beat the eggs, salt, pepper, and garlic for 1 to 2 minutes, or until well combined. 3. Fold in the spinach, mushrooms, shallot, and ¼ cup of the Swiss cheese. 4. Pour the egg mixture into the prepared cake pan, and sprinkle the remaining ¼ cup of Swiss over the top. 5. Place into the air fryer and bake for 18 to 20 minutes, or until the eggs are set in the center. 6. Remove from the air fryer and allow to cool for 5 minutes. Drizzle with hot sauce (if using) before serving.

Per Serving:
calories: 207 | fat: 13g | protein: 18g | carbs: 4g | fiber: 1g | sodium: 456mg

Turkish Egg Bowl

Prep time: 10 minutes | Cook time: 15 minutes | Serves 2

2 tablespoons ghee
½–1 teaspoon red chile flakes
2 tablespoons extra-virgin olive oil
1 cup full-fat goat's or sheep's milk yogurt
1 clove garlic, minced
1 tablespoon fresh lemon juice

Salt and black pepper, to taste
Dash of vinegar
4 large eggs
Optional: pinch of sumac
2 tablespoons chopped fresh cilantro or parsley

1. In a skillet, melt the ghee over low heat. Add the chile flakes and let it infuse while you prepare the eggs. Remove from the heat and mix with the extra-virgin olive oil. Set aside. Combine the yogurt, garlic, lemon juice, salt, and pepper. 2. Poach the eggs. Fill a medium saucepan with water and a dash of vinegar. Bring to a boil over high heat. Crack each egg individually into a ramekin or a cup. Using a spoon, create a gentle whirlpool in the water; this will help the egg white wrap around the egg yolk. Slowly lower the egg into the water in the center of the whirlpool. Turn off the heat and cook for 3 to 4 minutes. Use a slotted spoon to remove the egg from the water and place it on a plate. Repeat for all remaining eggs. 3. To assemble, place the yogurt mixture in a bowl and add the poached eggs. Drizzle with the infused oil, and garnish with cilantro. Add a pinch of sumac, if using. Eat warm.

Per Serving:
calories: 576 | fat: 46g | protein: 27g | carbs: 17g | fiber: 4g | sodium: 150mg

Bulgur Wheat Cereal with Apples and Almonds

Prep time: 2 minutes | Cook time: 23 minutes | Serves 1

½ teaspoon extra virgin olive oil
¼ cup medium-grain uncooked bulgur wheat
½ medium apple (any variety), chopped
1 tablespoon raisins

¾ cup hot water
1teaspoon honey
1 tablespoon slivered or finely chopped almonds
Pinch of ground cinnamon

1. Add the olive oil to a small pan placed over medium heat. When the oil becomes hot, add the bulgur and sauté for 2–3 minutes, stirring frequently with a wooden spoon. 2. Add the apple, raisins, and hot water. When the mixture begins to boil, promptly remove the pan from the heat, cover, and set it aside for 10 minutes. After 10 minutes, add the honey and stir. 3. Top the cereal with the almonds and then sprinkle the cinnamon over the top. Serve warm.

Per Serving:
calories: 297 | fat: 8g | protein: 7g | carbs: 56g | fiber: 8g | sodium: 14mg

Chapter 3 Beef, Pork, and Lamb

Beef and Goat Cheese Stuffed Peppers

Prep time: 10 minutes | Cook time: 30 minutes | Serves 4

1 pound (454 g) lean ground beef	1 teaspoon salt
½ cup cooked brown rice	½ teaspoon black pepper
2 Roma tomatoes, diced	¼ teaspoon ground allspice
3 garlic cloves, minced	2 bell peppers, halved and seeded
½ yellow onion, diced	4 ounces (113 g) goat cheese
2 tablespoons fresh oregano, chopped	¼ cup fresh parsley, chopped

1. Preheat the air fryer to 360°F(182ºC). 2. In a large bowl, combine the ground beef, rice, tomatoes, garlic, onion, oregano, salt, pepper, and allspice. Mix well. 3. Divide the beef mixture equally into the halved bell peppers and top each with about 1 ounce (28 g a quarter of the total) of the goat cheese. 4. Place the peppers into the air fryer basket in a single layer, making sure that they don't touch each other. Bake for 30 minutes. 5. Remove the peppers from the air fryer and top with fresh parsley before serving.

Per Serving:
calories: 298 | fat: 12g | protein: 32g | carbs: 17g | fiber: 3g | sodium: 695mg

Stewed Pork with Greens

Prep time: 10 minutes | Cook time: 1 hour 40 minutes | Serves 3

¾ teaspoon fine sea salt, divided	1 medium onion (any variety), chopped
½ teaspoon freshly ground black pepper, divided	2 spring onions, sliced (white parts only)
1¼ pounds (567g) pork shoulder, trimmed and cut into 1½-inch chunks	1 leek, sliced (white parts only)
6 tablespoons extra virgin olive oil, divided	¼ cup chopped fresh dill
1 bay leaf	1 pound (454 g) Swiss chard, roughly chopped
3 allspice berries	3 tablespoons fresh lemon juice plus more for serving
2 tablespoons dry red wine	

1. Sprinkle ¼ teaspoon of the sea salt and ¼ teaspoon of the black pepper over the pork. Rub the seasonings into the meat. 2. Add 1 tablespoon of the olive oil to a heavy pan over medium-high heat. Add the bay leaf and allspice berries, then add the meat and brown for 2–3 minutes per side. 3. Add the red wine and let it bubble, then use a wooden spatula to scrape the browned bits from the pan. Continue simmering until the liquid has evaporated, about 3 minutes, then transfer the meat and juices to a plate. Set aside. 4. Heat 4 tablespoons of the olive oil in a large pot placed over medium heat. Add the onion, spring onions, and leeks, and sauté until soft, about 5 minutes, then add the dill and sauté for 1–2 minutes more. 5. Add the meat and juices to the pot and sprinkle another ¼ teaspoon sea salt and ¼ teaspoon black pepper over the meat. Add just enough hot water to cover the meat halfway (start with less water), then cover and reduce the heat to low. Simmer for about 1 hour or until the meat is tender. 6. Remove the lid and add the chard and lemon juice. Use tongs to toss the chard and mix well. Continue simmering for about 5 minutes, then drizzle in the last tablespoon of olive oil and mix again. Cover and simmer for another 20 minutes, mixing occasionally, until the greens are wilted, then remove the pot from the heat. 7. Let stand covered for 10 minutes, then add a squeeze of lemon before serving. Allow to cool completely before covering and storing in the refrigerator for up to 2 days.

Per Serving:
calories: 565 | fat: 38g | protein: 39g | carbs: 15g | fiber: 4g | sodium: 592mg

Greek Stuffed Tenderloin

Prep time: 10 minutes | Cook time: 10 minutes | Serves 4

1½ pounds (680 g) venison or beef tenderloin, pounded to ¼ inch thick	¼ cup finely chopped onions
3 teaspoons fine sea salt	2 cloves garlic, minced
1 teaspoon ground black pepper	For Garnish/Serving (Optional):
2 ounces (57 g) creamy goat cheese	Prepared yellow mustard
½ cup crumbled feta cheese (about 2 ounces / 57 g)	Halved cherry tomatoes
	Extra-virgin olive oil
	Sprigs of fresh rosemary
	Lavender flowers

1. Spray the air fryer basket with avocado oil. Preheat the air fryer to 400ºF (204ºC). 2. Season the tenderloin on all sides with the salt and pepper. 3. In a medium-sized mixing bowl, combine the goat cheese, feta, onions, and garlic. Place the mixture in the center of the tenderloin. Starting at the end closest to you, tightly roll the tenderloin like a jelly roll. Tie the rolled tenderloin tightly with kitchen twine. 4. Place the meat in the air fryer basket and air fry for 5 minutes. Flip the meat over and cook for another 5 minutes, or until the internal temperature reaches 135ºF (57ºC) for medium-rare. 5. To serve, smear a line of prepared yellow mustard on a platter, then place the meat next to it and add halved cherry tomatoes on the side, if desired. Drizzle with olive oil and garnish with rosemary sprigs and lavender flowers, if desired. 6. Best served fresh. Store leftovers in an airtight container in the fridge for 3 days. Reheat in a preheated 350ºF (177ºC) air fryer for 4 minutes, or until heated through.

Per Serving:
calories: 345 | fat: 17g | protein: 43g | carbs: 2g | fiber: 0g | sodium: 676mg

Calabrian Braised Beef with Caramelized Onions and Potatoes

Prep time: 10 minutes | Cook time: 4 hours 30 minutes | Serves 6 to 8

5 tablespoons olive oil, divided
3 medium onions, thinly sliced
4 cloves garlic, very thinly sliced
1½ teaspoons salt, divided
2 pounds (907 g) top sirloin steak
½ teaspoon freshly ground black pepper
2 tablespoons chopped fresh

thyme, divided
3 medium potatoes, peeled and thinly sliced
2 sprigs fresh rosemary, leaves picked and finely chopped, divided
¼ cup grated Parmesan cheese, plus 4 tablespoons, divided
1 (28-ounce / 794-g) can crushed tomatoes

1. Preheat the oven to 325°F(165ºC). 2. Heat 2 tablespoons of olive oil in a large skillet over medium heat. Add the onions and garlic along with ½ teaspoon of salt, reduce the heat to medium-low, and cook, stirring frequently, until they become very soft and golden brown, about 20 minutes. Remove from the heat. 3. Add 1 tablespoon of olive oil to a Dutch oven over medium-high heat. Pat the meat dry with paper towels and sprinkle with the remaining 1 teaspoon of salt and the pepper. Brown the meat on both sides in the Dutch oven, about 10 minutes. 4. Place about half of the cooked onions on top of the meat in an even layer. Sprinkle 1 tablespoon of thyme over the onions, then top with half of the potato slices, arranging them in an even layer. Drizzle with 1 tablespoon of olive oil, and top with half of the rosemary, and 2 tablespoons of cheese. Pour half of the tomatoes over the top. Repeat with the remaining onions, thyme, potatoes, the remaining tablespoon of olive oil, rosemary, 2 tablespoons of cheese, and the tomatoes. Place the lid on the Dutch oven and cook in the preheated oven for about 4 hours, until the meat is very tender. Sprinkle the remaining ¼ cup of cheese over the top and cook under the broiler for a few minutes, until the cheese is melted and golden brown. Serve hot.

Per Serving:
calories: 399 | fat: 23g | protein: 29g | carbs: 19g | fiber: 4g | sodium: 516mg

Greek Meatball Soup

Prep time: 20 minutes | Cook time: 45 minutes | Serves 5

1 pound (454 g) ground beef
⅓ cup orzo
4 large eggs
1 onion, finely chopped
2 garlic cloves, minced
2 tablespoons finely chopped

fresh Italian parsley
Sea salt
Freshly ground black pepper
½ cup all-purpose flour
5 to 6 cups chicken broth
Juice of 2 lemons

1. In a large bowl, combine the ground beef, orzo, 1 egg, the onion, garlic, and parsley and stir until well mixed. Season with salt and pepper and mix again. 2. Place the flour in a small bowl. 3. Roll the meat mixture into a ball about the size of a golf ball and dredge it in the flour to coat, shaking off any excess. Place the meatball in a stockpot and repeat with the remaining meat mixture. 4. Pour enough broth into the pot to cover the meatballs by about 1 inch. Bring the broth to a boil over high heat. Reduce the heat to low, cover, and simmer for 30 to 45 minutes, until the meatballs are cooked through. 5. While the meatballs are simmering, in a small bowl, whisk the 3 remaining eggs until frothy. Add the lemon juice and whisk well. 6. When the meatballs are cooked, while whisking continuously, slowly pour 1½ cups of the hot broth into the egg mixture. Pour the egg mixture back into the pot and mix well. Bring back to a simmer, then remove from the heat and serve.

Per Serving:
calories: 297 | fat: 9g | protein: 27g | carbs: 28g | fiber: 1g | sodium: 155mg

Beef Ragù

Prep time: 15 minutes | Cook time: 4½ hours | Serves 6

1 medium yellow onion, diced small
3 cloves garlic, minced
6 tablespoons tomato paste
3 tablespoons chopped fresh oregano leaves (or 3 teaspoons dried oregano)

1 (4-pound / 1.8-kg) beef chuck roast, halved
Coarse sea salt
Black pepper
2 cups beef stock
2 tablespoons red wine vinegar

1. Combine the onion, garlic, tomato paste, and oregano in the slow cooker. 2. Season the roast halves with salt and pepper and place on top of the onion mixture in the slow cooker. Add the beef stock. 3. Cover and cook until meat is tender and can easily be pulled apart with a fork, on high for 4½ hours, or on low for 9 hours. Let cool 10 minutes. 4. Shred the meat while it is still in the slow cooker using two forks. Stir the vinegar into the sauce. Serve hot, over pasta.

Per Serving:
calories: 482 | fat: 19g | protein: 67g | carbs: 13g | fiber: 1g | sodium: 292mg

Tenderloin with Crispy Shallots

Prep time: 30 minutes | Cook time: 18 to 20 minutes | Serves 6

1½ pounds (680 g) beef tenderloin steaks
Sea salt and freshly ground black pepper, to taste

4 medium shallots
1 teaspoon olive oil or avocado oil

1. Season both sides of the steaks with salt and pepper, and let them sit at room temperature for 45 minutes. 2. Set the air fryer to 400°F (204ºC) and let it preheat for 5 minutes. 3. Working in batches if necessary, place the steaks in the air fryer basket in a single layer and air fry for 5 minutes. Flip and cook for 5 minutes longer, until an instant-read thermometer inserted in the center of the steaks registers 120ºF (49ºC) for medium-rare (or as desired). Remove the steaks and tent with aluminum foil to rest. 4. Set the air fryer to 300ºF (149ºC). In a medium bowl, toss the shallots with the oil. Place the shallots in the basket and air fry for 5 minutes, then give them a toss and cook for 3 to 5 minutes more, until crispy and golden brown. 5. Place the steaks on serving plates and arrange the shallots on top.

Per Serving:
calories: 166 | fat: 8g | protein: 24g | carbs: 1g | fiber: 0g | sodium: 72mg

Southern Chili

Prep time: 20 minutes | Cook time: 25 minutes | Serves 4

1 pound (454 g) ground beef (85% lean)
1 cup minced onion
1 (28-ounce / 794-g) can tomato purée
1 (15-ounce / 425-g) can diced

tomatoes with green chilies
1 (15-ounce / 425-g) can light red kidney beans, rinsed and drained
¼ cup Chili seasoning

1. Preheat the air fryer to 400ºF (204ºC). 2. In a baking pan, mix the ground beef and onion. Place the pan in the air fryer. 3. Cook for 4 minutes. Stir and cook for 4 minutes more until browned. Remove the pan from the fryer. Drain the meat and transfer to a large bowl. 4. Reduce the air fryer temperature to 350ºF (177ºC). 5. To the bowl with the meat, add in the tomato purée, diced tomatoes and green chilies, kidney beans, and Chili seasoning. Mix well. Pour the mixture into the baking pan. 6. Cook for 25 minutes, stirring every 10 minutes, until thickened.

Per Serving:
calories: 455 | fat: 18g | protein: 32g | carbs: 44g | fiber: 11g | sodium: 815mg

Bulgur and Beef–Stuffed Peppers

Prep time: 15 minutes | Cook time: 26 minutes | Serves 4

½ cup bulgur wheat
1 cup vegetable broth
2 tablespoons olive oil
1 medium white onion, peeled and diced
1 clove garlic, peeled and minced
1 medium Roma tomato, seeded and chopped
1 teaspoon minced fresh rosemary

1 teaspoon fresh thyme leaves
½ teaspoon salt
½ teaspoon ground black pepper
½ pound (227 g) 90% lean ground beef
4 large red bell peppers, tops removed and seeded
½ cup marinara sauce
1 cup water
½ cup grated Parmesan cheese

1. Add bulgur and broth to the Instant Pot® and stir well. Close lid, set steam release to Sealing, press the Rice button, adjust pressure to Low, and set time to 12 minutes. When the timer beeps, quick-release the pressure until the float valve drops. Open lid and fluff bulgur with a fork, then transfer to a medium bowl and set aside to cool. 2. Press the Sauté button and heat oil. Add onion and cook until tender, about 5 minutes. Add garlic, tomato, rosemary, thyme, salt, and pepper. Cook until garlic and herbs are fragrant, about 1 minute. 3. Add ground beef and cook, crumbling well, until no longer pink, about 5 minutes. Press the Cancel button. 4. Add beef mixture to bulgur and mix well. Divide mixture between bell peppers, making sure not to compact the mixture too much. Top each pepper with marinara sauce. 5. Clean out pot, add water, and place rack in pot. Carefully stand peppers on rack. Close lid, set steam release to Sealing, press the Manual button, and set time to 3 minutes. When the timer beeps, quick-release the pressure until the float valve drops. Open lid and carefully transfer peppers with tongs to plates. Top with cheese and serve immediately.

Per Serving:
calories: 363 | fat: 17g | protein: 21g | carbs: 31g | fiber: 7g | sodium: 594mg

Greek Kebabs

Prep time: 10 minutes | Cook time: 10 minutes | Serves 6

• 1/4 cup olive oil
• Juice of 1 lemon
• 1 tablespoon dried oregano
• 2 cloves garlic, minced
• 5 bay leaves

• Sea salt and freshly ground pepper, to taste
• 2 pounds beef sirloin, cut into 2-inch cubes

1. Combine all the ingredients except the meat in a plastic bag. Add the meat and shake to coat. 2. Marinate for up to 24 hours and drain. 3. Skewer the meat onto 8-inch skewers and grill on medium heat for 8–10 minutes, turning the skewers halfway through the cooking time.

Mustard Lamb Chops

Prep time: 5 minutes | Cook time: 14 minutes | Serves 4

Oil, for spraying
1 tablespoon Dijon mustard
2 teaspoons lemon juice
½ teaspoon dried tarragon
¼ teaspoon salt

¼ teaspoon freshly ground black pepper
4 (1¼-inch-thick) loin lamb chops

1. Preheat the air fryer to 390ºF (199ºC). Line the air fryer basket with parchment and spray lightly with oil. 2. In a small bowl, mix together the mustard, lemon juice, tarragon, salt, and black pepper. 3. Pat dry the lamb chops with a paper towel. Brush the chops on both sides with the mustard mixture. 4. Place the chops in the prepared basket. You may need to work in batches, depending on the size of your air fryer. 5. Cook for 8 minutes, flip, and cook for another 6 minutes, or until the internal temperature reaches 125ºF (52ºC) for rare, 145ºF (63ºC) for medium-rare, or 155ºF (68ºC) for medium.

Per Serving:
calories: 96 | fat: 4g | protein: 14g | carbs: 0g | fiber: 0g | sodium: 233mg

Onion Pork Kebabs

Prep time: 22 minutes | Cook time: 18 minutes | Serves 3

2 tablespoons tomato purée
½ fresh serrano, minced
⅓ teaspoon paprika
1 pound (454 g) pork, ground
½ cup green onions, finely chopped

3 cloves garlic, peeled and finely minced
1 teaspoon ground black pepper, or more to taste
1 teaspoon salt, or more to taste

1. Thoroughly combine all ingredients in a mixing dish. Then form your mixture into sausage shapes. 2. Cook for 18 minutes at 355ºF (179ºC). Mound salad on a serving platter, top with air-fried kebabs and serve warm. Bon appétit!

Per Serving:
calories: 216 | fat: 6g | protein: 35g | carbs: 4g | fiber: 1g | sodium: 855mg

Beef and Wild Mushroom Stew

Prep time: 15 minutes | Cook time: 1 hour 15 minutes | Serves 8

2 pounds (907 g) fresh porcini or morel mushrooms	chopped
⅓ cup olive oil	1 clove garlic, minced
2 pounds (907 g) lean, boneless beef, cut into 2-inch cubes	1 cup dry white wine
2 medium onions, finely	1 teaspoon thyme, minced
	Sea salt and freshly ground pepper, to taste

1. Wash the mushrooms carefully by soaking them in cold water and swirling them around. 2. Trim away any soft parts of the mushrooms. 3. Heat the olive oil in a heavy stew pot over medium-high heat. Brown the meat evenly on all sides, and set aside on a plate. 4. Add the onions, garlic, and mushrooms to the olive oil, and cook for 5–8 minutes, or until the onions are tender, stirring frequently. 5. Add the remaining ingredients and return the browned meat to the pot. Cover and bring to a boil, then reduce heat to low and simmer. Simmer for 1 hour, or until the meat is tender and flavorful. 6. Season with sea salt and freshly ground pepper to taste.

Per Serving:
calories: 343 | fat: 22g | protein: 26g | carbs: 9g | fiber: 2g | sodium: 93mg

Cheesy Low-Carb Lasagna

Prep time: 10 minutes | Cook time: 10 minutes | Serves 4

Meat Layer:	Cheese Layer:
Extra-virgin olive oil	8 ounces (227 g) ricotta cheese
1 pound (454 g) 85% lean ground beef	1 cup shredded Mozzarella cheese
1 cup prepared marinara sauce	½ cup grated Parmesan cheese
¼ cup diced celery	2 large eggs
¼ cup diced red onion	1 teaspoon dried Italian seasoning, crushed
½ teaspoon minced garlic	½ teaspoon each minced garlic, garlic powder, and black pepper
Kosher salt and black pepper, to taste	

1. For the meat layer: Grease a cake pan with 1 teaspoon olive oil. 2. In a large bowl, combine the ground beef, marinara, celery, onion, garlic, salt, and pepper. Place the seasoned meat in the pan. 3. Place the pan in the air fryer basket. Set the air fryer to 375ºF (191ºC) for 10 minutes. 4. Meanwhile, for the cheese layer: In a medium bowl, combine the ricotta, half the Mozzarella, the Parmesan, lightly beaten eggs, Italian seasoning, minced garlic, garlic powder, and pepper. Stir until well blended. 5. At the end of the cooking time, spread the cheese mixture over the meat mixture. Sprinkle with the remaining ½ cup Mozzarella. Set the air fryer to 375ºF (191ºC) for 10 minutes, or until the cheese is browned and bubbling. 6. At the end of the cooking time, use a meat thermometer to ensure the meat has reached an internal temperature of 160ºF (71ºC). 7. Drain the fat and liquid from the pan. Let stand for 5 minutes before serving.

Per Serving:
calories: 555 | fat: 36g | protein: 45g | carbs: 10g | fiber: 2g | sodium: 248mg

Baked Lamb Kofta Meatballs

Prep timePrep Time: 15 minutes | Cook Time: 30 minutes | Serves 2

¼ cup walnuts	¼ teaspoon salt
½ small onion	¼ teaspoon cumin
1 garlic clove	¼ teaspoon allspice
1 roasted piquillo pepper	Pinch cayenne pepper
2 tablespoons fresh parsley	8 ounces (227 g) lean ground lamb
2 tablespoons fresh mint	

1. Preheat the oven to 350°F (180ºC) and set the rack to the middle position. Line a baking sheet with foil. 2. In the bowl of a food processor, combine the walnuts, onion, garlic, roasted pepper, parsley, mint, salt, cumin, allspice, and cayenne pepper. Pulse about 10 times to combine everything. 3. Transfer the spice mixture to the bowl and add the lamb. With your hands or a spatula, mix the spices into the lamb. 4. Roll into 1½-inch balls (about the size of golf balls). 5. Place the meatballs on the foil-lined baking sheet and bake for 30 minutes, or until cooked to an internal temperature of 160°F(71ºC).

Per Serving:
calories: 408 | fat: 23g | protein: 22g | carbs: 7g | fiber: 3g | sodium: 429mg

Lebanese Malfouf (Stuffed Cabbage Rolls)

Prep time: 15 minutes | Cook time: 33 minutes | Serves 4

1 head green cabbage	1 teaspoon ground cinnamon
1 pound (454 g) lean ground beef	2 tablespoons chopped fresh mint
½ cup long-grain brown rice	Juice of 1 lemon
4 garlic cloves, minced	Olive oil cooking spray
1 teaspoon salt	½ cup beef broth
½ teaspoon black pepper	1 tablespoon olive oil

1. Cut the cabbage in half and remove the core. Remove 12 of the larger leaves to use for the cabbage rolls. 2. Bring a large pot of salted water to a boil, then drop the cabbage leaves into the water, boiling them for 3 minutes. Remove from the water and set aside. 3. In a large bowl, combine the ground beef, rice, garlic, salt, pepper, cinnamon, mint, and lemon juice, and mix together until combined. Divide this mixture into 12 equal portions. 4. Preheat the air fryer to 360°F(182ºC). Lightly coat a small casserole dish with olive oil cooking spray. 5. Place a cabbage leaf on a clean work surface. Place a spoonful of the beef mixture on one side of the leaf, leaving space on all other sides. Fold the two perpendicular sides inward and then roll forward, tucking tightly as rolled (similar to a burrito roll). Place the finished rolls into the baking dish, stacking them on top of each other if needed. 6. Pour the beef broth over the top of the cabbage rolls so that it soaks down between them, and then brush the tops with the olive oil. 7. Place the casserole dish into the air fryer basket and bake for 30 minutes.

Per Serving:
calories: 329 | fat: 10g | protein: 29g | carbs: 33g | fiber: 7g | sodium: 700mg

Braised Lamb Shanks with Bell Pepper and Harissa

Prep time: 10 minutes | Cook time: 1 hour 20 minutes | Serves 4

4 (10- to 12-ounce/ 283- to 340-g) lamb shanks, trimmed
¾ teaspoon salt, divided
1 tablespoon extra-virgin olive oil
1 onion, chopped
1 red bell pepper, stemmed, seeded, and cut into 1-inch pieces
¼ cup harissa, divided
4 garlic cloves, minced
1 tablespoon tomato paste
½ cup chicken broth
1 bay leaf
2 tablespoons chopped fresh mint

1. Pat lamb shanks dry with paper towels and sprinkle with ½ teaspoon salt. Using highest sauté function, heat oil in Instant Pot for 5 minutes (or until just smoking). Brown 2 shanks on all sides, 8 to 10 minutes; transfer to plate. Repeat with remaining shanks; transfer to plate. 2. Add onion, bell pepper, and remaining ¼ teaspoon salt to fat left in pot and cook, using highest sauté function, until vegetables are softened, about 5 minutes. Stir in 2 tablespoons harissa, garlic, and tomato paste and cook until fragrant, about 30 seconds. Stir in broth and bay leaf, scraping up any browned bits. Nestle shanks into pot and add any accumulated juices. Lock lid in place and close pressure release valve. Select high pressure cook function and cook for 60 minutes. 3. Turn off Instant Pot and let pressure release naturally for 15 minutes. Quick-release any remaining pressure, then carefully remove lid, allowing steam to escape away from you. Transfer shanks to serving dish, tent with aluminum foil, and let rest while finishing sauce. 4. Strain braising liquid through fine-mesh strainer into fat separator. Discard bay leaf and transfer solids to blender. Let braising liquid settle for 5 minutes, then pour ¾ cup defatted liquid into blender with solids; discard remaining liquid. Add remaining 2 tablespoons harissa and process until smooth, about 1 minute. Season with salt and pepper to taste. Pour portion of sauce over shanks and sprinkle with mint. Serve, passing remaining sauce separately.

Per Serving:
calories: 450 | fat: 33g | protein: 28g | carbs: 9g | fiber: 3g | sodium: 780mg

Asian Glazed Meatballs

Prep time: 15 minutes | Cook time: 10 minutes per batch | Serves 4 to 6

1 large shallot, finely chopped
2 cloves garlic, minced
1 tablespoon grated fresh ginger
2 teaspoons fresh thyme, finely chopped
1½ cups brown mushrooms, very finely chopped (a food processor works well here)
2 tablespoons soy sauce
Freshly ground black pepper, to taste
1 pound (454 g) ground beef
½ pound (227 g) ground pork
3 egg yolks
1 cup Thai sweet chili sauce (spring roll sauce)
¼ cup toasted sesame seeds
2 scallions, sliced

1. Combine the shallot, garlic, ginger, thyme, mushrooms, soy sauce, freshly ground black pepper, ground beef and pork, and egg yolks in a bowl and mix the ingredients together. Gently shape the mixture into 24 balls, about the size of a golf ball. 2. Preheat the air fryer to 380ºF (193ºC). 3. Working in batches, air fry the meatballs for 8 minutes, turning the meatballs over halfway through the cooking time. Drizzle some of the Thai sweet chili sauce on top of each meatball and return the basket to the air fryer, air frying for another 2 minutes. Reserve the remaining Thai sweet chili sauce for serving. 4. As soon as the meatballs are done, sprinkle with toasted sesame seeds and transfer them to a serving platter. Scatter the scallions around and serve warm.

Per Serving:
calories: 274 | fat: 11g | protein: 29g | carbs: 14g | fiber: 4g | sodium: 802mg

Mediterranean Chimichurri Skirt Steak

Prep time: 10 minutes | Cook time: 15 minutes | Serves 4

¾ cup fresh mint
¾ cup fresh parsley
⅔ cup extra-virgin olive oil
⅓ cup lemon juice
Zest of 1 lemon
2 tablespoons dried oregano
4 garlic cloves, peeled
½ teaspoon red pepper flakes
½ teaspoon kosher salt
1 to 1½ pounds (454 to 680 g) skirt steak, cut in half if longer than grill pan

1. In a food processor or blender, add the mint, parsley, olive oil, lemon juice, lemon zest, oregano, garlic, red pepper flakes, and salt. Process until the mixture reaches your desired consistency—anywhere from a slightly chunky to smooth purée. Remove a half cup of the chimichurri mixture and set aside. 2. Pour the remaining chimichurri mixture into a medium bowl or zip-top bag and add the steak. Mix together well and marinate for at least 30 minutes, and up to 8 hours in the refrigerator. 3. In a grill pan over medium-high heat, add the steak and cook 4 minutes on each side (for medium rare). Cook an additional 1 to 2 minutes per side for medium. 4. Place the steak on a cutting board, tent with foil to keep it warm, and let it rest for 10 minutes. Thinly slice the steak crosswise against the grain and serve with the reserved sauce.

Per Serving:
calories: 460 | fat: 38g | protein: 28g | carbs: 5g | fiber: 2g | sodium: 241mg

Garlic Balsamic London Broil

Prep time: 30 minutes | Cook time: 8 to 10 minutes | Serves 8

2 pounds (907 g) London broil
3 large garlic cloves, minced
3 tablespoons balsamic vinegar
3 tablespoons whole-grain mustard
2 tablespoons olive oil
Sea salt and ground black pepper, to taste
½ teaspoon dried hot red pepper flakes

1. Score both sides of the cleaned London broil. 2. Thoroughly combine the remaining ingredients; massage this mixture into the meat to coat it on all sides. Let it marinate for at least 3 hours. 3. Set the air fryer to 400ºF (204ºC); Then cook the London broil for 15 minutes. Flip it over and cook another 10 to 12 minutes. Bon appétit!

Per Serving:
calories: 240 | fat: 15g | protein: 23g | carbs: 2g | fiber: 0g | sodium: 141mg

Kofta with Vegetables in Tomato Sauce

Prep time: 15 minutes | Cook time: 6 to 8 hours | Serves 4

1 pound (454 g) raw ground beef
1 small white or yellow onion, finely diced
2 garlic cloves, minced
1 tablespoon dried parsley
2 teaspoons ground coriander
1 teaspoon ground cumin
½ teaspoon sea salt
½ teaspoon freshly ground black pepper
¼ teaspoon ground nutmeg
¼ teaspoon dried mint
¼ teaspoon paprika
1 (28-ounce/ 794-g) can no-salt-added diced tomatoes
2 or 3 zucchini, cut into 1½-inch-thick rounds
4 ounces (113 g) mushrooms
1 large red onion, chopped
1 green bell pepper, seeded and chopped

1. In large bowl, mix together the ground beef, white or yellow onion, garlic, parsley, coriander, cumin, salt, pepper, nutmeg, mint, and paprika until well combined and all of the spices and onion are well blended into the meat. Form the meat mixture into 10 to 12 oval patties. Set aside. 2. In a slow cooker, combine the tomatoes, zucchini, mushrooms, red onion, and bell pepper. Stir to mix well. 3. Place the kofta patties on top of the tomato mixture. 4. Cover the cooker and cook for 6 to 8 hours on Low heat.

Per Serving:
calories: 263 | fat: 9g | protein: 27g | carbs: 23g | fiber: 7g | sodium: 480mg

Lamb Chops with Shaved Zucchini Salad

Prep time: 20 minutes | Cook time: 40 minutes | Serves 4

4 (8- to 12-ounce/ 227- to 340-g) lamb shoulder chops (blade or round bone), about ¾ inch thick, trimmed
¾ teaspoon table salt, divided
¾ teaspoon pepper, divided
2 tablespoons extra-virgin olive oil, divided
1 onion, chopped
5 garlic cloves, minced
½ cup chicken broth
1 bay leaf
4 zucchini (6 ounces / 170 g each), sliced lengthwise into ribbons
1 teaspoon grated lemon zest plus 1 tablespoon juice
2 ounces (57 g) goat cheese, crumbled (½ cup)
¼ cup chopped fresh mint
2 tablespoons raisins

1. Pat lamb chops dry with paper towels and sprinkle with ½ teaspoon salt and ½ teaspoon pepper. Using highest sauté function, heat 1½ teaspoons oil in Instant Pot for 5 minutes (or until just smoking). Brown half of chops on both sides, 6 to 8 minutes; transfer to plate. Repeat with 1½ teaspoons oil and remaining chops; transfer to plate. 2. Add onion to fat left in pot and cook, using highest sauté function, until softened, about 5 minutes. Stir in garlic and cook until fragrant, about 30 seconds. Stir in broth and bay leaf, scraping up any browned bits. Return chops to pot along with any accumulated juices (chops will overlap). Lock lid in place and close pressure release valve. Select high pressure cook function and cook for 20 minutes. 3. Turn off Instant Pot and let pressure release naturally for 15 minutes. Quick-release any remaining pressure, then carefully remove lid, allowing steam to escape away from you. Transfer chops to serving dish. Gently toss zucchini with lemon zest and juice, remaining 1 tablespoon oil, remaining ¼

teaspoon salt, and remaining ¼ teaspoon pepper in bowl. Arrange zucchini on serving dish with lamb, and sprinkle with goat cheese, mint, and raisins. Serve.

Per Serving:
calories: 390 | fat: 20g | protein: 38g | carbs: 14g | fiber: 2g | sodium: 720mg

Moroccan Flank Steak with Harissa Couscous

Prep time: 5 minutes | Cook time: 15 minutes | Serves 4

1½ teaspoons coriander seeds
1¼ teaspoons ground ginger
½ teaspoon ground cumin
¾ teaspoon ground cinnamon
¼ teaspoon ground cloves
1½ pounds (680 g) flank steak
3 tablespoons olive oil
¾ cup chicken broth
1 tablespoon harissa
½ cup chopped pitted dried dates
1 cup uncooked couscous
Sea salt
Freshly ground black pepper
¼ cup chopped fresh Italian parsley

1. In a small bowl, combine the coriander, ginger, cumin, cinnamon, and cloves. Rub the steak all over with the seasoning mix. 2. In a large sauté pan, heat the olive oil over medium-high heat. Add the steak and cook for 2 to 3 minutes on each side for medium-rare. Transfer the steak to a plate and set aside to rest for 10 minutes. 3. In the same pan, mix together the meat juices with the broth, harissa, and dates. Bring to a boil over medium-high heat. Add the couscous, remove from the heat, cover, and let stand for 5 minutes. Season with salt and pepper. 4. Cut the steak across the grain into thin strips. 5. Serve the steak with the couscous, garnished with parsley.

Per Serving:
calories: 516 | fat: 16g | protein: 43g | carbs: 49g | fiber: 4g | sodium: 137mg

Garlic Butter Steak Bites

Prep time: 5 minutes | Cook time: 16 minutes | Serves 3

Oil, for spraying
1 pound (454 g) boneless steak, cut into 1-inch pieces
2 tablespoons olive oil
1 teaspoon Worcestershire
sauce
½ teaspoon granulated garlic
½ teaspoon salt
¼ teaspoon freshly ground black pepper

1. Preheat the air fryer to 400°F (204°C). Line the air fryer basket with parchment and spray lightly with oil. 2. In a medium bowl, combine the steak, olive oil, Worcestershire sauce, garlic, salt, and black pepper and toss until evenly coated. 3. Place the steak in a single layer in the prepared basket. You may have to work in batches, depending on the size of your air fryer. 4. Cook for 10 to 16 minutes, flipping every 3 to 4 minutes. The total cooking time will depend on the thickness of the meat and your preferred doneness. If you want it well done, it may take up to 5 additional minutes.

Per Serving:
calories: 293| fat: 17g | protein: 32g | carbs: 1g | fiber: 0g | sodium: 494mg

Hearty Stewed Beef in Tomato Sauce

Prep time: 20 minutes | Cook time: 1 hour 45 minutes | Serves 5

3 tablespoons extra virgin olive oil	4 cloves
2 pounds (907 g) boneless beef chuck, cut into 2-inch (5cm) chunks	4 allspice berries
	1 bay leaf
	¼ teaspoon freshly ground black pepper
1 medium onion (any variety), diced	15 ounces (425 g) canned crushed tomatoes or chopped fresh tomatoes
4 garlic cloves, minced	
⅓ cup white wine	1 cup hot water
2 tablespoons tomato paste	½ teaspoon fine sea salt
1 cinnamon stick	

1. Add the olive oil to a deep pan over medium heat. When the oil starts to shimmer, place half the beef in the pan. Brown the meat until a crust develops, about 3–4 minutes per side, then transfer the meat to a plate, and set aside. Repeat with the remaining pieces. 2. Add the onions to the pan and sauté for 3 minutes or until soft, using a wooden spatula to scrape the browned bits from the bottom of the pan. Add the garlic and sauté for 1 minute, then add the wine and deglaze the pan for 1 more minute, again using the wooden spatula to scrape any browned bits from the bottom of the pan. 3. Add the tomato paste to the pan while stirring rapidly, then add the cinnamon stick, cloves, allspice berries, bay leaf, black pepper, crushed tomatoes, and hot water. Mix well. 4. Add the beef back to the pan. Stir, then cover and reduce the heat to low. Simmer for 1 hour 30 minutes or until the beef is cooked through and tender, and the sauce has thickened. (If the sauce becomes too dry, add more hot water as needed.) 5. About 10 minutes before the cooking time is complete, add the sea salt and stir. When ready to serve, remove the cinnamon stick, bay leaf, allspice berries, and cloves. Store in the refrigerator for up to 3 days.

Per Serving:
calories: 357 | fat: 19g | protein: 39g | carbs: 8g | fiber: 2g | sodium: 403mg

Grilled Filet Mignon with Red Wine–Mushroom Sauce

Prep timePrep Time: 20 minutes | Cook Time: 20 minutes | Serves 2

2 (3-ounce / 85-g) pieces filet mignon	1 cup low-sodium chicken stock
2 tablespoons olive oil, divided	½ teaspoon dried thyme
8 ounces (227 g) baby bella (cremini) mushrooms, quartered	1 sprig fresh rosemary
1 large shallot, minced (about ⅓ cup)	1 teaspoon herbes de Provence
	¼ teaspoon salt
2 teaspoons flour	¼ teaspoon garlic powder
2 teaspoons tomato paste	¼ teaspoon onion powder
½ cup red wine	Pinch freshly ground black pepper

1. Preheat the oven to 425°F (220°C) and set the oven rack to the middle position. 2. Remove the filets from the refrigerator about 30 minutes before you're ready to cook them. Pat them dry with a paper towel and let them rest while you prepare the mushroom sauce. 3. In a sauté pan, heat 1 tablespoon of olive oil over medium-high heat. Add the mushrooms and shallot and sauté for 10 minutes. 4. Add the flour and tomato paste and cook for another 30 seconds. Add the wine and scrape up any browned bits from the sauté pan. Add the chicken stock, thyme, and rosemary. 5. Stir the sauce so the flour doesn't form lumps and bring it to a boil. Once the sauce thickens, reduce the heat to the lowest setting and cover the pan to keep the sauce warm. 6. In a small bowl, combine the herbes de Provence, salt, garlic powder, onion powder, and pepper. 7. Rub the beef with the remaining 1 tablespoon of olive oil and season it on both sides with the herb mixture. 8. Heat an oven-safe sauté pan over medium-high heat. Add the beef and sear for 2½ minutes on each side. Then, transfer the pan to the oven for 5 more minutes to finish cooking. Use a meat thermometer to check the internal temperature and remove it at 130°F (54°C) for medium-rare. 9. Tent the meat with foil and let it rest for 5 minutes before serving topped with the mushroom sauce.

Per Serving:
calories: 385 | fat: 20g | protein: 25g | carbs: 15g | fiber: 0g | sodium: 330mg

Meatballs in Creamy Almond Sauce

Prep time: 15 minutes | Cook time: 35 minutes | Serves 4 to 6

8 ounces (227 g) ground veal or pork	½ teaspoon ground nutmeg
8 ounces (227 g) ground beef	2 teaspoons chopped fresh flat-leaf Italian parsley, plus ¼ cup, divided
½ cup finely minced onion, divided	
1 large egg, beaten	½ cup extra-virgin olive oil, divided
¼ cup almond flour	
1½ teaspoons salt, divided	¼ cup slivered almonds
1 teaspoon garlic powder	1 cup dry white wine or chicken broth
½ teaspoon freshly ground black pepper	¼ cup unsweetened almond butter

1. In a large bowl, combine the veal, beef, ¼ cup onion, and the egg and mix well with a fork. In a small bowl, whisk together the almond flour, 1 teaspoon salt, garlic powder, pepper, and nutmeg. Add to the meat mixture along with 2 teaspoons chopped parsley and incorporate well. Form the mixture into small meatballs, about 1 inch in diameter, and place on a plate. Let sit for 10 minutes at room temperature. 2. In a large skillet, heat ¼ cup oil over medium-high heat. Add the meatballs to the hot oil and brown on all sides, cooking in batches if necessary, 2 to 3 minutes per side. Remove from skillet and keep warm. 3. In the hot skillet, sauté the remaining ¼ cup minced onion in the remaining ¼ cup olive oil for 5 minutes. Reduce the heat to medium-low and add the slivered almonds. Sauté until the almonds are golden, another 3 to 5 minutes. 4. In a small bowl, whisk together the white wine, almond butter, and remaining ½ teaspoon salt. Add to the skillet and bring to a boil, stirring constantly. Reduce the heat to low, return the meatballs to skillet, and cover. Cook until the meatballs are cooked through, another 8 to 10 minutes. 5. Remove from the heat, stir in the remaining ¼ cup chopped parsley, and serve the meatballs warm and drizzled with almond sauce.

Per Serving:
calories: 447 | fat: 36g | protein: 20g | carbs: 7g | fiber: 2g | sodium: 659mg

Garlic-Marinated Flank Steak

Prep time: 30 minutes | Cook time: 8 to 10 minutes |
Serves 6

½ cup avocado oil
¼ cup coconut aminos
1 shallot, minced
1 tablespoon minced garlic
2 tablespoons chopped fresh oregano, or 2 teaspoons dried

1½ teaspoons sea salt
1 teaspoon freshly ground black pepper
¼ teaspoon red pepper flakes
2 pounds (907 g) flank steak

1. In a blender, combine the avocado oil, coconut aminos, shallot, garlic, oregano, salt, black pepper, and red pepper flakes. Process until smooth. 2. Place the steak in a zip-top plastic bag or shallow dish with the marinade. Seal the bag or cover the dish and marinate in the refrigerator for at least 2 hours or overnight. 3. Remove the steak from the bag and discard the marinade. 4. Set the air fryer to 400ºF (204ºC). Place the steak in the air fryer basket (if needed, cut into sections and work in batches). Air fry for 4 to 6 minutes, flip the steak, and cook for another 4 minutes or until the internal temperature reaches 120ºF (49ºC) in the thickest part for medium-rare (or as desired).

Per Serving:
calories: 373 | fat: 26g | protein: 33g | carbs: 1g | fiber: 0g | sodium: 672mg

Lamb Burger with Feta and Olives

Prep time: 10 minutes | Cook time: 20 minutes |
Serves 3 to 4

2 teaspoons olive oil
⅓ onion, finely chopped
1 clove garlic, minced
1 pound (454 g) ground lamb
2 tablespoons fresh parsley, finely chopped
1½ teaspoons fresh oregano, finely chopped

½ cup black olives, finely chopped
⅓ cup crumbled feta cheese
½ teaspoon salt
Freshly ground black pepper, to taste
4 thick pita breads

1. Preheat a medium skillet over medium-high heat on the stovetop. Add the olive oil and cook the onion until tender, but not browned, about 4 to 5 minutes. Add the garlic and cook for another minute. Transfer the onion and garlic to a mixing bowl and add the ground lamb, parsley, oregano, olives, feta cheese, salt and pepper. Gently mix the ingredients together. 2. Divide the mixture into 3 or 4 equal portions and then form the hamburgers, being careful not to over-handle the meat. One good way to do this is to throw the meat back and forth between your hands like a baseball, packing the meat each time you catch it. Flatten the balls into patties, making an indentation in the center of each patty. Flatten the sides of the patties as well to make it easier to fit them into the air fryer basket. 3. Preheat the air fryer to 370ºF (188ºC). 4. If you don't have room for all four burgers, air fry two or three burgers at a time for 8 minutes at 370ºF (188ºC). Flip the burgers over and air fry for another 8 minutes. If you cooked your burgers in batches, return the first batch of burgers to the air fryer for the last two minutes of cooking to re-heat. This should give you a medium-well burger. If you'd prefer a medium-rare burger, shorten the cooking time to about 13 minutes. Remove the burgers to a resting plate and let the burgers rest for a few minutes before dressing and serving. 5. While the burgers are resting, toast the pita breads in the air fryer for 2 minutes. Tuck the burgers into the toasted pita breads, or wrap the pitas around the burgers and serve with a tzatziki sauce or some mayonnaise.

Per Serving:
calories: 380 | fat: 21g | protein: 28g | carbs: 20g | fiber: 2g | sodium: 745mg

Beef Meatballs in Garlic Cream Sauce

Prep time: 15 minutes | Cook time: 6 to 8 hours |
Serves 4

For the Sauce:
1 cup low-sodium vegetable broth or low-sodium chicken broth
1 tablespoon extra-virgin olive oil
2 garlic cloves, minced
1 tablespoon dried onion flakes
1 teaspoon dried rosemary
2 tablespoons freshly squeezed lemon juice
Pinch sea salt
Pinch freshly ground black pepper

For the Meatballs:
1 pound (454 g) raw ground beef
1 large egg
2 tablespoons bread crumbs
1 teaspoon ground cumin
1 teaspoon salt
½ teaspoon freshly ground black pepper
TO FINISH
2 cups plain Greek yogurt
2 tablespoons chopped fresh parsley

Make the Sauce: In a medium bowl, whisk together the vegetable broth, olive oil, garlic, onion flakes, rosemary, lemon juice, salt, and pepper until combined. Make the Meatballs: In a large bowl, mix together the ground beef, egg, bread crumbs, cumin, salt, and pepper until combined. Shape the meat mixture into 10 to 12 (2½-inch) meatballs. 1. Pour the sauce into the slow cooker. 2. Add the meatballs to the slow cooker. 3. Cover the cooker and cook for 6 to 8 hours on Low heat. 4. Stir in the yogurt. Replace the cover on the cooker and cook for 15 to 30 minutes on Low heat, or until the sauce has thickened. 5. Garnish with fresh parsley for serving.

Per Serving:
calories: 345 | fat: 20g | protein: 29g | carbs: 13g | fiber: 1g | sodium: 842mg

Greek Lamb Chops

Prep time: 10 minutes | Cook time: 6 to 8 hours |
Serves 6

3 pounds (1.4 kg) lamb chops
½ cup low-sodium beef broth
Juice of 1 lemon
1 tablespoon extra-virgin olive oil

2 garlic cloves, minced
1 teaspoon dried oregano
1 teaspoon sea salt
½ teaspoon freshly ground black pepper

1. Put the lamb chops in a slow cooker. 2. In a small bowl, whisk together the beef broth, lemon juice, olive oil, garlic, oregano, salt, and pepper until blended. Pour the sauce over the lamb chops. 3. Cover the cooker and cook for 6 to 8 hours on Low heat.

Per Serving:
calories: 325 | fat: 13g | protein: 47g | carbs: 1g | fiber: 0g | sodium: 551mg

Parmesan Herb Filet Mignon

Prep time: 20 minutes | Cook time: 13 minutes | Serves 4

1 pound (454 g) filet mignon	1 teaspoon dried rosemary
Sea salt and ground black	1 teaspoon dried thyme
pepper, to taste	1 tablespoon sesame oil
½ teaspoon cayenne pepper	1 small-sized egg, well-whisked
1 teaspoon dried basil	½ cup Parmesan cheese, grated

1. Season the filet mignon with salt, black pepper, cayenne pepper, basil, rosemary, and thyme. Brush with sesame oil. 2. Put the egg in a shallow plate. Now, place the Parmesan cheese in another plate. 3. Coat the filet mignon with the egg; then lay it into the Parmesan cheese. Set the air fryer to 360ºF (182ºC). 4. Cook for 10 to 13 minutes or until golden. Serve with mixed salad leaves and enjoy!

Per Serving:
calories: 252 | fat: 13g | protein: 32g | carbs: 1g | fiber: 0g | sodium: 96mg

Seasoned Beef Kebabs

Prep time: 15 minutes | Cook time: 10 minutes | Serves 6

2 pounds beef fillet	⅓ cup extra-virgin olive oil
1½ teaspoons salt	1 large onion, cut into 8
1 teaspoon freshly ground black	quarters
pepper	1 large red bell pepper, cut into
½ teaspoon ground allspice	1-inch cubes
½ teaspoon ground nutmeg	

1. Preheat a grill, grill pan, or lightly oiled skillet to high heat. 2. Cut the beef into 1-inch cubes and put them in a large bowl. 3. In a small bowl, mix together the salt, black pepper, allspice, and nutmeg. 4. Pour the olive oil over the beef and toss to coat the beef. Then evenly sprinkle the seasoning over the beef and toss to coat all pieces. 5. Skewer the beef, alternating every 1 or 2 pieces with a piece of onion or bell pepper. 6. To cook, place the skewers on the grill or skillet, and turn every 2 to 3 minutes until all sides have cooked to desired doneness, 6 minutes for medium-rare, 8 minutes for well done. Serve warm.

Per Serving:
calories: 326 | fat: 21g | protein: 32g | carbs: 4g | fiber: 1g | sodium: 714mg

Roasted Pork with Apple-Dijon Sauce

Prep time: 15 minutes | Cook time: 40 minutes | Serves 8

1½ tablespoons extra-virgin	¼ cup apple jelly
olive oil	¼ cup apple juice
1 (12-ounce/ 340-g) pork	2 to 3 tablespoons Dijon
tenderloin	mustard
¼ teaspoon kosher salt	½ tablespoon cornstarch
¼ teaspoon freshly ground	½ tablespoon cream
black pepper	

1. Preheat the oven to 325°F(165°C). 2. In a large sauté pan or skillet, heat the olive oil over medium heat. 3. Add the pork to the skillet, using tongs to turn and sear the pork on all sides. Once seared, sprinkle pork with salt and pepper, and set it on a small baking sheet. 4. In the same skillet, with the juices from the pork, mix the apple jelly, juice, and mustard into the pan juices. Heat thoroughly over low heat, stirring consistently for 5 minutes. Spoon over the pork. 5. Put the pork in the oven and roast for 15 to 17 minutes, or 20 minutes per pound. Every 10 to 15 minutes, baste the pork with the apple-mustard sauce. 6. Once the pork tenderloin is done, remove it from the oven and let it rest for 15 minutes. Then, cut it into 1-inch slices. 7. In a small pot, blend the cornstarch with cream. Heat over low heat. Add the pan juices into the pot, stirring for 2 minutes, until thickened. Serve the sauce over the pork.

Per Serving:
calories: 146 | fat: 7g | protein: 13g | carbs: 8g | fiber: 0g | sodium: 192mg

Beef, Mushroom, and Green Bean Soup

Prep time: 10 minutes | Cook time: 45 minutes | Serves 4

2 tablespoons olive oil	½ cup white wine
1 pound (454 g) chuck or round	8 cups chicken broth
beef roast, cut into 2-inch	1 pound (454 g) green beans
pieces	8 ounces (227 g) cremini (baby
1 large onion, diced	bella) mushrooms, chopped
½ teaspoon sea salt	3 tablespoons tomato paste
¼ teaspoon freshly ground	½ teaspoon dried oregano
black pepper	

1. In a large stockpot, heat the olive oil over medium-high heat. Add the beef and brown, 5 to 7 minutes. Add the onion, salt, and pepper and cook for 5 minutes. Add the wine and cook for 4 minutes. Add the broth, green beans, mushrooms, tomato paste, and oregano and stir to combine. 2. Bring to a boil, reduce the heat to low, cover, and simmer for 35 to 45 minutes, until the meat is cooked through. Serve.

Per Serving:
calories: 307 | fat: 14g | protein: 28g | carbs: 17g | fiber: 5g | sodium: 265mg

Spice-Rubbed Pork Loin

Prep time: 5 minutes | Cook time: 20 minutes | Serves 6

1 teaspoon paprika	1 (1½-pound / 680-g) boneless
½ teaspoon ground cumin	pork loin
½ teaspoon chili powder	½ teaspoon salt
½ teaspoon garlic powder	¼ teaspoon ground black
2 tablespoons coconut oil	pepper

1. In a small bowl, mix paprika, cumin, chili powder, and garlic powder. 2. Drizzle coconut oil over pork. Sprinkle pork loin with salt and pepper, then rub spice mixture evenly on all sides. 3. Place pork loin into ungreased air fryer basket. Adjust the temperature to 400ºF (204ºC) and air fry for 20 minutes, turning pork halfway through cooking. Pork loin will be browned and have an internal temperature of at least 145ºF (63ºC) when done. Serve warm.

Per Serving:
calories: 192 | fat: 9g | protein: 26g | carbs: 1g | fiber: 0g | sodium: 257mg

Italian Pot Roast

Prep time: 15 minutes | Cook time: 6 hours | Serves 8

1 (3-pound / 1.4-kg) beef chuck roast, trimmed and halved crosswise
4 cloves garlic, halved lengthwise
1½ teaspoons coarse sea salt
1 teaspoon black pepper
1 tablespoon olive oil
1 large yellow onion, cut into 8 wedges
1¼ pounds (567 g) small white potatoes
1 (28-ounce / 794-g) can whole tomatoes in purée
1 tablespoon chopped fresh rosemary leaves (or 1 teaspoon dried and crumbled rosemary)

1. With a sharp paring knife, cut four slits in each of the beef roast halves, and stuff the slits with one-half of the garlic halves. Generously season the beef with the salt and pepper. 2. In a large skillet, heat the olive oil over medium-high heat, swirling to coat the bottom of the pan. Cook the beef until browned on all sides, about 5 minutes. 3. Combine the beef, onion, potatoes, tomatoes, rosemary, and the remaining garlic in the slow cooker. 4. Cover and cook until the meat is fork-tender, on high for about 6 hours. 5. Transfer the meat to a cutting board. Thinly slice, and discard any fat or gristle. 6. Skim the fat from the top of the sauce in the slow cooker. 7. Serve hot, dividing the beef and vegetables among the eight bowls, and generously spooning the sauce over the top.

Per Serving:
calories: 317 | fat: 12g | protein: 37g | carbs: 17g | fiber: 4g | sodium: 605mg

Smoked Paprika and Lemon Marinated Pork Kabobs

Prep time: 10 minutes | Cook time: 10 minutes | Serves 4

⅓ cup finely chopped flat-leaf parsley
¼ cup olive oil
2 tablespoons minced red onion
1 tablespoon lemon juice
1 tablespoon smoked paprika
2 teaspoons ground cumin
1 clove garlic, minced
¼ teaspoon cayenne pepper
½ teaspoon salt
2 pork tenderloins, each about 1 pound (454 g), trimmed of silver skin and any excess fat, cut into 1¼-inch cubes
1 lemon, cut into wedges, for serving

1. In a large bowl, whisk together the parsley, olive oil, onion, lemon juice, smoked paprika, cumin, garlic, cayenne, and salt. Add the pork and toss to coat well. Cover and refrigerate, stirring occasionally, for at least 4 hours (or as long as overnight). 2. Soak bamboo skewers in water for 30 minutes. 3. Preheat the grill to high heat. 4. Remove the meat from the marinade, discarding the marinade. Thread the meat onto the soaked skewers and place the skewers on the grill. Cook, with the lid closed, turning occasionally, until the pork is cooked through and browned on all sides, about 8 to 10 minutes total. 5. Transfer the skewers to a serving platter and serve immediately with the lemon wedges.

Per Serving:
calories: 447 | fat: 21g | protein: 60g | carbs: 3g | fiber: 1g | sodium: 426mg

Pepper Steak

Prep time: 30 minutes | Cook time: 16 to 20 minutes | Serves 4

1 pound (454 g) cube steak, cut into 1-inch pieces
1 cup Italian dressing
1½ cups beef broth
1 tablespoon soy sauce
½ teaspoon salt
¼ teaspoon freshly ground black pepper
¼ cup cornstarch
1 cup thinly sliced bell pepper, any color
1 cup chopped celery
1 tablespoon minced garlic
1 to 2 tablespoons oil

1. In a large resealable bag, combine the beef and Italian dressing. Seal the bag and refrigerate to marinate for 8 hours. 2. In a small bowl, whisk the beef broth, soy sauce, salt, and pepper until blended. 3. In another small bowl, whisk ¼ cup water and the cornstarch until dissolved. Stir the cornstarch mixture into the beef broth mixture until blended. 4. Preheat the air fryer to 375°F (191°C). 5. Pour the broth mixture into a baking pan. Cook for 4 minutes. Stir and cook for 4 to 5 minutes more. Remove and set aside. 6. Increase the air fryer temperature to 400°F (204°C). Line the air fryer basket with parchment paper. 7. Remove the steak from the marinade and place it in a medium bowl. Discard the marinade. Stir in the bell pepper, celery, and garlic. 8. Place the steak and pepper mixture on the parchment. Spritz with oil. 9. Cook for 4 minutes. Shake the basket and cook for 4 to 7 minutes more, until the vegetables are tender and the meat reaches an internal temperature of 145°F (63°C). Serve with the gravy.

Per Serving:
calories: 302 | fat: 14g | protein: 27g | carbs: 15g | fiber: 1g | sodium: 635mg

Blackened Cajun Pork Roast

Prep time: 20 minutes | Cook time: 33 minutes | Serves 4

2 pounds (907 g) bone-in pork loin roast
2 tablespoons oil
¼ cup Cajun seasoning
½ cup diced onion
½ cup diced celery
½ cup diced green bell pepper
1 tablespoon minced garlic

1. Cut 5 slits across the pork roast. Spritz it with oil, coating it completely. Evenly sprinkle the Cajun seasoning over the pork roast. 2. In a medium bowl, stir together the onion, celery, green bell pepper, and garlic until combined. Set aside. 3. Preheat the air fryer to 360°F (182°C). Line the air fryer basket with parchment paper. 4. Place the pork roast on the parchment and spritz with oil. 5. Cook for 5 minutes. Flip the roast and cook for 5 minutes more. Continue to flip and cook in 5-minute increments for a total cook time of 20 minutes. 6. Increase the air fryer temperature to 390°F (199°C). 7. Cook the roast for 8 minutes more and flip. Add the vegetable mixture to the basket and cook for a final 5 minutes. Let the roast sit for 5 minutes before serving.

Per Serving:
calories: 400 | fat: 16g | protein: 52g | carbs: 8g | fiber: 2g | sodium: 738mg

Pork Tenderloin with Vegetable Ragu

Prep time: 25 minutes | Cook time: 18 minutes | Serves 6

2 tablespoons light olive oil, divided
1 (1½-pound / 680-g) pork tenderloin
¼ teaspoon salt
¼ teaspoon ground black pepper
1 medium zucchini, trimmed and sliced
1 medium yellow squash, sliced
1 medium onion, peeled and chopped
1 medium carrot, peeled and

grated
1 (14½-ounce / 411-g) can diced tomatoes, drained
2 cloves garlic, peeled and minced
¼ teaspoon crushed red pepper flakes
1 tablespoon chopped fresh basil
1 tablespoon chopped fresh oregano
1 sprig fresh thyme
½ cup red wine

1. Press the Sauté button on the Instant Pot® and heat 1 tablespoon oil. Season pork with salt and black pepper. Brown pork lightly on all sides, about 2 minutes per side. Transfer pork to a plate and set aside. 2. Add remaining 1 tablespoon oil to the pot. Add zucchini and squash, and cook until tender, about 5 minutes. Add onion and carrot, and cook until just softened, about 5 minutes. Add tomatoes, garlic, crushed red pepper flakes, basil, oregano, thyme, and red wine to pot, and stir well. Press the Cancel button. 3. Top vegetable mixture with browned pork. Close lid, set steam release to Sealing, press the Manual button, and set time to 3 minutes. When the timer beeps, quick-release the pressure until the float valve drops and open lid. Transfer pork to a cutting board and cut into 1" slices. Pour sauce on a serving platter and arrange pork slices on top. Serve immediately.

Per Serving:
calories: 190 | fat: 7g | protein: 23g | carbs: 9g | fiber: 2g | sodium: 606mg

One-Pan Greek Pork and Vegetables

Prep time: 10 minutes | Cook time: 40 minutes | Serves 3

1 pound (454 g) pork shoulder, cut into 1-inch cubes
¾ teaspoon fine sea salt, divided
½ teaspoon freshly ground black pepper, divided, plus more for serving
4 tablespoons extra virgin olive oil, divided
1 medium red onion, sliced

1 medium green bell pepper, seeded and sliced
1 medium carrot, peeled and julienned
¼ cup dry red wine
15 cherry tomatoes, halved
2 tablespoons hot water
½ teaspoon dried oregano

1. Scatter the cubed pork onto a cutting board and sprinkle with ¼ teaspoon of sea salt and ¼ teaspoon of black pepper. Flip the pieces over and sprinkle an additional ¼ teaspoon of sea salt and the remaining ¼ teaspoon of black pepper. 2. In a large pan wide enough to hold all the pork in a single layer, heat 3 tablespoons of olive oil over high heat. Once the oil is hot, add the pork pieces and brown for 2 minutes, then flip the pork pieces and brown for 2 more minutes. (Do not stir.) 3. Add the onions and sauté for 2 minutes and then add the bell peppers and carrots and sauté for 2 more minutes, ensuring all vegetables are coated with the oil. Reduce the heat to medium, cover the pan loosely, and cook for 5 minutes, stirring occasionally. 4. Add the wine and continue cooking for

about 4 minutes, using a wooden spatula to scrape any browned bits from the bottom of the pan. Add about 20 cherry tomato halves and stir gently, then drizzle with the remaining 1 tablespoon of olive oil and add the hot water. Reduce the heat to low and simmer for 15–20 minutes or until all the liquids are absorbed. Remove the pan from the heat. 5. Sprinkle the oregano over the top. Top with the remaining cherry tomato halves and season to taste with the remaining ¼ teaspoon of sea salt and additional black pepper before serving. Store covered in the refrigerator for up to 3 days.

Per Serving:
calories: 407 | fat: 27g | protein: 30g | carbs: 8g | fiber: 2g | sodium: 700mg

Mexican-Style Shredded Beef

Prep time: 5 minutes | Cook time: 35 minutes | Serves 6

1 (2-pound / 907-g) beef chuck roast, cut into 2-inch cubes
1 teaspoon salt
½ teaspoon ground black

pepper
½ cup no-sugar-added chipotle sauce

1. In a large bowl, sprinkle beef cubes with salt and pepper and toss to coat. Place beef into ungreased air fryer basket. Adjust the temperature to 400ºF (204ºC) and air fry for 30 minutes, shaking the basket halfway through cooking. Beef will be done when internal temperature is at least 160ºF (71ºC). 2. Place cooked beef into a large bowl and shred with two forks. Pour in chipotle sauce and toss to coat. 3. Return beef to air fryer basket for an additional 5 minutes at 400ºF (204ºC) to crisp with sauce. Serve warm.
Per Serving:
calories: 204 | fat: 9g | protein: 31g | carbs: 0g | fiber: 0g | sodium: 539mg

Goat Cheese-Stuffed Flank Steak

Prep time: 10 minutes | Cook time: 14 minutes | Serves 6

1 pound (454 g) flank steak
1 tablespoon avocado oil
½ teaspoon sea salt
½ teaspoon garlic powder
¼ teaspoon freshly ground

black pepper
2 ounces (57 g) goat cheese, crumbled
1 cup baby spinach, chopped

1. Place the steak in a large zip-top bag or between two pieces of plastic wrap. Using a meat mallet or heavy-bottomed skillet, pound the steak to an even ¼-inch thickness. 2. Brush both sides of the steak with the avocado oil. 3. Mix the salt, garlic powder, and pepper in a small dish. Sprinkle this mixture over both sides of the steak. 4. Sprinkle the goat cheese over top, and top that with the spinach. 5. Starting at one of the long sides, roll the steak up tightly. Tie the rolled steak with kitchen string at 3-inch intervals. 6. Set the air fryer to 400ºF (204ºC). Place the steak roll-up in the air fryer basket. Air fry for 7 minutes. Flip the steak and cook for an additional 7 minutes, until an instant-read thermometer reads 120ºF (49ºC) for medium-rare (adjust the cooking time for your desired doneness).

Per Serving:
calories: 151 | fat: 8g | protein: 18g | carbs: 0g | fiber: 0g | sodium: 281mg

Mini Greek Meatloaves

Prep time: 5 minutes |Cook time: 25 minutes|

Serves: 6

Nonstick cooking spray
1 tablespoon extra-virgin olive oil
½ cup minced onion (about ¼ onion)
1 garlic clove, minced (about ½ teaspoon)
1 pound (454 g) ground beef (93% lean)
½ cup whole-wheat bread crumbs
½ cup crumbled feta cheese

(about 2 ounces/ 57 g)
1 large egg
½ teaspoon dried oregano, crushed between your fingers
¼ teaspoon freshly ground black pepper
½ cup 2% plain Greek yogurt
⅓ cup chopped and pitted Kalamata olives
2 tablespoons olive brine
Romaine lettuce or pita bread, for serving (optional)

1. Preheat the oven to 400°F(205ºC). Coat a 12-cup muffin pan with nonstick cooking spray and set aside. 2. In a small skillet over medium heat, heat the oil. Add the onion and cook for 4 minutes, stirring frequently. Add the garlic and cook for 1 more minute, stirring frequently. Remove from the heat. 3. In a large mixing bowl, combine the onion and garlic with the ground beef, bread crumbs, feta, egg, oregano, and pepper. Gently mix together with your hands. 4. Divide into 12 portions and place in the muffin cups. Cook for 18 to 20 minutes, or until the internal temperature of the meat is 160°F(71ºC) on a meat thermometer. 5. While the meatloaves are baking, in a small bowl, whisk together the yogurt, olives, and olive brine. 6. When you're ready to serve, place the meatloaves on a serving platter and spoon the olive-yogurt sauce on top. You can also serve them on a bed of lettuce or with cut-up pieces of pita bread.

Per Serving:
calories: 226 | fat: 11g | protein: 21g | carbs: 10g | fiber: 1g | sodium: 311mg

Pork Meatballs

Prep time: 10 minutes | Cook time: 12 minutes |

Makes 18 meatballs

1 pound (454 g) ground pork
1 large egg, whisked
½ teaspoon garlic powder
½ teaspoon salt
½ teaspoon ground ginger

¼ teaspoon crushed red pepper flakes
1 medium scallion, trimmed and sliced

1. Combine all ingredients in a large bowl. Spoon out 2 tablespoons mixture and roll into a ball. Repeat to form eighteen meatballs total. 2. Place meatballs into ungreased air fryer basket. Adjust the temperature to 400ºF (204ºC) and air fry for 12 minutes, shaking the basket three times throughout cooking. Meatballs will be browned and have an internal temperature of at least 145ºF (63ºC) when done. Serve warm.

Per Serving:
1 meatball: calories: 35 | fat: 1g | protein: 6g | carbs: 0g | fiber: 0g | sodium: 86mg

Tarragon Lamb Shanks with Cannellini Beans

Prep time: 20 minutes | Cook time: 10 hours | Serves 12

four 1½-pound lamb shanks
one 19-ounce can cannellini or other white beans, rinsed and drained
2 medium-sized carrots, diced
1 large yellow onion, chopped
1 large stalk celery, chopped

2 cloves garlic, thinly sliced
2 teaspoons tarragon
½ teaspoon sea salt
¼ teaspoon black pepper
one 28-ounce can diced tomatoes, with the juice

1. Trim the fat from the lamb shanks. 2. Put the beans, carrots, onion, celery, and garlic in the slow cooker and stir to combine. 3. Place lamb shanks on the bean mixture, and sprinkle with the tarragon, salt, and pepper. 4. Pour the tomatoes over the lamb. Cover and cook on high for 1 hour. 5. Reduce heat to low, and cook 9 hours or until the lamb is very tender. Remove the lamb shanks from slow cooker and place on a plate. 6. Pour the bean mixture through a colander or sieve over a bowl, reserving the liquid. Let the liquid stand for 5 minutes. Skim the fat from the surface of the liquid. Return the bean mixture to the liquid. Return to the slow cooker. 7. Remove the lamb from the bones. Discard the bones. Return the lamb to the slow cooker. Cover and cook to reheat, about 15 minutes. 8. Serve the lamb hot with the bean mixture.

Flank Steak with Artichokes

Prep time: 15 minutes | Cook time: 60 minutes |

Serves 4 to 6

4 tablespoons grapeseed oil, divided
2 pounds (907 g) flank steak
1 (14-ounce/ 397-g) can artichoke hearts, drained and roughly chopped
1 onion, diced
8 garlic cloves, chopped
1 (32-ounce/ 907-g) container low-sodium beef broth
1 (14½-ounce / 411-g) can

diced tomatoes, drained
1 cup tomato sauce
2 tablespoons tomato paste
1 teaspoon dried oregano
1 teaspoon dried parsley
1 teaspoon dried basil
½ teaspoon ground cumin
3 bay leaves
2 to 3 cups cooked couscous (optional)

1. Preheat the oven to 450ºF(235ºC). 2. In an oven-safe sauté pan or skillet, heat 3 tablespoons of oil on medium heat. Sear the steak for 2 minutes per side on both sides. Transfer the steak to the oven for 30 minutes, or until desired tenderness. 3. Meanwhile, in a large pot, combine the remaining 1 tablespoon of oil, artichoke hearts, onion, and garlic. Pour in the beef broth, tomatoes, tomato sauce, and tomato paste. Stir in oregano, parsley, basil, cumin, and bay leaves. 4. Cook the vegetables, covered, for 30 minutes. Remove bay leaf and serve with flank steak and ½ cup of couscous per plate, if using.

Per Serving:
calories: 577 | fat: 21g | protein: 45g | carbs: 54g | fiber: 5g | sodium: 150mg

Pork Casserole with Fennel and Potatoes

Prep time: 20 minutes | Cook time: 6 to 8 hours | Serves 6

2 large fennel bulbs
3 pounds (1.4 kg) pork tenderloin, cut into 1½-inch pieces
2 pounds (907 g) red potatoes, quartered
1 cup low-sodium chicken broth
4 garlic cloves, minced

1½ teaspoons dried thyme
1 teaspoon dried parsley
1 teaspoon sea salt
Freshly ground black pepper
⅓ cup shredded Parmesan cheese

1. Cut the stalks off the fennel bulbs. Trim a little piece from the bottom of the bulbs to make them stable, then cut straight down through the bulbs to halve them. Cut the halves into quarters. Peel off and discard any wilted outer layers. Cut the fennel pieces crosswise into slices. 2. In a slow cooker, combine the fennel, pork, and potatoes. Stir to mix well. 3. In a small bowl, whisk together the chicken broth, garlic, thyme, parsley, and salt until combined. Season with pepper and whisk again. Pour the sauce over the pork. 4. Cover the cooker and cook for 6 to 8 hours on Low heat. 5. Top with Parmesan cheese for serving.

Per Serving:
calories: 412 | fat: 7g | protein: 55g | carbs: 31g | fiber: 5g | sodium: 592mg

Steak Gyro Platter

Prep time: 30 minutes | Cook time: 8 to 10 minutes | Serves 4

1 pound (454 g) flank steak
1 teaspoon garlic powder
1 teaspoon ground cumin
½ teaspoon sea salt
½ teaspoon freshly ground black pepper
5 ounces (142 g) shredded romaine lettuce

½ cup crumbled feta cheese
½ cup peeled and diced cucumber
⅓ cup sliced red onion
¼ cup seeded and diced tomato
2 tablespoons pitted and sliced black olives
Tzatziki sauce, for serving

1. Pat the steak dry with paper towels. In a small bowl, combine the garlic powder, cumin, salt, and pepper. Sprinkle this mixture all over the steak, and allow the steak to rest at room temperature for 45 minutes. 2. Preheat the air fryer to 400°F (204°C). Place the steak in the air fryer basket and air fry for 4 minutes. Flip the steak and cook 4 to 6 minutes more, until an instant-read thermometer reads 120°F (49°C) at the thickest point for medium-rare (or as desired). Remove the steak from the air fryer and let it rest for 5 minutes. 3. Divide the romaine among plates. Top with the feta, cucumber, red onion, tomato, and olives.

Per Serving:
calories: 229 | fat: 10g | protein: 28g | carbs: 5g | fiber: 2g | sodium: 559mg

Chapter 4 Fish and Seafood

Southern-Style Catfish

Prep time: 10 minutes | Cook time: 12 minutes | Serves 4

4 (7-ounce / 198-g) catfish
fillets
⅓ cup heavy whipping cream
1 tablespoon lemon juice
1 cup blanched finely ground

almond flour
2 teaspoons Old Bay seasoning
½ teaspoon salt
¼ teaspoon ground black
pepper

1. Place catfish fillets into a large bowl with cream and pour in lemon juice. Stir to coat. 2. In a separate large bowl, mix flour and Old Bay seasoning. 3. Remove each fillet and gently shake off excess cream. Sprinkle with salt and pepper. Press each fillet gently into flour mixture on both sides to coat. 4. Place fillets into ungreased air fryer basket. Adjust the temperature to 400°F (204°C) and air fry for 12 minutes, turning fillets halfway through cooking. Catfish will be golden brown and have an internal temperature of at least 145°F (63°C) when done. Serve warm.

Per Serving:
calories: 438 | fat: 28g | protein: 41g | carbs: 7g | fiber: 4g | sodium: 387mg

Southern Italian Seafood Stew in Tomato Broth

Prep time: 15 minutes | Cook time: 1 hour 20 minutes | Serves 6

½ cup olive oil
1 fennel bulb, cored and finely
chopped
2 stalks celery, finely chopped
1 medium onion, finely chopped
1 tablespoon dried oregano
½ teaspoon crushed red pepper
flakes
1½ pounds (680 g) cleaned
squid, bodies cut into ½-inch
rings, tentacles halved
2 cups dry white wine
1 (28-ounce / 794-g) can tomato

purée
1 bay leaf
1 teaspoon salt
½ teaspoon freshly ground
black pepper
1 cup bottled clam juice
1 pound (454 g) whole head-on
prawns
1½ pounds (680 g) mussels,
scrubbed
1 lemon, cut into wedges, for
serving

1. In a large Dutch oven, heat the olive oil over medium-high heat. Add the fennel, celery, onion, oregano, and red pepper flakes and reduce the heat to medium. Cook, stirring occasionally, for about 15 minutes, until the vegetables soften. Stir in the squid, reduce the heat to low, and simmer for 15 minutes. 2. Add the wine to the pot, raise the heat to medium-high, and bring to a boil. Cook, stirring occasionally, until the wine has evaporated. Reduce the heat again to low and add the tomato purée, bay leaf, salt, and pepper. Cook gently, stirring every once in a while, for about 40 minutes, until the mixture becomes very thick. 3. Stir in 2 cups of water and the clam juice, raise the heat again to medium-high, and bring to a boil. 4. Add the shrimp and mussels and cook, covered, for 5 minutes or so, until the shells of the mussels have opened and the prawns are pink and cooked through. 5. To serve, ladle the seafood and broth into bowls and garnish with the lemon wedges. Serve hot.

Per Serving:
calories: 490 | fat: 23g | protein: 48g | carbs: 22g | fiber: 5g | sodium: 899mg

Crispy Fish Sticks

Prep time: 15 minutes | Cook time: 10 minutes | Serves 4

1 ounce (28 g) pork rinds, finely
ground
¼ cup blanched finely ground
almond flour
½ teaspoon Old Bay seasoning

1 tablespoon coconut oil
1 large egg
1 pound (454 g) cod fillet, cut
into ¾-inch strips

1. Place ground pork rinds, almond flour, Old Bay seasoning, and coconut oil into a large bowl and mix together. In a medium bowl, whisk egg. 2. Dip each fish stick into the egg and then gently press into the flour mixture, coating as fully and evenly as possible. Place fish sticks into the air fryer basket. 3. Adjust the temperature to 400°F (204°C) and air fry for 10 minutes or until golden. 4. Serve immediately.

Per Serving:
calories: 223 | fat: 14g | protein: 21g | carbs: 2g | fiber: 1g | sodium: 390mg

Balsamic-Glazed Black Pepper Salmon

Prep time: 5 minutes | Cook time: 8 minutes | Serves 4

½ cup balsamic vinegar
1 tablespoon honey
4 (8-ounce / 227-g) salmon
fillets

Sea salt and freshly ground
pepper, to taste
1 tablespoon olive oil

1. Heat a cast-iron skillet over medium-high heat. Mix the vinegar and honey in a small bowl. 2. Season the salmon fillets with the sea salt and freshly ground pepper; brush with the honey-balsamic glaze. 3. Add olive oil to the skillet, and sear the salmon fillets, cooking for 3–4 minutes on each side until lightly browned and medium rare in the center. 4. Let sit for 5 minutes before serving.

Per Serving:
calories: 478 | fat: 17g | protein: 65g | carbs: 10g | fiber: 0g | sodium: 246mg

River Trout with Herb Sauce

Prep time: 10 minutes | Cook time: 3 minutes | Serves 4

4 (½-pound / 227-g) fresh river trout, rinsed and patted dry
1 teaspoon salt, divided
1 teaspoon white wine vinegar
½ cup water
½ cup minced fresh flat-leaf parsley

2 tablespoons chopped fresh oregano
1 teaspoon fresh thyme leaves
1 small shallot, peeled and minced
2 tablespoons olive oil
½ teaspoon lemon juice

1. Sprinkle trout with ¾ teaspoon salt inside and out. Combine vinegar and water, pour into the Instant Pot®, and place rack inside. Place trout on rack. 2. Close lid, set steam release to Sealing, press the Manual button, and set time to 3 minutes. When the timer beeps, let pressure release naturally for 3 minutes. Quick-release any remaining pressure until the float valve drops and then open lid. 3. Transfer fish to a serving plate. Peel and discard skin from fish. Remove and discard the heads if desired. 4. In a small bowl, mix together parsley, oregano, thyme, shallot, olive oil, lemon juice, and remaining ¼ teaspoon salt. Pour evenly over fish. Serve immediately.

Per Serving:
calories: 344 | fat: 18g | protein: 45g | carbs: 1g | fiber: 0g | sodium: 581mg

Monkfish with Sautéed Leeks, Fennel, and Tomatoes

Prep time: 20 minutes | Cook time: 35 minutes | Serves 4

1 to 1½ pounds (454 to 680 g) monkfish
3 tablespoons lemon juice, divided
1 teaspoon kosher salt, divided
⅛ teaspoon freshly ground black pepper
2 tablespoons extra-virgin olive oil
1 leek, white and light green parts only, sliced in half lengthwise and thinly sliced

½ onion, julienned
3 garlic cloves, minced
2 bulbs fennel, cored and thinly sliced, plus ¼ cup fronds for garnish
1 (14½-ounce / 411-g) can no-salt-added diced tomatoes
2 tablespoons fresh parsley, chopped
2 tablespoons fresh oregano, chopped
¼ teaspoon red pepper flakes

1. Place the fish in a medium baking dish and add 2 tablespoons of the lemon juice, ¼ teaspoon of the salt, and the black pepper. Place in the refrigerator. 2. Heat the olive oil in a large skillet or sauté pan over medium heat. Add the leek and onion and sauté until translucent, about 3 minutes. Add the garlic and sauté for 30 seconds. Add the fennel and sauté 4 to 5 minutes. Add the tomatoes and simmer for 2 to 3 minutes. 3. Stir in the parsley, oregano, red pepper flakes, the remaining ¾ teaspoon salt, and the remaining 1 tablespoon lemon juice. Place the fish on top of the leek mixture, cover, and simmer for 20 to 25 minutes, turning over halfway through, until the fish is opaque and pulls apart easily. Garnish with the fennel fronds.

Per Serving:
calories: 220 | fat: 9g | protein: 22g | carbs: 11g | fiber: 3g | sodium: 345mg

Roasted Red Snapper

Prep time: 5 minutes | Cook time: 45 minutes | Serves 4

1 (2 to 2½ pounds / 907 g to 1.1 kg) whole red snapper, cleaned and scaled
2 lemons, sliced (about 10 slices)

3 cloves garlic, sliced
4 or 5 sprigs of thyme
3 tablespoons cold salted butter, cut into small cubes, divided

1. Preheat the oven to 350°F(180°C). 2. Cut a piece of foil to about the size of your baking sheet; put the foil on the baking sheet. 3. Make a horizontal slice through the belly of the fish to create a pocket. 4. Place 3 slices of lemon on the foil and the fish on top of the lemons. 5. Stuff the fish with the garlic, thyme, 3 lemon slices and butter. Reserve 3 pieces of butter. 6. Place the reserved 3 pieces of butter on top of the fish, and 3 or 4 slices of lemon on top of the butter. Bring the foil together and seal it to make a pocket around the fish. 7. Put the fish in the oven and bake for 45 minutes. Serve with remaining fresh lemon slices.

Per Serving:
calories: 345 | fat: 13g | protein: 54g | carbs: 12g | fiber: 3g | sodium: 170mg

Poached Octopus

Prep time: 10 minutes | Cook time: 16 minutes | Serves 8

2 pounds (907 g) potatoes (about 6 medium)
3 teaspoons salt, divided
1 (2-pound / 907-g) frozen octopus, thawed, cleaned, and rinsed
3 cloves garlic, peeled, divided

1 bay leaf
2 teaspoons whole peppercorns
½ cup olive oil
¼ cup white wine vinegar
½ teaspoon ground black pepper
½ cup chopped fresh parsley

1. Place potatoes in the Instant Pot® with 2 teaspoons salt and enough water to just cover the potatoes halfway. Close lid, set steam release to Sealing, press the Manual button, and set time to 6 minutes. When the timer beeps, quick-release the pressure until the float valve drops and open lid. Press the Cancel button. 2. Remove potatoes with tongs (reserve the cooking water), and peel them as soon as you can handle them. Dice potatoes into bite-sized pieces. Set aside. 3. Add octopus to potato cooking water in the pot and add more water to cover if needed. Add 1 garlic clove, bay leaf, and peppercorns. Close lid, set steam release to Sealing, press the Manual button, and set time to 10 minutes. When the timer beeps, quick-release the pressure until the float valve drops and open lid. Remove and discard bay leaf. 4. Check octopus for tenderness by seeing if a fork will sink easily into the thickest part of the flesh. If not, close the top and bring it to pressure for another minute or two and check again. 5. Remove octopus and drain. Chop head and tentacles into small, bite-sized chunks. 6. Crush remaining 2 garlic cloves and place in a small jar or plastic container. Add olive oil, vinegar, remaining 1 teaspoon salt, and pepper. Close the lid and shake well. 7. In a large serving bowl, mix potatoes with octopus, cover with vinaigrette, and sprinkle with parsley.

Per Serving:
calories: 301 | fat: 15g | protein: 15g | carbs: 30g | fiber: 2g | sodium: 883mg

Baked Grouper with Tomatoes and Garlic

Prep time: 5 minutes | Cook time: 12 minutes | Serves 4

4 grouper fillets
½ teaspoon salt
3 garlic cloves, minced
1 tomato, sliced
¼ cup sliced Kalamata olives
¼ cup fresh dill, roughly chopped
Juice of 1 lemon
¼ cup olive oil

1. Preheat the air fryer to 380°F(193ºC). 2. Season the grouper fillets on all sides with salt, then place into the air fryer basket and top with the minced garlic, tomato slices, olives, and fresh dill. 3. Drizzle the lemon juice and olive oil over the top of the grouper, then bake for 10 to 12 minutes, or until the internal temperature reaches 145°F(63ºC).

Per Serving:
calories: 379 | fat: 17g | protein: 51g | carbs: 3g | fiber: 1g | sodium: 492mg

Asian Marinated Salmon

Prep time: 30 minutes | Cook time: 6 minutes | Serves 2

Marinade:
¼ cup wheat-free tamari or coconut aminos
2 tablespoons lime or lemon juice
2 tablespoons sesame oil
2 tablespoons Swerve confectioners'-style sweetener, or a few drops liquid stevia
2 teaspoons grated fresh ginger
2 cloves garlic, minced
½ teaspoon ground black pepper
2 (4-ounce / 113-g) salmon fillets (about 1¼ inches thick)

Sliced green onions, for garnish
Sauce (Optional):
¼ cup beef broth
¼ cup wheat-free tamari
3 tablespoons Swerve confectioners'-style sweetener or equivalent amount of liquid or powdered sweetener
1 tablespoon tomato sauce
1 teaspoon stevia glycerite (optional)
⅛ teaspoon guar gum or xanthan gum (optional, for thickening)

1. Make the marinade: In a medium-sized shallow dish, stir together all the ingredients for the marinade until well combined. Place the salmon in the marinade. Cover and refrigerate for at least 2 hours or overnight. 2. Preheat the air fryer to 400ºF (204°C). 3. Remove the salmon fillets from the marinade and place them in the air fryer, leaving space between them. Air fry for 6 minutes, or until the salmon is cooked through and flakes easily with a fork. 4. While the salmon cooks, make the sauce, if using: Place all the sauce ingredients except the guar gum in a medium-sized bowl and stir until well combined. Taste and adjust the sweetness to your liking. While whisking slowly, add the guar gum. Allow the sauce to thicken for 3 to 5 minutes. (The sauce can be made up to 3 days ahead and stored in an airtight container in the fridge.) Drizzle the sauce over the salmon before serving. 5. Garnish the salmon with sliced green onions before serving. Store leftovers in an airtight container in the fridge for up to 3 days. Reheat in a preheated 350ºF (177°C) air fryer for 3 minutes, or until heated through.

Per Serving:
calories: 431 | fat: 19g | protein: 32g | carbs: 34g | fiber: 0g | sodium: 168mg

Lemon Mahi-Mahi

Prep time: 5 minutes | Cook time: 14 minutes | Serves 2

Oil, for spraying
2 (6-ounce / 170-g) mahi-mahi fillets
1 tablespoon lemon juice
1 tablespoon olive oil
¼ teaspoon salt
¼ teaspoon freshly ground black pepper
1 tablespoon chopped fresh dill
2 lemon slices

1. Line the air fryer basket with parchment and spray lightly with oil. 2. Place the mahi-mahi in the prepared basket. 3. In a small bowl, whisk together the lemon juice and olive oil. Brush the mixture evenly over the mahi-mahi. 4. Sprinkle the mahi-mahi with the salt and black pepper and top with the dill. 5. Air fry at 400ºF (204°C) for 12 to 14 minutes, depending on the thickness of the fillets, until they flake easily. 6. Transfer to plates, top each with a lemon slice, and serve.

Per Serving:
calories: 218 | fat: 8g | protein: 32g | carbs: 3g | fiber: 1g | sodium: 441mg

Fish Tagine

Prep time: 25 minutes | Cook time: 12 minutes | Serves 4

2 tablespoons extra-virgin olive oil, plus extra for drizzling
1 large onion, halved and sliced ¼ inch thick
1 pound (454 g) carrots, peeled, halved lengthwise, and sliced ¼ inch thick
2 (2-inch) strips orange zest, plus 1 teaspoon grated zest
¾ teaspoon table salt, divided
2 tablespoons tomato paste
4 garlic cloves, minced, divided
1¼ teaspoons paprika
1 teaspoon ground cumin
¼ teaspoon red pepper flakes
¼ teaspoon saffron threads, crumbled
1 (8-ounce / 227-g) bottle clam juice
1½ pounds (680 g) skinless halibut fillets, 1½ inches thick, cut into 2-inch pieces
¼ cup pitted oil-cured black olives, quartered
2 tablespoons chopped fresh parsley
1 teaspoon sherry vinegar

1. Using highest sauté function, heat oil in Instant Pot until shimmering. Add onion, carrots, orange zest strips, and ¼ teaspoon salt, and cook until vegetables are softened and lightly browned, 10 to 12 minutes. Stir in tomato paste, three-quarters of garlic, paprika, cumin, pepper flakes, and saffron and cook until fragrant, about 30 seconds. Stir in clam juice, scraping up any browned bits. 2. Sprinkle halibut with remaining ½ teaspoon salt. Nestle halibut into onion mixture and spoon some of cooking liquid on top of pieces. Lock lid in place and close pressure release valve. Select high pressure cook function and set cook time for 0 minutes. Once Instant Pot has reached pressure, immediately turn off pot and quick-release pressure. 3. Discard orange zest. Gently stir in olives, parsley, vinegar, grated orange zest, and remaining garlic. Season with salt and pepper to taste. Drizzle extra oil over individual portions before serving.

Per Serving:
calories: 310 | fat: 15g | protein: 34g | carbs: 18g | fiber: 4g | sodium: 820mg

Italian Breaded Shrimp

Prep time: 10 minutes | Cook time: 5 minutes | Serves 4

2 large eggs
2 cups seasoned Italian breadcrumbs
1 teaspoon salt

1 cup flour
1 pound (454 g) large shrimp (21-25), peeled and deveined
Extra-virgin olive oil

1. In a small bowl, beat the eggs with 1 tablespoon water, then transfer to a shallow dish. 2. Add the breadcrumbs and salt to a separate shallow dish; mix well. 3. Place the flour into a third shallow dish. 4. Coat the shrimp in the flour, then egg, and finally the breadcrumbs. Place on a plate and repeat with all of the shrimp. 5. Preheat a skillet over high heat. Pour in enough olive oil to coat the bottom of the skillet. Cook the shrimp in the hot skillet for 2 to 3 minutes on each side. Take the shrimp out and drain on a paper towel. Serve warm.

Per Serving:
calories: 459 | fat: 6g | protein: 36g | carbs: 63g | fiber: 3g | sodium: 617mg

Burgundy Salmon

Prep time: 10 minutes | Cook time: 26 minutes | Serves 4

4 salmon steaks
Sea salt and freshly ground pepper, to taste
1 tablespoon olive oil
1 shallot, minced
2 cups high-quality Burgundy

wine
½ cup beef stock
2 tablespoons tomato paste
1 teaspoon fresh thyme, chopped

1. Preheat the oven to 350ºF (180ºC). 2. Season the salmon steaks with sea salt and freshly ground pepper. Wrap the salmon steaks in aluminum foil and bake for 10–13 minutes. 3. Heat the olive oil in a deep skillet on medium heat. Add the shallot and cook for 3 minutes, or until tender. 4. Add the wine, beef stock, and tomato paste, and simmer for 10 minutes, or until sauce thickens and reduces by ⅓. 5. Place the fish on a serving platter and spoon the sauce over it. Sprinkle the fish with the fresh thyme, and serve.

Per Serving:
calories: 546 | fat: 17g | protein: 66g | carbs: 6g | fiber: 0g | sodium: 303mg

Salmon with Cauliflower

Prep time: 10 minutes | Cook time: 25 minutes | Serves 4

1 pound (454 g) salmon fillet, diced
1 cup cauliflower, shredded
1 tablespoon dried cilantro

1 tablespoon coconut oil, melted
1 teaspoon ground turmeric
¼ cup coconut cream

1. Mix salmon with cauliflower, dried cilantro, ground turmeric, coconut cream, and coconut oil. 2. Transfer the salmon mixture into the air fryer and cook the meal at 350ºF (177ºC) for 25 minutes. Stir the meal every 5 minutes to avoid the burning.

Per Serving:
calories: 232 | fat: 14g | protein: 24g | carbs: 3g | fiber: 1g | sodium: 94mg

Citrus–Marinated Salmon with Fennel Cream

Prep time: 15 minutes | Cook time: 25 minutes | Serves 4

2 tablespoons extra-virgin olive oil
¼ cup orange juice
½ teaspoon unrefined sea salt or salt
Freshly ground pepper
4 salmon fillets (4 ounces / 113

g each), skin-on
1 fennel bulb, thinly sliced (reserve fronds)
½ sweet onion, thinly sliced
1 cup plain Greek yogurt
2 oranges, 1 zested, 1 thinly sliced

1. In a small bowl, whisk the olive oil, orange juice, salt, and pepper together until emulsified. 2. Place the salmon fillets in a glass baking dish and pour marinade over the top. Allow to marinate for 1 hour. 3. Preheat the oven to 400ºF (205ºC). 4. Scatter fennel and onion around the sides of the salmon, and cover the baking dish with aluminum foil. Bake until the fish flakes easily with a fork and is opaque in color, 20 to 25 minutes. 5. While the fish is baking, combine the Greek yogurt with 2 tablespoons (6 g) fennel fronds, finely chopped, and orange zest. 6. Remove the fish from oven and place on a serving plate. Dollop each with about ¼ of yogurt mixture and garnish with orange slices.

Per Serving:
calories: 312 | fat: 14g | protein: 27g | carbs: 20g | fiber: 4g | sodium: 438mg

Cod Stew with Olives

Prep time: 20 minutes | Cook time: 15 minutes | Serves 4

3 tablespoons olive oil
1 medium onion, peeled and diced
1 stalk celery, diced
1 medium carrot, peeled and chopped
2 cloves garlic, peeled and minced
1 tablespoon chopped fresh oregano
½ teaspoon ground fennel

1 sprig fresh thyme
1 (14½-ounce / 411-g) can diced tomatoes
1½ cups vegetable broth
1 pound (454 g) cod fillets, cut into 1" pieces
⅓ cup sliced green olives
¼ teaspoon ground black pepper
2 tablespoons chopped fresh dill

1. Press the Sauté button on the Instant Pot® and heat oil. Add onion, celery, and carrot. Cook until vegetables are soft, about 6 minutes. Add garlic, oregano, fennel, and thyme. Cook for 30 seconds, then add tomatoes and vegetable broth. Stir well. Press the Cancel button. 2. Close lid, set steam release to Sealing, press the Manual button, and set time to 3 minutes. 3. When the timer beeps, quick-release the pressure until the float valve drops and open lid. Press the Cancel button, then press the Sauté button and add fish, olives, and pepper. Cook until fish is opaque, 3–5 minutes. Sprinkle with dill and serve hot.

Per Serving:
calories: 200 | fat: 16g | protein: 7g | carbs: 14g | fiber: 3g | sodium: 379mg

Steamed Cod with Capers and Lemon

Prep time: 10 minutes | Cook time: 3 minutes | Serves 4

1 cup water
4 (4-ounce / 113-g) cod fillets, rinsed and patted dry
½ teaspoon ground black pepper
1 small lemon, thinly sliced
2 tablespoons extra-virgin olive oil
¼ cup chopped fresh parsley
2 tablespoons capers
1 tablespoon chopped fresh chives

1. Add water to the Instant Pot® and place the rack inside. 2. Season fish fillets with pepper. Top each fillet with three slices of lemon. Place fillets on rack. Close lid, set steam release to Sealing, press the Steam button, and set time to 3 minutes. 3. While fish cooks, combine olive oil, parsley, capers, and chives in a small bowl and mix well. Set aside. 4. When the timer beeps, quick-release the pressure until the float valve drops. Press the Cancel button and open lid. Place cod fillets on a serving platter. Remove and discard lemon slices and drizzle fish with olive oil mixture, making sure each fillet has herbs and capers on top. Serve immediately.

Per Serving:
calories: 140 | fat: 10g | protein: 14g | carbs: 0g | fiber: 0g | sodium: 370mg

Sicilian Baked Cod with Herbed Breadcrumbs

Prep time: 5 minutes | Cook time: 25 minutes | Serves 4

2 tablespoons olive oil, divided
1 medium red onion, halved and cut into half circles
1 tablespoon red wine vinegar
¾ teaspoon salt, divided, plus more for seasoning
¼ teaspoon freshly ground black pepper, plus more for seasoning
½ teaspoon anchovy paste
3 tablespoons dried breadcrumbs
2 tablespoons chopped flat-leaf parsley
2 tablespoons chopped fresh mint leaves
2 tablespoons chopped fresh basil leaves
4 (6-ounce / 170-g) cod fillets
½ cup dry white wine

1. Preheat the oven to 400ºF (205ºC). 2. Heat 1 tablespoon of olive oil in a medium skillet over medium-high heat. Add the onion and cook, stirring frequently, until softened, about 5 minutes. Add the vinegar and season with the salt and pepper. Cook for about 30 seconds more. Spread the onions into an even layer in a baking dish large enough to hold the fish in a single layer. 3. Heat the remaining 1 tablespoon of olive oil in the same skillet over low heat. Add the anchovy paste and cook, stirring, for about 1 minute. Add the breadcrumbs and toss to coat them in oil. Remove the breadcrumbs to a bowl and let them cool a bit. Add the parsley, mint, and basil, ¼ teaspoon of salt, and a pinch of pepper. 4. Arrange the fish fillets on top of the onions and season with the remaining ½ teaspoon of salt and ¼ teaspoon of pepper. Sprinkle the breadcrumbs equally over the fillets. Pour the wine into the dish. 5. Bake, adding a little more wine or water if necessary until cooked through, about 10 to 15 minutes, depending on the thickness of the fish fillets. Serve hot.

Per Serving:
calories: 299 | fat: 10g | protein: 40g | carbs: 8g | fiber: 1g | sodium: 652mg

Tuna Steak

Prep time: 10 minutes | Cook time: 12 minutes | Serves 4

1 pound (454 g) tuna steaks, boneless and cubed
1 tablespoon mustard
1 tablespoon avocado oil
1 tablespoon apple cider vinegar

1. Mix avocado oil with mustard and apple cider vinegar. 2. Then brush tuna steaks with mustard mixture and put in the air fryer basket. 3. Cook the fish at 360ºF (182ºC) for 6 minutes per side.

Per Serving:
calories: 197 | fat: 9g | protein: 27g | carbs: 0g | fiber: 0g | sodium: 87mg

Herb-Marinated Flounder

Prep time: 5 minutes | Cook time: 10 minutes | Serves 4

½ cup lightly packed flatleaf parsley
¼ cup olive oil
4 garlic cloves, peeled and halved
2 tablespoons fresh rosemary
2 tablespoons fresh thyme
leaves
2 tablespoons fresh sage
2 tablespoons lemon zest
Sea salt and freshly ground pepper, to taste
4 flounder fillets

1. Preheat the oven to 350ºF (180ºC). 2. Place all the ingredients except the fish in a food processor. Blend to form a thick paste. 3. Place the fillets on a baking sheet, and brush this paste on them. Refrigerate for at least 1 hour. 4. Bake for 8–10 minutes, or until the flounder is slightly firm and opaque. Season with sea salt and freshly ground pepper.

Per Serving:
calories: 283 | fat: 18g | protein: 27g | carbs: 3g | fiber: 1g | sodium: 322mg

Seasoned Steamed Crab

Prep time: 10 minutes | Cook time: 3 minutes | Serves 2

1 tablespoon extra-virgin olive oil
½ teaspoon Old Bay seafood seasoning
½ teaspoon smoked paprika
¼ teaspoon cayenne pepper
2 cloves garlic, peeled and minced
2 (2-pound / 907-g) Dungeness crabs
1 cup water

1. In a medium bowl, combine oil, seafood seasoning, smoked paprika, cayenne pepper, and garlic. Mix well. Coat crabs in seasoning mixture and place in the steamer basket. 2. Add water to the Instant Pot® and place steamer basket inside. Close lid, set steam release to Sealing, press the Manual button, and set time to 3 minutes. 3. When the timer beeps, quick-release the pressure until the float valve drops. Press the Cancel button and open lid. Transfer crabs to a serving platter. Serve hot.

Per Serving:
calories: 185 | fat: 8g | protein: 25g | carbs: 1g | fiber: 0g | sodium: 434mg

Lemon and Herb Fish Packets

Prep time: 10 minutes | Cook time: 5 minutes | Serves 4

1 cup water
4 (4-ounce / 113-g) halibut or other white fish fillets
½ teaspoon salt
½ teaspoon ground black pepper
1 small lemon, thinly sliced

¼ cup chopped fresh dill
¼ cup chopped fresh chives
2 tablespoons chopped fresh tarragon
2 tablespoons extra-virgin olive oil

1. Add water to the Instant Pot® and place the rack inside. 2. Season fish fillets with salt and pepper. Measure out four pieces of foil large enough to wrap around fish fillets. Lay fish fillets on foil. Top with lemon, dill, chives, and tarragon, and drizzle each with olive oil. Carefully wrap fish loosely in foil. 3. Place packets on rack. Close lid, set steam release to Sealing, press the Steam button, and set time to 5 minutes. 4. When the timer beeps, quick-release the pressure until the float valve drops. Press the Cancel button and open lid. Serve immediately.

Per Serving:
calories: 185 | fat: 9g | protein: 23g | carbs: 0g | fiber: 0g | sodium: 355mg

Steamed Shrimp and Asparagus

Prep time: 15 minutes | Cook time: 1 minute | Serves 4

1 cup water
1 bunch asparagus, trimmed
½ teaspoon salt, divided
1 pound (454 g) shrimp, peeled

and deveined
1½ tablespoons lemon juice
2 tablespoons olive oil

1. Pour water into the Instant Pot®. Insert rack and place steamer basket onto rack. 2. Spread asparagus on the bottom of the steamer basket. Sprinkle with ¼ teaspoon salt. Add shrimp. Drizzle with lemon juice and sprinkle with remaining ¼ teaspoon salt. Drizzle olive oil over shrimp. 3. Close lid, set steam release to Sealing, press the Manual button, and set time to 1 minute. When the timer beeps, quick-release the pressure until the float valve drops and open lid. 4. Transfer shrimp and asparagus to a platter and serve.

Per Serving:
calories: 145 | fat: 8g | protein: 19g | carbs: 1g | fiber: 0g | sodium: 295mg

Parmesan Mackerel with Coriander

Prep time: 10 minutes | Cook time: 7 minutes | Serves 2

12 ounces (340 g) mackerel fillet
2 ounces (57 g) Parmesan,

grated
1 teaspoon ground coriander
1 tablespoon olive oil

1. Sprinkle the mackerel fillet with olive oil and put it in the air fryer basket. 2. Top the fish with ground coriander and Parmesan. 3. Cook the fish at 390ºF (199ºC) for 7 minutes.

Per Serving:
calories: 522 | fat: 39g | protein: 42g | carbs: 1g | fiber: 0g | sodium: 544mg

Shrimp and Fish Chowder

Prep time: 20 minutes | Cook time: 4 to 6 hours |
Serves 4

3 cups low-sodium vegetable broth
1 (28-ounce / 794-g) can no-salt-added crushed tomatoes
1 large bell pepper, any color, seeded and diced
1 large onion, diced
2 zucchini, chopped
3 garlic cloves, minced
1 teaspoon dried thyme

1 teaspoon dried basil
½ teaspoon sea salt
¼ teaspoon freshly ground black pepper
¼ teaspoon red pepper flakes
8 ounces (227 g) whole raw medium shrimp, peeled and deveined
8 ounces (227 g) fresh cod fillets, cut into 1-inch pieces

1. In a slow cooker, combine the vegetable broth, tomatoes, bell pepper, onion, zucchini, garlic, thyme, basil, salt, black pepper, and red pepper flakes. Stir to mix well. 2. Cover the cooker and cook for 4 to 6 hours on Low heat. 3. Stir in the shrimp and cod. Replace the cover on the cooker and cook for 15 to 30 minutes on Low heat, or until the shrimp have turned pink and the cod is firm and flaky.

Per Serving:
calories: 201 | fat: 1g | protein: 26g | carbs: 24g | fiber: 7g | sodium: 598mg

Seared Scallops with White Bean Purée

Prep time: 15 minutes | Cook time: 15 minutes | Serves 2

4 tablespoons olive oil, divided
2 garlic cloves
2 teaspoons minced fresh rosemary
1 (15-ounce / 425-g) can white cannellini beans, drained and rinsed

½ cup low-sodium chicken stock
Salt
Freshly ground black pepper
10 ounces (283 g) sea scallops (about 6)

1. To make the bean purée, heat 2 tablespoons of olive oil in a saucepan over medium-high heat. Add the garlic and sauté for 30 seconds, or just until it's fragrant. Don't let it burn. Add the rosemary and remove the pan from the heat. 2. Add the white beans and chicken stock to the pan, return it to the heat, and stir. Bring the beans to a boil. Reduce the heat to low and simmer for 5 minutes. 3. Transfer the beans to a blender and purée them for 30 seconds, or until they're smooth. Taste and season with salt and pepper. Let them sit in the blender with the lid on to keep them warm while you prepare the scallops. 4. Pat the scallops dry with a paper towel and season them with salt and pepper. 5. Heat the remaining 2 tablespoons of olive oil in a large sauté pan. When the oil is shimmering, add the scallops, flat-side down. 6. Cook the scallops for 2 minutes, or until they're golden on the bottom. Flip them over and cook for another 1 to 2 minutes, or until opaque and slightly firm. 7. To serve, divide the bean purée between two plates and top with the scallops.

Per Serving:
calories: 465 | fat: 29g | protein: 30g | carbs: 21g | fiber: 8g | sodium: 319mg

Caramelized Fennel and Sardines with Penne

Prep time: 15 minutes | Cook time: 30 minutes | Serves 4

8 ounces (227 g) whole-wheat penne
2 tablespoons extra-virgin olive oil
1 bulb fennel, cored and thinly sliced, plus ¼ cup fronds
2 celery stalks, thinly sliced, plus ½ cup leaves
4 garlic cloves, sliced
¾ teaspoon kosher salt
¼ teaspoon freshly ground black pepper
Zest of 1 lemon
Juice of 1 lemon
2 (4.4-ounce / 125-g) cans boneless/skinless sardines packed in olive oil, undrained

1. Cook the penne according to the package directions. Drain, reserving 1 cup pasta water. 2. Heat the olive oil in a large skillet or sauté pan over medium heat. Add the fennel and celery and cook, stirring often, until tender and golden, about 10 to 12 minutes. Add the garlic and cook for 1 minute. 3. Add the penne, reserved pasta water, salt, and black pepper. Increase the heat to medium-high and cook for 1 to 2 minutes. 4. Remove the pan from the heat and stir in the lemon zest, lemon juice, fennel fronds, and celery leaves. Break the sardines into bite-size pieces and gently mix in, along with the oil they were packed in.

Per Serving:
calories: 400 | fat: 15g | protein: 22g | carbs: 46g | fiber: 6g | sodium: 530mg

Paprika-Spiced Fish

Prep time: 5 minutes | Cook time: 10 minutes | Serves 4

4 (5-ounce / 142-g) sea bass fillets
½ teaspoon salt
1 tablespoon smoked paprika
3 tablespoons unsalted butter
Lemon wedges

1. Season the fish on both sides with the salt. Repeat with the paprika. 2. Preheat a skillet over high heat. Melt the butter. 3. Once the butter is melted, add the fish and cook for 4 minutes on each side. 4. Once the fish is done cooking, move to a serving dish and squeeze lemon over the top.

Per Serving:
calories: 257 | fat: 34g | protein: 34g | carbs: 1g | fiber: 1g | sodium: 416mg

Balsamic Tilapia

Prep time: 5 minutes | Cook time: 15 minutes | Serves 4

4 tilapia fillets, boneless
2 tablespoons balsamic vinegar
1 teaspoon avocado oil
1 teaspoon dried basil

1. Sprinkle the tilapia fillets with balsamic vinegar, avocado oil, and dried basil. 2. Then put the fillets in the air fryer basket and cook at 365ºF (185ºC) for 15 minutes.

Per Serving:
calories: 129 | fat: 3g | protein: 23g | carbs: 1g | fiber: 0g | sodium: 92mg

Tuna Cakes

Prep time: 10 minutes | Cook time: 10 minutes | Serves 4

4 (3-ounce / 85-g) pouches tuna, drained
1 large egg, whisked
2 tablespoons peeled and chopped white onion
½ teaspoon Old Bay seasoning

1. In a large bowl, mix all ingredients together and form into four patties. 2. Place patties into ungreased air fryer basket. Adjust the temperature to 400ºF (204ºC) and air fry for 10 minutes. Patties will be browned and crispy when done. Let cool 5 minutes before serving.

Per Serving:
calories: 113 | fat: 2g | protein: 22g | carbs: 1g | fiber: 0g | sodium: 56mg

Fire-Roasted Salmon à l'Orange

Prep time: 10 minutes | Cook time: 25 minutes | Serves 4

½ cup extra-virgin olive oil, divided
2 tablespoons balsamic vinegar
2 tablespoons garlic powder, divided
1 tablespoon cumin seeds
1 teaspoon sea salt, divided
1 teaspoon freshly ground black pepper, divided
2 teaspoons smoked paprika
4 (8-ounce / 227-g) salmon fillets, skinless
2 small red onion, thinly sliced
½ cup halved Campari tomatoes
1 small fennel bulb, thinly
sliced lengthwise
1 large carrot, thinly sliced
8 medium portobello mushrooms
8 medium radishes, sliced ⅛ inch thick
½ cup dry white wine
½ lime, zested
Handful cilantro leaves
½ cup halved pitted kalamata olives
1 orange, thinly sliced
4 roasted sweet potatoes, cut in wedges lengthwise

1. Preheat the oven to 375ºF. 2. In a medium bowl, mix 6 tablespoons of olive oil, the balsamic vinegar, 1 tablespoon of garlic powder, the cumin seeds, ¼ teaspoon of sea salt, ¼ teaspoon of pepper, and the paprika. Put the salmon in the bowl and marinate while preparing the vegetables, about 10 minutes. 3. Heat an oven-safe sauté pan or skillet on medium-high heat and sear the top of the salmon for about 2 minutes, or until lightly brown. Set aside. 4. Add the remaining 2 tablespoons of olive oil to the same skillet. Once it's hot, add the onion, tomatoes, fennel, carrot, mushrooms, radishes, the remaining 1 teaspoon of garlic powder, ¾ teaspoon of salt, and ¾ teaspoon of pepper. Mix well and cook for 5 to 7 minutes, until fragrant. Add wine and mix well. 5. Place the salmon on top of the vegetable mixture, browned-side up. Sprinkle the fish with lime zest and cilantro and place the olives around the fish. Put orange slices over the fish and cook for about 7 additional minutes. While this is baking, add the sliced sweet potato wedges on a baking sheet and bake this alongside the skillet. 6. Remove from the oven, cover the skillet tightly, and let rest for about 3 minutes.

Per Serving:
calories: 873 | fat: 41g | protein: 57g | carbs: 68g | fiber: 12g | sodium: 667mg

Chopped Tuna Salad

Prep time: 15 minutes | Cook time: 0 minutes | Serves 4

2 tablespoons extra-virgin olive oil
2 tablespoons lemon juice
2 teaspoons Dijon mustard
½ teaspoon kosher salt
¼ teaspoon freshly ground black pepper
12 olives, pitted and chopped
½ cup celery, diced
½ cup red onion, diced
½ cup red bell pepper, diced
½ cup fresh parsley, chopped
2 (6-ounce / 170-g) cans no-salt-added tuna packed in water, drained
6 cups baby spinach

1. In a medium bowl, whisk together the olive oil, lemon juice, mustard, salt, and black pepper. Add in the olives, celery, onion, bell pepper, and parsley and mix well. Add the tuna and gently incorporate. 2. Divide the spinach evenly among 4 plates or bowls. Spoon the tuna salad evenly on top of the spinach.

Per Serving:
calories: 220 | fat: 11g | protein: 25g | carbs: 7g | fiber: 2g | sodium: 396mg

Baked Salmon with Tomatoes and Olives

Prep time: 5 minutes | Cook time: 8 minutes | Serves 4

2 tablespoons olive oil
4 (1½-inch-thick) salmon fillets
½ teaspoon salt
¼ teaspoon cayenne
1 teaspoon chopped fresh dill
2 Roma tomatoes, diced
¼ cup sliced Kalamata olives
4 lemon slices

1. Preheat the air fryer to 380°F(193°C). 2. Brush the olive oil on both sides of the salmon fillets, and then season them lightly with salt, cayenne, and dill. 3. Place the fillets in a single layer in the basket of the air fryer, then layer the tomatoes and olives over the top. Top each fillet with a lemon slice. 4. Bake for 8 minutes, or until the salmon has reached an internal temperature of 145°F(63°C).

Per Serving:
calories: 483 | fat: 22g | protein: 66g | carbs: 3g | fiber: 1g | sodium: 593mg

Lemon-Pepper Trout

Prep time: 5 minutes | Cook time: 15 minutes | Serves 4

4 trout fillets
2 tablespoons olive oil
½ teaspoon salt
1 teaspoon black pepper
2 garlic cloves, sliced
1 lemon, sliced, plus additional wedges for serving

1. Preheat the air fryer to 380°F(193°C). 2. Brush each fillet with olive oil on both sides and season with salt and pepper. Place the fillets in an even layer in the air fryer basket. 3. Place the sliced garlic over the tops of the trout fillets, then top the garlic with lemon slices and roast for 12 to 15 minutes, or until it has reached an internal temperature of 145°F(63°C). 4. Serve with fresh lemon wedges.

Per Serving:
calories: 185 | fat: 12g | protein: 17g | carbs: 2g | fiber: 1g | sodium: 333mg

Tuna Slow-Cooked in Olive Oil

Prep time: 5 minutes | Cook time: 45 minutes | Serves 4

1 cup extra-virgin olive oil, plus more if needed
4 (3- to 4-inch) sprigs fresh rosemary
8 (3- to 4-inch) sprigs fresh thyme
2 large garlic cloves, thinly sliced
2 (2-inch) strips lemon zest
1 teaspoon salt
½ teaspoon freshly ground black pepper
1 pound (454 g) fresh tuna steaks (about 1 inch thick)

1. Select a thick pot just large enough to fit the tuna in a single layer on the bottom. The larger the pot, the more olive oil you will need to use. Combine the olive oil, rosemary, thyme, garlic, lemon zest, salt, and pepper over medium-low heat and cook until warm and fragrant, 20 to 25 minutes, lowering the heat if it begins to smoke. 2. Remove from the heat and allow to cool for 25 to 30 minutes, until warm but not hot. 3. Add the tuna to the bottom of the pan, adding additional oil if needed so that tuna is fully submerged, and return to medium-low heat. Cook for 5 to 10 minutes, or until the oil heats back up and is warm and fragrant but not smoking. Lower the heat if it gets too hot. 4. Remove the pot from the heat and let the tuna cook in warm oil 4 to 5 minutes, to your desired level of doneness. For a tuna that is rare in the center, cook for 2 to 3 minutes. 5. Remove from the oil and serve warm, drizzling 2 to 3 tablespoons seasoned oil over the tuna. 6. To store for later use, remove the tuna from the oil and place in a container with a lid. Allow tuna and oil to cool separately. When both have cooled, remove the herb stems with a slotted spoon and pour the cooking oil over the tuna. Cover and store in the refrigerator for up to 1 week. Bring to room temperature to allow the oil to liquify before serving.

Per Serving:
calories: 606 | fat: 55g | protein: 28g | carbs: 1g | fiber: 0g | sodium: 631mg

Mediterranean Cod

Prep time: 15 minutes | Cook time: 6 minutes | Serves 2

1 cup water
2 (5-ounce / 142-g) cod fillets
2 teaspoons olive oil
½ teaspoon salt
10 Kalamata olives, pitted and
halved
1 small Roma tomato, diced
3 tablespoons chopped fresh basil leaves, divided

1. Add water to the Instant Pot® and place the rack inside. 2. Place each piece of cod on a 10" × 10" square of aluminum foil. Drizzle each fillet with 1 teaspoon oil and sprinkle with ¼ teaspoon salt. Add 5 olives, half of the tomatoes, and 1 tablespoon basil on top of each fillet. Bring up the sides of the foil and crimp at the top to create a foil pocket. 3. Place both fish packets on rack. Close lid, set steam release to Sealing, press the Manual button, and set time to 6 minutes. When the timer beeps, quick-release the pressure until the float valve drops and open lid. 4. Remove foil packets and transfer fish and toppings to two plates. Garnish each serving with half of the remaining 1 tablespoon basil.

Per Serving:
calories: 181 | fat: 8g | protein: 26g | carbs: 2g | fiber: 1g | sodium: 662mg

Paprika Crab Burgers

Prep time: 30 minutes | Cook time: 14 minutes | Serves 3

2 eggs, beaten
1 shallot, chopped
2 garlic cloves, crushed
1 tablespoon olive oil
1 teaspoon yellow mustard
1 teaspoon fresh cilantro, chopped

10 ounces (283 g) crab meat
1 teaspoon smoked paprika
½ teaspoon ground black pepper
Sea salt, to taste
¾ cup Parmesan cheese

1. In a mixing bowl, thoroughly combine the eggs, shallot, garlic, olive oil, mustard, cilantro, crab meat, paprika, black pepper, and salt. Mix until well combined. 2. Shape the mixture into 6 patties. Roll the crab patties over grated Parmesan cheese, coating well on all sides. Place in your refrigerator for 2 hours. 3. Spritz the crab patties with cooking oil on both sides. Cook in the preheated air fryer at 360°F (182°C) for 14 minutes. Serve on dinner rolls if desired. Bon appétit!

Per Serving:
calories: 288 | fat: 16g | protein: 32g | carbs: 4g | fiber: 1g | sodium: 355mg

Olive Oil–Poached Fish over Citrus Salad

Prep time: 10 minutes | Cook time: 25 minutes | Serves 4

Fish
4 skinless white fish fillets (1¼ to 1½ pounds / 567 to 680 g total), such as halibut, sole, or cod, ¾'–1' thick
¼ teaspoon kosher salt
¼ teaspoon ground black pepper
5–7 cups olive oil
1 lemon, thinly sliced
Salad
¼ cup white wine vinegar
1 Earl Grey tea bag
2 blood oranges or tangerines

1 ruby red grapefruit or pomelo
6 kumquats, thinly sliced, or 2 clementines, peeled and sectioned
4 cups baby arugula
½ cup pomegranate seeds
¼ cup extra-virgin olive oil
2 teaspoons minced shallot
½ teaspoon kosher salt
¼ teaspoon ground black pepper
¼ cup mint leaves, coarsely chopped

1. Make the fish: Season the fish with the salt and pepper and set aside for 30 minutes. 2. Preheat the oven to 225°F. 3. In a large high-sided ovenproof skillet or roasting pan over medium heat, warm 1' to 1½' of the oil and the lemon slices until the temperature reaches 120°F (use a candy thermometer). Add the fish fillets to the oil, without overlapping, making sure they're completely submerged. 4. Transfer the skillet or pan to the oven, uncovered. Bake for 25 minutes. Transfer the fish to a rack to drain for 5 minutes. 5. Make the salad: In a small saucepan, heat the vinegar until almost boiling. Add the tea bag and set aside to steep for 10 minutes. 6. Meanwhile, with a paring knife, cut off enough of the top and bottom of 1 of the oranges or tangerines to reveal the flesh. Cut along the inside of the peel, between the pith and the flesh, taking off as much pith as possible. Over a large bowl, hold the orange in 1 hand. With the paring knife, cut along the membranes between each section, allowing the fruit to fall into the bowl. Once all the fruit segments have been released, squeeze the remaining membranes over a small bowl. Repeat with the second orange and the grapefruit or pomelo. 7. In the large bowl with the segmented fruit, add the kumquats or clementines, arugula, and pomegranate seeds. Gently toss to distribute. 8. Remove the tea bag from the vinegar and squeeze out as much liquid as possible. Discard the bag and add the vinegar to the small bowl with the citrus juice. Slowly whisk in the oil, shallot, salt, and pepper. Drizzle 3 to 4 tablespoons over the salad and gently toss. (Store the remaining vinaigrette in the refrigerator for up to 1 week.) 9. Sprinkle the salad with the mint and serve with the fish.

Per Serving:
calories: 280 | fat: 7g | protein: 29g | carbs: 25g | fiber: 6g | sodium: 249mg

Moroccan–Style Grilled Tuna

Prep time: 10 minutes | Cook time: 6 to 8 minutes | Serves 4

2 tablespoons finely chopped cilantro
2 tablespoons finely chopped parsley
6 cloves garlic, minced
½ teaspoon unrefined sea salt or salt

½ teaspoon paprika
1 lemon, juiced and zested
3 tablespoons extra-virgin olive oil
4 tuna steaks (4 ounces / 113 g each)

1. In a medium bowl, mix the cilantro, parsley, garlic, salt, paprika, and lemon juice and zest together. Whisk in the olive oil. 2. Place the fish in a glass baking dish and pour half of the chermoula sauce over the top. Cover with plastic wrap and allow to marinate for 1 hour. 3. Preheat grill to medium-high heat. 4. Grill the fish, turning once, until firm, 6 to 8 minutes. Transfer to a platter, spread with the remaining chermoula sauce, and let stand for 5 minutes to absorb the flavors.

Per Serving:
calories: 217 | fat: 11g | protein: 25g | carbs: 3g | fiber: 0g | sodium: 335mg

Lemony Salmon

Prep time: 30 minutes | Cook time: 10 minutes | Serves 4

1½ pounds (680 g) salmon steak
½ teaspoon grated lemon zest
Freshly cracked mixed peppercorns, to taste
⅓ cup lemon juice

Fresh chopped chives, for garnish
½ cup dry white wine
½ teaspoon fresh cilantro, chopped
Fine sea salt, to taste

1. To prepare the marinade, place all ingredients, except for salmon steak and chives, in a deep pan. Bring to a boil over medium-high flame until it has reduced by half. Allow it to cool down. 2. After that, allow salmon steak to marinate in the refrigerator approximately 40 minutes. Discard the marinade and transfer the fish steak to the preheated air fryer. 3. Air fry at 400°F (204°C) for 9 to 10 minutes. To finish, brush hot fish steaks with the reserved marinade, garnish with fresh chopped chives, and serve right away!

Per Serving:
calories: 244 | fat: 8g | protein: 35g | carbs: 3g | fiber: 0g | sodium: 128mg

Shrimp with Arugula Pesto and Zucchini Noodles

Prep time: 20 minutes | Cook time: 5 minutes | Serves 2

3 cups lightly packed arugula
½ cup lightly packed basil leaves
3 medium garlic cloves
¼ cup walnuts
3 tablespoons olive oil
2 tablespoons grated Parmesan cheese
1 tablespoon freshly squeezed

lemon juice
Salt
Freshly ground black pepper
1 (10-ounce / 283-g) package zucchini noodles
8 ounces (227 g) cooked, shelled shrimp
2 Roma tomatoes, diced

1. Combine the arugula, basil, garlic, walnuts, olive oil, Parmesan cheese, and lemon juice in a food processor fitted with the chopping blade. Process until smooth, scraping down the sides as needed. Season with salt and pepper. 2. Heat a sauté pan over medium heat. Add the pesto, zucchini noodles, and shrimp. Toss to combine the sauce over the noodles and shrimp, and cook until warmed through. Don't overcook or the zucchini will become limp. 3. Taste and add additional salt and pepper if needed. Top with the diced tomatoes.

Per Serving:
calories: 434 | fat: 30g | protein: 33g | carbs: 15g | fiber: 5g | sodium: 412mg

Seasoned Sole

Prep time: 5 minutes | Cook time: 2 to 4 hours | Serves 4

Nonstick cooking spray
2 pounds (907 g) fresh sole fillets
3 tablespoons freshly squeezed lime juice
2 tablespoons extra-virgin olive

oil
2 garlic cloves, minced
1 tablespoon ground cumin
1½ teaspoons paprika
1 teaspoon sea salt
¼ cup fresh cilantro

1. Coat a slow-cooker insert with cooking spray, or line the bottom and sides with parchment paper or aluminum foil. 2. Place the sole in the prepared slow cooker in a single layer, cutting it into pieces to fit if needed. 3. In a small bowl, whisk together the lime juice, olive oil, garlic, cumin, paprika, and salt until blended. Pour the sauce over the fish. 4. Cover the cooker and cook for 2 to 4 hours on Low heat. 5. Garnish with fresh cilantro for serving.

Per Serving:
calories: 234 | fat: 12g | protein: 29g | carbs: 2g | fiber: 1g | sodium: 713mg

Ahi Tuna Steaks

Prep time: 5 minutes | Cook time: 14 minutes | Serves 2

2 (6-ounce / 170-g) ahi tuna steaks
2 tablespoons olive oil

3 tablespoons everything bagel seasoning

1. Drizzle both sides of each steak with olive oil. Place seasoning on a medium plate and press each side of tuna steaks into seasoning to form a thick layer. 2. Place steaks into ungreased air fryer basket.

Adjust the temperature to 400ºF (204ºC) and air fry for 14 minutes, turning steaks halfway through cooking. Steaks will be done when internal temperature is at least 145ºF (63ºC) for well-done. Serve warm.

Per Serving:
calories: 305 | fat: 14g | protein: 42g | carbs: 0g | fiber: 0g | sodium: 377mg

Weeknight Sheet Pan Fish Dinner

Prep time: 10 minutes |Cook time: 10 minutes| Serves: 4

Nonstick cooking spray
2 tablespoons extra-virgin olive oil
1 tablespoon balsamic vinegar
4 (4-ounce / 113-g) fish fillets, such as cod or tilapia (½ inch

thick)
2½ cups green beans (about 12 ounces)
1 pint cherry or grape tomatoes (about 2 cups)

1. Preheat the oven to 400°F(205ºC). Coat two large, rimmed baking sheets with nonstick cooking spray. 2. In a small bowl, whisk together the oil and vinegar. Set aside. 3. Place two pieces of fish on each baking sheet. 4. In a large bowl, combine the beans and tomatoes. Pour in the oil and vinegar, and toss gently to coat. Pour half of the green bean mixture over the fish on one baking sheet, and the remaining half over the fish on the other. Turn the fish over, and rub it in the oil mixture to coat. Spread the vegetables evenly on the baking sheets so hot air can circulate around them. 5. Bake for 5 to 8 minutes, until the fish is just opaque and not translucent. The fish is done and ready to serve when it just begins to separate into flakes (chunks) when pressed gently with a fork.

Per Serving:
calories: 190 | fat: 8g | protein: 22g | carbs: 8g | fiber: 3g | sodium: 70mg

Herbed Shrimp Pita

Prep time: 5 minutes | Cook time: 8 minutes | Serves 4

1 pound (454 g) medium shrimp, peeled and deveined
2 tablespoons olive oil
1 teaspoon dried oregano
½ teaspoon dried thyme
½ teaspoon garlic powder
¼ teaspoon onion powder
½ teaspoon salt

¼ teaspoon black pepper
4 whole wheat pitas
4 ounces (113 g) feta cheese, crumbled
1 cup shredded lettuce
1 tomato, diced
¼ cup black olives, sliced
1 lemon

1. Preheat the oven to 380°F(193ºC). 2. In a medium bowl, combine the shrimp with the olive oil, oregano, thyme, garlic powder, onion powder, salt, and black pepper. 3. Pour shrimp in a single layer in the air fryer basket and roast for 6 to 8 minutes, or until cooked through. 4. Remove from the air fryer and divide into warmed pitas with feta, lettuce, tomato, olives, and a squeeze of lemon.

Per Serving:
calories: 320 | fat: 14g | protein: 30g | carbs: 20g | fiber: 3g | sodium: 813mg

Summer Mackerel Niçoise Platter

Prep time: 10 minutes | Cook time: 15 minutes | Serves 2

For the Dressing:
3 tablespoons red wine vinegar
4 tablespoons olive oil
1 teaspoon Dijon mustard
¼ teaspoon salt
Pinch freshly ground black pepper
For the Salad:
2 teaspoons salt

2 small red potatoes
1 cup tender green beans
2 cups baby greens
2 hard-boiled eggs
½ cup cherry tomatoes, halved
⅓ cup Niçoise olives
2 (4-ounce / 113-g) tins of mackerel fillets, drained

Make the Dressing: Combine the vinegar, olive oil, Dijon mustard, salt, and pepper in a lidded jar. Shake or whisk the dressing until thoroughly combined. Taste and add more salt and pepper to taste, if needed. Make the Salad: 1. Fill a large saucepan with about 3 inches of water, add salt, and bring to a boil. Add the potatoes and cook for 10 to 15 minutes, or until you can pierce them with a sharp knife, but they are still firm. 2. Remove the potatoes and add the green beans to the water. Reduce the heat and let the beans simmer for 5 minutes. 3. Place both the potatoes and green beans in a colander and run it under cold water until vegetables are cool. 4. Lay the baby greens on a large platter. 5. Slice the potatoes and arrange them on one section of the platter. Add the green beans to another section of the platter. Slice the hard-boiled eggs and arrange them in another section. 6. Continue with the tomatoes, olives, and mackerel fillets. Pour the dressing over the salad.

Per Serving:
calories: 657 | fat: 47g | protein: 25g | carbs: 38g | fiber: 7g | sodium: 355mg

Saffron Rice with Whitefish

Prep time: 10 minutes | Cook time: 35 minutes | Serves 4

4 tablespoons extra-virgin olive oil, divided
1 large onion, chopped
3 cod fillets, rinsed and patted dry

4½ cups water
1 teaspoon saffron threads
1½ teaspoons salt
1 teaspoon turmeric
2 cups long-grain rice, rinsed

1. In a large pot over medium heat, cook 2 tablespoons of olive oil and the onions for 5 minutes. 2. While the onions are cooking, preheat another large pan over high heat. Add the remaining 2 tablespoons of olive oil and the cod fillets. Cook the cod for 2 minutes on each side, then remove from the pan and set aside. 3. Once the onions are done cooking, add the water, saffron, salt, turmeric, and rice, stirring to combine. Cover and cook for 12 minutes. 4. Cut the cod up into 1-inch pieces. Place the cod pieces in the rice, lightly toss, cover, and cook for another 10 minutes. 5. Once the rice is done cooking, fluff with a fork, cover, and let stand for 5 minutes. Serve warm.

Per Serving:
calories: 564 | fat: 15g | protein: 26g | carbs: 78g | fiber: 2g | sodium: 945mg

Citrus Swordfish

Prep time: 10 minutes | Cook time: 1½ hours | Serves 2

Nonstick cooking oil spray
1½ pounds (680 g) swordfish fillets
Sea salt
Black pepper
1 yellow onion, chopped
5 tablespoons chopped fresh

flat-leaf parsley
1 tablespoon olive oil
2 teaspoons lemon zest
2 teaspoons orange zest
Orange and lemon slices, for garnish
Fresh parsley sprigs, for garnish

1. Coat the interior of the slow cooker crock with nonstick cooking oil spray. 2. Season the fish fillets with salt and pepper. Place the fish in the slow cooker. 3. Distribute the onion, parsley, olive oil, lemon zest, and orange zest over fish. 4. Cover and cook on low for 1½ hours. 5. Serve hot, garnished with orange and lemon slices and sprigs of fresh parsley.

Per Serving:
calories: 578 | fat: 30g | protein: 68g | carbs: 7g | fiber: 2g | sodium: 283mg

Snapper with Shallot and Tomato

Prep time: 20 minutes | Cook time: 15 minutes | Serves 2

2 snapper fillets
1 shallot, peeled and sliced
2 garlic cloves, halved
1 bell pepper, sliced
1 small-sized serrano pepper, sliced
1 tomato, sliced

1 tablespoon olive oil
¼ teaspoon freshly ground black pepper
½ teaspoon paprika
Sea salt, to taste
2 bay leaves

1. Place two parchment sheets on a working surface. Place the fish in the center of one side of the parchment paper. 2. Top with the shallot, garlic, peppers, and tomato. Drizzle olive oil over the fish and vegetables. Season with black pepper, paprika, and salt. Add the bay leaves. 3. Fold over the other half of the parchment. Now, fold the paper around the edges tightly and create a half moon shape, sealing the fish inside. 4. Cook in the preheated air fryer at 390ºF (199ºC) for 15 minutes. Serve warm.

Per Serving:
calories: 325 | fat: 10g | protein: 47g | carbs: 11g | fiber: 2g | sodium: 146mg

Chapter 5 Poultry

Turkey Kofta Casserole

Prep time: 20 minutes | Cook time: 6 to 8 hours | Serves 4

For the Kofta:
2 pounds (907 g) raw ground turkey
1 small onion, diced
3 garlic cloves, minced
2 tablespoons chopped fresh parsley
1 tablespoon ground coriander
2 teaspoons ground cumin
1 teaspoon sea salt
1 teaspoon freshly ground black pepper
½ teaspoon ground nutmeg
½ teaspoon dried mint

½ teaspoon paprika
For the Casserole:
Nonstick cooking spray
4 large (about 2½ pounds / 1.1 kg) potatoes, peeled and cut into ¼-inch-thick rounds
4 large (about 3 pounds / 1.4 kg) tomatoes, cut into ¼-inch-thick rounds
Salt
Freshly ground black pepper
1 (8-ounce / 227-g) can no-salt-added, no-sugar-added tomato sauce

Make the Kofta: 1. In a large bowl, mix together the turkey, onion, garlic, parsley, coriander, cumin, salt, pepper, nutmeg, mint, and paprika until combined. 2. Form the kofta mixture into 13 to 15 equal patties, using about 2 to 3 tablespoons of the meat mixture per patty. Make the Casserole: 1. Coat a slow-cooker insert with cooking spray. 2. Layer the kofta patties, potatoes, and tomatoes in the prepared slow cooker, alternating the ingredients as you go, like a ratatouille. Season with salt and pepper. 3. Spread the tomato sauce over the ingredients. 4. Cover the cooker and cook for 6 to 8 hours on Low heat, or until the potatoes are tender.

Per Serving:
calories: 588 | fat: 17g | protein: 52g | carbs: 61g | fiber: 11g | sodium: 833mg

Greek Roasted Lemon Chicken with Potatoes

Prep time: 10 minutes | Cook time: 1 hour 20 minutes | Serves 4

2 pounds (907 g) potatoes (russet or white varieties), peeled
1½ pounds (680 g) chicken pieces (breasts, thighs, legs)
1 cup wine (any variety), for rinsing
1½ teaspoons freshly ground black pepper, divided

2 tablespoons dried oregano, divided
1 teaspoon salt, divided
½ cup extra virgin olive oil
2 tablespoons fresh lemon juice
2 to 3 allspice berries
2 to 3 cloves
2 garlic cloves, cut into quarters

1. Preheat the oven to 375°F (190°C). Place the peeled potatoes in a large bowl and cover them with cold water. Set aside. 2. Rinse the chicken pieces with the wine, pat dry with paper towels, and transfer to a large plate. In a small bowl, mix 1 teaspoon of black pepper, 1 tablespoon of oregano, and ½ teaspoon of salt to make a rub. Apply the rub to the chicken pieces and then set aside. 3. Remove the potatoes from the water. Rinse and pat dry the potatoes, then cut them into wedges and then cut again into half wedges. Place them in a large bowl. 4. Add the olive oil, lemon juice, remaining tablespoon of the oregano, remaining ½ teaspoon of the black pepper, and remaining ½ teaspoon of salt to the potatoes. Mix until all the potatoes are coated with the spices and olive oil. 5. Transfer the potatoes to a large baking dish and spread them into a single layer. Place the chicken pieces on top of the potatoes and then scatter the allspice berries, cloves, and garlic around the chicken. 6. Add hot water to one corner of the dish and then tilt the dish until the water is distributed throughout and fills about ¼ of the depth of the dish. (Do not pour the water directly over the potatoes because it will rinse off the olive oil and spices.) 7. Transfer to the oven and roast for 20 minutes, then reduce the oven temperature to 350°F (180°C) and roast for 1 more hour or until the potatoes and chicken are done. (If the water in the dish evaporates too quickly, add more hot water, ¼ cup at a time.) The potatoes are done when they have a golden color and a knife can be inserted easily. Serve hot. Store in the refrigerator for up to 3 days.

Per Serving:
calories: 629 | fat: 34g | protein: 38g | carbs: 43g | fiber: 3g | sodium: 761mg

Smoky Chicken Leg Quarters

Prep time: 30 minutes | Cook time: 23 to 27 minutes | Serves 6

½ cup avocado oil
2 teaspoons smoked paprika
1 teaspoon sea salt
1 teaspoon garlic powder
½ teaspoon dried rosemary

½ teaspoon dried thyme
½ teaspoon freshly ground black pepper
2 pounds (907 g) bone-in, skin-on chicken leg quarters

1. In a blender or small bowl, combine the avocado oil, smoked paprika, salt, garlic powder, rosemary, thyme, and black pepper. 2. Place the chicken in a shallow dish or large zip-top bag. Pour the marinade over the chicken, making sure all the legs are coated. Cover and marinate for at least 2 hours or overnight. 3. Place the chicken in a single layer in the air fryer basket, working in batches if necessary. Set the air fryer to 400°F (204°C) and air fry for 15 minutes. Flip the chicken legs, then reduce the temperature to 350°F (177°C). Cook for 8 to 12 minutes more, until an instant-read thermometer reads 160°F (71°C) when inserted into the thickest piece of chicken. 4. Allow to rest for 5 to 10 minutes before serving.

Per Serving:
calories: 347 | fat: 25g | protein: 29g | carbs: 1g | fiber: 0g | sodium: 534mg

Pesto-Glazed Chicken Breasts

Prep time: 5 minutes | Cook time: 20 minutes | Serves 4

¼ cup plus 1 tablespoon extra-virgin olive oil, divided
4 boneless, skinless chicken breasts
½ teaspoon salt
¼ teaspoon freshly ground
black pepper
1 packed cup fresh basil leaves
1 garlic clove, minced
¼ cup grated Parmesan cheese
¼ cup pine nuts

1. In a large, heavy skillet, heat 1 tablespoon of the olive oil over medium-high heat. 2. Season the chicken breasts on both sides with salt and pepper and place in the skillet. Cook for 10 minutes on the first side, then turn and cook for 5 minutes. 3. Meanwhile, in a blender or food processor, combine the basil, garlic, Parmesan cheese, and pine nuts, and blend on high. Gradually pour in the remaining ¼ cup olive oil and blend until smooth. 4. Spread 1 tablespoon pesto on each chicken breast, cover the skillet, and cook for 5 minutes. Serve the chicken pesto side up.

Per Serving:
calories: 531 | fat: 28g | protein: 64g | carbs: 2g | fiber: 0g | sodium: 572mg

Classic Chicken Kebab

Prep time: 35 minutes | Cook time: 25 minutes | Serves 4

¼ cup olive oil
1 teaspoon garlic powder
1 teaspoon onion powder
1 teaspoon ground cumin
½ teaspoon dried oregano
½ teaspoon dried basil
¼ cup lemon juice
1 tablespoon apple cider vinegar
Olive oil cooking spray
1 pound (454 g) boneless skinless chicken thighs, cut into 1-inch pieces
1 red bell pepper, cut into 1-inch pieces
1 red onion, cut into 1-inch pieces
1 zucchini, cut into 1-inch pieces
12 cherry tomatoes

1. In a large bowl, mix together the olive oil, garlic powder, onion powder, cumin, oregano, basil, lemon juice, and apple cider vinegar. 2. Spray six skewers with olive oil cooking spray. 3. On each skewer, slide on a piece of chicken, then a piece of bell pepper, onion, zucchini, and finally a tomato and then repeat. Each skewer should have at least two pieces of each item. 4. Once all of the skewers are prepared, place them in a 9-by-13-inch baking dish and pour the olive oil marinade over the top of the skewers. Turn each skewer so that all sides of the chicken and vegetables are coated. 5. Cover the dish with plastic wrap and place it in the refrigerator for 30 minutes. 6. After 30 minutes, preheat the air fryer to 380°F(193°C). (If using a grill attachment, make sure it is inside the air fryer during preheating.) 7. Remove the skewers from the marinade and lay them in a single layer in the air fryer basket. If the air fryer has a grill attachment, you can also lay them on this instead. 8. Cook for 10 minutes. Rotate the kebabs, then cook them for 15 minutes more. 9. Remove the skewers from the air fryer and let them rest for 5 minutes before serving.

Per Serving:
calories: 306 | fat: 19g | protein: 24g | carbs: 10g | fiber: 3g | sodium: 119mg

Baked Chicken Caprese

Prep time: 5minutes |Cook time: 25 minutes| Serves: 4

Nonstick cooking spray
1 pound (454 g) boneless, skinless chicken breasts
2 tablespoons extra-virgin olive oil
¼ teaspoon freshly ground black pepper
¼ teaspoon kosher or sea salt
1 large tomato, sliced thinly
1 cup shredded mozzarella or 4 ounces (113 g) fresh mozzarella cheese, diced
1 (14½-ounce / 411-g) can low-sodium or no-salt-added crushed tomatoes
2 tablespoons fresh torn basil leaves
4 teaspoons balsamic vinegar

1. Set one oven rack about 4 inches below the broiler element. Preheat the oven to 450°F(235°C). Line a large, rimmed baking sheet with aluminum foil. Place a wire cooling rack on the aluminum foil, and spray the rack with nonstick cooking spray. Set aside. 2. Cut the chicken into 4 pieces (if they aren't already). Put the chicken breasts in a large zip-top plastic bag. With a rolling pin or meat mallet, pound the chicken so it is evenly flattened, about ¼-inch thick. Add the oil, pepper, and salt to the bag. Reseal the bag, and massage the ingredients into the chicken. Take the chicken out of the bag and place it on the prepared wire rack. 3. Cook the chicken for 15 to 18 minutes, or until the internal temperature of the chicken is 165°F(74°C) on a meat thermometer and the juices run clear. Turn the oven to the high broiler setting. Layer the tomato slices on each chicken breast, and top with the mozzarella. Broil the chicken for another 2 to 3 minutes, or until the cheese is melted (don't let the chicken burn on the edges). Remove the chicken from the oven. 4. While the chicken is cooking, pour the crushed tomatoes into a small, microwave-safe bowl. Cover the bowl with a paper towel, and microwave for about 1 minute on high, until hot. When you're ready to serve, divide the tomatoes among four dinner plates. Place each chicken breast on top of the tomatoes. Top with the basil and a drizzle of balsamic vinegar.

Per Serving:
calories: 304 | fat: 15g | protein: 34g | carbs: 7g | fiber: 3g | sodium: 215mg

Blackened Chicken

Prep time: 10 minutes | Cook time: 20 minutes | Serves 4

1 large egg, beaten
¾ cup Blackened seasoning
2 whole boneless, skinless
chicken breasts (about 1 pound / 454 g each), halved
1 to 2 tablespoons oil

1. Place the beaten egg in one shallow bowl and the Blackened seasoning in another shallow bowl. 2. One at a time, dip the chicken pieces in the beaten egg and the Blackened seasoning, coating thoroughly. 3. Preheat the air fryer to 360°F (182°C). Line the air fryer basket with parchment paper. 4. Place the chicken pieces on the parchment and spritz with oil. 5. Cook for 10 minutes. Flip the chicken, spritz it with oil, and cook for 10 minutes more until the internal temperature reaches 165°F (74°C) and the chicken is no longer pink inside. Let sit for 5 minutes before serving.

Per Serving:
calories: 225 | fat: 10g | protein: 28g | carbs: 8g | fiber: 6g | sodium: 512mg

Jerk Chicken Kebabs

Prep time: 10 minutes | Cook time: 14 minutes | Serves 4

8 ounces (227 g) boneless, skinless chicken thighs, cut into 1-inch cubes
2 tablespoons jerk seasoning
2 tablespoons coconut oil
½ medium red bell pepper, seeded and cut into 1-inch pieces
¼ medium red onion, peeled and cut into 1-inch pieces
½ teaspoon salt

1. Place chicken in a medium bowl and sprinkle with jerk seasoning and coconut oil. Toss to coat on all sides. 2. Using eight (6-inch) skewers, build skewers by alternating chicken, pepper, and onion pieces, about three repetitions per skewer. 3. Sprinkle salt over skewers and place into ungreased air fryer basket. Adjust the temperature to 370ºF (188ºC) and air fry for 14 minutes, turning skewers halfway through cooking. Chicken will be golden and have an internal temperature of at least 165ºF (74ºC) when done. Serve warm.

Per Serving:
calories: 142 | fat: 9g | protein: 12g | carbs: 4g | fiber: 1g | sodium: 348mg

Old Delhi Butter Chicken

Prep time: 15 minutes | Cook time: 3 to 7 hours | Serves 6

Tomato Sauce:
3 medium red onions, roughly chopped
2 to 3 fresh green chiles
1 tablespoon freshly grated ginger
6 garlic cloves, roughly chopped
2¾-inch piece cassia bark
5 green cardamom pods
4 cloves
10 black peppercorns
1 teaspoon salt
10 ripe red tomatoes, roughly chopped, or 1 (14-ounce / 397-g) can plum tomatoes
1 tablespoon tomato paste
½ teaspoon turmeric
1 tablespoon Kashmiri chili powder
2 teaspoons coriander seeds, ground
2 cups hot water
Chicken:
2 tablespoons ghee or butter
1 tablespoon cumin seeds
12 chicken thighs, skinned, trimmed, and cut into cubes
1 to 2 tablespoons honey
1 tablespoon dried fenugreek leaves
⅓ cup heavy cream (optional)
1 tablespoon butter (optional)
Coriander leaves to garnish (optional)

Make the Tomato Sauce: 1. Heat the slow cooker to high and add the onion, chiles, ginger, garlic, cassia bark, green cardamom pods, cloves, black peppercorns, salt, tomatoes, tomato paste, turmeric, chili powder, ground coriander seeds, and water. 2. Cover and cook on high for 1 to 2 hours, or on low for 3 hours. By the end, the tomatoes should have broken down. 3. Remove the cassia bark (this is important, because if you grind the cassia in the sauce it will turn out much darker) and blend the sauce with an immersion or regular blender until it's smooth. You can strain this to get a fine, glossy sauce, if you'd like, or leave it as it is. Return the sauce to the slow cooker. Make the Chicken: 4. In a frying pan, heat the ghee. Add cumin seeds and cook until fragrant, about 1 minute. Pour into the sauce in the slow cooker. 5. Add the diced chicken, cover the slow cooker, and cook on high for 2 hours, or on low for 4 hours. 6. When the chicken is cooked, stir in the honey, dried fenugreek leaves, and cream (if using). If you want to thicken the sauce you can turn the cooker to high and reduce for a while with the cover off. Add some butter, a little extra drizzle of cream, and garnish with coriander leaves (if using) just before serving.

Per Serving:
calories: 600 | fat: 21g | protein: 80g | carbs: 22g | net carbs: 17g | sugars: 12g | fiber: 5g | sodium: 814mg | cholesterol: 373mg

Pork Rind Fried Chicken

Prep time: 30 minutes | Cook time: 20 minutes | Serves 4

¼ cup buffalo sauce
4 (4-ounce / 113-g) boneless, skinless chicken breasts
½ teaspoon paprika
½ teaspoon garlic powder
¼ teaspoon ground black pepper
2 ounces (57 g) plain pork rinds, finely crushed

1. Pour buffalo sauce into a large sealable bowl or bag. Add chicken and toss to coat. Place sealed bowl or bag into refrigerator and let marinate at least 30 minutes up to overnight. 2. Remove chicken from marinade but do not shake excess sauce off chicken. Sprinkle both sides of thighs with paprika, garlic powder, and pepper. 3. Place pork rinds into a large bowl and press each chicken breast into pork rinds to coat evenly on both sides. 4. Place chicken into ungreased air fryer basket. Adjust the temperature to 400ºF (204ºC) and roast for 20 minutes, turning chicken halfway through cooking. Chicken will be golden and have an internal temperature of at least 165ºF (74ºC) when done. Serve warm.

Per Serving:
calories: 217 | fat: 8g | protein: 35g | carbs: 1g | fiber: 0g | sodium: 400mg

Bomba Chicken with Chickpeas

Prep time: 10 minutes | Cook time: 30 minutes | Serves 4

2 pounds (907 g) boneless, skinless chicken thighs
Sea salt
Freshly ground black pepper
2 tablespoons olive oil, divided
1 onion, chopped
3 garlic cloves, minced
1 cup chicken broth
1 tablespoon bomba sauce or harissa
2 (15-ounce / 425-g) cans chickpeas, drained and rinsed
¼ cup chopped fresh Italian parsley

1. Season the chicken thighs generously with salt and pepper. 2. In a large skillet, heat 1 tablespoon of olive oil over medium-high heat. Add the chicken and cook until browned, 2 to 3 minutes per side. Transfer the chicken to a plate and set aside. 3. In the same skillet, heat the remaining 1 tablespoon of olive oil. Add the onion and garlic and sauté for 4 to 5 minutes, until softened. Return the chicken to the skillet, then add the broth and bomba sauce. Bring to a boil, reduce the heat to low, cover, and simmer for 15 minutes, or until the chicken is cooked through. 4. Add the chickpeas and simmer for 5 minutes more. 5. Garnish with the parsley and serve.

Per Serving:
calories: 552 | fat: 19g | protein: 56g | carbs: 37g | fiber: 10g | sodium: 267mg

Sumac Chicken with Cauliflower and Carrots

Prep time: 15 minutes | Cook time: 40 minutes | Serves 4

3 tablespoons extra-virgin olive oil
1 tablespoon ground sumac
1 teaspoon kosher salt
½ teaspoon ground cumin
¼ teaspoon freshly ground black pepper
1½ pounds (680 g) bone-in chicken thighs and drumsticks
1 medium cauliflower, cut into 1-inch florets
2 carrots, peeled and cut into 1-inch rounds
1 lemon, cut into ¼-inch-thick slices
1 tablespoon lemon juice
¼ cup fresh parsley, chopped
¼ cup fresh mint, chopped

1. Preheat the oven to 425ºF (220ºC). Line a baking sheet with parchment paper or foil. 2. In a large bowl, whisk together the olive oil, sumac, salt, cumin, and black pepper. Add the chicken, cauliflower, and carrots and toss until thoroughly coated with the oil and spice mixture. 3. Arrange the cauliflower, carrots, and chicken in a single layer on the baking sheet. Top with the lemon slices. Roast for 40 minutes, tossing the vegetables once halfway through. Sprinkle the lemon juice over the chicken and vegetables and garnish with the parsley and mint.

Per Serving:
calories: 510 | fat: 38g | protein: 31g | carbs: 13g | fiber: 4g | sodium: 490mg

Chicken with Lentils and Butternut Squash

Prep time: 15 minutes | Cook time: 28 minutes | Serves 4

2 large shallots, halved and sliced thin, divided
5 teaspoons extra-virgin olive oil, divided
½ teaspoon grated lemon zest plus 2 teaspoons juice
1 teaspoon table salt, divided
4 (5- to 7-ounce / 142- to 198-g) bone-in chicken thighs, trimmed
¼ teaspoon pepper
2 garlic cloves, minced
1½ teaspoons caraway seeds
1 teaspoon ground coriander
1 teaspoon ground cumin
½ teaspoon paprika
⅛ teaspoon cayenne pepper
2 cups chicken broth
1 cup French green lentils, picked over and rinsed
2 pounds (907 g) butternut squash, peeled, seeded, and cut into 1½-inch pieces
1 cup fresh parsley or cilantro leaves

1. Combine half of shallots, 1 tablespoon oil, lemon zest and juice, and ¼ teaspoon salt in bowl; set aside. Pat chicken dry with paper towels and sprinkle with ½ teaspoon salt and pepper. Using highest sauté function, heat remaining 2 teaspoons oil in Instant Pot for 5 minutes (or until just smoking). Place chicken skin side down in pot and cook until well browned on first side, about 5 minutes; transfer to plate. 2. Add remaining shallot and remaining ¼ teaspoon salt to fat left in pot and cook, using highest sauté function, until shallot is softened, about 2 minutes. Stir in garlic, caraway, coriander, cumin, paprika, and cayenne and cook until fragrant, about 30 seconds. Stir in broth, scraping up any browned bits, then stir in lentils. 3. Nestle chicken skin side up into lentils and add any accumulated juices. Arrange squash on top. Lock lid in place and close pressure release valve. Select high pressure cook function and cook for 15 minutes. 4. Turn off Instant Pot and quick-release pressure. Carefully remove lid, allowing steam to escape away from you. Transfer chicken to plate and discard skin, if desired. Season lentil mixture with salt and pepper to taste. Add parsley to shallot mixture and toss to combine. Serve chicken with lentil mixture, topping individual portions with shallot-parsley salad.

Per Serving:
calories: 513 | fat: 14g | protein: 42g | carbs: 60g | fiber: 17g | sodium: 773mg

Turkey Breast Romano

Prep time: 15 minutes | Cook time: 20 minutes | Serves 8

½ cup all-purpose flour
½ teaspoon salt
½ teaspoon ground black pepper
2 pounds (907 g) boneless, skinless turkey breast, cut into bite-sized pieces
2 tablespoons olive oil
1 large sweet onion, peeled and diced
4 cloves garlic, peeled and minced
1 tablespoon dried oregano
1 teaspoon dried basil
2 tablespoons tomato paste
½ cup low-sodium chicken broth
1 (8-ounce / 227-g) can tomato sauce
1 teaspoon balsamic vinegar
2 (4-ounce / 113-g) cans sliced mushrooms, drained
1 tablespoon sugar
1 pound (454 g) spaghetti, cooked
8 ounces (227 g) Romano cheese, grated

1. Place flour, salt, and pepper in a large zip-top plastic bag. Seal and shake to mix. Add turkey to the bag, seal, and shake to coat turkey in flour mixture. 2. Press the Sauté button on the Instant Pot® and heat oil. Add turkey and onion, and cook until turkey begins to brown and onion is translucent, about 5 minutes. 3. Stir in garlic, oregano, basil, and tomato paste, and cook for 2 minutes. Stir in broth, tomato sauce, vinegar, mushrooms, and sugar. Press the Cancel button. 4. Close lid, set steam release to Sealing, press the Manual button, and set time to 12 minutes. When the timer beeps, let pressure release naturally for 10 minutes. 5. Quick-release any remaining pressure until the float valve drops. Open lid and stir turkey and sauce, pour over pasta, and top with grated Romano cheese.

Per Serving:
calories: 498 | fat: 11g | protein: 47g | carbs: 53g | fiber: 4g | sodium: 734mg

Teriyaki Chicken Legs

Prep time: 12 minutes | Cook time: 18 to 20 minutes | Serves 2

4 tablespoons teriyaki sauce
1 tablespoon orange juice
1 teaspoon smoked paprika
4 chicken legs
Cooking spray

1. Mix together the teriyaki sauce, orange juice, and smoked paprika. Brush on all sides of chicken legs. 2. Spray the air fryer basket with nonstick cooking spray and place chicken in basket. 3. Air fry at 360ºF (182ºC) for 6 minutes. Turn and baste with sauce. Cook for 6 more minutes, turn and baste. Cook for 6 to 8 minutes more, until juices run clear when chicken is pierced with a fork.

Per Serving:
calories: 392 | fat: 13g | protein: 59g | carbs: 7g | fiber: 1g | sodium: 641mg

Ginger Turmeric Chicken Thighs

Prep time: 5 minutes | Cook time: 25 minutes | Serves 4

4 (4-ounce / 113-g) boneless, skin-on chicken thighs	½ teaspoon salt
2 tablespoons coconut oil, melted	½ teaspoon garlic powder
	½ teaspoon ground ginger
½ teaspoon ground turmeric	¼ teaspoon ground black pepper

1. Place chicken thighs in a large bowl and drizzle with coconut oil. Sprinkle with remaining ingredients and toss to coat both sides of thighs. 2. Place thighs skin side up into ungreased air fryer basket. Adjust the temperature to 400°F (204°C) and air fry for 25 minutes. After 10 minutes, turn thighs. When 5 minutes remain, flip thighs once more. Chicken will be done when skin is golden brown and the internal temperature is at least 165°F (74°C). Serve warm.

Per Serving:
calories: 392 | fat: 31g | protein: 25g | carbs: 1g | fiber: 0g | sodium: 412mg

Za'atar Chicken

Prep time: 5 minutes | Cook time: 40 minutes |
Serves 4 to 6

⅓ cup plus 1 tablespoon za'atar spice	⅓ cup extra-virgin olive oil
2 tablespoons garlic, minced	1 teaspoon salt
⅓ cup lemon juice	8 pieces chicken thighs and drumsticks, skin on

1. Preheat the oven to 400°F(205°C). 2. In a small bowl, combine the ⅓ cup za'atar spice with the garlic, lemon juice, olive oil, and salt. 3. Place the chicken in a baking dish, and pat dry with a paper towel. 4. Pour the za'atar mixture over the chicken, making sure the pieces are completely and evenly coated. 5. Put the chicken in the oven and cook for 40 minutes. 6. Once the chicken is done cooking, sprinkle it with the remaining tablespoon of za'atar spice. Serve with potatoes, rice, or salad.

Per Serving:
calories: 426 | fat: 23g | protein: 51g | carbs: 2g | fiber: 0g | sodium: 633mg

Chicken and Shrimp Paella

Prep time: 20 minutes | Cook time: 40 minutes | Serves 6

3 tablespoons olive oil	diced tomatoes, with their juices
1 onion, chopped (about 2 cups)	
5 garlic cloves, minced	Zest and juice of 1 lemon
1 pound (454 g) chicken breasts, cut into 1-inch pieces	½ teaspoon salt
1 cup Arborio rice	1 cup thawed frozen peas
1 teaspoon ground cumin	1 medium zucchini, cut into cubes (about 2 cups)
1 teaspoon smoked paprika	
½ teaspoon ground turmeric	8 ounces (227 g) uncooked shrimp, thawed, peeled, and deveined
1½ cups low-sodium chicken broth	
1 (14½-ounce / 411-g) can	2 tablespoons chopped fresh parsley

1. In a large saucepan, heat 2 tablespoons of the olive oil over medium heat. Add the onion and cook, occasionally stirring, for 5 minutes, or until softened. Add the garlic, chicken, rice, and remaining 1 tablespoon olive oil. Stir until the rice is coated with the oil. 2. Add the cumin, smoked paprika, turmeric, broth, tomatoes with their juices, lemon zest, lemon juice, and salt. Spread the rice mixture evenly in the pan. Bring to a boil. Reduce the heat to medium-low, cover, and cook for 25 minutes—do not stir. 3. Remove the lid and stir in the peas and zucchini. Add the shrimp, nestling them into the rice. Cover and cook for 8 to 10 minutes. Remove from the heat and let stand for 10 minutes. 4. Top with the parsley and serve.

Per Serving:
calories: 310 | fat: 18g | protein: 26g | carbs: 18g | fiber: 7g | sodium: 314mg

Cilantro Lime Chicken Thighs

Prep time: 15 minutes | Cook time: 22 minutes | Serves 4

4 bone-in, skin-on chicken thighs	2 teaspoons chili powder
	1 teaspoon cumin
1 teaspoon baking powder	2 medium limes
½ teaspoon garlic powder	¼ cup chopped fresh cilantro

1. Pat chicken thighs dry and sprinkle with baking powder. 2. In a small bowl, mix garlic powder, chili powder, and cumin and sprinkle evenly over thighs, gently rubbing on and under chicken skin. 3. Cut one lime in half and squeeze juice over thighs. Place chicken into the air fryer basket. 4. Adjust the temperature to 380°F (193°C) and roast for 22 minutes. 5. Cut other lime into four wedges for serving and garnish cooked chicken with wedges and cilantro.

Per Serving:
calories: 445 | fat: 32g | protein: 32g | carbs: 6g | fiber: 2g | sodium: 198mg

Classic Whole Chicken

Prep time: 5 minutes | Cook time: 50 minutes | Serves 4

Oil, for spraying	½ teaspoon salt
1 (4-pound / 1.8-kg) whole chicken, giblets removed	½ teaspoon freshly ground black pepper
1 tablespoon olive oil	¼ teaspoon finely chopped fresh parsley, for garnish
1 teaspoon paprika	
½ teaspoon granulated garlic	

1. Line the air fryer basket with parchment and spray lightly with oil. 2. Pat the chicken dry with paper towels. Rub it with the olive oil until evenly coated. 3. In a small bowl, mix together the paprika, garlic, salt, and black pepper and sprinkle it evenly over the chicken. 4. Place the chicken in the prepared basket, breast-side down. 5. Air fry at 360°F (182°C) for 30 minutes, flip, and cook for another 20 minutes, or until the internal temperature reaches 165°F (74°C) and the juices run clear. 6. Sprinkle with the parsley before serving.

Per Serving:
calories: 549 | fat: 11g | protein: 105g | carbs: 0g | fiber: 0g | sodium: 523mg

Chicken and Chickpea Skillet with Berbere Spice

Prep time: 15 minutes | Cook time: 45 minutes | Serves 6

2 tablespoons olive oil
1 (3-to 4-pound / 1.4-to 1.8-kg) whole chicken, cut into 8 pieces
3 teaspoons Berbere or baharat spice blend
1 large onion, preferably Spanish, thinly sliced into half-moons
2 garlic cloves, minced
2 cups 1-inch cubes peeled butternut squash, or 1 (12-ounce / 340-g) bag pre-cut squash
1 (15-ounce / 425-g) can no-salt-added chickpeas, undrained
½ cup golden raisins
Hot cooked rice, for serving

1. In a 12-inch skillet, heat 1 tablespoon olive oil over medium-high heat. Sprinkle the chicken with 2 teaspoons of the Berbere spice. Add half the chicken to the skillet and cook until browned, 4 to 6 minutes per side. Transfer the chicken to a plate and repeat to brown the remaining chicken. Set aside. 2. In the same skillet, heat the remaining 1 tablespoon olive oil. Add the onion and cook, stirring, until softened, about 5 minutes. Add the remaining 1 teaspoon Berbere spice, the garlic, squash, chickpeas, and raisins and stir to combine. Return the chicken to skillet, pushing the pieces between the vegetables, and bring to a boil. Reduce the heat to maintain a simmer, cover tightly, and cook for 20 to 25 minutes, until the chicken is cooked through and an instant-read thermometer inserted into the thickest part registers 165ºF (74ºC), and the squash is tender. 3. Serve over hot cooked rice.

Per Serving:
1 cup: calories: 507 | fat: 26g | protein: 42g | carbs: 33g | fiber: 9g | sodium: 218mg

Fiesta Chicken Plate

Prep time: 15 minutes | Cook time: 12 to 15 minutes | Serves 4

1 pound (454 g) boneless, skinless chicken breasts (2 large breasts)
2 tablespoons lime juice
1 teaspoon cumin
½ teaspoon salt
½ cup grated Pepper Jack cheese
1 (16-ounce / 454-g) can refried
beans
½ cup salsa
2 cups shredded lettuce
1 medium tomato, chopped
2 avocados, peeled and sliced
1 small onion, sliced into thin rings
Sour cream
Tortilla chips (optional)

1. Split each chicken breast in half lengthwise. 2. Mix lime juice, cumin, and salt together and brush on all surfaces of chicken breasts. 3. Place in air fryer basket and air fry at 390ºF (199ºC) for 12 to 15 minutes, until well done. 4. Divide the cheese evenly over chicken breasts and cook for an additional minute to melt cheese. 5. While chicken is cooking, heat refried beans on stovetop or in microwave. 6. When ready to serve, divide beans among 4 plates. Place chicken breasts on top of beans and spoon salsa over. Arrange the lettuce, tomatoes, and avocados artfully on each plate and scatter with the onion rings. 7. Pass sour cream at the table and serve with tortilla chips if desired.

Per Serving:
calories: 497 | fat: 27g | protein: 38g | carbs: 26g | fiber: 12g | sodium: 722mg

Turkey Meatloaf

Prep time: 10 minutes | Cook time: 50 minutes | Serves 4

8 ounces (227 g) sliced mushrooms
1 small onion, coarsely chopped
2 cloves garlic
1½ pounds (680 g) 85% lean ground turkey
2 eggs, lightly beaten
1 tablespoon tomato paste
¼ cup almond meal
2 tablespoons almond milk
1 tablespoon dried oregano
1 teaspoon salt
½ teaspoon freshly ground black pepper
1 Roma tomato, thinly sliced

1. Preheat the air fryer to 350ºF (177ºC). Lightly coat a round pan with olive oil and set aside. 2. In a food processor fitted with a metal blade, combine the mushrooms, onion, and garlic. Pulse until finely chopped. Transfer the vegetables to a large mixing bowl. 3. Add the turkey, eggs, tomato paste, almond meal, milk, oregano, salt, and black pepper. Mix gently until thoroughly combined. Transfer the mixture to the prepared pan and shape into a loaf. Arrange the tomato slices on top. 4. Air fry for 50 minutes or until the meatloaf is nicely browned and a thermometer inserted into the thickest part registers 165ºF (74ºC). Remove from the air fryer and let rest for about 10 minutes before slicing.

Per Serving:
calories: 353 | fat: 20g | protein: 38g | carbs: 7g | fiber: 2g | sodium: 625mg

Mediterranean Roasted Turkey Breast

Prep time: 15 minutes | Cook time: 6 to 8 hours | Serves 4

3 garlic cloves, minced
1 teaspoon sea salt
1 teaspoon dried oregano
½ teaspoon freshly ground black pepper
½ teaspoon dried basil
½ teaspoon dried parsley
½ teaspoon dried rosemary
½ teaspoon dried thyme
¼ teaspoon dried dill
¼ teaspoon ground nutmeg
2 tablespoons extra-virgin olive oil
2 tablespoons freshly squeezed lemon juice
1 (4- to 6-pound / 1.8- to 2.7-kg) boneless or bone-in turkey breast
1 onion, chopped
½ cup low-sodium chicken broth
4 ounces (113 g) whole Kalamata olives, pitted
1 cup sun-dried tomatoes (packaged, not packed in oil), chopped

1. In a small bowl, stir together the garlic, salt, oregano, pepper, basil, parsley, rosemary, thyme, dill, and nutmeg. 2. Drizzle the olive oil and lemon juice all over the turkey breast and generously season it with the garlic-spice mix. 3. In a slow cooker, combine the onion and chicken broth. Place the seasoned turkey breast on top of the onion. Top the turkey with the olives and sun-dried tomatoes. 4. Cover the cooker and cook for 6 to 8 hours on Low heat. 5. Slice or shred the turkey for serving.

Per Serving:
calories: 676 | fat: 19g | protein: 111g | carbs: 14g | fiber: 3g | sodium: 626mg

Greek Yogurt–Marinated Chicken Breasts

Prep time: 15 minutes | Cook time: 30 minutes | Serves 2

½ cup plain Greek yogurt
3 garlic cloves, minced
2 tablespoons minced fresh oregano (or 1 tablespoon dried oregano)

Zest of 1 lemon
1 tablespoon olive oil
½ teaspoon salt
2 (4-ounce / 113-g) boneless, skinless chicken breasts

1. In a medium bowl, add the yogurt, garlic, oregano, lemon zest, olive oil, and salt and stir to combine. If the yogurt is very thick, you may need to add a few tablespoons of water or a squeeze of lemon juice to thin it a bit. 2. Add the chicken to the bowl and toss it in the marinade to coat it well. Cover and refrigerate the chicken for at least 30 minutes or up to overnight. 3. Preheat the oven to 350°F(180°C) and set the rack to the middle position. 4. Place the chicken in a baking dish and roast for 30 minutes, or until chicken reaches an internal temperature of 165°F(74°C).
Per Serving:
calories: 255 | fat: 13g | protein: 29g | carbs: 8g | fiber: 2g | sodium: 694mg

Chicken Chili Verde over Rice

Prep time: 15 minutes | Cook time: 6 hours | Serves 2

1 cup diced tomatillos
1 onion, halved and sliced thin
2 garlic cloves, minced
1 jalapeño pepper, seeds and membranes removed, minced
1 teaspoon ground cumin
1 teaspoon ground coriander
1 teaspoon extra-virgin olive oil

½ cup long-grain brown rice
1 cup low-sodium chicken broth
2 boneless, skinless chicken breasts, about 8 ounces (227 g) each, cut into 4-inch tenders
¼ cup fresh cilantro

1. Combine the tomatillos, onion, garlic, jalapeño, cumin, and coriander in a food processor. Pulse until it has a sauce-like consistency but is still slightly chunky. 2. Grease the inside of the slow cooker with the olive oil. 3. Add the rice to the slow cooker and pour in the chicken broth. Gently stir to make sure the rice grains are fully submerged. 4. Place the chicken on top of the rice and pour the tomatillo salsa over the top. 5. Cover and cook on low for 6 hours.
Per Serving:
calories: 536 | fat: 11g | protein: 59g | carbs: 48g | net carbs: 44g | sugars: 6g | fiber: 4g | sodium: 148mg | cholesterol: 166mg

Chicken Marinara and Zucchini

Prep time: 10 minutes | Cook time: 15 minutes | Serves 4

2 large zucchini, trimmed and chopped
4 (6-ounce / 170-g) chicken breast halves
3 cups marinara sauce

1 tablespoon Italian seasoning
½ teaspoon salt
1 cup shredded mozzarella cheese

1. Place zucchini on the bottom of the Instant Pot®. Place chicken on zucchini. Pour marinara sauce over chicken. Sprinkle with Italian seasoning and salt. 2. Close lid, set steam release to Sealing,

press the Poultry button, and cook for the default time of 15 minutes. When the timer beeps, let pressure release naturally for 10 minutes. Quick-release any remaining pressure until the float valve drops and then open lid. Check chicken using a meat thermometer to ensure the internal temperature is at least 165°F (74°C). 3. Sprinkle chicken with cheese. Close lid and let stand on the Keep Warm setting for 5 minutes to allow the cheese to melt. 4. Transfer chicken and zucchini to a serving platter. Serve hot.
Per Serving:
calories: 21 | fat: 13g | protein: 51g | carbs: 21g | fiber: 5g | sodium: 442mg

Lebanese Garlic Chicken Flatbreads

Prep time: 5 minutes | Cook time: 20 minutes | Serves 6

8 cloves garlic
½ teaspoon kosher salt
¼ cup olive oil
2 tablespoons fresh lemon juice
½ teaspoon ground sumac

1 pound (454 g) boneless, skinless chicken thighs
1 cup thinly sliced cucumber
6 whole wheat flatbreads

1. In a medium bowl, muddle the garlic and salt together using the end of a wooden spoon, or use a mortar and pestle if you have one. Add the oil, lemon juice, and sumac and stir into a thick paste. 2. Place the chicken thighs in a gallon-size resealable plastic bag and pour the garlic mixture over the top. Massage the marinade into the chicken and place in the fridge for 6 hours or overnight. 3. Coat a grill rack or grill pan with olive oil and prepare to medium-high heat. 4. Remove the chicken from the marinade and discard the marinade. Grill the chicken until grill marks form and a thermometer inserted in the thickest part reaches 165°F(74°C), about 10 minutes per side. 5. Slice the chicken into bite-size pieces and distribute, along with the cucumber slices, among 6 flatbreads. Roll the flatbreads around the chicken and serve.
Per Serving:
calories: 407 | fat: 13g | protein: 37g | carbs:379g | fiber: 5g | sodium: 154mg

Cajun-Breaded Chicken Bites

Prep time: 10 minutes | Cook time: 12 minutes | Serves 4

1 pound (454 g) boneless, skinless chicken breasts, cut into 1-inch cubes
½ cup heavy whipping cream
½ teaspoon salt
¼ teaspoon ground black

pepper
1 ounce (28 g) plain pork rinds, finely crushed
¼ cup unflavored whey protein powder
½ teaspoon Cajun seasoning

1. Place chicken in a medium bowl and pour in cream. Stir to coat. Sprinkle with salt and pepper. 2. In a separate large bowl, combine pork rinds, protein powder, and Cajun seasoning. Remove chicken from cream, shaking off any excess, and toss in dry mix until fully coated. 3. Place bites into ungreased air fryer basket. Adjust the temperature to 400°F (204°C) and air fry for 12 minutes, shaking the basket twice during cooking. Bites will be done when golden brown and have an internal temperature of at least 165°F (74°C). Serve warm.
Per Serving:
calories: 272 | fat: 13g | protein: 35g | carbs: 2g | fiber: 1g | sodium: 513mg

Turkish Chicken Kebabs

Prep time: 30 minutes | Cook time: 15 minutes | Serves 4

¼ cup plain Greek yogurt
1 tablespoon minced garlic
1 tablespoon tomato paste
1 tablespoon fresh lemon juice
1 tablespoon vegetable oil
1 teaspoon kosher salt
1 teaspoon ground cumin

1 teaspoon sweet Hungarian paprika
½ teaspoon ground cinnamon
½ teaspoon black pepper
½ teaspoon cayenne pepper
1 pound (454 g) boneless, skinless chicken thighs, quartered crosswise

1. In a large bowl, combine the yogurt, garlic, tomato paste, lemon juice, vegetable oil, salt, cumin, paprika, cinnamon, black pepper, and cayenne. Stir until the spices are blended into the yogurt. 2. Add the chicken to the bowl and toss until well coated. Marinate at room temperature for 30 minutes, or cover and refrigerate for up to 24 hours. 3. Arrange the chicken in a single layer in the air fryer basket. Set the air fryer to 375°F (191°C) for 10 minutes. Turn the chicken and cook for 5 minutes more. Use a meat thermometer to ensure the chicken has reached an internal temperature of 165°F (74°C).

Per Serving:
calories: 188 | fat: 8g | protein: 24g | carbs: 4g | fiber: 1g | sodium: 705mg

Chapter 6 Beans and Grains

Brown Rice Vegetable Bowl with Roasted Red Pepper Dressing

Prep time: 10 minutes | Cook time: 22 minutes | Serves 2

¼ cup chopped roasted red bell pepper
2 tablespoons extra-virgin olive oil
1 tablespoon red wine vinegar
1 teaspoon honey
2 tablespoons light olive oil
2 cloves garlic, peeled and minced
½ teaspoon ground black pepper
¼ teaspoon salt
1 cup brown rice
1 cup vegetable broth
¼ cup chopped fresh flat-leaf parsley
2 tablespoons chopped fresh chives
2 tablespoons chopped fresh dill
½ cup diced tomato
½ cup chopped red onion
½ cup diced cucumber
½ cup chopped green bell pepper

1. Place roasted red pepper, extra-virgin olive oil, red wine vinegar, and honey in a blender. Purée until smooth, about 1 minute. Refrigerate until ready to serve. 2. Press the Sauté button on the Instant Pot® and heat light olive oil. Add garlic and cook until fragrant, about 30 seconds. Add black pepper, salt, and rice and stir well. Press the Cancel button. 3. Stir in broth. Close lid, set steam release to Sealing, press the Manual button, and set time to 22 minutes.

Per Serving:
calories: 561 | fat: 23g | protein: 10g | carbs: 86g | fiber: 5g | sodium: 505mg

South Indian Split Yellow Pigeon Peas with Mixed Vegetables

Prep time: 20 minutes | Cook time: 4½ to 6½ minutes | Serves 6

Sambar Masala :
1 teaspoon rapeseed oil
3 tablespoons coriander seeds
2 tablespoons split gram
1 teaspoon black peppercorns
½ teaspoon fenugreek seeds
½ teaspoon mustard seeds
¼ teaspoon cumin seeds
12 whole dried red chiles
Sambar :
1½ cups split yellow pigeon peas, washed
2 fresh green chiles, sliced lengthwise
2 garlic cloves, chopped
6 pearl onions
4 to 5 tablespoons sambar masala
2 teaspoons salt
1 to 2 carrots, peeled and chopped
1 red potato, peeled and diced
1 white radish (mooli), peeled and chopped into 2¾-inch sticks
1 tomato, roughly chopped
4 cups water
2 to 3 moringa seed pods, or ⅓ pound (151 g) green beans or asparagus, chopped into 2¾-inch lengths
2 tablespoons tamarind paste
½ teaspoon asafetida
2 teaspoons coconut oil
1 teaspoon mustard seeds
20 curry leaves
2 dried red chilies
Handful fresh coriander leaves, chopped (optional)

Make the Sambar Masala: 1. Add the oil to a medium nonstick skillet. Add all of the remaining ingredients and roast for a few minutes until fragrant. The spices will brown a little, but don't let them burn. 2. Remove from the heat and pour onto a plate to cool. Once cooled, place into your spice grinder or mortar and pestle and grind to a powder. Set aside. Make the Sambar: 3. Heat the slow cooker to high and add the pigeon peas, green chiles, garlic, pearl onions, sambar masala, salt, carrots, potatoes, radish, tomato, and water. 4. Cover and cook for 4 hours on high, or for 6 hours on low. 5. Add the moringa (or green beans or asparagus), tamarind paste, and asafetida. Cover and cook for another 30 minutes. 6. When you're ready to serve, heat the coconut oil in a frying pan and pop the mustard seeds with the curry leaves and dried chiles. Pour over the sambar. Top with coriander leaves (if using) and serve.

Per Serving:
calories: 312 | fat: 7g | protein: 12g | carbs: 59g | net carbs: 43g | sugars: 12g | fiber: 16g | sodium: 852mg | cholesterol: 0mg

Tomato Bulgur

Prep time: 10 minutes | Cook time: 25 minutes | Serves 4

3 tablespoons olive oil
1 onion, diced
1 garlic clove, minced
1 tablespoon tomato paste
½ teaspoon paprika
3 Roma (plum) tomatoes, finely chopped, or 1 cup canned crushed tomatoes with their juices
Juice of ½ lemon
¼ teaspoon sea salt, plus more as needed
1 cup dried bulgur
2 cups vegetable broth, chicken broth, or water

1. In a large saucepan, heat the olive oil over medium-high heat. Add the onion and garlic and sauté for 4 to 5 minutes, until the onion is soft. Add the tomato paste and paprika and stir for about 30 seconds. 2. Add the chopped tomatoes, lemon juice, and salt and cook for 1 to 2 minutes more. 3. Add the bulgur and stir for about 30 seconds. Add the broth, bring to a simmer, reduce the heat to low, cover, and simmer for 13 to 15 minutes, until the liquid has been absorbed. Uncover and stir, then remove from the heat, cover, and let stand for 5 minutes. 4. Taste and adjust the seasoning, then serve.

Per Serving:
calories: 243 | fat: 11g | protein: 6g | carbs: 34g | fiber: 6g | sodium: 92mg

Lentil Bowl

1 cup dried lentils, any color, rinsed well under cold water and picked over to remove debris
3 cups low-sodium vegetable broth
1 (15-ounce/ 425-g) can no-salt-added diced tomatoes
1 small onion, chopped
3 celery stalks, chopped
3 carrots, chopped
3 garlic cloves, minced
2 tablespoons Italian seasoning
1 teaspoon sea salt
½ teaspoon freshly ground black pepper
2 bay leaves
1 tablespoon freshly squeezed lemon juice

1. In a slow cooker, combine the lentils, vegetable broth, tomatoes, onion, celery, carrots, garlic, Italian seasoning, salt, pepper, and bay leaves. Stir to mix well. 2. Cover the cooker and cook for 6 to 8 hours on Low heat. 3. Stir in the lemon juice before serving.

Per Serving:
calories: 152 | fat: 1g | protein: 10g | carbs: 29g | fiber: 13g | sodium: 529mg

Barley Salad with Lemon-Tahini Dressing

1½ cups pearl barley
5 tablespoons extra-virgin olive oil, divided
1½ teaspoons table salt, for cooking barley
¼ cup tahini
1 teaspoon grated lemon zest plus ¼ cup juice (2 lemons)
1 tablespoon sumac, divided
1 garlic clove, minced
¾ teaspoon table salt
1 English cucumber, cut into ½-inch pieces
1 carrot, peeled and shredded
1 red bell pepper, stemmed, seeded, and chopped
4 scallions, sliced thin
2 tablespoons finely chopped jarred hot cherry peppers
¼ cup coarsely chopped fresh mint

1. Combine 6 cups water, barley, 1 tablespoon oil, and 1½ teaspoons salt in Instant Pot. Lock lid in place and close pressure release valve. Select high pressure cook function and cook for 8 minutes. Turn off Instant Pot and let pressure release naturally for 15 minutes. Quick-release any remaining pressure, then carefully remove lid, allowing steam to escape away from you. Drain barley, spread onto rimmed baking sheet, and let cool completely, about 15 minutes. 2. Meanwhile, whisk remaining ¼ cup oil, tahini, 2 tablespoons water, lemon zest and juice, 1 teaspoon sumac, garlic, and ¾ teaspoon salt in large bowl until combined; let sit for 15 minutes. 3. Measure out and reserve ½ cup dressing for serving. Add barley, cucumber, carrot, bell pepper, scallions, and cherry peppers to bowl with dressing and gently toss to combine. Season with salt and pepper to taste. Transfer salad to serving dish and sprinkle with mint and remaining 2 teaspoons sumac. Serve, passing reserved dressing separately.

Per Serving:
calories: 370 | fat: 18g | protein: 8g | carbs: 47g | fiber: 10g | sodium: 510mg

Creamy Pea Soup

1 pound (454 g) dried split green peas
2 tablespoons olive oil
1 onion, coarsely chopped
2 garlic cloves, coarsely chopped
3 cups vegetable broth or
chicken broth
6 ounces (170 g) plain full-fat Greek yogurt, at room temperature
Sea salt
Freshly ground black pepper

1. Place the split peas in a large stockpot and add water to cover by about 2 inches. Bring the water to a boil over high heat, reduce the heat to low, and simmer until the peas are tender, 20 to 30 minutes. Drain the peas and set aside in a medium bowl. 2. In the same stockpot, heat the olive oil over medium-high heat. Add the onion and garlic and sauté for 5 to 7 minutes, or until the onion is soft. Return the cooked peas to the pot, add the broth, and purée with an immersion blender. Cook over medium heat until heated through, about 5 minutes. 3. Add the yogurt and season with salt and pepper. Taste, adjust the seasonings, and serve.

Per Serving:
calories: 513 | fat: 10g | protein: 29g | carbs: 81g | fiber: 30g | sodium: 82mg

French Lentils with Swiss Chard

2 tablespoons extra-virgin olive oil, plus extra for drizzling
12 ounces (340 g) Swiss chard, stems chopped fine, leaves sliced into ½-inch-wide strips
1 onion, chopped fine
½ teaspoon table salt
2 garlic cloves, minced
1 teaspoon minced fresh thyme or ¼ teaspoon dried
2½ cups water
1 cup French green lentils, picked over and rinsed
3 tablespoons whole-grain mustard
½ teaspoon grated lemon zest plus 1 teaspoon juice
3 tablespoons sliced almonds, toasted
2 tablespoons chopped fresh parsley

1. Using highest sauté function, heat oil in Instant Pot until shimmering. Add chard stems, onion, and salt and cook until vegetables are softened, about 5 minutes. Stir in garlic and thyme and cook until fragrant, about 30 seconds. Stir in water and lentils. 2. Lock lid in place and close pressure release valve. Select high pressure cook function and cook for 11 minutes. Turn off Instant Pot and let pressure release naturally for 15 minutes. Quick-release any remaining pressure, then carefully remove lid, allowing steam to escape away from you. 3. Stir chard leaves into lentils, 1 handful at a time, and let cook in residual heat until wilted, about 5 minutes. Stir in mustard and lemon zest and juice. Season with salt and pepper to taste. Transfer to serving dish, drizzle with extra oil, and sprinkle with almonds and parsley. Serve.

Per Serving:
calories: 190 | fat: 8g | protein: 9g | carbs: 23g | fiber: 6g | sodium: 470mg

Southwestern Rice Casserole

Prep time: 20 minutes | Cook time: 4 to 6 hours | Serves 2

1 teaspoon extra-virgin olive oil	1 teaspoon dried oregano
1 cup brown rice	⅛ teaspoon cayenne pepper
1 cup canned black beans, drained and rinsed	⅛ teaspoon sea salt
1 cup frozen corn, thawed	1½ cups low-sodium vegetable broth or water
1 cup canned fire-roasted diced tomatoes, undrained	¼ cup fresh cilantro
	¼ cup sharp cheddar cheese

1. Grease the inside of the slow cooker with the olive oil. 2. Add the brown rice, beans, corn, tomatoes, oregano, cayenne, and salt. Pour in the broth and stir to mix thoroughly. 3. Cover and cook on low for 4 to 6 hours. 4. Stir in the cilantro and cheddar cheese before serving.

Per Serving:
calories: 681 | fat: 12g | protein: 25g | carbs: 126g | net carbs: 109g | sugars: 11g | fiber: 17g | sodium: 490mg | cholesterol: 140mg

Herbed Barley

Prep time: 10 minutes | Cook time: 30 minutes | Serves 4

2 tablespoons olive oil	1 bay leaf
½ cup diced onion	½ teaspoon thyme
½ cup diced celery	½ teaspoon rosemary
1 carrot, peeled and diced	¼ cup walnuts or pine nuts
3 cups water or chicken broth	Sea salt and freshly ground pepper, to taste
1 cup barley	

1. Heat the olive oil in a medium saucepan over medium-high heat. Sauté the onion, celery, and carrot over medium heat until they are tender. 2. Add the water or chicken broth, barley, and seasonings, and bring to a boil. Reduce the heat and simmer for 25 minutes, or until tender. 3. Stir in the nuts and season to taste.

Per Serving:
calories: 283 | fat: 11g | protein: 6g | carbs: 43g | fiber: 9g | sodium: 26mg

Wild Rice and Mushroom Soup

Prep time: 15 minutes | Cook time: 35 minutes | Serves 8

2 tablespoons olive oil	minced
2 medium carrots, peeled and chopped	1 teaspoon dried thyme
2 stalks celery, chopped	1 teaspoon dried oregano
1 medium yellow onion, peeled and chopped	½ teaspoon salt
2 (8-ounce/ 227-g) containers sliced button mushrooms	½ teaspoon ground black pepper
3 cloves garlic, peeled and	1 cup wild rice blend
	6 cups vegetable broth

1. Press the Sauté button on the Instant Pot® and heat oil. Add carrots, celery, and onion. Cook until vegetables are just tender, about 5 minutes. Add mushrooms and cook until they begin to release their juices, about 4 minutes. 2. Add garlic, thyme, oregano, salt, pepper, and rice, and sauté until garlic is fragrant, about 1 minute. Press the Cancel button, add broth, and stir well. Close lid, set steam release to Sealing, press the Manual button, and set time to 25 minutes. 3. When the timer beeps, quick-release the pressure until the float valve drops, open lid, and stir well. Serve hot.

Per Serving:
calories: 141 | fat: 4g | protein: 4g | carbs: 24g | fiber: 3g | sodium: 722mg

Lentil and Spinach Curry

Prep time: 10 minutes | Cook time: 17 minutes | Serves 4

1 tablespoon olive oil	½ teaspoon ground coriander
½ cup diced onion	½ teaspoon ground turmeric
1 clove garlic, peeled and minced	½ teaspoon curry powder
1 cup dried yellow lentils, rinsed and drained	½ cup diced tomatoes
4 cups water	5 ounces (142 g) baby spinach leaves

1. Press the Sauté button on the Instant Pot® and heat oil. Add onion and cook until translucent, about 5 minutes. Add garlic and cook for 30 seconds. Add lentils and toss to combine. Press the Cancel button. 2. Pour in water. Close lid, set steam release to Sealing, press the Manual button, and set time to 6 minutes. When the timer beeps, quick-release the pressure until the float valve drops and open lid. Press the Cancel button. Drain any residual liquid. Stir in coriander, turmeric, curry powder, tomatoes, and spinach. 3. Press the Sauté button, press the Adjust button to change the heat to Less, and simmer uncovered until tomatoes are heated through and spinach has wilted, about 5 minutes. 4. Transfer to a dish and serve.

Per Serving:
calories: 195 | fat: 4g | protein: 13g | carbs: 26g | fiber: 8g | sodium: 111mg

Roasted White Beans with Peppers

Prep time: 5 minutes | Cook time: 15 minutes | Serves 4

Olive oil cooking spray	3 garlic cloves, minced
2 (15-ounce/ 425-g) cans white beans, or cannellini beans, drained and rinsed	1 tablespoon olive oil
	¼ to ½ teaspoon salt
1 red bell pepper, diced	½ teaspoon black pepper
½ red onion, diced	1 rosemary sprig
	1 bay leaf

1. Preheat the air fryer to 360°F (182°C). Lightly coat the inside of a 5-cup capacity casserole dish with olive oil cooking spray. (The shape of the casserole dish will depend upon the size of the air fryer, but it needs to be able to hold at least 5 cups.) 2. In a large bowl, combine the beans, bell pepper, onion, garlic, olive oil, salt, and pepper. 3. Pour the bean mixture into the prepared casserole dish, place the rosemary and bay leaf on top, and then place the casserole dish into the air fryer. 4. Roast for 15 minutes. 5. Remove the rosemary and bay leaves, then stir well before serving.

Per Serving:
calories: 77 | fat: 4.2g | protein: 2.2g | carbs: 9.6g | fiber: 3.3g | sodium: 150mg

Spicy Black Beans with Root Veggies

Prep time: 20 minutes | Cook time: 8 hours | Serves 2

1 onion, chopped
1 leek, white part only, sliced
3 garlic cloves, minced
1 jalapeño pepper, minced
2 Yukon Gold potatoes, peeled and cubed
1 parsnip, peeled and cubed
1 carrot, sliced
1 cup dried black beans, sorted and rinsed

2 cups vegetable broth
2 teaspoons chili powder
½ teaspoon dried marjoram leaves
½ teaspoon salt
⅛ teaspoon freshly ground black pepper
⅛ teaspoon crushed red pepper flakes

1. In the slow cooker, combine all the ingredients. 2. Cover and cook on low for 7 to 8 hours, or until the beans and vegetables are tender, and serve.

Per Serving:
calories: 597 | fat: 2g | protein: 27g | carbs: 124g | net carbs: 99g | sugars: 13g | fiber: 25g | sodium: 699mg | cholesterol: 0mg

Quinoa Salad with Tomatoes

Prep time: 10 minutes | Cook time: 22 minutes | Serves 4

2 tablespoons olive oil
2 cloves garlic, peeled and minced
1 cup diced fresh tomatoes
¼ cup chopped fresh Italian flat-leaf parsley

1 tablespoon lemon juice
1 cup quinoa, rinsed and drained
2 cups water
1 teaspoon salt

1. Press the Sauté button on the Instant Pot® and heat oil. Add garlic and cook 30 seconds, then add tomatoes, parsley, and lemon juice. Cook an additional 1 minute. Transfer mixture to a small bowl and set aside. Press the Cancel button. 2. Add quinoa and water to the Instant Pot®. Close lid, set steam release to Sealing, press the Multigrain button, and set time to 20 minutes. 3. When timer beeps, let pressure release naturally, about 20 minutes, then open lid. Fluff with a fork and stir in tomato mixture and salt. Serve immediately.

Per Serving:
calories: 223 | fat: 10g | protein: 6g | carbs: 29g | fiber: 3g | sodium: 586mg

Lemon Orzo with Fresh Herbs

Prep time: 10 minutes | Cook time: 10 minutes | Serves 4

2 cups orzo
½ cup fresh parsley, finely chopped
½ cup fresh basil, finely chopped
2 tablespoons lemon zest

½ cup extra-virgin olive oil
⅓ cup lemon juice
1 teaspoon salt
½ teaspoon freshly ground black pepper

1. Bring a large pot of water to a boil. Add the orzo and cook for 7 minutes. Drain and rinse with cold water. Let the orzo sit in a strainer to completely drain and cool. 2. Once the orzo has cooled, put it in a large bowl and add the parsley, basil, and lemon zest. 3.

In a small bowl, whisk together the olive oil, lemon juice, salt, and pepper. Add the dressing to the pasta and toss everything together. Serve at room temperature or chilled.

Per Serving:
calories: 568 | fat: 29g | protein: 11g | carbs: 65g | fiber: 4g | sodium: 586mg

Barley Risotto

Prep time: 10 minutes | Cook time: 30 minutes | Serves 6

2 tablespoons olive oil
1 large onion, peeled and diced
1 clove garlic, peeled and minced
1 stalk celery, finely minced
1½ cups pearl barley, rinsed and drained
⅓ cup dried mushrooms

4 cups low-sodium chicken broth
2¼ cups water
1 cup grated Parmesan cheese
2 tablespoons minced fresh parsley
¼ teaspoon salt

1. Press the Sauté button on the Instant Pot® and heat oil. Add onion and sauté 5 minutes. Add garlic and cook 30 seconds. Stir in celery, barley, mushrooms, broth, and water. Press the Cancel button. 2. Close lid, set steam release to Sealing, press the Manual button, and set time to 18 minutes. When the timer beeps, quick-release the pressure until the float valve drops and open the lid. 3. Drain off excess liquid, leaving enough to leave the risotto slightly soupy. Press the Cancel button, then press the Sauté button and cook until thickened, about 5 minutes. Stir in cheese, parsley, and salt. Serve immediately.

Per Serving:
calories: 175 | fat: 9g | protein: 10g | carbs: 13g | fiber: 2g | sodium: 447mg

Greek Yogurt Corn Bread

Prep time: 15 minutes | Cook time: 25 minutes | Serves 4 to 6

⅓ cup olive oil, plus extra for greasing
1 cup cornmeal
1 cup all-purpose flour
¼ cup sugar
½ teaspoon baking soda

½ teaspoon baking powder
1 teaspoon sea salt
1 cup plain full-fat Greek yogurt
1 large egg
¼ cup crumbled feta cheese

1. Preheat the oven to 375°F(190°C). Lightly grease an 8-inch square baking dish with olive oil. 2. In a large bowl, stir together the cornmeal, flour, sugar, baking soda, baking powder, and salt until well mixed. Add the yogurt, olive oil, and egg and stir until smooth. Stir in the feta. 3. Pour the batter into the prepared baking dish and bake until a toothpick inserted into the center of the corn bread comes out clean, about 30 minutes. 4. Remove the corn bread from the oven, cut it into 9 squares, and serve.

Per Serving:
calories: 546 | fat: 24g | protein: 11g | carbs: 71g | fiber: 2g | sodium: 584mg

Earthy Lentil and Rice Pilaf

Prep time: 5 minutes | Cook time: 50 minutes | Serves 6

¼ cup extra-virgin olive oil
1 large onion, chopped
6 cups water
1 teaspoon ground cumin

1 teaspoon salt
2 cups brown lentils, picked over and rinsed
1 cup basmati rice

1. In a medium pot over medium heat, cook the olive oil and onions for 7 to 10 minutes until the edges are browned. 2. Turn the heat to high, add the water, cumin, and salt, and bring this mixture to a boil, boiling for about 3 minutes. 3. Add the lentils and turn the heat to medium-low. Cover the pot and cook for 20 minutes, stirring occasionally. 4. Stir in the rice and cover; cook for an additional 20 minutes. 5. Fluff the rice with a fork and serve warm.

Per Serving:
calories: 397 | fat: 11g | protein: 18g | carbs: 60g | fiber: 18g | sodium: 396mg

Spanish Rice

Prep time: 10 minutes | Cook time: 20 minutes | Serves 4

2 tablespoons extra-virgin olive oil
1 medium onion, finely chopped
1 large tomato, finely diced
2 tablespoons tomato paste

1 teaspoon smoked paprika
1 teaspoon salt
1½ cups basmati rice
3 cups water

1. In a medium pot over medium heat, cook the olive oil, onion, and tomato for 3 minutes. 2. Stir in the tomato paste, paprika, salt, and rice. Cook for 1 minute. 3. Add the water, cover the pot, and turn the heat to low. Cook for 12 minutes. 4. Gently toss the rice, cover, and cook for another 3 minutes.

Per Serving:
calories: 328 | fat: 7g | protein: 6g | carbs: 60g | fiber: 2g | sodium: 651mg

Black Lentil Dhal

Prep time: 10 minutes | Cook time: 8 to 10 hours | Serves 6

2 cups dry whole black lentils
1 medium onion, finely chopped
1 heaped tablespoon freshly grated ginger
3 garlic cloves, chopped
3 fresh tomatoes, puréed, or 7 to 8 ounces (198 to 227 g) canned tomatoes, blended
2 fresh green chiles, chopped
2 tablespoons ghee
½ teaspoon turmeric
1 teaspoon chili powder

2 teaspoons coriander seeds, ground
1 teaspoon cumin seeds, ground
1 teaspoon sea salt
6⅓ cups water
1 to 2 tablespoons butter (optional)
1 teaspoon garam masala
1 teaspoon dried fenugreek leaves
Handful fresh coriander leaves, chopped

1. Preheat the slow cooker on high. 2. Clean and wash the black lentils. 3. Put the lentils, onion, ginger, garlic, tomatoes, chiles, ghee, turmeric, chili powder, coriander seeds, cumin seeds, salt, and water into the slow cooker. Cover and cook for 10 hours on low or for 8 hours on high. 4. When the lentils are cooked and creamy, stir in the butter (if using), garam masala, and fenugreek leaves to make the dhal rich and delicious. Garnish with a sprinkle of fresh coriander leaves and serve.

Per Serving:
calories: 271 | fat: 3g | protein: 17g | carbs: 47g | net carbs: 38g | sugars: 4g | fiber: 9g | sodium: 415mg | cholesterol: 5mg

White Bean Cassoulet

Prep time: 30 minutes | Cook time: 45 minutes | Serves 8

1 tablespoon olive oil
1 medium onion, peeled and diced
2 cups dried cannellini beans, soaked overnight and drained
1 medium parsnip, peeled and diced
2 medium carrots, peeled and diced
2 stalks celery, diced
1 medium zucchini, trimmed

and chopped
½ teaspoon fennel seed
¼ teaspoon ground nutmeg
½ teaspoon garlic powder
1 teaspoon sea salt
½ teaspoon ground black pepper
2 cups vegetable broth
1 (14½-ounce / 411-g) can diced tomatoes, including juice
2 sprigs rosemary

1. Press the Sauté button on the Instant Pot® and heat oil. Add onion and cook until translucent, about 5 minutes. Add beans and toss. 2. Add a layer of parsnip, then a layer of carrots, and next a layer of celery. Finally, add a layer of zucchini. Sprinkle in fennel seed, nutmeg, garlic powder, salt, and pepper. Press the Cancel button. 3. Gently pour in broth and canned tomatoes. Top with rosemary. 4. Close lid, set steam release to Sealing, press the Bean button, and cook for the default time of 30 minutes. When the timer beeps, let pressure release naturally for 10 minutes. Quick-release any remaining pressure until the float valve drops and open lid. Press the Cancel button. 5. Press the Sauté button, then press the Adjust button to change the temperature to Less, and simmer bean mixture uncovered for 10 minutes to thicken. Transfer to a serving bowl and carefully toss. Remove and discard rosemary and serve.

Per Serving:
calories: 128 | fat: 2g | protein: 6g | carbs: 21g | fiber: 5g | sodium: 387mg

Couscous with Apricots

Prep time: 10 minutes | Cook time: 15 minutes | Serves 4

2 tablespoons olive oil
1 small onion, diced
1 cup whole-wheat couscous
2 cups water or broth
½ cup dried apricots, soaked in

water overnight
½ cup slivered almonds or pistachios
½ teaspoon dried mint
½ teaspoon dried thyme

1. Heat the olive oil in a large skillet over medium-high heat. Add the onion and cook until translucent and soft. 2. Stir in the couscous and cook for 2–3 minutes. 3. Add the water or broth, cover, and cook for 8–10 minutes until the water is mostly absorbed. 4. Remove from the heat and let stand for a few minutes. 5. Fluff with a fork and fold in the apricots, nuts, mint, and thyme.

Per Serving:
calories: 294 | fat: 15g | protein: 8g | carbs: 38g | fiber: 6g | sodium: 6mg

Moroccan White Beans with Lamb

Prep time: 25 minutes | Cook time: 22 minutes | Serves 6 to 8

1½ tablespoons table salt, for brining
1 pound (454 g) dried great Northern beans, picked over and rinsed
1 (12-ounce/ 340-g) lamb shoulder chop (blade or round bone), ¾ to 1 inch thick, trimmed and halved
½ teaspoon table salt
2 tablespoons extra-virgin olive oil, plus extra for serving
1 onion, chopped

1 red bell pepper, stemmed, seeded, and chopped
2 tablespoons tomato paste
3 garlic cloves, minced
2 teaspoons paprika
2 teaspoons ground cumin
1½ teaspoons ground ginger
¼ teaspoon cayenne pepper
½ cup dry white wine
2 cups chicken broth
2 tablespoons minced fresh parsley

1. Dissolve 1½ tablespoons salt in 2 quarts cold water in large container. Add beans and soak at room temperature for at least 8 hours or up to 24 hours. Drain and rinse well. 2. Pat lamb dry with paper towels and sprinkle with ½ teaspoon salt. Using highest sauté function, heat oil in Instant Pot for 5 minutes (or until just smoking). Brown lamb, about 5 minutes per side; transfer to plate. 3. Add onion and bell pepper to fat left in pot and cook, using highest sauté function, until softened, about 5 minutes. Stir in tomato paste, garlic, paprika, cumin, ginger, and cayenne and cook until fragrant, about 30 seconds. Stir in wine, scraping up any browned bits, then stir in broth and beans. 4. Nestle lamb into beans and add any accumulated juices. Lock lid in place and close pressure release valve. Select high pressure cook function and cook for 1 minute. Turn off Instant Pot and let pressure release naturally for 15 minutes. Quick-release any remaining pressure, then carefully remove lid, allowing steam to escape away from you. 5. Transfer lamb to cutting board, let cool slightly, then shred into bite-size pieces using 2 forks; discard excess fat and bones. Stir lamb and parsley into beans, and season with salt and pepper to taste. Drizzle individual portions with extra oil before serving.

Per Serving:
calories: 350 | fat: 12g | protein: 20g | carbs: 40g | fiber: 15g | sodium: 410mg

Wheat Berry Pilaf

Prep time: 15 minutes | Cook time: 7 hours | Makes 7 cups

1 cup wheat berries
1 onion, chopped
1 leek, white part only, chopped
1 cup sliced cremini mushrooms
3 cups vegetable broth
1 tablespoon freshly squeezed

lemon juice
½ teaspoon dried thyme leaves
½ teaspoon salt
⅛ teaspoon freshly ground black pepper

1. Rinse the wheat berries well, and drain. 2. In the slow cooker, combine all the ingredients, and stir. 3. Cover and cook on low for 7 hours, or until the wheat berries and vegetables are tender.

Per Serving:
calories: 90 | fat: 0g | protein: 3g | carbs: 20g | net carbs: 17g | sugars: 2g | fiber: 3g | sodium: 173mg | cholesterol: 0mg

Slow Cooker Vegetarian Chili

Prep time: 20 minutes | Cook time: 4 to 6 hours | Serves 4

1 (28-ounce/ 794-g) can chopped whole tomatoes, with the juice
1 medium green bell pepper, chopped
1 (15-ounce / 425-g) can red beans, drained and rinsed
1 (15-ounce / 425-g) can black beans, drained and rinsed
1 yellow onion, chopped

1 tablespoon olive oil
1 tablespoon onion powder
1 teaspoon garlic powder
1 teaspoon cayenne pepper
1 teaspoon paprika
½ teaspoon sea salt
½ teaspoon black pepper
1 large hass avocado, pitted, peeled, and chopped, for garnish

1. Combine the tomatoes, bell pepper, red beans, black beans, and onion in the slow cooker. Sprinkle with the onion powder, garlic powder, cayenne pepper, paprika, ½ teaspoon salt, and ½ teaspoon black pepper. 2. Cover and cook on high for 4 to 6 hours or on low for 8 hours, or until thick. 3. Season with salt and black pepper if needed. Served hot, garnished with some of the avocado.

Per Serving:
calories:446 | fat: 15.4g | protein: 20.9g | carbs: 61g | fiber: 21.5g | sodium: 599mg

Vegetable Barley Soup

Prep time: 30 minutes | Cook time: 26 minutes | Serves 8

2 tablespoons olive oil
½ medium yellow onion, peeled and chopped
1 medium carrot, peeled and chopped
1 stalk celery, chopped
2 cups sliced button mushrooms
2 cloves garlic, peeled and minced
½ teaspoon dried thyme
½ teaspoon ground black pepper
1 large russet potato, peeled and cut into ½" pieces
1(14½-ounce / 411-g) can

fire-roasted diced tomatoes, undrained
½ cup medium pearl barley, rinsed and drained
4 cups vegetable broth
2 cups water
1 (15-ounce / 425-g) can corn, drained
1 (15-ounce / 425-g) can cut green beans, drained
1 (15-ounce / 425-g) can Great Northern beans, drained and rinsed
½ teaspoon salt

1. Press the Sauté button on the Instant Pot® and heat oil. Add onion, carrot, celery, and mushrooms. Cook until just tender, about 5 minutes. Add garlic, thyme, and pepper. Cook 30 seconds. Press the Cancel button. 2. Add potato, tomatoes, barley, broth, and water to pot. Close lid, set steam release to Sealing, press the Soup button, and cook for the default time of 20 minutes. 3. When the timer beeps, let pressure release naturally, about 15 minutes. Open lid and stir soup, then add corn, green beans, and Great Northern beans. Close lid and let stand on the Keep Warm setting for 10 minutes. Stir in salt. Serve hot.

Per Serving:
calories: 190 | fat: 4g | protein: 7g | carbs: 34g | fiber: 8g | sodium: 548mg

Savory Gigantes Plaki (Baked Giant White Beans)

Prep time: 5 minutes | Cook time: 30 minutes | Serves 4

Olive oil cooking spray
1 (15-ounce/ 425-g) can cooked butter beans, drained and rinsed
1 cup diced fresh tomatoes
½ tablespoon tomato paste
2 garlic cloves, minced
½ yellow onion, diced
½ teaspoon salt
¼ cup olive oil
¼ cup fresh parsley, chopped

1. Preheat the air fryer to 380°F(193°C). Lightly coat the inside of a 5-cup capacity casserole dish with olive oil cooking spray. (The shape of the casserole dish will depend upon the size of the air fryer, but it needs to be able to hold at least 5 cups.) 2. In a large bowl, combine the butter beans, tomatoes, tomato paste, garlic, onion, salt, and olive oil, mixing until all ingredients are combined. 3. Pour the mixture into the prepared casserole dish and top with the chopped parsley. 4. Bake in the air fryer for 15 minutes. Stir well, then return to the air fryer and bake for 15 minutes more.

Per Serving:
calories: 199 | fat: 18.6g | protein: 2g | carbs: 8g | fiber: 3g | sodium: 300mg

Rice with Blackened Fish

Prep time: 10 minutes | Cook time: 2 to 4 hours | Serves 4

1 teaspoon ground cumin
1 teaspoon ground coriander
1 teaspoon garlic powder
1 teaspoon paprika
½ teaspoon sea salt
½ teaspoon freshly ground black pepper
½ teaspoon onion powder
1 pound (454 g) fresh salmon fillets
1 cup raw long-grain brown rice, rinsed
2½ cups low-sodium chicken broth
¼ cup diced tomato

1. In a small bowl, stir together the cumin, coriander, garlic powder, paprika, salt, pepper, and onion powder. Generously season the salmon fillets with the blackening seasoning. 2. In a slow cooker, combine the rice, chicken broth, and tomato. Stir to mix well. 3. Place the seasoned salmon on top of the rice mixture. 4. Cover the cooker and cook for 2 to 4 hours on Low heat.

Per Serving:
calories: 318 | fat: 6g | protein: 29g | carbs: 38g | fiber: 3g | sodium: 337mg

Farro Salad with Tomatoes and Olives

Prep time: 10 minutes | Cook time: 20 minutes | Serves 6

10 ounces (283 g) farro, rinsed and drained
4 cups water
4 Roma tomatoes, seeded and chopped
4 scallions, green parts only, thinly sliced
½ cup sliced black olives
¼ cup minced fresh flat-leaf parsley
¼ cup extra-virgin olive oil
2 tablespoons balsamic vinegar
¼ teaspoon ground black pepper

1. Place farro and water in the Instant Pot®. Close lid and set steam release to Sealing. Press the Multigrain button and set time to 20 minutes. When the timer beeps, let pressure release naturally, about 30 minutes. 2. Open lid and fluff with a fork. Transfer to a bowl and cool 30 minutes. Add tomatoes, scallions, black olives, and parsley and mix well. 3. In a small bowl, whisk together oil, balsamic vinegar, and pepper. Pour over salad and toss to evenly coat. Refrigerate for at least 4 hours before serving. Serve chilled or at room temperature.

Per Serving:
calories: 288 | fat: 14g | protein: 7g | carbs: 31g | fiber: 3g | sodium: 159mg

Revithosoupa (Chickpea Soup)

Prep time: 10 minutes | Cook time: 30 minutes | Serves 8

1 pound (454 g) dried chickpeas
4 cups water
¾ teaspoon salt
½ teaspoon ground black pepper
10 strands saffron
2 medium onions, peeled and
diced
1 cup extra-virgin olive oil
1 teaspoon dried oregano
3 tablespoons lemon juice
2 tablespoons chopped fresh parsley

1. Add chickpeas, water, salt, pepper, saffron, onions, oil, and oregano to the Instant Pot® and stir well. Close lid, set steam release to Sealing, press the Bean button, and cook for the default time of 30 minutes. 2. When the timer beeps, let pressure release naturally, about 25 minutes. Open lid. Serve hot or cold, sprinkled with lemon juice. Garnish with chopped parsley.

Per Serving:
calories: 464 | fat: 30g | protein: 12g | carbs: 38g | fiber: 10g | sodium: 236mg

Creamy Lima Bean Soup

Prep time: 10 minutes | Cook time: 17 minutes | Serves 6

1 tablespoon olive oil
1 small onion, peeled and diced
1 clove garlic, peeled and minced
2 cups vegetable stock
½ cup water
2 cups dried lima beans, soaked
overnight and drained
½ teaspoon salt
½ teaspoon ground black pepper
2 tablespoons thinly sliced chives

1. Press the Sauté button on the Instant Pot® and heat oil. Add onion and cook until golden brown, about 10 minutes. Add garlic and cook until fragrant, about 30 seconds. Press the Cancel button. 2. Add stock, water, and lima beans. Close lid, set steam release to Sealing, press the Manual button, and set time to 6 minutes. When the timer beeps, let pressure release naturally, about 20 minutes. 3. Open lid and purée soup with an immersion blender or in batches in a blender. Season with salt and pepper, then sprinkle with chives before serving.

Per Serving:
calories: 67 | fat: 2g | protein: 2g | carbs: 9g | fiber: 2g | sodium: 394mg

Tomato Rice

Prep time: 10 minutes | Cook time: 25 minutes | Serves 3

2 tablespoons extra virgin olive oil
1 medium onion (any variety), chopped
1 garlic clove, finely chopped
1 cup uncooked medium-grain rice
1 tablespoon tomato paste
1 pound (454 g) canned crushed

tomatoes, or 1 pound (454 g) fresh tomatoes (puréed in a food processor)
¾ teaspoon fine sea salt
1 teaspoon granulated sugar
2 cups hot water
2 tablespoons chopped fresh mint or basil

1. Heat the olive oil in a wide, deep pan over medium heat. When the oil begins to shimmer, add the onion and sauté for 3–4 minutes or until soft, then add the garlic and sauté for an additional 30 seconds. 2. Add the rice and stir until the rice is coated with the oil, then add the tomato paste and stir rapidly. Add the tomatoes, sea salt, and sugar, and then stir again. 3. Add the hot water, stir, then reduce the heat to low and simmer, covered, for 20 minutes or until the rice is soft. (If the rice appears to need more cooking time, add a small amount of hot water to the pan and continue cooking.) Remove the pan from the heat. 4. Add the chopped mint or basil, and let the rice sit for 10 minutes before serving. Store covered in the refrigerator for up to 4 days.

Per Serving:
calories: 359 | fat: 11g | protein: 7g | carbs: 60g | fiber: 6g | sodium: 607mg

Mediterranean Creamed Green Peas

Prep time: 5 minutes | Cook time: 25 minutes | Serves 4

1 cup cauliflower florets, fresh or frozen
½ white onion, roughly chopped
2 tablespoons olive oil
½ cup unsweetened almond milk
3 cups green peas, fresh or frozen
3 garlic cloves, minced

2 tablespoons fresh thyme leaves, chopped
1 teaspoon fresh rosemary leaves, chopped
½ teaspoon salt
½ teaspoon black pepper
Shredded Parmesan cheese, for garnish
Fresh parsley, for garnish

1. Preheat the air fryer to 380°F(193°C). 2. In a large bowl, combine the cauliflower florets and onion with the olive oil and toss well to coat. 3. Put the cauliflower-and-onion mixture into the air fryer basket in an even layer and bake for 15 minutes. 4. Transfer the cauliflower and onion to a food processor. Add the almond milk and pulse until smooth. 5. In a medium saucepan, combine the cauliflower purée, peas, garlic, thyme, rosemary, salt, and pepper and mix well. Cook over medium heat for an additional 10 minutes, stirring regularly. 6. Serve with a sprinkle of Parmesan cheese and chopped fresh parsley.

Per Serving:
calories: 313 | fat: 16.4g | protein: 14.7g | carbs: 28.8g | fiber: 8.3g | sodium: 898mg

Black Chickpeas

Prep time: 11 minutes | Cook time: 9 to 11 hours | Serves 6

1 tablespoon rapeseed oil
2 teaspoons cumin seeds
2 cups dried whole black chickpeas, washed
4 cups hot water
1 onion, roughly chopped
2-inch piece fresh ginger, peeled and roughly chopped
4 garlic cloves

3 fresh green chiles
1 tomato, roughly chopped
1 teaspoon turmeric
1 teaspoon Kashmiri chili powder
1 teaspoon sea salt
Handful fresh coriander leaves, chopped
Juice of 1 lemon

1. Heat the oil in a frying pan (or in the slow cooker if you have a sear setting). Add the cumin seeds until they sizzle, then pour them into the cooker. 2. Heat the slow cooker to high, and then add the chickpeas and water. 3. In a blender, purée the onion, ginger, garlic, chiles, and tomato to make a paste. Add it to the cooker, along with the turmeric, chili powder, and salt. 4. Cover and cook for 9 hours on high, or for 11 hours on low. 5. When the chickpeas are cooked, check the seasoning. Add the coriander leaves and lemon juice, and serve.

Per Serving:
calories: 129 | fat: 4g | protein: 5g | carbs: 19g | net carbs: 14g | sugars: 6g | fiber: 5g | sodium: 525mg | cholesterol: 0mg

Red Lentils with Kale and Feta

Prep time: 10 minutes | Cook time: 10 minutes | Serves 6

1 tablespoon olive oil
1 medium yellow onion, peeled and chopped
1 clove garlic, peeled and minced
3 cups chopped kale
1 cup dried red lentils, rinsed and drained
2 cups water
3 tablespoons chopped fresh

mint
2 tablespoons chopped fresh flat-leaf parsley
1 tablespoon lemon juice
¼ teaspoon ground allspice
¼ teaspoon salt
¼ teaspoon ground black pepper
½ cup crumbled feta cheese

1. Press the Sauté button on the Instant Pot® and heat oil. Add onion and cook until just tender, about 3 minutes. Add garlic and cook until fragrant, about 30 seconds. Add kale and toss to coat in onion mixture. Cook until starting to wilt, about 1 minute. Press the Cancel button. 2. Add lentils and water to pot. Close lid, set steam release to Sealing, press the Manual button, and set time to 5 minutes. When the timer beeps, let pressure release naturally for 5 minutes, then quick-release any remaining pressure until the float valve drops. Open lid and drain off any excess liquid. 3. Add mint, parsley, lemon juice, allspice, salt, and pepper, and toss to mix. Transfer to a serving bowl and top with feta. Serve warm or at room temperature.

Per Serving:
calories: 244 | fat: 6g | protein: 17g | carbs: 33g | fiber: 12g | sodium: 338mg

Garlic-Asparagus Israeli Couscous

Prep time: 5 minutes |Cook time: 25 minutes| Serves: 6

1 cup garlic-and-herb goat cheese (about 4 ounces/ 113 g)
1½ pounds (680 g) asparagus spears, ends trimmed and stalks chopped into 1-inch pieces (about 2¾ to 3 cups chopped)
1 tablespoon extra-virgin olive oil
1 garlic clove, minced (about ½ teaspoon)
¼ teaspoon freshly ground black pepper
1¾ cups water
1 (8-ounce/ 227-g) box uncooked whole-wheat or regular Israeli couscous (about 1⅓ cups)
¼ teaspoon kosher or sea salt

1. Preheat the oven to 425°F (220ºC). Put the goat cheese on the counter to bring to room temperature. 2. In a large bowl, mix together the asparagus, oil, garlic, and pepper. Spread the asparagus on a large, rimmed baking sheet and roast for 10 minutes, stirring a few times. Remove the pan from the oven, and spoon the asparagus into a large serving bowl. 3. While the asparagus is roasting, in a medium saucepan, bring the water to a boil. Add the couscous and salt. Reduce the heat to medium-low, cover, and cook for 12 minutes, or until the water is absorbed. 4. Pour the hot couscous into the bowl with the asparagus. Add the goat cheese, mix thoroughly until completely melted, and serve.

Per Serving:
calories: 98 | fat: 1.3g | protein: 10.2g | carbs: 13.5g | fiber:3.67g | sodium: 262mg

Quinoa and Artichoke Hearts Salad

Prep time: 10 minutes | Cook time: 5 minutes | Serves 4

1 cup raw pecan halves
1 cup quinoa, rinsed and drained
2½ cups water
2 cups frozen artichoke hearts, thawed and drained
2 cups halved cherry tomatoes
½ small red onion, peeled and thinly sliced
¼ cup Italian salad dressing
4 large Belgian endive leaves

1. Press the Sauté button on the Instant Pot®. Roughly chop pecans and add them to the Instant Pot®. Dry-roast for several minutes, stirring continuously to prevent burning. Pecans are sufficiently toasted when they're fragrant and slightly brown. Transfer to a medium bowl and set aside to cool. Press the Cancel button. 2. Clean and dry pot. Add quinoa and water to the Instant Pot®. Close lid, set steam release to Sealing, press the Manual button, and set time to 2 minutes. When the timer beeps, let pressure release naturally for 10 minutes. Quick-release any remaining pressure until the float valve drops and open lid. Transfer to a colander, drain excess liquid, and rinse under cold water. Drain well and transfer to a large bowl. 3. While quinoa is cooking, cook artichoke hearts according to package directions and then plunge into cold water to cool and stop the cooking process. Drain and cut into quarters. 4. Stir artichoke hearts into quinoa along with tomatoes and red onion. Toss with salad dressing. Cover and refrigerate for 1 hour before serving. 5. Place endive leaves on four plates. Top each with ¼ cup quinoa mixture. Sprinkle toasted pecans over the top of each endive boat and serve.

Per Serving:
calories: 414 | fat: 24g | protein: 11g | carbs: 42g | fiber: 10g | sodium: 327mg

Moroccan Vegetables and Chickpeas

Prep time: 25 minutes | Cook time: 6 hours | Serves 6

1 large carrot, cut into ¼-inch rounds
2 large baking potatoes, peeled and cubed
1 large bell pepper, any color, chopped
6 ounces (170 g) green beans, trimmed and cut into bite-size pieces
1 large yellow onion, chopped
2 garlic cloves, minced
1 teaspoon peeled, grated fresh ginger
1 (15-ounce / 425-g) can diced tomatoes, with the juice
3 cups canned chickpeas, rinsed and drained
1¾ cups vegetable stock
1 tablespoon ground coriander
1 teaspoon ground cumin
¼ teaspoon ground red pepper
Sea salt
Black pepper
8 ounces (227 g) fresh baby spinach
¼ cup diced dried apricots
¼ cup diced dried figs
1 cup plain greek yogurt

1. Put the carrot, potatoes, bell pepper, green beans, onion, garlic, and ginger in the slow cooker. Stir in the diced tomatoes, chickpeas, and vegetable stock. Sprinkle with coriander, cumin, red pepper, salt, and black pepper. 2. Cover and cook on high for 6 hours or until the vegetables are tender. 3. Add the spinach, apricots, figs, and Greek yogurt, and cook and stir until the spinach wilts, about 4 minutes. Serve hot.

Per Serving:
calories: 307 | fat: 5g | protein: 13g | carbs: 57g | fiber: 12g | sodium: 513mg

Lemon and Garlic Rice Pilaf

Prep time: 10 minutes | Cook time: 34 minutes | Serves 8

2 tablespoons olive oil
1 medium yellow onion, peeled and chopped
4 cloves garlic, peeled and minced
1 tablespoon grated lemon zest
½ teaspoon ground black pepper
1 teaspoon dried thyme
1 teaspoon dried oregano
¼ teaspoon salt
2 tablespoons white wine
2 tablespoons lemon juice
2 cups brown rice
2 cups vegetable broth

1. Press the Sauté button on the Instant Pot® and heat oil. Add onion and cook until soft, about 6 minutes. Add garlic and cook until fragrant, about 30 seconds. Add lemon zest, pepper, thyme, oregano, and salt. Cook until fragrant, about 1 minute. 2. Add wine and lemon juice and cook, stirring well, until liquid has almost evaporated, about 1 minute. Add rice and cook, stirring constantly, until coated and starting to toast, about 3 minutes. Press the Cancel button. 3. Stir in broth. Close lid, set steam release to Sealing, press the Manual button, and set time to 22 minutes. 4. When the timer beeps, let pressure release naturally for 10 minutes, then quick-release the remaining pressure until the float valve drops. Open lid and fluff rice with a fork. Serve warm.

Per Serving:
calories: 202 | fat: 5g | protein: 4g | carbs: 37g | fiber: 1g | sodium: 274mg

Chicken Artichoke Rice Bake

Prep time: 10 minutes | Cook time: 3 to 5 hours | Serves 4

Nonstick cooking spray
1 cup raw long-grain brown rice, rinsed
2½ cups low-sodium chicken broth
1 (14-ounce/ 397-g) can artichoke hearts, drained and rinsed
½ small onion, diced
2 garlic cloves, minced
10 ounces (283 g) fresh spinach, chopped
1 teaspoon dried thyme
½ teaspoon sea salt
½ teaspoon freshly ground black pepper
1 pound (454 g) boneless, skinless chicken breast

1. Generously coat a slow-cooker insert with cooking spray. Put the rice, chicken broth, artichoke hearts, onion, garlic, spinach, thyme, salt, and pepper in a slow cooker. Gently stir to mix well. 2. Place the chicken on top of the rice mixture. 3. Cover the cooker and cook for 3 to 5 hours on Low heat. 4. Remove the chicken from the cooker, shred it, and stir it back into the rice in the cooker.

Per Serving:
calories: 323 | fat: 4g | protein: 32g | carbs: 44g | fiber: 6g | sodium: 741mg

Venetian-Style Pasta E Fagioli

Prep time: 15 minutes | Cook time: 50 minutes | Serves 2

1 cup uncooked borlotti (cranberry) beans or pinto beans
3 tablespoons extra virgin olive oil, divided
1 small carrot, finely chopped
½ medium onion (white or red), finely chopped
1 celery stalk, finely chopped
1 bay leaf
1 tablespoon tomato paste
2 cups cold water
1 rosemary sprig plus ½ teaspoon chopped fresh
rosemary needles
¼ teaspoon fine sea salt
¼ teaspoon freshly ground black pepper plus more to taste
1½ ounces (43 g) uncooked egg fettuccine or other egg noodles
1 garlic clove, peeled and finely sliced
¼ teaspoon red pepper flakes
2 teaspoons grated Parmesan cheese
Pinch of coarse sea salt, for serving

1. Place the beans in a large bowl and cover with cold water by 3 inches (7.5cm) to allow for expansion. Soak for 12 hours or overnight, then drain and rinse. 2. Add 2 tablespoons of the olive oil to a medium pot over medium heat. When the oil begins to shimmer, add the carrot, onions, celery, and bay leaf. Sauté for 3 minutes, then add the tomato paste and continue sautéing and stirring for 2 more minutes. 3. Add the beans, cold water, and rosemary sprig. Cover, bring to a boil, then reduce the heat to low and simmer for 30–40 minutes or until the beans are soft, but not falling apart. Remove the rosemary sprig and bay leaf. Use a slotted spoon to remove about 1 cup of the beans. Set aside. 4. Using an immersion blender, blend the remaining beans in the pot, then add the whole beans back to the pot along with the sea salt and ¼ teaspoon of the black pepper. Increase the heat to medium. When the mixture begins to bubble, add the pasta and cook until done, about 3 minutes. 5. While the pasta is cooking, heat 1 teaspoon of the olive oil in a small pan over medium heat. Add the garlic, red pepper flakes, and chopped rosemary needles. Sauté for 2 minutes, then transfer the mixture to the beans and stir. 6. When the pasta is done cooking, remove from the heat and set aside to cool for 5 minutes before dividing between 2 plates. Drizzle 1 teaspoon of the olive oil and sprinkle 1 teaspoon of the grated Parmesan over each serving. Season with freshly ground pepper to taste and a pinch of coarse sea salt. This dish is best served promptly, but can be stored in the refrigerator for up to 2 days.

Per Serving:
calories: 409 | fat: 22g | protein: 12g | carbs: 42g | fiber: 11g | sodium: 763mg

Brown Rice Salad with Zucchini and Tomatoes

Prep time: 5 minutes | Cook time: 22 minutes | Serves 6

1 cup brown basmati rice
1¼ cups vegetable broth
5 tablespoons olive oil, divided
2 cups chopped zucchini
2 cups sliced cherry tomatoes
¼ cup minced red onion
2 tablespoons lemon juice
¼ teaspoon salt
¼ teaspoon ground black pepper
¼ cup chopped fresh flat-leaf parsley
¼ cup toasted slivered almonds
¼ cup crumbled feta cheese

1. Place rice, broth, and 1 tablespoon olive oil in the Instant Pot® and stir well. Close lid, set steam release to Sealing, press the Manual button, and set time to 22 minutes. 2. When the timer beeps, let pressure release naturally for 10 minutes, then quick-release the remaining pressure. Open lid and fluff rice with a fork. Transfer to a large bowl and set aside to cool to room temperature. 3. Add zucchini, tomatoes, and onion to rice. In a small bowl, whisk remaining 4 tablespoons olive oil, lemon juice, salt, and pepper. Pour over rice and toss. Top with parsley, almonds, and feta. Serve warm or at room temperature.

Per Serving:
calories: 209 | fat: 12g | protein: 5g | carbs: 21g | fiber: 2g | sodium: 380mg

Asparagus-Spinach Farro

Prep time: 5 minutes | Cook time: 16 minutes | Serves 4

2 tablespoons olive oil
1 cup quick-cooking farro
½ shallot, finely chopped
4 garlic cloves, minced
Sea salt
Freshly ground black pepper
2½ cups water, vegetable broth,
or chicken broth
8 ounces (227 g) asparagus, woody ends trimmed, cut into 2-inch pieces
3 ounces (85 g) fresh baby spinach
½ cup grated Parmesan cheese

1. In a large skillet, heat the olive oil over medium-high heat. Add the farro, shallot, and garlic, season with salt and pepper, and cook for about 4 minutes. Add the water and bring the mixture to a boil. Reduce the heat to low, cover, and simmer for 10 minutes (or for the time recommended on the package of farro). 2. Add the asparagus and cook until tender, about 5 minutes. Add the spinach and cook for 30 seconds more, or until wilted. 3. Top with the Parmesan and serve.

Per Serving:
calories: 277 | fat: 11g | protein: 10g | carbs: 38g | fiber: 7g | sodium: 284mg

Three-Grain Pilaf

Prep time: 10 minutes | Cook time: 10 minutes | Serves 6

2 tablespoons extra-virgin olive oil	drained
½ cup sliced scallions	2½ cups vegetable stock
1 cup jasmine rice	¼ teaspoon salt
½ cup millet	¼ teaspoon ground black pepper
½ cup quinoa, rinsed and	

1. Press the Sauté button on the Instant Pot® and heat oil. Add scallions and cook until just tender, 2 minutes. Add rice, millet, and quinoa and cook for 3 minutes to toast. Add stock and stir well. Press the Cancel button. 2. Close lid, set steam release to Sealing, press the Manual button, and set time to 4 minutes. When the timer beeps, quick-release the pressure until the float valve drops and open the lid. Fluff pilaf with a fork and stir in salt and pepper. Serve warm.

Per Serving:
calories: 346 | fat: 7g | protein: 8g | carbs: 61g | fiber: 4g | sodium: 341mg

Pesto Rice with Olives and Goat Cheese

Prep time: 5 minutes | Cook time: 22 minutes | Serves 8

2 cups brown basmati rice	½ cup chopped mixed olives
2¼ cups vegetable broth	¼ cup chopped fresh basil
½ cup pesto	¼ cup crumbled goat cheese

1. Place rice, broth, and pesto in the Instant Pot® and stir well. Close lid, set steam release to Sealing, press the Manual button, and set time to 22 minutes. 2. When the timer beeps, let pressure release naturally for 10 minutes, then quick-release the remaining pressure. Open lid, add olives and basil, and fluff rice with a fork. Serve warm, topped with goat cheese.

Per Serving:
calories: 219 | fat: 6g | protein: 6g | carbs: 36g | fiber: 1g | sodium: 148mg

Simple Herbed Rice

Prep time: 10 minutes | Cook time: 32 minutes | Serves 8

2 tablespoons extra-virgin olive oil	2¼ cups brown rice
½ medium yellow onion, peeled and chopped	2 cups water
4 cloves garlic, peeled and minced	¼ cup chopped fresh flat-leaf parsley
¼ teaspoon salt	¼ cup chopped fresh basil
½ teaspoon ground black pepper	2 tablespoons chopped fresh oregano
	2 teaspoons fresh thyme leaves

1. Press the Sauté button on the Instant Pot® and heat oil. Add onion and cook until soft, about 6 minutes. Add garlic, salt, and pepper and cook until fragrant, about 30 seconds. Add rice and cook, stirring constantly, until well-coated and starting to toast,

about 3 minutes. Press the Cancel button. 2. Stir in water. Close lid, set steam release to Sealing, press the Manual button, and set time to 22 minutes. When the timer beeps, let pressure release naturally for 10 minutes, then quick-release the remaining pressure. Open lid and fold in parsley, basil, oregano, and thyme. Serve warm.

Per Serving:
calories: 102 | fat: 4g | protein: 2g | carbs: 15g | fiber: 1g | sodium: 96mg

Herbed Lima Beans

Prep time: 10 minutes | Cook time: 6 minutes | Serves 6

1 pound (454 g) frozen baby lima beans, thawed	oil
2 cloves garlic, peeled and minced	3 cups water
2 thyme sprigs	1 tablespoon chopped fresh dill
1 bay leaf	1 tablespoon chopped fresh tarragon
2 tablespoons extra-virgin olive	1 tablespoon chopped fresh mint

1. Add lima beans, garlic, thyme, bay leaf, oil, and water to the Instant Pot®. Close lid, set steam release to Sealing, press the Manual button, and set time to 6 minutes. When the timer beeps, quick-release the pressure until the float valve drops. Open lid, remove and discard thyme and bay leaf, and stir well. 2. Stir in dill, tarragon, and mint, and let stand for 10 minutes on the Keep Warm setting before serving.

Per Serving:
calories: 134 | fat: 5g | protein: 5g | carbs: 17g | fiber: 4g | sodium: 206mg

Bulgur with Red Pepper and Goat Cheese

Prep time: 10 minutes | Cook time: 16 minutes | Serves 4

1 tablespoon light olive oil	¼ teaspoon salt
1 medium red bell pepper, seeded and chopped	1 cup bulgur wheat
½ medium yellow onion, peeled and chopped	2 cups water
1 clove garlic, peeled and minced	¼ cup chopped fresh chives
½ teaspoon ground black pepper	¼ cup chopped fresh flat-leaf parsley
	2 ounces (57 g) crumbled goat cheese

1. Press the Sauté button on the Instant Pot® and heat oil. Add bell pepper and onion, and cook until just softened, about 3 minutes. Add garlic, black pepper, and salt. Cook until garlic is fragrant, about 30 seconds. Press the Cancel button. 2. Add bulgur and water to the Instant Pot® and stir well. Close lid, set steam release to Sealing, press the Rice button, adjust pressure to Low, and set time to 12 minutes. When the timer beeps, quick-release the pressure until the float valve drops. Open lid and fluff bulgur with a fork. 3. Add chives and parsley to pot and toss. Transfer rice mixture to a serving dish and top with goat cheese. Serve warm.

Per Serving:
calories: 123 | fat: 7g | protein: 4g | carbs: 12g | fiber: 4g | sodium: 227mg

White Beans with Garlic and Tomatoes

Prep time: 10 minutes | Cook time: 40 minutes | Serves 6

1 cup dried cannellini beans, soaked overnight and drained
4 cups water
4 cups vegetable stock
1 tablespoon olive oil
1 teaspoon salt

2 cloves garlic, peeled and minced
½ cup diced tomato
½ teaspoon dried sage
½ teaspoon ground black pepper

1. Add beans and water to the Instant Pot®. Close lid, set steam release to Sealing, press the Bean button, and cook for default time of 30 minutes. When timer beeps, quick-release the pressure until the float valve drops. 2. Press the Cancel button, open lid, drain and rinse beans, and return to pot along with stock. Soak for 1 hour. 3. Add olive oil, salt, garlic, tomato, sage, and pepper to beans. Close lid, set steam release to Sealing, press the Manual button, and set time to 10 minutes. When the timer beeps, quick-release the pressure until the float valve drops and open lid. Serve hot.

Per Serving:
calories: 128 | fat: 2g | protein: 7g | carbs: 20g | fiber: 4g | sodium: 809mg

Crunchy Pea and Barley Salad

Prep time: 10 minutes | Cook time: 15 minutes | Serves 4

2 cups water
1 cup quick-cooking barley
2 cups sugar snap pea pods
Small bunch flat-leaf parsley, chopped

½ small red onion, diced
2 tablespoons olive oil
Juice of 1 lemon
Sea salt and freshly ground pepper, to taste

1. Bring water to boil in a saucepan. Stir in the barley and cover. 2. Simmer for 10 minutes until all water is absorbed, and then let stand about 5 minutes covered. 3. Rinse the barley under cold water and combine it with the peas, parsley, onion, olive oil, and lemon juice. 4. Season with sea salt and freshly ground pepper to taste.

Per Serving:
calories: 277 | fat: 8g | protein: 8g | carbs: 47g | fiber: 11g | sodium: 19mg

Chapter 7 Pasta

Bowtie Pesto Pasta Salad

Prep time: 5 minutes | Cook time: 4 minutes | Serves 8

1 pound (454 g) whole-wheat bowtie pasta
4 cups water
1 tablespoon extra-virgin olive oil
2 cups halved cherry tomatoes

2 cups baby spinach
½ cup chopped fresh basil
½ cup prepared pesto
½ teaspoon ground black pepper
½ cup grated Parmesan cheese

1. Add pasta, water, and olive oil to the Instant Pot®. Close lid, set steam release to Sealing, press the Manual button, and set time to 4 minutes. 2. When the timer beeps, quick-release the pressure until the float valve drops and open lid. Drain off any excess liquid. Allow pasta to cool to room temperature, about 30 minutes. Stir in tomatoes, spinach, basil, pesto, pepper, and cheese. Refrigerate for 2 hours. Stir well before serving.

Per Serving:
calories: 360 | fat: 13g | protein: 16g | carbs: 44g | fiber: 7g | sodium: 372mg

Creamy Spring Vegetable Linguine

Prep time: 10 minutes | Cook time: 10 minutes | Serves 4 to 6

1 pound (454 g) linguine
5 cups water, plus extra as needed
1 tablespoon extra-virgin olive oil
1 teaspoon table salt
1 cup jarred whole baby artichokes packed in water, quartered

1 cup frozen peas, thawed
4 ounces (113 g) finely grated Pecorino Romano (2 cups), plus extra for serving
½ teaspoon pepper
2 teaspoons grated lemon zest
2 tablespoons chopped fresh tarragon

1. Loosely wrap half of pasta in dish towel, then press bundle against corner of counter to break noodles into 6-inch lengths; repeat with remaining pasta. 2. Add pasta, water, oil, and salt to Instant Pot, making sure pasta is completely submerged. Lock lid in place and close pressure release valve. Select high pressure cook function and cook for 4 minutes. Turn off Instant Pot and quick-release pressure. Carefully remove lid, allowing steam to escape away from you. 3. Stir artichokes and peas into pasta, cover, and let sit until heated through, about 3 minutes. Gently stir in Pecorino and pepper until cheese is melted and fully combined, 1 to 2 minutes. Adjust consistency with extra hot water as needed. Stir in lemon zest and tarragon, and season with salt and pepper to taste. Serve, passing extra Pecorino separately.

Per Serving:
calories: 390 | fat: 8g | protein: 17g | carbs: 59g | fiber: 4g | sodium: 680mg

Couscous with Crab and Lemon

Prep time: 10 minutes | Cook time: 7 minutes | Serves 4

1 cup couscous
1 clove garlic, peeled and minced
2 cups water
3 tablespoons extra-virgin olive oil, divided
¼ cup minced fresh flat-leaf parsley

1 tablespoon minced fresh dill
8 ounces (227 g) jumbo lump crabmeat
3 tablespoons lemon juice
½ teaspoon ground black pepper
¼ cup grated Parmesan cheese

1. Place couscous, garlic, water, and 1 tablespoon oil in the Instant Pot® and stir well. Close lid, set steam release to Sealing, press the Manual button, and set time to 7 minutes. When the timer beeps, let pressure release naturally for 10 minutes, then quick-release the remaining pressure and open lid. 2. Fluff couscous with a fork. Add parsley, dill, crabmeat, lemon juice, pepper, and remaining 2 tablespoons oil, and stir until combined. Top with cheese and serve immediately.

Per Serving:
calories: 360 | fat: 15g | protein: 22g | carbs: 34g | fiber: 2g | sodium: 388mg

Spaghetti with Fresh Mint Pesto and Ricotta Salata

Prep time: 5 minutes | Cook time: 15 minutes | Serves 4

1 pound (454 g) spaghetti
¼ cup slivered almonds
2 cups packed fresh mint leaves, plus more for garnish
3 medium garlic cloves
1 tablespoon lemon juice and ½ teaspoon lemon zest from 1

lemon
⅓ cup olive oil
¼ teaspoon freshly ground black pepper
½ cup freshly grated ricotta salata, plus more for garnish

1. Set a large pot of salted water over high heat to boil for the pasta. 2. In a food processor, combine the almonds, mint leaves, garlic, lemon juice and zest, olive oil, and pepper and pulse to a smooth paste. Add the cheese and pulse to combine. 3. When the water is boiling, add the pasta and cook according to the package instructions. Drain the pasta and return it to the pot. Add the pesto to the pasta and toss until the pasta is well coated. Serve hot, garnished with additional mint leaves and cheese, if desired.

Per Serving:
calories: 619 | fat: 31g | protein: 21g | carbs: 70g | fiber: 4g | sodium: 113mg

Baked Ziti

Prep time: 10 minutes | Cook time: 55 minutes | Serves 8

For the Marinara Sauce:
2 tablespoons olive oil
¼ medium onion, diced (about 3 tablespoons)
3 cloves garlic, chopped
1 (28-ounce / 794-g) can whole, peeled tomatoes, roughly chopped
Sprig of fresh thyme
½ bunch fresh basil
Sea salt and freshly ground

pepper, to taste
For the Ziti:
1 pound (454 g) whole-wheat ziti
3½ cups marinara sauce
1 cup low-fat cottage cheese
1 cup grated, low-fat mozzarella cheese, divided
¾ cup freshly grated, low-fat Parmesan cheese, divided

Make the marinara sauce: 1. Heat the olive oil in a medium saucepan over medium-high heat. 2. Sauté the onion and garlic, stirring until lightly browned, about 3 minutes. 3. Add the tomatoes and the herb sprigs, and bring to a boil. Lower the heat and simmer, covered, for 10 minutes. Remove and discard the herb sprigs. 4. Stir in sea salt and season with freshly ground pepper to taste. Make the ziti: 1. Preheat the oven to 375ºF (190ºC). 2. Prepare the pasta according to package directions. Drain pasta. Combine the pasta in a bowl with 2 cups marinara sauce, the cottage cheese, and half the mozzarella and Parmesan cheeses. 3. Spread the mixture in a baking dish, and top with the remaining marinara sauce and cheese. 4. Bake for 30–40 minutes, or until bubbly and golden brown.

Per Serving:
calories: 389 | fat: 12g | protein: 18g | carbs: 56g | fiber: 9g | sodium: 369mg

Whole-Wheat Spaghetti à la Puttanesca

Prep time: 5 minutes | Cook time: 20 minutes | Serves 6

1 pound (454 g) dried whole-wheat spaghetti
⅓ cup olive oil
5 garlic cloves, minced or pressed
4 anchovy fillets, chopped
½ teaspoon red pepper flakes
1 teaspoon salt
½ teaspoon freshly ground

black pepper
1 (28-ounce / 794-g) can tomato purée
1 pint cherry tomatoes, halved
½ cup pitted green olives, halved
2 tablespoons drained capers
¾ cup coarsely chopped basil

1. Cook the pasta according to the package instructions. 2. Meanwhile, heat the oil in a large skillet over medium-high heat. Add the garlic, anchovies, red pepper flakes, salt, and pepper. Cook, stirring frequently, until the garlic just begins to turn golden brown, 2 to 3 minutes. Add the tomato purée, olives, cherry tomatoes, and capers and let the mixture simmer, reducing the heat if necessary, and stirring occasionally, until the pasta is done, about 10 minutes. 3. Drain the pasta in a colander and then add it to the sauce, tossing with tongs until the pasta is well coated. Serve hot, garnished with the basil.

Per Serving:
calories: 464 | fat: 17g | protein: 12g | carbs: 70g | fiber: 12g | sodium: 707mg

Rotini with Spinach, Cherry Tomatoes, and Feta

Prep time: 5 minutes | Cook time: 30 minutes | Serves 2

6 ounces (170 g) uncooked rotini pasta (penne pasta will also work)
1 garlic clove, minced
3 tablespoons extra virgin olive oil, divided
1½ cups cherry tomatoes, halved and divided

9 ounces (255 g) baby leaf spinach, washed and chopped
1½ ounces (43 g) crumbled feta, divided
Kosher salt, to taste
Freshly ground black pepper, to taste

1. Cook the pasta according to the package instructions, reserving ½ cup of the cooking water. Drain and set aside. 2. While the pasta is cooking, combine the garlic with 2 tablespoons of the olive oil in a small bowl. Set aside. 3. Add the remaining tablespoon of olive oil to a medium pan placed over medium heat and then add 1 cup of the tomatoes. Cook for 2–3 minutes, then use a fork to mash lightly. 4. Add the spinach to the pan and continue cooking, stirring occasionally, until the spinach is wilted and the liquid is absorbed, about 4–5 minutes. 5. Transfer the cooked pasta to the pan with the spinach and tomatoes. Add 3 tablespoons of the pasta water, the garlic and olive oil mixture, and 1 ounce (28 g) of the crumbled feta. Increase the heat to high and cook for 1 minute. 6. Top with the remaining cherry tomatoes and feta, and season to taste with kosher salt and black pepper. Store covered in the refrigerator for up to 2 days.

Per Serving:
calories: 602 | fat: 27g | protein: 19g | carbs: 74g | fiber: 7g | sodium: 307mg

Simple Pesto Pasta

**Prep time: 10 minutes | Cook time: 10 minutes |
Serves 4 to 6**

1 pound (454 g) spaghetti
4 cups fresh basil leaves, stems removed
3 cloves garlic
1 teaspoon salt
½ teaspoon freshly ground

black pepper
¼ cup lemon juice
½ cup pine nuts, toasted
½ cup grated Parmesan cheese
1 cup extra-virgin olive oil

1. Bring a large pot of salted water to a boil. Add the spaghetti to the pot and cook for 8 minutes. 2. Put basil, garlic, salt, pepper, lemon juice, pine nuts, and Parmesan cheese in a food processor bowl with chopping blade and purée. 3. While the processor is running, slowly drizzle the olive oil through the top opening. Process until all the olive oil has been added. 4. Reserve ½ cup of the pasta water. Drain the pasta and put it into a bowl. Immediately add the pesto and pasta water to the pasta and toss everything together. Serve warm.

Per Serving:
calories: 1067 | fat: 72g | protein: 23g | carbs: 91g | fiber: 6g | sodium: 817mg

Tahini Soup

Prep time: 5 minutes | Cook time: 4 minutes | Serves 6

2 cups orzo	½ teaspoon ground black
8 cups water	pepper
1 tablespoon olive oil	½ cup tahini
1 teaspoon salt	¼ cup lemon juice

1. Add pasta, water, oil, salt, and pepper to the Instant Pot®. Close lid, set steam release to Sealing, press the Manual button, and set time to 4 minutes. When the timer beeps, quick-release the pressure until the float valve drops, and open lid. Set aside. 2. Add tahini to a small mixing bowl and slowly add lemon juice while whisking constantly. Once lemon juice has been incorporated, take about ½ cup hot broth from the pot and slowly add to tahini mixture while whisking, until creamy smooth. 3. Pour mixture into the soup and mix well. Serve immediately.

Per Serving:
calories: 338 | fat: 13g | protein: 12g | carbs: 49g | fiber: 5g | sodium: 389mg

Penne with Tuna and Green Olives

Prep time: 5 minutes | Cook time: 5 minutes | Serves 4

2 tablespoons olive oil	olive oil (don't drain off the oil)
3 garlic cloves, minced	½ teaspoon wine vinegar
½ cup green olives	12 ounces (340 g) penne pasta,
½ teaspoon salt	cooked according to package
¼ teaspoon freshly ground	directions
black pepper	2 tablespoons chopped flat-leaf
2 (6-ounce / 170-g) cans tuna in	parsley

1. Heat the olive oil in a medium skillet over medium heat. Add the garlic and cook, stirring, 2 to 3 minutes, just until the garlic begins to brown. Add the olives, salt, pepper, and the tuna along with its oil. Cook, stirring, for a minute or two to heat the ingredients through. Remove from the heat and stir in the vinegar. 2. Add the cooked pasta to the skillet and toss to combine the pasta with the sauce. Serve immediately, garnished with the parsley.

Per Serving:
calories: 511 | fat: 22g | protein: 31g | carbs: 52g | fiber: 1g | sodium: 826mg

Avgolemono

Prep time: 10 minutes | Cook time: 3 minutes | Serves 6

6 cups chicken stock	pepper
½ cup orzo	¼ cup lemon juice
1 tablespoon olive oil	2 large eggs
12 ounces (340 g) cooked	2 tablespoons chopped fresh
chicken breast, shredded	dill
½ teaspoon salt	1 tablespoon chopped fresh flat-
½ teaspoon ground black	leaf parsley

1. Add stock, orzo, and olive oil to the Instant Pot®. Close lid, set steam release to Sealing, press the Manual button, and set time to 3 minutes. When the timer beeps, quick-release the pressure until the float valve drops. Open lid and stir in chicken, salt, and pepper. 2. In a medium bowl, combine lemon juice and eggs, then slowly whisk in hot cooking liquid from the pot, ¼ cup at a time, until 1 cup of liquid has been added. Immediately add egg mixture to soup and stir well. Let stand on the Keep Warm setting, stirring occasionally, for 10 minutes. Add dill and parsley. Serve immediately.

Per Serving:
calories: 193 | fat: 5g | protein: 21g | carbs: 15g | fiber: 1g | sodium: 552mg

Rotini with Red Wine Marinara

Prep time: 10 minutes | Cook time: 25 minutes | Serves 6

1 pound (454 g) rotini	crushed tomatoes
4 cups water	½ cup red wine
1 tablespoon olive oil	1 teaspoon sugar
½ medium yellow onion, peeled	2 tablespoons chopped fresh
and diced	basil
3 cloves garlic, peeled and	½ teaspoon salt
minced	¼ teaspoon ground black
1 (15-ounce / 425-g) can	pepper

1. Add pasta and water to the Instant Pot®. Close lid, set steam release to Sealing, press the Manual button, and set time to 4 minutes. When the timer beeps, quick-release the pressure until the float valve drops and open the lid. Press the Cancel button. Drain pasta and set aside. 2. Clean pot and return to machine. Press the Sauté button and heat oil. Add onion and cook until it begins to caramelize, about 10 minutes. Add garlic and cook 30 seconds. Add tomatoes, red wine, and sugar, and simmer for 10 minutes. Add basil, salt, pepper, and pasta. Serve immediately.

Per Serving:
calories: 320 | fat: 4g | protein: 10g | carbs: 59g | fiber: 4g | sodium: 215mg

Quick Shrimp Fettuccine

Prep time: 10 minutes | Cook time: 10 minutes |
Serves 4 to 6

8 ounces (227 g) fettuccine	⅓ cup lemon juice
pasta	1 tablespoon lemon zest
¼ cup extra-virgin olive oil	½ teaspoon salt
3 tablespoons garlic, minced	½ teaspoon freshly ground
1 pound (454 g) large shrimp	black pepper
(21-25), peeled and deveined	

1. Bring a large pot of salted water to a boil. Add the fettuccine and cook for 8 minutes. 2. In a large saucepan over medium heat, cook the olive oil and garlic for 1 minute. 3. Add the shrimp to the saucepan and cook for 3 minutes on each side. Remove the shrimp from the pan and set aside. 4. Add the lemon juice and lemon zest to the saucepan, along with the salt and pepper. 5. Reserve ½ cup of the pasta water and drain the pasta. 6. Add the pasta water to the saucepan with the lemon juice and zest and stir everything together. Add the pasta and toss together to evenly coat the pasta. Transfer the pasta to a serving dish and top with the cooked shrimp. Serve warm.

Per Serving:
calories: 615 | fat: 17g | protein: 33g | carbs: 89g | fiber: 4g | sodium: 407mg

Pine Nut and Currant Couscous with Butternut Squash

Prep time: 10 minutes | Cook time: 50 minutes | Serves 4

3 tablespoons olive oil
1 medium onion, chopped
3 cloves garlic, minced
6 canned plum tomatoes, crushed
1 cinnamon stick
1 teaspoon ground coriander
1 teaspoon ground cumin
1 teaspoon salt, divided
¼ teaspoon red pepper flakes
1½ pounds (680 g) diced butternut squash

1 (16-ounce / 454-g) can chickpeas, drained and rinsed
4½ cups vegetable broth, divided
1-inch strip lemon zest
½ cup currants
4 cups (about 5 ounces / 142 g) chopped spinach
Juice of ½ lemon
¼ teaspoon pepper
1 cup whole-wheat couscous
¼ cup toasted pine nuts

1. Heat the olive oil in a medium saucepan set over medium heat. Add the onion and cook, stirring frequently, until softened and lightly browned, about 10 minutes. Stir in the garlic, tomatoes, cinnamon stick, coriander, cumin, ½ teaspoon of the salt, and the red pepper flakes and cook for about 3 minutes more, until the tomatoes begin to break down. Stir in the butternut squash, chickpeas, 3 cups broth, lemon zest, and currants and bring to a simmer. 2. Partially cover the pan and cook for about 25 minutes, until the squash is tender. Add the spinach and cook, stirring, for 2 or 3 more minutes, until the spinach is wilted. Stir in the lemon juice. 3. While the vegetables are cooking, prepare the couscous. Combine the remaining 1½ cups broth, the remaining ½ teaspoon of salt, and the pepper in a small saucepan and bring to a boil. Remove the pan from the heat and stir in the couscous. Cover immediately and let sit for about 5 minutes, until the liquid has been fully absorbed. Fluff with a fork. 4. Spoon the couscous into serving bowls, top with the vegetable and chickpea mixture, and sprinkle some of the pine nuts over the top of each bowl. Serve immediately.

Per Serving:
calories: 549 | fat: 19g | protein: 16g | carbs: 84g | fiber: 14g | sodium: 774mg

Neapolitan Pasta and Zucchini

Prep time: 5 minutes | Cook time: 28 minutes | Serves 3

⅓ cup extra virgin olive oil
1 large onion (any variety), diced
1 teaspoon fine sea salt, divided
2 large zucchini, quartered lengthwise and cut into ½-inch pieces
10 ounces (283 g) uncooked spaghetti, broken into 1-inch

pieces
2 tablespoons grated Parmesan cheese
2 ounces (57 g) grated or shaved Parmesan cheese for serving
½ teaspoon freshly ground black pepper

1. Add the olive oil to a medium pot over medium heat. When the oil begins to shimmer, add the onions and ¼ teaspoon of the sea salt. Sauté for 3 minutes, add the zucchini, and continue sautéing for 3 more minutes. 2. Add 2 cups of hot water to the pot or enough to just cover the zucchini (the amount of water may vary depending on the size of the pot). Cover, reduce the heat to low, and simmer for 10 minutes. 3. Add the pasta to the pot, stir, then add 2 more cups of hot water. Continue simmering, stirring occasionally, until the pasta is cooked and the mixture has thickened, about 12 minutes. (If the pasta appears to be dry or undercooked, add small amounts of hot water to the pot to ensure the pasta is covered in the water.). When the pasta is cooked, remove the pot from the heat. Add 2 tablespoons of the grated Parmesan and stir. 4. Divide the pasta into three servings and then top each with 1 ounce (28 g) of the grated or shaved Parmesan. Sprinkle the remaining sea salt and black pepper over the top of each serving. Store covered in the refrigerator for up to 3 days.

Per Serving:
calories: 718 | fat: 33g | protein: 24g | carbs: 83g | fiber: 6g | sodium: 815mg

Puglia-Style Pasta with Broccoli Sauce

Prep time: 15 minutes | Cook time: 25 minutes | Serves 3

1 pound (454 g) fresh broccoli, washed and cut into small florets
7 ounces (198 g) uncooked rigatoni pasta
2 tablespoons extra virgin olive oil, plus 1½ tablespoons for serving
3 garlic cloves, thinly sliced
2 tablespoons pine nuts

4 canned packed-in-oil anchovies
½ teaspoon kosher salt
3 teaspoons fresh lemon juice
3 ounces (85 g) grated or shaved Parmesan cheese, divided
½ teaspoon freshly ground black pepper

1. Place the broccoli in a large pot filled with enough water to cover the broccoli. Bring the pot to a boil and cook for 12 minutes or until the stems can be easily pierced with a fork. Use a slotted spoon to transfer the broccoli to a plate, but do not discard the cooking water. Set the broccoli aside. 2. Add the pasta to the pot with the broccoli water and cook according to package instructions. 3. About 3 minutes before the pasta is ready, place a large, deep pan over medium heat and add 2 tablespoons of the olive oil. When the olive oil is shimmering, add the garlic and sauté for 1 minute, stirring continuously, until the garlic is golden, then add the pine nuts and continue sautéing for 1 more minute. 4. Stir in the anchovies, using a wooden spoon to break them into smaller pieces, then add the broccoli. Continue cooking for 1 additional minute, stirring continuously and using the spoon to break the broccoli into smaller pieces. 5. When the pasta is ready, remove the pot from the heat and drain, reserving ¼ cup of the cooking water. 6. Add the pasta and 2 tablespoons of the cooking water to the pan, stirring until all the ingredients are well combined. Cook for 1 minute, then remove the pan from the heat. 7. Promptly divide the pasta among three plates. Top each serving with a pinch of kosher salt, 1 teaspoon of the lemon juice, 1 ounce (28 g) of the Parmesan, 1½ teaspoons of the remaining olive oil, and a pinch of fresh ground pepper. Store covered in the refrigerator for up to 3 days.

Per Serving:
calories: 610 | fat: 31g | protein: 24g | carbs: 66g | fiber: 12g | sodium: 654mg

No-Drain Pasta alla Norma

Prep time: 5 minutes |Cook time: 25 minutes| Serves: 6

1 medium globe eggplant (about 1 pound / 454 g), cut into ¾-inch cubes	part-skim ricotta cheese
	3 Roma tomatoes, chopped (about 2 cups)
1 tablespoon extra-virgin olive oil	2 garlic cloves, minced (about 1 teaspoon)
1 cup chopped onion (about ½ medium onion)	¼ teaspoon kosher or sea salt
	½ cup loosely packed fresh basil leaves
8 ounces (227 g) uncooked thin spaghetti	Grated Parmesan cheese, for serving (optional)
1 (15-ounce / 425-g) container	

1. Lay three paper towels on a large plate, and pile the cubed eggplant on top. (Don't cover the eggplant.) Microwave the eggplant on high for 5 minutes to dry and partially cook it. 2. In a large stockpot over medium-high heat, heat the oil. Add the eggplant and the onion and cook for 5 minutes, stirring occasionally. 3. Add the spaghetti, ricotta, tomatoes, garlic, and salt. Cover with water by a ½ inch (about 4 cups of water). Cook uncovered for 12 to 15 minutes, or until the pasta is just al dente (tender with a bite), stirring occasionally to prevent the pasta from sticking together or sticking to the bottom of the pot. 4. Remove the pot from the heat and let the pasta stand for 3 more minutes to absorb more liquid while you tear the basil into pieces. Sprinkle the basil over the pasta and gently stir. Serve with Parmesan cheese, if desired.

Per Serving:
calories: 299 | fat: 9g | protein: 15g | carbs: 41g | fiber: 5g | sodium: 174mg

Roasted Asparagus Caprese Pasta

Prep time: 10 minutes |Cook time: 15 minutes| Serves: 6

8 ounces (227 g) uncooked small pasta, like orecchiette (little ears) or farfalle (bow ties)	oil
	¼ teaspoon freshly ground black pepper
1½ pounds (680 g) fresh asparagus, ends trimmed and stalks chopped into 1-inch pieces (about 3 cups)	¼ teaspoon kosher or sea salt
	2 cups fresh mozzarella, drained and cut into bite-size pieces (about 8 ounces / 227 g)
1 pint grape tomatoes, halved (about 1½ cups)	⅓ cup torn fresh basil leaves
2 tablespoons extra-virgin olive	2 tablespoons balsamic vinegar

1. Preheat the oven to 400°F(205°C). 2. In a large stockpot, cook the pasta according to the package directions. Drain, reserving about ¼ cup of the pasta water. 3. While the pasta is cooking, in a large bowl, toss the asparagus, tomatoes, oil, pepper, and salt together. Spread the mixture onto a large, rimmed baking sheet and bake for 15 minutes, stirring twice as it cooks. 4. Remove the vegetables from the oven, and add the cooked pasta to the baking sheet. Mix with a few tablespoons of pasta water to help the sauce become smoother and the saucy vegetables stick to the pasta. 5. Gently mix in the mozzarella and basil. Drizzle with the balsamic vinegar. Serve from the baking sheet or pour the pasta into a large bowl. 6. If you want to make this dish ahead of time or to serve it cold, follow the recipe up to step 4, then refrigerate the pasta and vegetables. When you are ready to serve, follow step 5 either with

the cold pasta or with warm pasta that's been gently reheated in a pot on the stove.

Per Serving:
calories: 317 | fat: 12g | protein: 16g | carbs: 38g | fiber: 7g | sodium: 110mg

Zucchini with Bow Ties

Prep time: 5 minutes |Cook time: 25 minutes| Serves: 4

3 tablespoons extra-virgin olive oil	¼ teaspoon ground nutmeg
	8 ounces (227 g) uncooked farfalle (bow ties) or other small pasta shape
2 garlic cloves, minced (about 1 teaspoon)	
3 large or 4 medium zucchini, diced (about 4 cups)	½ cup grated Parmesan or Romano cheese (about 2 ounces / 57 g)
½ teaspoon freshly ground black pepper	1 tablespoon freshly squeezed lemon juice (from ½ medium lemon)
¼ teaspoon kosher or sea salt	
½ cup 2% milk	

1. In a large skillet over medium heat, heat the oil. Add the garlic and cook for 1 minute, stirring frequently. Add the zucchini, pepper, and salt. Stir well, cover, and cook for 15 minutes, stirring once or twice. 2. In a small, microwave-safe bowl, warm the milk in the microwave on high for 30 seconds. Stir the milk and nutmeg into the skillet and cook uncovered for another 5 minutes, stirring occasionally. 3. While the zucchini is cooking, in a large stockpot, cook the pasta according to the package directions. 4. Drain the pasta in a colander, saving about 2 tablespoons of pasta water. Add the pasta and pasta water to the skillet. Mix everything together and remove from the heat. Stir in the cheese and lemon juice and serve.

Per Serving:
calories: 405 | fat: 16g | protein: 12g | carbs: 57g | fiber: 9g | sodium: 407mg

Walnut Spaghetti

Prep time: 10 minutes | Cook time: 20 minutes | Serves 6

1 pound (454 g) whole-wheat spaghetti	cheese
	½ cup freshly grated, lowfat Parmesan cheese
½ cup olive oil	¼ cup flat-leaf parsley, chopped
4 cloves garlic, minced	Sea salt and freshly ground pepper, to taste
¾ cup walnuts, toasted and finely chopped	
2 tablespoons low-fat ricotta	

1. Prepare the spaghetti in boiling water according to package directions for al dente, reserving 1 cup of the pasta water. 2. Heat the olive oil in a large skillet on medium-low heat. Add the garlic and sauté for 1–2 minutes. 3. Ladle ½ cup of the pasta water into the skillet, and continue to simmer for 5–10 minutes. 4. Add the chopped walnuts and ricotta cheese. 5. Toss the walnut sauce with the spaghetti in a large serving bowl. Top with the Parmesan cheese and parsley. Season and serve.

Per Serving:
calories: 551 | fat: 31g | protein: 16g | carbs: 60g | fiber: 7g | sodium: 141mg

Chapter 8 Pizzas, Wraps, and Sandwiches

Turkish Pizza

Prep time: 20 minutes | Cook time: 10 minutes | Serves 4

4 ounces (113 g) ground lamb or 85% lean ground beef
¼ cup finely chopped green bell pepper
¼ cup chopped fresh parsley
1 small plum tomato, seeded and finely chopped
2 tablespoons finely chopped yellow onion
1 garlic clove, minced
2 teaspoons tomato paste
¼ teaspoon sweet paprika

¼ teaspoon ground cumin
⅛ to ¼ teaspoon red pepper flakes
⅛ teaspoon ground allspice
⅛ teaspoon kosher salt
⅛ teaspoon black pepper
4 (6-inch) flour tortillas
For Serving:
Chopped fresh mint
Extra-virgin olive oil
Lemon wedges

1. In a medium bowl, gently mix the ground lamb, bell pepper, parsley, chopped tomato, onion, garlic, tomato paste, paprika, cumin, red pepper flakes, allspice, salt, and black pepper until well combined. 2. Divide the meat mixture evenly among the tortillas, spreading it all the way to the edge of each tortilla. 3. Place 1 tortilla in the air fryer basket. Set the air fryer to 400ºF (204ºC) for 10 minutes, or until the meat topping has browned and the edge of the tortilla is golden. Transfer to a plate and repeat to cook the remaining tortillas. 4. Serve the pizzas warm, topped with chopped fresh mint and a drizzle of extra-virgin olive oil and with lemon wedges alongside.

Per Serving:
calories: 172 | fat: 8g | protein: 8g | carbs: 18g | fiber: 2g | sodium: 318mg

Beans and Greens Pizza

Prep time: 11 minutes | Cook time: 14 to 19 minutes | Serves 4

¾ cup whole-wheat pastry flour
½ teaspoon low-sodium baking powder
1 tablespoon olive oil, divided
1 cup chopped kale
2 cups chopped fresh baby spinach

1 cup canned no-salt-added cannellini beans, rinsed and drained
½ teaspoon dried thyme
1 piece low-sodium string cheese, torn into pieces

1. In a small bowl, mix the pastry flour and baking powder until well combined. 2. Add ¼ cup of water and 2 teaspoons of olive oil. Mix until a dough forms. 3. On a floured surface, press or roll the dough into a 7-inch round. Set aside while you cook the greens. 4. In a baking pan, mix the kale, spinach, and remaining teaspoon of the olive oil. Air fry at 350ºF (177ºC) for 3 to 5 minutes, until the greens are wilted. Drain well. 5. Put the pizza dough into the air fryer basket. Top with the greens, cannellini beans, thyme, and string cheese. Air fry for 11 to 14 minutes, or until the crust is golden brown and the cheese is melted. Cut into quarters to serve.

Per Serving:
calories: 181 | fat: 6g | protein: 8g | carbs: 27g | fiber: 6g | sodium: 103mg

Dill Salmon Salad Wraps

Prep time: 10 minutes |Cook time: 10 minutes| Serves:6

1 pound (454 g) salmon filet, cooked and flaked, or 3 (5-ounce / 142-g) cans salmon
½ cup diced carrots (about 1 carrot)
½ cup diced celery (about 1 celery stalk)
3 tablespoons chopped fresh dill
3 tablespoons diced red onion (a little less than ⅛ onion)

2 tablespoons capers
1½ tablespoons extra-virgin olive oil
1 tablespoon aged balsamic vinegar
½ teaspoon freshly ground black pepper
¼ teaspoon kosher or sea salt
4 whole-wheat flatbread wraps or soft whole-wheat tortillas

1. In a large bowl, mix together the salmon, carrots, celery, dill, red onion, capers, oil, vinegar, pepper, and salt. 2. Divide the salmon salad among the flatbreads. Fold up the bottom of the flatbread, then roll up the wrap and serve.

Per Serving:
calories: 185 | fat: 8g | protein: 17g | carbs: 12g | fiber: 2g | sodium: 237mg

Barbecue Chicken Pita Pizza

Prep time: 5 minutes | Cook time: 5 to 7 minutes per batch | Makes 4 pizzas

1 cup barbecue sauce, divided
4 pita breads
2 cups shredded cooked chicken
2 cups shredded Mozzarella

cheese
½ small red onion, thinly sliced
2 tablespoons finely chopped fresh cilantro

1. Measure ½ cup of the barbecue sauce in a small measuring cup. Spread 2 tablespoons of the barbecue sauce on each pita. 2. In a medium bowl, mix together the remaining ½ cup of barbecue sauce and chicken. Place ½ cup of the chicken on each pita. Top each pizza with ½ cup of the Mozzarella cheese. Sprinkle the tops of the pizzas with the red onion. 3. Place one pizza in the air fryer. Air fry at 400ºF (204ºC) for 5 to 7 minutes. Repeat this process with the remaining pizzas. 4. Top the pizzas with the cilantro.

Per Serving:
calories: 530 | fat: 19g | protein: 40g | carbs: 47g | fiber: 2g | sodium: 672mg

Za'atar Pizza

Prep time: 10 minutes | Cook time: 15 minutes | Serves 4 to 6

1 sheet puff pastry
¼ cup extra-virgin olive oil

⅓ cup za'atar seasoning

1. Preheat the oven to 350°F(180°C). 2. Put the puff pastry on a parchment-lined baking sheet. Cut the pastry into desired slices. 3. Brush the pastry with olive oil. Sprinkle with the za'atar. 4. Put the pastry in the oven and bake for 10 to 12 minutes or until edges are lightly browned and puffed up. Serve warm or at room temperature.

Per Serving:
calories: 374 | fat: 30g | protein: 3g | carbs: 20g | fiber: 1g | sodium: 166mg

Grilled Eggplant and Feta Sandwiches

Prep time: 10 minutes | Cook time: 8 minutes | Serves 2

1 medium eggplant, sliced into ½-inch-thick slices
2 tablespoons olive oil
Sea salt and freshly ground pepper, to taste
5 to 6 tablespoons hummus

4 slices whole-wheat bread, toasted
1 cup baby spinach leaves
2 ounces (57 g) feta cheese, softened

1. Preheat a gas or charcoal grill to medium-high heat. 2. Salt both sides of the sliced eggplant, and let sit for 20 minutes to draw out the bitter juices. 3. Rinse the eggplant and pat dry with a paper towel. 4. Brush the eggplant slices with olive oil and season with sea salt and freshly ground pepper. 5. Grill the eggplant until lightly charred on both sides but still slightly firm in the middle, about 3–4 minutes a side. 6. Spread the hummus on the bread and top with the spinach leaves, feta, and eggplant. Top with the other slice of bread and serve warm.

Per Serving:
calories: 516 | fat: 27g | protein: 14g | carbs: 59g | fiber: 14g | sodium: 597mg

Mediterranean Tuna Salad Sandwiches

Prep time: 10 minutes | Cook time: 5 minutes | Serves 2

1 can white tuna, packed in water or olive oil, drained
1 roasted red pepper, diced
½ small red onion, diced
10 low-salt olives, pitted and finely chopped
¼ cup plain Greek yogurt

1 tablespoon flat-leaf parsley, chopped
Juice of 1 lemon
Sea salt and freshly ground pepper, to taste
4 whole-grain pieces of bread

1. In a small bowl, combine all of the ingredients except the bread, and mix well. 2. Season with sea salt and freshly ground pepper to taste. Toast the bread or warm in a pan. 3. Make the sandwich and serve immediately.

Per Serving:
calories: 307 | fat: 7g | protein: 30g | carbs: 31g | fiber: 5g | sodium: 564mg

Vegetable Pita Sandwiches

Prep time: 15 minutes | Cook time: 9 to 12 minutes | Serves 4

1 baby eggplant, peeled and chopped
1 red bell pepper, sliced
½ cup diced red onion
½ cup shredded carrot

1 teaspoon olive oil
⅓ cup low-fat Greek yogurt
½ teaspoon dried tarragon
2 low-sodium whole-wheat pita breads, halved crosswise

1. In a baking pan, stir together the eggplant, red bell pepper, red onion, carrot, and olive oil. Put the vegetable mixture into the air fryer basket and roast at 390°F (199°C) for 7 to 9 minutes, stirring once, until the vegetables are tender. Drain if necessary. 2. In a small bowl, thoroughly mix the yogurt and tarragon until well combined. 3. Stir the yogurt mixture into the vegetables. Stuff one-fourth of this mixture into each pita pocket. 4. Place the sandwiches in the air fryer and cook for 2 to 3 minutes, or until the bread is toasted. Serve immediately.

Per Serving:
calories: 115 | fat: 2g | protein: 4g | carbs: 22g | fiber: 6g | sodium: 90mg

Mediterranean-Pita Wraps

Prep time: 5 minutes | Cook time: 14 minutes | Serves 4

1 pound (454 g) mackerel fish fillets
2 tablespoons olive oil
1 tablespoon Mediterranean seasoning mix
½ teaspoon chili powder

Sea salt and freshly ground black pepper, to taste
2 ounces (57 g) feta cheese, crumbled
4 tortillas

1. Toss the fish fillets with the olive oil; place them in the lightly oiled air fryer basket. 2. Air fry the fish fillets at 400°F (204°C) for about 14 minutes, turning them over halfway through the cooking time. 3. Assemble your pitas with the chopped fish and remaining ingredients and serve warm.

Per Serving:
calories: 275 | fat: 13g | protein: 27g | carbs: 13g | fiber: 2g | sodium: 322mg

Pesto Chicken Mini Pizzas

Prep time: 5 minutes | Cook time: 10 minutes | Serves 4

2 cups shredded cooked chicken
¾ cup pesto
4 English muffins, split

2 cups shredded Mozzarella cheese

1. In a medium bowl, toss the chicken with the pesto. Place one-eighth of the chicken on each English muffin half. Top each English muffin with ¼ cup of the Mozzarella cheese. 2. Put four pizzas at a time in the air fryer and air fry at 350°F (177°C) for 5 minutes. Repeat this process with the other four pizzas.

Per Serving:
calories: 617 | fat: 36g | protein: 45g | carbs: 29g | fiber: 3g | sodium: 544mg

Cucumber Basil Sandwiches

Prep time: 10 minutes | Cook time: 0 minutes | Serves 2

Cucumber Basil Sandwiches
Prep time: 10 minutes | Cook
time: 0 minutes | Serves 2
4 slices whole-grain bread

¼ cup hummus
1 large cucumber, thinly sliced
4 whole basil leaves

1. Spread the hummus on 2 slices of bread, and layer the cucumbers onto it. Top with the basil leaves and close the sandwiches. 2. Press down lightly and serve immediately.
Per Serving:
calories: 209 | fat: 5g | protein: 9g | carbs: 32g | fiber: 6g | sodium: 275mg

Jerk Chicken Wraps

Prep time: 30 minutes | Cook time: 15 minutes | Serves 4

1 pound (454 g) boneless, skinless chicken tenderloins
1 cup jerk marinade
Olive oil
4 large low-carb tortillas

1 cup julienned carrots
1 cup peeled cucumber ribbons
1 cup shredded lettuce
1 cup mango or pineapple chunks

1. In a medium bowl, coat the chicken with the jerk marinade, cover, and refrigerate for 1 hour. 2. Spray the air fryer basket lightly with olive oil. 3. Place the chicken in the air fryer basket in a single layer and spray lightly with olive oil. You may need to cook the chicken in batches. Reserve any leftover marinade. 4. Air fry at 375°F (191°C) for 8 minutes. Turn the chicken over and brush with some of the remaining marinade. Cook until the chicken reaches an internal temperature of at least 165°F (74°C), an additional 5 to 7 minutes. 5. To assemble the wraps, fill each tortilla with ¼ cup carrots, ¼ cup cucumber, ¼ cup lettuce, and ¼ cup mango. Place one quarter of the chicken tenderloins on top and roll up the tortilla. These are great served warm or cold.
Per Serving:
calories: 241 | fat: 4g | protein: 28g | carbs: 23g | fiber: 4g | sodium: 85mg

Margherita Open-Face Sandwiches

Prep time: 10 minutes |Cook time: 5 minutes| Serves 4

2 (6- to 7-inch) whole-wheat submarine or hoagie rolls, sliced open horizontally
1 tablespoon extra-virgin olive oil
1 garlic clove, halved
1 large ripe tomato, cut into 8 slices

¼ teaspoon dried oregano
1 cup fresh mozzarella (about 4 ounces / 113 g), patted dry and sliced
¼ cup lightly packed fresh basil leaves, torn into small pieces
¼ teaspoon freshly ground black pepper

1. Preheat the broiler to high with the rack 4 inches under the heating element. 2. Place the sliced bread on a large, rimmed baking sheet. Place under the broiler for 1 minute, until the bread is just lightly toasted. Remove from the oven. 3. Brush each piece of the toasted bread with the oil, and rub a garlic half over each piece. 4. Place the toasted bread back on the baking sheet. Evenly distribute the tomato slices on each piece, sprinkle with the oregano, and layer the cheese on top. 5. Place the baking sheet under the broiler. Set the timer for 1½ minutes, but check after 1 minute. When the cheese is melted and the edges are just starting to get dark brown, remove the sandwiches from the oven (this can take anywhere from 1½ to 2 minutes). 6. Top each sandwich with the fresh basil and pepper.
Per Serving:
calories: 176 | fat: 9g | protein: 10g | carbs: 14g | fiber: 2g | sodium: 119mg

Mexican Pizza

Prep time: 10 minutes | Cook time: 7 to 9 minutes | Serves 4

¾ cup refried beans (from a 16-ounce / 454-g can)
½ cup salsa
10 frozen precooked beef meatballs, thawed and sliced
1 jalapeño pepper, sliced

4 whole-wheat pita breads
1 cup shredded pepper Jack cheese
½ cup shredded Colby cheese
⅓ cup sour cream

1. In a medium bowl, combine the refried beans, salsa, meatballs, and jalapeño pepper. 2. Preheat the air fryer for 3 to 4 minutes or until hot. 3. Top the pitas with the refried bean mixture and sprinkle with the cheeses. 4. Bake at 370°F (188°C) for 7 to 9 minutes or until the pizza is crisp and the cheese is melted and starts to brown. 5. Top each pizza with a dollop of sour cream and serve warm.
Per Serving:
calories: 484 | fat: 30g | protein: 24g | carbs: 32g | fiber: 7g | sodium: 612mg

Greek Salad Wraps

Prep time: 15 minutes |Cook time: 0 minutes| Serves: 4

1½ cups seedless cucumber, peeled and chopped (about 1 large cucumber)
1 cup chopped tomato (about 1 large tomato)
½ cup finely chopped fresh mint
1 (2¼-ounce / 64-g) can sliced black olives (about ½ cup), drained
¼ cup diced red onion (about ¼

onion)
2 tablespoons extra-virgin olive oil
1 tablespoon red wine vinegar
¼ teaspoon freshly ground black pepper
¼ teaspoon kosher or sea salt
½ cup crumbled goat cheese (about 2 ounces / 57 g)
4 whole-wheat flatbread wraps or soft whole-wheat tortillas

1. In a large bowl, mix together the cucumber, tomato, mint, olives, and onion until well combined. 2. In a small bowl, whisk together the oil, vinegar, pepper, and salt. Drizzle the dressing over the salad, and mix gently. 3. With a knife, spread the goat cheese evenly over the four wraps. Spoon a quarter of the salad filling down the middle of each wrap. 4. Fold up each wrap: Start by folding up the bottom, then fold one side over and fold the other side over the top. Repeat with the remaining wraps and serve.
Per Serving:
calories: 217 | fat: 14g | protein: 7g | carbs: 17g | fiber: 3g | sodium: 329mg

Greek Salad Pita

Prep time: 15 minutes | Cook time: 0 minutes | Serves 4

1 cup chopped romaine lettuce
1 tomato, chopped and seeded
½ cup baby spinach leaves
½ small red onion, thinly sliced
½ small cucumber, chopped and deseeded
2 tablespoons olive oil

1 tablespoon crumbled feta cheese
½ tablespoon red wine vinegar
1 teaspoon Dijon mustard
Sea salt and freshly ground pepper, to taste
1 whole-wheat pita

1. Combine everything except the sea salt, freshly ground pepper, and pita bread in a medium bowl. 2. Toss until the salad is well combined. 3. Season with sea salt and freshly ground pepper to taste. Fill the pita with the salad mixture, serve, and enjoy!

Per Serving:
calories: 123 | fat: 8g | protein: 3g | carbs: 12g | fiber: 2g | sodium: 125mg

Avocado and Asparagus Wraps

Prep time: 10 minutes | Cook time: 10 minutes | Serves 6

12 spears asparagus
1 ripe avocado, mashed slightly
Juice of 1 lime
2 cloves garlic, minced
2 cups brown rice, cooked and chilled

3 tablespoons Greek yogurt
Sea salt and freshly ground pepper, to taste
3 (8-inch) whole-grain tortillas
½ cup cilantro, diced
2 tablespoons red onion, diced

1. Steam asparagus in microwave or stove top steamer until tender. Mash the avocado, lime juice, and garlic in a medium mixing bowl. In a separate bowl, mix the rice and yogurt. 2. Season both mixtures with sea salt and freshly ground pepper to taste. Heat the tortillas in a dry nonstick skillet. 3. Spread each tortilla with the avocado mixture, and top with the rice, cilantro, and onion, followed by the asparagus. 4. Fold up both sides of the tortilla, and roll tightly to close. Cut in half diagonally before serving.

Per Serving:
calories: 361 | fat: 9g | protein: 9g | carbs: 63g | fiber: 7g | sodium: 117mg

Grilled Chicken Salad Pita

Prep time: 15 minutes | Cook time: 16 minutes | Serves 1

1 boneless, skinless chicken breast
Sea salt and freshly ground pepper, to taste
1 cup baby spinach
1 roasted red pepper, sliced
1 tomato, chopped

½ small red onion, thinly sliced
½ small cucumber, chopped
1 tablespoon olive oil
Juice of 1 lemon
1 whole-wheat pita pocket
2 tablespoons crumbled feta cheese

1. Preheat a gas or charcoal grill to medium-high heat. 2. Season the chicken breast with sea salt and freshly ground pepper, and grill until cooked through, about 7–8 minutes per side. 3. Allow chicken to rest for 5 minutes before slicing into strips. 4. While the chicken is cooking, put all the chopped vegetables into a medium-mixing bowl and season with sea salt and freshly ground pepper. 5. Chop

the chicken into cubes and add to salad. Add the olive oil and lemon juice and toss well. 6. Stuff the mixture onto a pita pocket and top with the feta cheese. Serve immediately.

Per Serving:
calories: 653 | fat: 26g | protein: 71g | carbs: 34g | fiber: 6g | sodium: 464mg

Open-Faced Eggplant Parmesan Sandwich

Prep time: 10 minutes | Cook time: 10 minutes | Serves 2

1 small eggplant, sliced into ¼-inch rounds
Pinch sea salt
2 tablespoons olive oil
Sea salt and freshly ground pepper, to taste

2 slices whole-grain bread, thickly cut and toasted
1 cup marinara sauce (no added sugar)
¼ cup freshly grated, low-fat Parmesan cheese

1. Preheat broiler to high heat. 2. Salt both sides of the sliced eggplant, and let sit for 20 minutes to draw out the bitter juices. 3. Rinse the eggplant and pat dry with a paper towel. 4. Brush the eggplant with the olive oil, and season with sea salt and freshly ground pepper. 5. Lay the eggplant on a sheet pan, and broil until crisp, about 4 minutes. Flip over and crisp the other side. 6. Lay the toasted bread on a sheet pan. Spoon some marinara sauce on each slice of bread, and layer the eggplant on top. 7. Sprinkle half of the cheese on top of the eggplant and top with more marinara sauce. 8. Sprinkle with remaining cheese. 9. Put the sandwiches under the broiler until the cheese has melted, about 2 minutes. 10. Using a spatula, transfer the sandwiches to plates and serve.

Per Serving:
calories: 355 | fat: 19g | protein: 10g | carbs: 38g | fiber: 13g | sodium: 334mg

Classic Margherita Pizza

Prep time: 10 minutes | Cook time: 10 minutes | Serves 4

All-purpose flour, for dusting
1 pound (454 g) premade pizza dough
1 (15-ounce / 425-g) can crushed San Marzano tomatoes, with their juices
2 garlic cloves

1 teaspoon Italian seasoning
Pinch sea salt, plus more as needed
1½ teaspoons olive oil, for drizzling
10 slices mozzarella cheese
12 to 15 fresh basil leaves

1. Preheat the oven to 475°F (245°C). 2. On a floured surface, roll out the dough to a 12-inch round and place it on a lightly floured pizza pan or baking sheet. 3. In a food processor, combine the tomatoes with their juices, garlic, Italian seasoning, and salt and process until smooth. Taste and adjust the seasoning. 4. Drizzle the olive oil over the pizza dough, then spoon the pizza sauce over the dough and spread it out evenly with the back of the spoon, leaving a 1-inch border. Evenly distribute the mozzarella over the pizza. 5. Bake until the crust is cooked through and golden, 8 to 10 minutes. Remove from the oven and let sit for 1 to 2 minutes. Top with the basil right before serving.

Per Serving:
calories: 570 | fat: 21g | protein: 28g | carbs: 66g | fiber: 4g | sodium: 570mg

Chapter 9 Snacks and Appetizers

Classic Hummus with Tahini

Prep time: 5 minutes | Cook time: 0 minutes | Makes about 2 cups

2 cups drained canned chickpeas, liquid reserved
½ cup tahini
¼ cup olive oil, plus more for garnish
2 cloves garlic, peeled, or to taste
Juice of 1 lemon, plus more as needed

1 tablespoon ground cumin
Salt
Freshly ground black pepper
1 teaspoon paprika, for garnish
2 tablespoons chopped flat-leaf parsley, for garnish
4 whole-wheat pita bread or flatbread rounds, warmed

1. In a food processor, combine the chickpeas, tahini, oil, garlic, lemon juice, and cumin. Season with salt and pepper, and process until puréed. With the food processor running, add the reserved chickpea liquid until the mixture is smooth and reaches the desired consistency. 2. Spoon the hummus into a serving bowl, drizzle with a bit of olive oil, and sprinkle with the paprika and parsley. 3. Serve immediately, with warmed pita bread or flatbread, or cover and refrigerate for up to 2 days. Bring to room temperature before serving.

Per Serving:
¼ cup: calories: 309 | fat: 16g | protein: 9g | carbs: 36g | fiber: 7g | sodium: 341mg

Salmon Niçoise Salad with Dijon-Chive Dressing

Prep time: 10 minutes | Cook time: 20 minutes | Serves 4

1 pound (454 g) baby or fingerling potatoes
½ pound (227 g) green beans
6 tablespoons olive oil
4 (4-ounce / 113-g) salmon fillets
¼ teaspoon freshly ground black pepper
2 teaspoons Dijon mustard
3 tablespoons red wine vinegar

1 tablespoon, plus 1 teaspoon finely chopped fresh chives
1 head romaine lettuce, sliced cross-wise
2 hard-boiled eggs, quartered
¼ cup Niçoise or other small black olives
1 cup cherry tomatoes, quartered

1. Put potatoes in a large saucepan and add cold water to cover. Bring the water to a boil, then reduce the heat to maintain a simmer and cook for 12 to 15 minutes, until fork-tender. Drain and set aside until cool enough to handle, then cut into cubes. Set aside. 2. Meanwhile, bring a medium saucepan of water to a boil. Add the green beans and cook for 3 minutes. Drain and rinse with cold water to stop the cooking. Set aside. 3. In a large skillet, heat 1 tablespoon of the olive oil over medium-high heat. Season the salmon with pepper. Add the salmon to the pan and cook for 4 to 5 minutes on each side. Transfer to a platter; keep warm. 4. In a small bowl, whisk together the mustard, vinegar, 1 tablespoon of chives, and remaining 5 tablespoons olive oil. 5. Divide the lettuce evenly among four plates. Add 1 salmon fillet to each plate. Divide the potatoes, green beans, eggs, olives, and tomatoes among the plates and drizzle with the dressing. 6.Sprinkle with the remaining 1 teaspoon chives and serve.

Per Serving:
1 cup: calories: 398 | fat: 25g | protein: 15g | carbs: 30g | fiber: 8g | sodium: 173mg

Goat Cheese and Garlic Crostini

Prep time: 3 minutes | Cook time: 5 minutes | Serves 4

1 whole wheat baguette
¼ cup olive oil
2 garlic cloves, minced

4 ounces (113 g) goat cheese
2 tablespoons fresh basil, minced

1. Preheat the air fryer to 380°F(193°C). 2. Cut the baguette into ½-inch-thick slices. 3. In a small bowl, mix together the olive oil and garlic, then brush it over one side of each slice of bread. 4. Place the olive-oil-coated bread in a single layer in the air fryer basket and bake for 5 minutes. 5. Meanwhile, in a small bowl, mix together the goat cheese and basil. 6. Remove the toast from the air fryer, then spread a thin layer of the goat cheese mixture over the top of each piece and serve.

Per Serving:
calories: 315 | fat: 24g | protein: 11g | carbs: 14g | fiber: 1g | sodium: 265mg

Taco-Spiced Chickpeas

Prep time: 5 minutes | Cook time: 17 minutes | Serves 3

Oil, for spraying
1 (15½-ounce / 439-g) can chickpeas, drained
1 teaspoon chili powder

½ teaspoon ground cumin
½ teaspoon salt
½ teaspoon granulated garlic
2 teaspoons lime juice

1. Line the air fryer basket with parchment and spray lightly with oil. Place the chickpeas in the prepared basket. 2. Air fry at 390ºF (199°C) for 17 minutes, shaking or stirring the chickpeas and spraying lightly with oil every 5 to 7 minutes. 3. In a small bowl, mix together the chili powder, cumin, salt, and garlic. 4. When 2 to 3 minutes of cooking time remain, sprinkle half of the seasoning mix over the chickpeas. Finish cooking. 5. Transfer the chickpeas to a medium bowl and toss with the remaining seasoning mix and the lime juice. Serve immediately.

Per Serving:
calories: 208 | fat: 4g | protein: 11g | carbs: 34g | fiber: 10g | sodium: 725mg

Sardine and Herb Bruschetta

Prep time: 5 minutes | Cook time: 10 minutes | Serves 4

8 (1-inch) thick whole-grain baguette slices
1½ tablespoons extra virgin olive oil
4 ounces (113 g) olive oil–packed sardines
2 tablespoons fresh lemon juice
1 teaspoon red wine vinegar

2 tablespoons capers, drained
3 tablespoons finely chopped onion (any variety)
½ teaspoon dried oregano
1 tablespoon finely chopped fresh mint
1 garlic clove, halved

1. Preheat the oven to 400°F (205°C). 2. Place the baguette slices on a large baking sheet and brush them with the olive oil. Transfer to the oven and toast until the slices are golden, about 10 minutes. 3. While the baguette slices are toasting, make the sardine topping by combining the sardines, lemon juice, and vinegar in a medium bowl. Mash with a fork. Add the capers, onions, oregano, and mint, and stir to combine. 4. When the baguette slices are done toasting, remove them from the oven and rub them with the garlic. 5. Transfer the slices to a serving platter. Place 1 heaping tablespoon of the topping onto each baguette slice. Store the sardine topping in the refrigerator for up to 3 days.

Per Serving:
calories: 249 | fat: 11g | protein: 14g | carbs: 24g | fiber: 4g | sodium: 387mg

Salmon-Stuffed Cucumbers

Prep time: 10 minutes | Cook time: 0 minutes | Serves 4

2 large cucumbers, peeled
1 (4-ounce / 113-g) can red salmon
1 medium very ripe avocado, peeled, pitted, and mashed
1 tablespoon extra-virgin olive oil

Zest and juice of 1 lime
3 tablespoons chopped fresh cilantro
½ teaspoon salt
¼ teaspoon freshly ground black pepper

1. Slice the cucumber into 1-inch-thick segments and using a spoon, scrape seeds out of center of each segment and stand up on a plate. 2. In a medium bowl, combine the salmon, avocado, olive oil, lime zest and juice, cilantro, salt, and pepper and mix until creamy. 3. Spoon the salmon mixture into the center of each cucumber segment and serve chilled.

Per Serving:
calories: 173 | fat: 13g | protein: 8g | carbs: 8g | fiber: 4g | sodium: 420mg

Lemon-Pepper Chicken Drumsticks

Prep time: 30 minutes | Cook time: 30 minutes | Serves 2

2 teaspoons freshly ground coarse black pepper
1 teaspoon baking powder
½ teaspoon garlic powder

4 chicken drumsticks (4 ounces / 113 g each)
Kosher salt, to taste
1 lemon

1. In a small bowl, stir together the pepper, baking powder, and garlic powder. Place the drumsticks on a plate and sprinkle evenly with the baking powder mixture, turning the drumsticks so they're well coated. Let the drumsticks stand in the refrigerator for at least 1 hour or up to overnight. 2. Sprinkle the drumsticks with salt, then transfer them to the air fryer, standing them bone-end up and leaning against the wall of the air fryer basket. Air fry at 375°F (191°C) until cooked through and crisp on the outside, about 30 minutes. 3. Transfer the drumsticks to a serving platter and finely grate the zest of the lemon over them while they're hot. Cut the lemon into wedges and serve with the warm drumsticks.

Per Serving:
calories: 438 | fat: 24g | protein: 48g | carbs: 6g | fiber: 2g | sodium: 279mg

Savory Mackerel & Goat'S Cheese "Paradox" Balls

Prep time: 10 minutes | Cook time: 0 minutes |
Makes 10 fat bombs

2 smoked or cooked mackerel fillets, boneless, skin removed
4.4 ounces (125 g) soft goat's cheese
1 tablespoon fresh lemon juice
1 teaspoon Dijon or yellow

mustard
1 small red onion, finely diced
2 tablespoons chopped fresh chives or herbs of choice
¾ cup pecans, crushed
10 leaves baby gem lettuce

1. In a food processor, combine the mackerel, goat's cheese, lemon juice, and mustard. Pulse until smooth. Transfer to a bowl, add the onion and herbs, and mix with a spoon. Refrigerate for 20 to 30 minutes, or until set. 2. Using a large spoon or an ice cream scoop, divide the mixture into 10 balls, about 40 g/1.4 ounces each. Roll each ball in the crushed pecans. Place each ball on a small lettuce leaf and serve. Keep the fat bombs refrigerated in a sealed container for up to 5 days.

Per Serving:
1 fat bomb: calories: 165 | fat: 12g | protein: 12g | carbs: 2g | fiber: 1g | sodium: 102mg

Red Lentils with Sumac

Prep time: 5 minutes | Cook time: 20 minutes |
Serves 6 to 8

1 cup red lentils, picked through and rinsed
1 teaspoon ground sumac

½ teaspoon salt
Pita chips, warm pita bread, or raw vegetables, for serving

1. In a medium saucepan, combine the lentils, sumac, and 2 cups water. Bring the water to a boil. Reduce the heat to maintain a simmer and cook for 15 minutes, or until the lentils are softened and most of the water has been absorbed. Stir in the salt and cook until the lentils have absorbed all the water, about 5 minutes more. 2. Serve with pita chips, warm pita bread, or as a dip for raw vegetables.

Per Serving:
1 cup: calories: 162 | fat: 1g | protein: 11g | carbs: 30g | fiber: 9g | sodium: 219mg

Lebanese Muhammara

Prep time: 15 minutes | Cook time: 15 minutes | Serves 6

2 large red bell peppers
¼ cup plus 2 tablespoons extra-virgin olive oil
1 cup walnut halves
1 tablespoon agave nectar or honey
1 teaspoon fresh lemon juice

1 teaspoon ground cumin
1 teaspoon kosher salt
1 teaspoon red pepper flakes
Raw vegetables (such as cucumber, carrots, zucchini slices, or cauliflower) or toasted pita chips, for serving

1. Drizzle the peppers with 2 tablespoons of the olive oil and place in the air fryer basket. Set the air fryer to 400ºF (204ºC) for 10 minutes. 2. Add the walnuts to the basket, arranging them around the peppers. Set the air fryer to 400ºF (204ºC) for 5 minutes. 3. Remove the peppers, seal in a resealable plastic bag, and let rest for 5 to 10 minutes. Transfer the walnuts to a plate and set aside to cool. 4. Place the softened peppers, walnuts, agave, lemon juice, cumin, salt, and ½ teaspoon of the pepper flakes in a food processor and purée until smooth. 5. Transfer the dip to a serving bowl and make an indentation in the middle. Pour the remaining ¼ cup olive oil into the indentation. Garnish the dip with the remaining ½ teaspoon pepper flakes. 6. Serve with vegetables or toasted pita chips.

Per Serving:
calories: 219 | fat: 20g | protein: 3g | carbs: 9g | fiber: 2g | sodium: 391mg

Five-Ingredient Falafel with Garlic-Yogurt Sauce

Prep time: 5 minutes | Cook time: 15 minutes | Serves 4

Falafel:
1 (15-ounce / 425-g) can chickpeas, drained and rinsed
½ cup fresh parsley
2 garlic cloves, minced
½ tablespoon ground cumin
1 tablespoon whole wheat flour

Salt
Garlic-Yogurt Sauce:
1 cup nonfat plain Greek yogurt
1 garlic clove, minced
1 tablespoon chopped fresh dill
2 tablespoons lemon juice

Make the Falafel: 1. Preheat the air fryer to 360°F(182°C). 2. Put the chickpeas into a food processor. Pulse until mostly chopped, then add the parsley, garlic, and cumin and pulse for another 1 to 2 minutes, or until the ingredients are combined and turning into a dough. 3. Add the flour. Pulse a few more times until combined. The dough will have texture, but the chickpeas should be pulsed into small bits. 4. Using clean hands, roll the dough into 8 balls of equal size, then pat the balls down a bit so they are about ½-thick disks. 5. Spray the basket of the air fryer with olive oil cooking spray, then place the falafel patties in the basket in a single layer, making sure they don't touch each other. 6. Fry in the air fryer for 15 minutes. Make the garlic-yogurt sauce 7. In a small bowl, combine the yogurt, garlic, dill, and lemon juice. 8. Once the falafel are done cooking and nicely browned on all sides, remove them from the air fryer and season with salt. 9. Serve hot with a side of dipping sauce.

Per Serving:
calories: 150 | fat: 3g | protein: 10g | carbs: 23g | fiber: 6g | sodium: 194mg

Cherry Tomato Bruschetta

Prep time: 15 minutes | Cook time: 0 minutes | Serves 4

8 ounces (227 g) assorted cherry tomatoes, halved
⅓ cup fresh herbs, chopped (such as basil, parsley, tarragon, dill)
1 tablespoon extra-virgin olive oil

¼ teaspoon kosher salt
⅛ teaspoon freshly ground black pepper
¼ cup ricotta cheese
4 slices whole-wheat bread, toasted

1. Combine the tomatoes, herbs, olive oil, salt, and black pepper in a medium bowl and mix gently. 2. Spread 1 tablespoon of ricotta cheese onto each slice of toast. Spoon one-quarter of the tomato mixture onto each bruschetta. If desired, garnish with more herbs.

Per Serving:
calories: 100 | fat: 1g | protein: 4g | carbs: 10g | fiber: 2g | sodium: 135mg

Sweet Potato Hummus

Prep time: 10 minutes | Cook time: 1 hour | Serves 8 to 10

1 pound (454 g) sweet potatoes (about 2)
1 (15-ounce / 425-g) can chickpeas, drained
4 garlic cloves, minced
2 tablespoons olive oil

2 tablespoons fresh lemon juice
2 teaspoons ground cumin
1 teaspoon Aleppo pepper or red pepper flakes
Pita chips, pita bread, or fresh vegetables, for serving

1. Preheat the oven to 400ºF (205ºC). 2. Prick the sweet potatoes in a few places with a small, sharp knife and place them on a baking sheet. Roast until cooked through, about 1 hour, then set aside to cool. Peel the sweet potatoes and put the flesh in a blender or food processor. 3. Add the chickpeas, garlic, olive oil, lemon juice, cumin, and ⅓ cup water. Blend until smooth. Add the Aleppo pepper. 4. Serve with pita chips, pita bread, or as a dip for fresh vegetables.

Per Serving:
calories: 178 | fat: 5g | protein: 7g | carbs: 30g | fiber: 9g | sodium: 149mg

Air Fryer Popcorn with Garlic Salt

Prep time: 3 minutes | Cook time: 10 minutes | Serves 2

2 tablespoons olive oil
¼ cup popcorn kernels

1 teaspoon garlic salt

1. Preheat the air fryer to 380°F(193°C). 2. Tear a square of aluminum foil the size of the bottom of the air fryer and place into the air fryer. 3. Drizzle olive oil over the top of the foil, and then pour in the popcorn kernels. 4. Roast for 8 to 10 minutes, or until the popcorn stops popping. 5. Transfer the popcorn to a large bowl and sprinkle with garlic salt before serving.

Per Serving:
calories: 134 | fat: 14g | protein: 0g | carbs: 3g | fiber: 1g | sodium: 620mg

Stuffed Figs with Goat Cheese and Honey

Prep time: 5 minutes | Cook time: 10 minutes | Serves 4

8 fresh figs
2 ounces (57 g) goat cheese
¼ teaspoon ground cinnamon

1 tablespoon honey, plus more
for serving
1 tablespoon olive oil

1. Preheat the air fryer to 360°F(182°C). 2. Cut the stem off of each fig. 3. Cut an X into the top of each fig, cutting halfway down the fig. Leave the base intact. 4. In a small bowl, mix together the goat cheese, cinnamon, and honey. 5. Spoon the goat cheese mixture into the cavity of each fig. 6. Place the figs in a single layer in the air fryer basket. Drizzle the olive oil over top of the figs and roast for 10 minutes. 7. Serve with an additional drizzle of honey.

Per Serving:
calories: 152 | fat: 9g | protein: 5g | carbs: 16g | fiber: 2g | sodium: 62mg

Marinated Olives

Prep time: 5 minutes | Cook time: 5 minutes | Serves 8 to 10

3 tablespoons olive oil
Zest and juice of 1 lemon
½ teaspoon Aleppo pepper or
red pepper flakes
¼ teaspoon ground sumac

1 cup pitted Kalamata olives
1 cup pitted green olives, such
as Castelvetrano
2 tablespoons finely chopped
fresh parsley

1. In a medium skillet, heat the olive oil over medium heat. Add the lemon zest, Aleppo pepper, and sumac and cook for 1 to 2 minutes, occasionally stirring, until fragrant. Remove from the heat and stir in the olives, lemon juice, and parsley. 2. Transfer the olives to a bowl and serve immediately, or let cool, then transfer to an airtight container and store in the refrigerator for up to 1 week. The flavor will continue to develop and is best after 8 to 12 hours.

Per Serving:
1 cup: calories: 59 | fat: 6g | protein: 0g | carbs: 1g | fiber: 1g | sodium: 115mg

Roasted Rosemary Olives

Prep time: 5 minutes | Cook time: 25 minutes | Serves 4

1 cup mixed variety olives,
pitted and rinsed
2 tablespoons lemon juice
1 tablespoon extra-virgin olive

oil
6 garlic cloves, peeled
4 rosemary sprigs

1. Preheat the oven to 400°F (205°C). Line the baking sheet with parchment paper or foil. 2. Combine the olives, lemon juice, olive oil, and garlic in a medium bowl and mix together. Spread in a single layer on the prepared baking sheet. Sprinkle on the rosemary. Roast for 25 minutes, tossing halfway through. 3. Remove the rosemary leaves from the stem and place in a serving bowl. Add the olives and mix before serving.

Per Serving:
calories: 100 | fat: 9g | protein: 0g | carbs: 4g | fiber: 0g | sodium: 260mg

Tirokafteri (Spicy Feta and Yogurt Dip)

Prep time: 10 minutes | Cook time: 0 minutes | Serves 8

1 teaspoon red wine vinegar
1 small green chili, seeded and
sliced
2 teaspoons extra virgin olive

oil
9 ounces (255 g) full-fat feta
¾ cup full-fat Greek yogurt

1. Combine the vinegar, chili, and olive oil in a food processor. Blend until smooth. 2. In a small bowl, combine the feta and Greek yogurt, and use a fork to mash the ingredients until a paste is formed. Add the pepper mixture and stir until blended. 3. Cover and transfer to the refrigerator to chill for at least 1 hour before serving. Store covered in the refrigerator for up to 3 days.

Per Serving:
calories: 109 | fat: 8g | protein: 6g | carbs: 4g | fiber: 0g | sodium: 311mg

Savory Mediterranean Popcorn

Prep time: 5 minutes | Cook time: 2 minutes | Serves 4 to 6

3 tablespoons extra-virgin olive
oil
¼ teaspoon garlic powder
¼ teaspoon freshly ground
black pepper

¼ teaspoon sea salt
⅛ teaspoon dried thyme
⅛ teaspoon dried oregano
12 cups plain popped popcorn

1. In a large sauté pan or skillet, heat the oil over medium heat, until shimmering, and then add the garlic powder, pepper, salt, thyme, and oregano until fragrant. 2. In a large bowl, drizzle the oil over the popcorn, toss, and serve.

Per Serving:
calories: 183 | fat: 12g | protein: 3g | carbs: 19g | fiber: 4g | sodium: 146mg

Marinated Mushrooms and Pearl Onions

Prep time: 10 minutes | Cook time: 4 minutes | Serves 10

3 pounds (1.4 kg) button
mushrooms, trimmed
1 (15-ounce / 425-g) bag frozen
pearl onions, thawed
3 cloves garlic, peeled and
minced
1 cup vegetable broth
¼ cup balsamic vinegar

¼ cup red wine
2 tablespoons olive oil
2 sprigs fresh thyme
½ teaspoon ground black
pepper
¼ teaspoon crushed red pepper
flakes

1. Place all ingredients in the Instant Pot® and mix well. 2. Close lid, set steam release to Sealing, press the Manual button, and set time to 4 minutes. 3. When the timer beeps, quick-release the pressure until the float valve drops and open lid. Transfer mixture to a bowl and serve warm.

Per Serving:
calories: 90 | fat: 3g | protein: 4g | carbs: 9g | fiber: 2g | sodium: 92mg

Heart-Healthful Trail Mix

Prep time: 15 minutes | Cook time: 30 minutes |
Serves 10

1 cup raw almonds
1 cup walnut halves
1 cup pumpkin seeds
1 cup dried apricots, cut into thin strips
1 cup dried cherries, roughly

chopped
1 cup golden raisins
2 tablespoons extra-virgin olive oil
1 teaspoon salt

1. Preheat the oven to 300°F(150°C). Line a baking sheet with aluminum foil. 2. In a large bowl, combine the almonds, walnuts, pumpkin seeds, apricots, cherries, and raisins. Pour the olive oil over all and toss well with clean hands. Add salt and toss again to distribute. 3. Pour the nut mixture onto the baking sheet in a single layer and bake until the fruits begin to brown, about 30 minutes. Cool on the baking sheet to room temperature. 4. Store in a large airtight container or zipper-top plastic bag.

Per Serving:
calories: 346 | fat: 20g | protein: 8g | carbs: 39g | fiber: 5g | sodium: 240mg

Fried Baby Artichokes with Lemon-Garlic Aioli

Prep time: 5 minutes | Cook time: 50 minutes | Serves 10

Artichokes:
15 baby artichokes
½ lemon
3 cups olive oil
Kosher salt, to taste
Aioli:
1 egg

2 cloves garlic, chopped
1 tablespoon fresh lemon juice
½ teaspoon Dijon mustard
½ cup olive oil
Kosher salt and ground black pepper, to taste

1. Make the Artichokes: Wash and drain the artichokes. With a paring knife, strip off the coarse outer leaves around the base and stalk, leaving the softer leaves on. Carefully peel the stalks and trim off all but 2' below the base. Slice off the top ½' of the artichokes. Cut each artichoke in half. Rub the cut surfaces with a lemon half to keep from browning. 2. In a medium saucepan fitted with a deep-fry thermometer over medium heat, warm the oil to about 280°F(138°C). Working in batches, cook the artichokes in the hot oil until tender, about 15 minutes. Using a slotted spoon, remove and drain on a paper towel–lined plate. Repeat with all the artichoke halves. 3. Increase the heat of the oil to 375°F(190°C). In batches, cook the precooked baby artichokes until browned at the edges and crisp, about 1 minute. Transfer to a paper towel–lined plate. Season with the salt to taste. Repeat with the remaining artichokes. 4. Make the aioli: In a blender, pulse together the egg, garlic, lemon juice, and mustard until combined. With the blender running, slowly drizzle in the oil a few drops at a time until the mixture thickens like mayonnaise, about 2 minutes. Transfer to a bowl and season to taste with the salt and pepper. 5. Serve the warm artichokes with the aioli on the side.

Per Serving:
calories: 236 | fat: 17g | protein: 6g | carbs: 21g | fiber: 10g | sodium: 283mg

Baked Spanakopita Dip

Prep time: 10 minutes | Cook time: 15 minutes | Serves 2

Olive oil cooking spray
3 tablespoons olive oil, divided
2 tablespoons minced white onion
2 garlic cloves, minced
4 cups fresh spinach
4 ounces (113 g) cream cheese, softened
4 ounces (113 g) feta cheese,

divided
Zest of 1 lemon
¼ teaspoon ground nutmeg
1 teaspoon dried dill
½ teaspoon salt
Pita chips, carrot sticks, or sliced bread for serving (optional)

1. Preheat the air fryer to 360°F(182°C). Coat the inside of a 6-inch ramekin or baking dish with olive oil cooking spray. 2. In a large skillet over medium heat, heat 1 tablespoon of the olive oil. Add the onion, then cook for 1 minute. 3. Add in the garlic and cook, stirring for 1 minute more. 4. Reduce the heat to low and mix in the spinach and water. Let this cook for 2 to 3 minutes, or until the spinach has wilted. Remove the skillet from the heat. 5. In a medium bowl, combine the cream cheese, 2 ounces (57 g) of the feta, and the remaining 2 tablespoons of olive oil, along with the lemon zest, nutmeg, dill, and salt. Mix until just combined. 6. Add the vegetables to the cheese base and stir until combined. 7. Pour the dip mixture into the prepared ramekin and top with the remaining 2 ounces (57 g) of feta cheese. 8. Place the dip into the air fryer basket and cook for 10 minutes, or until heated through and bubbling. 9. Serve with pita chips, carrot sticks, or sliced bread.

Per Serving:
calories: 376 | fat: 32g | protein: 14g | carbs: 11g | fiber: 2g | sodium: 737mg

Sweet-and-Spicy Nuts

Prep time: 5 minutes | Cook time: 20 minutes |
Serves 10 to 12

Nonstick cooking spray
Zest and juice of 1 lemon
2 tablespoons honey
2 teaspoons Berbere or baharat

spice blend
1 teaspoon Aleppo pepper
1½ cups cashews
1½ cups dry-roasted peanuts

1. Preheat the oven to 375°F (190°C). Line a baking sheet with parchment paper and spray the parchment with cooking spray. 2. Spread the nuts in an even layer over the prepared baking sheet. Bake for 8 to 10 minutes, until fragrant. Remove from the oven and let cool slightly. Keep the oven on. 3. In a small bowl, stir together the lemon zest, lemon juice, honey, Berbere, and Aleppo pepper. 4. Transfer the nuts to a large bowl and pour over the honey-spice mixture. Toss to coat evenly. Return the nut mixture to the baking sheet and spread into an even layer. Bake for 8 to 10 minutes, until the nuts are caramelized. Remove from the oven and let cool completely before serving. 5. Can be stored refrigerated for up to 2 weeks.

Per Serving:
calories: 336 | fat: 27g | protein: 11g | carbs: 17g | fiber: 3g | sodium: 7mg

Greek Yogurt Deviled Eggs

Prep time: 15 minutes | Cook time: 15 minutes | Serves 4

4 eggs
¼ cup nonfat plain Greek yogurt
1 teaspoon chopped fresh dill
⅛ teaspoon salt

⅛ teaspoon paprika
⅛ teaspoon garlic powder
Chopped fresh parsley, for garnish

1. Preheat the air fryer to 260°F(127°C). 2. Place the eggs in a single layer in the air fryer basket and cook for 15 minutes. 3. Quickly remove the eggs from the air fryer and place them into a cold water bath. Let the eggs cool in the water for 10 minutes before removing and peeling them. 4. After peeling the eggs, cut them in half. 5. Spoon the yolk into a small bowl. Add the yogurt, dill, salt, paprika, and garlic powder and mix until smooth. 6. Spoon or pipe the yolk mixture into the halved egg whites. Serve with a sprinkle of fresh parsley on top.

Per Serving:
calories: 74 | fat: 4g | protein: 7g | carbs: 2g | fiber: 0g | sodium: 152mg

Stuffed Fried Mushrooms

Prep time: 20 minutes | Cook time: 10 to 11 minutes | Serves 10

½ cup panko bread crumbs
½ teaspoon freshly ground black pepper
½ teaspoon onion powder
½ teaspoon cayenne pepper
1 (8-ounce / 227-g) package

cream cheese, at room temperature
20 cremini or button mushrooms, stemmed
1 to 2 tablespoons oil

1. In a medium bowl, whisk the bread crumbs, black pepper, onion powder, and cayenne until blended. 2. Add the cream cheese and mix until well blended. Fill each mushroom top with 1 teaspoon of the cream cheese mixture 3. Preheat the air fryer to 360ºF (182ºC). Line the air fryer basket with a piece of parchment paper. 4. Place the mushrooms on the parchment and spritz with oil. 5. Cook for 5 minutes. Shake the basket and cook for 5 to 6 minutes more until the filling is firm and the mushrooms are soft.

Per Serving:
calories: 120 | fat: 9g | protein: 3g | carbs: 7g | fiber: 1g | sodium: 125mg

Lemon Shrimp with Garlic Olive Oil

Prep time: 5 minutes | Cook time: 6 minutes | Serves 4

1 pound (454 g) medium shrimp, cleaned and deveined
¼ cup plus 2 tablespoons olive oil, divided
Juice of ½ lemon
3 garlic cloves, minced and divided

½ teaspoon salt
¼ teaspoon red pepper flakes
Lemon wedges, for serving (optional)
Marinara sauce, for dipping (optional)

1. Preheat the air fryer to 380°F(193ºC). 2. In a large bowl, combine the shrimp with 2 tablespoons of the olive oil, as well as the lemon juice, ⅓ of the minced garlic, salt, and red pepper flakes. Toss to coat the shrimp well. 3. In a small ramekin, combine the remaining ¼ cup of olive oil and the remaining minced garlic. 4. Tear off a 12-by-12-inch sheet of aluminum foil. Pour the shrimp into the center of the foil, then fold the sides up and crimp the edges so that it forms an aluminum foil bowl that is open on top. Place this packet into the air fryer basket. 5. Roast the shrimp for 4 minutes, then open the air fryer and place the ramekin with oil and garlic in the basket beside the shrimp packet. Cook for 2 more minutes. 6. Transfer the shrimp on a serving plate or platter with the ramekin of garlic olive oil on the side for dipping. You may also serve with lemon wedges and marinara sauce, if desired.

Per Serving:
calories: 283 | fat: 21g | protein: 23g | carbs: 1g | fiber: 0g | sodium: 427mg

Asiago Shishito Peppers

Prep time: 5 minutes | Cook time: 10 minutes | Serves 4

Oil, for spraying
6 ounces (170 g) shishito peppers
1 tablespoon olive oil

½ teaspoon salt
½ teaspoon lemon pepper
⅓ cup grated Asiago cheese, divided

1. Line the air fryer basket with parchment and spray lightly with oil. 2. Rinse the shishitos and pat dry with paper towels. 3. In a large bowl, mix together the shishitos, olive oil, salt, and lemon pepper. Place the shishitos in the prepared basket. 4. Roast at 350ºF (177ºC) for 10 minutes, or until blistered but not burned. 5. Sprinkle with half of the cheese and cook for 1 more minute. 6. Transfer to a serving plate. Immediately sprinkle with the remaining cheese and serve.

Per Serving:
calories: 81 | fat: 6g | protein: 3g | carbs: 5g | fiber: 1g | sodium: 443mg

Baked Eggplant Baba Ganoush

Prep time: 10 minutes | Cook time: 1 hour | Makes about 4 cups

2 pounds (907 g, about 2 medium to large) eggplant
3 tablespoons tahini
Zest of 1 lemon
2 tablespoons lemon juice
¾ teaspoon kosher salt

½ teaspoon ground sumac, plus more for sprinkling (optional)
⅓ cup fresh parsley, chopped
1 tablespoon extra-virgin olive oil

1. Preheat the oven to 350ºF (180ºC). Place the eggplants directly on the rack and bake for 60 minutes, or until the skin is wrinkly. 2. In a food processor add the tahini, lemon zest, lemon juice, salt, and sumac. Carefully cut open the baked eggplant and scoop the flesh into the food processor. Process until the ingredients are well blended. 3. Place in a serving dish and mix in the parsley. Drizzle with the olive oil and sprinkle with sumac, if desired.

Per Serving:
calories: 50 | fat: 16g | protein: 4g | carbs: 2g | fiber: 1g | sodium: 110mg

Spanish Home Fries with Spicy Tomato Sauce

Prep time: 5 minutes | Cook time: 1 hour | Serves 6

4 russet potatoes, peeled, cut into large dice	1 teaspoon hot smoked paprika
¼ cup olive oil plus 1 tablespoon, divided	1 serrano chile, seeded and chopped
½ cup crushed tomatoes	½ teaspoon salt
1½ teaspoons red wine	¼ teaspoon freshly ground black pepper

1. Preheat the oven to 425°F(220ºC). 2. Toss the potatoes with ¼ cup of olive oil and spread on a large baking sheet. Season with salt and pepper and roast in the preheated oven for about 50 to 60 minutes, turning once in the middle, until the potatoes are golden brown and crisp. 3. Meanwhile, make the sauce by combining the tomatoes, the remaining 1 tablespoon olive oil, wine, paprika, chile, salt, and pepper in a food processor or blender and process until smooth. 4. Serve the potatoes hot with the sauce on the side for dipping or spooned over the top.

Per Serving:
calories: 201 | fat: 11g | protein: 3g | carbs: 25g | fiber: 4g | sodium: 243mg

Spiced Maple Nuts

Prep time: 5 minutes | Cook time:10 minutes | Makes about 2 cups

2 cups raw walnuts or pecans (or a mix of nuts)	½ teaspoon pure maple syrup
1 teaspoon extra-virgin olive oil	¼ teaspoon kosher salt
1 teaspoon ground sumac	¼ teaspoon ground ginger
	2 to 4 rosemary sprigs

1. Preheat the oven to 350ºF (180ºC). Line a baking sheet with parchment paper or foil. 2. In a large bowl, combine the nuts, olive oil, sumac, maple syrup, salt, and ginger; mix together. Spread in a single layer on the prepared baking sheet. Add the rosemary. Roast for 8 to 10 minutes, or until golden and fragrant. 3. Remove the rosemary leaves from the stems and place in a serving bowl. Add the nuts and toss to combine before serving.

Per Serving:
¼ cup: calories: 175 | fat: 18g | protein: 3g | carbs: 4g | fiber: 2g | sodium: 35mg

Roasted Chickpeas

Prep time: 5 minutes | Cook time: 15 minutes | Makes about 1 cup

1 (15-ounce / 425-g) can chickpeas, drained	¼ teaspoon salt
2 teaspoons curry powder	1 tablespoon olive oil

1. Drain chickpeas thoroughly and spread in a single layer on paper towels. Cover with another paper towel and press gently to remove extra moisture. Don't press too hard or you'll crush the chickpeas. 2. Mix curry powder and salt together. 3. Place chickpeas in a medium bowl and sprinkle with seasonings. Stir well to coat. 4. Add olive oil and stir again to distribute oil. 5. Air fry at 390ºF (199ºC) for 15 minutes, stopping to shake basket about halfway through cooking time. 6. Cool completely and store in airtight container.

Per Serving:
¼ cup: calories: 181 | fat: 6g | protein: 8g | carbs: 24g | fiber: 7g | sodium: 407mg

Roasted Pepper Bruschetta with Capers and Basil

Prep time: 10 minutes | Cook time: 15 minutes | Serves 6 to 8

2 red bell peppers	3 tablespoons red wine vinegar
2 yellow bell peppers	1 teaspoon Dijon mustard
2 orange bell peppers	1 clove garlic, minced
2 tablespoons olive oil, plus ¼ cup	2 tablespoons capers, drained
¾ teaspoon salt, divided	¼ cup chopped fresh basil leaves, divided
½ teaspoon freshly ground black pepper, divided	1 whole-wheat baguette or other crusty bread, thinly sliced

1. Preheat the broiler to high and line a large baking sheet with aluminum foil. 2. Brush the peppers all over with 2 tablespoons of the olive oil and sprinkle with ½ teaspoon of the salt and ¼ teaspoon of the pepper. 3. Broil the peppers, turning every 3 minutes or so, until the skin is charred on all sides. Place them in a bowl, cover with plastic wrap, and let steam for 10 minutes. Slip the skins off and discard them. Seed and dice the peppers. 4. In a large bowl, whisk together the vinegar, mustard, garlic, the remaining ¼ teaspoon salt, and the remaining ¼ teaspoon of pepper. Still whisking, slowly add the remaining ¼ cup oil in a thin stream until the dressing is emulsified. Stir in the capers, 2 tablespoons of the basil, and the diced peppers. 5. Toast the bread slices and then spoon the pepper mixture over them, drizzling with extra dressing. Garnish with the remaining basil and serve immediately.

Per Serving:
calories: 243 | fat: 6g | protein: 8g | carbs: 39g | fiber: 4g | sodium: 755mg

Sea Salt Potato Chips

Prep time: 30 minutes | Cook time: 27 minutes | Serves 4

Oil, for spraying	1 tablespoon oil
4 medium yellow potatoes	⅛ to ¼ teaspoon fine sea salt

1. Line the air fryer basket with parchment and spray lightly with oil. 2. Using a mandoline or a very sharp knife, cut the potatoes into very thin slices. 3. Place the slices in a bowl of cold water and let soak for about 20 minutes. 4. Drain the potatoes, transfer them to a plate lined with paper towels, and pat dry. 5. Drizzle the oil over the potatoes, sprinkle with the salt, and toss to combine. Transfer to the prepared basket. 6. Air fry at 200ºF (93ºC) for 20 minutes. Toss the chips, increase the heat to 400ºF (204ºC), and cook for another 5 to 7 minutes, until crispy.

Per Serving:
calories: 194 | fat: 4g | protein: 4g | carbs: 37g | fiber: 5g | sodium: 90mg

Sfougato

Prep time: 10 minutes | Cook time: 8 minutes | Serves 4

½ cup crumbled feta cheese
¼ cup bread crumbs
1 medium onion, peeled and minced
4 tablespoons all-purpose flour
2 tablespoons minced fresh mint
½ teaspoon salt
½ teaspoon ground black pepper
1 tablespoon dried thyme
6 large eggs, beaten
1 cup water

1. In a medium bowl, mix cheese, bread crumbs, onion, flour, mint, salt, pepper, and thyme. Stir in eggs. 2. Spray an 8" round baking dish with nonstick cooking spray. Pour egg mixture into dish. 3. Place rack in the Instant Pot® and add water. Fold a long piece of foil in half lengthwise. Lay foil over rack to form a sling and top with dish. Cover loosely with foil. Close lid, set steam release to Sealing, press the Manual button, and set time to 8 minutes. 4. When the timer beeps, quick-release the pressure until the float valve drops. Open lid. Let stand 5 minutes, then remove dish from pot.

Per Serving:
calories: 226 | fat: 12g | protein: 14g | carbs: 15g | fiber: 1g | sodium: 621mg

Goat Cheese–Mackerel Pâté

Prep time: 10 minutes | Cook time: 0 minutes | Serves 4

4 ounces (113 g) olive oil-packed wild-caught mackerel
2 ounces (57 g) goat cheese
Zest and juice of 1 lemon
2 tablespoons chopped fresh parsley
2 tablespoons chopped fresh arugula
1 tablespoon extra-virgin olive oil
2 teaspoons chopped capers
1 to 2 teaspoons fresh horseradish (optional)
Crackers, cucumber rounds, endive spears, or celery, for serving (optional)

1. In a food processor, blender, or large bowl with immersion blender, combine the mackerel, goat cheese, lemon zest and juice, parsley, arugula, olive oil, capers, and horseradish (if using). Process or blend until smooth and creamy. 2. Serve with crackers, cucumber rounds, endive spears, or celery. 3. Store covered in the refrigerator for up to 1 week.

Per Serving:
calories: 142 | fat: 10g | protein: 11g | carbs: 1g | fiber: 0g | sodium: 203mg

Stuffed Dates with Feta, Parmesan, and Pine Nuts

Prep time: 5 minutes | Cook time: 10 minutes | Serves 4

1 ounce (28 g) feta
1 ounce (28 g) Parmesan cheese
12 dried dates, pitted
½ tablespoon raw pine nuts
1 teaspoon extra virgin olive oil

1. Preheat the oven to 425°F (220°C). Line a small baking pan with parchment paper. 2. Cut the feta and Parmesan into 12 small thin sticks, each about ¾ inch long and ¼ inch thick. 3. Use a sharp knife to cut a small slit lengthwise into each date. Insert a piece of the Parmesan followed by a piece of the feta, and then press 2–3 pine nuts slightly into the feta. 4. Transfer the dates to the prepared baking pan and place in the oven to roast for 10 minutes. (The edges of the dates should begin to brown.) 5. Remove the dates from the oven and drizzle a few drops of the olive oil over each date. Serve promptly. (These do not store well and are best enjoyed fresh.)

Per Serving:
calories: 126 | fat: 5g | protein: 4g | carbs: 17g | fiber: 2g | sodium: 194mg

Pea and Arugula Crostini with Pecorino Romano

Prep time: 10 minutes | Cook time: 15 minutes | Serves 6 to 8

1½ cups fresh or frozen peas
1 loaf crusty whole-wheat bread, cut into thin slices
3 tablespoons olive oil, divided
1 small garlic clove, finely mined or pressed
Juice of ½ lemon
½ teaspoon salt
¼ teaspoon freshly ground black pepper
1 cup (packed) baby arugula
¼ cup thinly shaved Pecorino Romano

1. Preheat the oven to 350°F (180°C). 2. Fill a small saucepan with about ½ inch of water. Bring to a boil over medium-high heat. Add the peas and cook for 3 to 5 minutes, until tender. Drain and rinse with cold water. 3. Arrange the bread slices on a large baking sheet and brush the tops with 2 tablespoons olive oil. Bake in the preheated oven for about 8 minutes, until golden brown. 4. Meanwhile, in a medium bowl, mash the peas gently with the back of a fork. They should be smashed but not mashed into a paste. Add the remaining 1 tablespoon olive oil, lemon juice, garlic, salt, and pepper and stir to mix. 5. Spoon the pea mixture onto the toasted bread slices and top with the arugula and cheese. Serve immediately.

Per Serving:
calories: 301 | fat: 13g | protein: 14g | carbs: 32g | fiber: 6g | sodium: 833mg

Homemade Sweet Potato Chips

Prep time: 5 minutes | Cook time: 15 minutes | Serves 2

1 large sweet potato, sliced thin
⅛ teaspoon salt
2 tablespoons olive oil

1. Preheat the air fryer to 380°F (193°C). 2. In a small bowl, toss the sweet potatoes, salt, and olive oil together until the potatoes are well coated. 3. Put the sweet potato slices into the air fryer and spread them out in a single layer. 4. Fry for 10 minutes. Stir, then air fry for 3 to 5 minutes more, or until the chips reach the preferred level of crispiness.

Per Serving:
calories: 175 | fat: 14g | protein: 1g | carbs: 13g | fiber: 2g | sodium: 191mg

Cheesy Dates

Prep time: 15 minutes | Cook time: 10 minutes | Serves 12 to 15

1 cup pecans, shells removed
1 (8-ounce / 227-g) container

mascarpone cheese
20 Medjool dates

1. Preheat the oven to 350°F(180ºC). Put the pecans on a baking sheet and bake for 5 to 6 minutes, until lightly toasted and aromatic. Take the pecans out of the oven and let cool for 5 minutes. 2. Once cooled, put the pecans in a food processor fitted with a chopping blade and chop until they resemble the texture of bulgur wheat or coarse sugar. 3. Reserve ¼ cup of ground pecans in a small bowl. Pour the remaining chopped pecans into a larger bowl and add the mascarpone cheese. 4. Using a spatula, mix the cheese with the pecans until evenly combined. 5. Spoon the cheese mixture into a piping bag. 6. Using a knife, cut one side of the date lengthwise, from the stem to the bottom. Gently open and remove the pit. 7. Using the piping bag, squeeze a generous amount of the cheese mixture into the date where the pit used to be. Close up the date and repeat with the remaining dates. 8. Dip any exposed cheese from the stuffed dates into the reserved chopped pecans to cover it up. 9. Set the dates on a serving plate; serve immediately or chill in the fridge until you are ready to serve.

Per Serving:
calories: 253 | fat: 4g | protein: 2g | carbs: 31g | fiber: 4g | sodium: 7mg

Italian Crepe with Herbs and Onion

Prep time: 15 minutes | Cook time: 20 minutes per crepe | Serves 6

2 cups cold water
1 cup chickpea flour
½ teaspoon kosher salt
¼ teaspoon freshly ground black pepper
3½ tablespoons extra-virgin

olive oil, divided
½ onion, julienned
½ cup fresh herbs, chopped (thyme, sage, and rosemary are all nice on their own or as a mix)

1. In a large bowl, whisk together the water, flour, salt, and black pepper. Add 2 tablespoons of the olive oil and whisk. Let the batter sit at room temperature for at least 30 minutes. 2. Preheat the oven to 450ºF (235ºC). Place a 12-inch cast-iron pan or oven-safe skillet in the oven to warm as the oven comes to temperature. 3. Remove the hot pan from the oven carefully, add ½ tablespoon of the olive oil and one-third of the onion, stir, and place the pan back in the oven. Cook, stirring occasionally, until the onions are golden brown, 5 to 8 minutes. 4. Remove the pan from the oven and pour in one-third of the batter (about 1 cup), sprinkle with one-third of the herbs, and put it back in the oven. Bake for 10 minutes, or until firm and the edges are set. 5. Increase the oven setting to broil and cook 3 to 5 minutes, or until golden brown. Slide the crepe onto the cutting board and repeat twice more. Halve the crepes and cut into wedges. Serve warm or at room temperature.

Per Serving:
calories: 135 | fat: 9g | protein: 4g | carbs: 11g | fiber: 2g | sodium: 105mg

Savory Lentil Dip

Prep time: 10 minutes | Cook time: 32 minutes | Serves 16

2 tablespoons olive oil
½ medium yellow onion, peeled and diced
3 cloves garlic, peeled and minced
2 cups dried red lentils, rinsed and drained

4 cups water
1 teaspoon salt
¼ teaspoon ground black pepper
2 tablespoons minced fresh flat-leaf parsley

1. Press the Sauté button on the Instant Pot® and heat oil. Add onion and cook 2–3 minutes, or until translucent. Add garlic and cook until fragrant, about 30 seconds. Add lentils, water, and salt to pot, and stir to combine. Close lid, set steam release to Sealing, press the Bean button, and cook for the default time of 30 minutes. 2. When the timer beeps, let pressure release naturally for 10 minutes. Quick-release any remaining pressure until the float valve drops, then open lid. Transfer lentil mixture to a food processor and blend until smooth. Season with pepper and garnish with parsley. Serve warm.

Per Serving:
calories: 76 | fat: 2g | protein: 5g | carbs: 11g | fiber: 2g | sodium: 145mg

Greek Potato Skins with Olives and Feta

Prep time: 5 minutes | Cook time: 45 minutes | Serves 4

2 russet potatoes
3 tablespoons olive oil, divided, plus more for drizzling (optional)
1 teaspoon kosher salt, divided
¼ teaspoon black pepper

2 tablespoons fresh cilantro, chopped, plus more for serving
¼ cup Kalamata olives, diced
¼ cup crumbled feta
Chopped fresh parsley, for garnish (optional)

1. Preheat the air fryer to 380°F(193ºC). 2. Using a fork, poke 2 to 3 holes in the potatoes, then coat each with about ½ tablespoon olive oil and ½ teaspoon salt. 3. Place the potatoes into the air fryer basket and bake for 30 minutes. 4. Remove the potatoes from the air fryer, and slice in half. Using a spoon, scoop out the flesh of the potatoes, leaving a ½-inch layer of potato inside the skins, and set the skins aside. 5. In a medium bowl, combine the scooped potato middles with the remaining 2 tablespoons of olive oil, ½ teaspoon of salt, black pepper, and cilantro. Mix until well combined. 6. Divide the potato filling into the now-empty potato skins, spreading it evenly over them. Top each potato with a tablespoon each of the olives and feta. 7. Place the loaded potato skins back into the air fryer and bake for 15 minutes. 8. Serve with additional chopped cilantro or parsley and a drizzle of olive oil, if desired.

Per Serving:
calories: 209 | fat: 13g | protein: 4g | carbs: 20g | fiber: 2g | sodium: 635mg

Quick Garlic Mushrooms

Prep time: 10 minutes | Cook time: 10 minutes |
Serves 4 to 6

2 pounds (907 g) cremini
mushrooms, cleaned
3 tablespoons unsalted butter
2 tablespoons garlic, minced

½ teaspoon salt
½ teaspoon freshly ground
black pepper

1. Cut each mushroom in half, stem to top, and put them into a bowl. 2. Preheat a large sauté pan or skillet over medium heat. 3. Cook the butter and garlic in the pan for 2 minutes, stirring occasionally. 4. Add the mushrooms and salt to the pan and toss together with the garlic butter mixture. Cook for 7 to 8 minutes, stirring every 2 minutes. 5. Remove the mushrooms from the pan and pour into a serving dish. Top with black pepper.

Per Serving:
calories: 183 | fat: 9g | protein: 9g | carbs: 10g | fiber: 3g | sodium: 334mg

Crunchy Basil White Beans

Prep time: 2 minutes | Cook time: 19 minutes | Serves 2

1 (15-ounce / 425-g) can
cooked white beans
2 tablespoons olive oil
1 teaspoon fresh sage, chopped

¼ teaspoon garlic powder
¼ teaspoon salt, divided
1 teaspoon chopped fresh basil

1. Preheat the air fryer to 380°F(193°C). 2. In a medium bowl, mix together the beans, olive oil, sage, garlic, ⅛ teaspoon salt, and basil. 3. Pour the white beans into the air fryer and spread them out in a single layer. 4. Bake for 10 minutes. Stir and continue cooking for an additional 5 to 9 minutes, or until they reach your preferred level of crispiness. 5. Toss with the remaining ⅛ teaspoon salt before serving.

Per Serving:
calories: 418 | fat: 14g | protein: 21g | carbs: 54g | fiber: 14g | sodium: 304mg

Grilled Halloumi with Watermelon, Cherry Tomatoes, Olives, and Herb Oil

Prep time: 5 minutes | Cook time: 5 minutes | Serves 4

½ cup coarsely chopped fresh
basil
3 tablespoons coarsely chopped
fresh mint leaves, plus thinly
sliced mint for garnish
1 clove garlic, coarsely chopped
½ cup olive oil, plus more for
brushing
½ teaspoon salt, plus a pinch
½ teaspoon freshly ground

black pepper, plus a pinch
¾ pound (340 g) cherry
tomatoes
8 ounces (227 g) Halloumi
cheese, cut crosswise into 8
slices
2 cups thinly sliced watermelon,
rind removed
¼ cup sliced, pitted Kalamata
olives

1. Heat a grill or grill pan to high. 2. In a food processor or blender, combine the basil, chopped mint, and garlic and pulse to chop. While the machine is running, add the olive oil in a thin stream.

Strain the oil through a fine-meshed sieve and discard the solids. Stir in ½ teaspoon of salt and ½ teaspoon of pepper. 3. Brush the grill rack with olive oil. Drizzle 2 tablespoons of the herb oil over the tomatoes and cheese and season them with pinches of salt and pepper. Place the tomatoes on the grill and cook, turning occasionally, until their skins become blistered and begin to burst, about 4 minutes. Place the cheese on the grill and cook until grill marks appear and the cheese begins to get melty, about 1 minute per side. 4. Arrange the watermelon on a serving platter. Arrange the grilled cheese and tomatoes on top of the melon. Drizzle the herb oil over the top and garnish with the olives and sliced mint. Serve immediately.

Per Serving:
calories: 535 | fat: 50g | protein: 14g | carbs: 12g | fiber: 2g | sodium: 663mg

Mini Lettuce Wraps

Prep time: 10 minutes | Cook time: 0 minutes |
Makes about 1 dozen wraps

1 tomato, diced
1 cucumber, diced
1 red onion, sliced
1 ounce (28 g) low-fat feta
cheese, crumbled
Juice of 1 lemon

1 tablespoon olive oil
Sea salt and freshly ground
pepper, to taste
12 small, intact iceberg lettuce
leaves

1. Combine the tomato, cucumber, onion, and feta in a bowl with the lemon juice and olive oil. 2. Season with sea salt and freshly ground pepper. 3. Without tearing the leaves, gently fill each leaf with a tablespoon of the veggie mixture. 4. Roll them as tightly as you can, and lay them seam-side-down on a serving platter.

Per Serving:
1 wrap: calories: 26 | fat: 2g | protein: 1g | carbs: 2g | fiber: 1g | sodium: 20mg

Garlic Edamame

Prep time: 5 minutes | Cook time: 10 minutes |
Serves 4

Olive oil
1 (16-ounce / 454-g) bag frozen
edamame in pods
½ teaspoon salt
½ teaspoon garlic salt

¼ teaspoon freshly ground
black pepper
½ teaspoon red pepper flakes
(optional)

1. Spray the air fryer basket lightly with olive oil. 2. In a medium bowl, add the frozen edamame and lightly spray with olive oil. Toss to coat. 3. In a small bowl, mix together the salt, garlic salt, black pepper, and red pepper flakes (if using). Add the mixture to the edamame and toss until evenly coated. 4. Place half the edamame in the air fryer basket. Do not overfill the basket. 5. Air fry at 375°F (191°C) for 5 minutes. Shake the basket and cook until the edamame is starting to brown and get crispy, 3 to 5 more minutes. 6. Repeat with the remaining edamame and serve immediately.

Per Serving:
calories: 125 | fat: 5g | protein: 12g | carbs: 10g | fiber: 5g | sodium: 443mg

Roasted Stuffed Figs

Prep time: 5 minutes | Cook time: 10 minutes | Serves 5

10 medium fresh figs
1½ tablespoons finely chopped walnuts
1½ tablespoons finely chopped almonds
½ teaspoon ground cinnamon

½ teaspoon sesame seeds
Pinch of salt
1½ teaspoons honey

1. Preheat the oven to 300°F (150ºC). Line a large baking sheet with foil, and grease the foil with olive oil. 2. Using a sharp knife, make a small vertical cut into the side of each fig, making sure not to cut all the way through the fig. Set aside. 3. In a small bowl, combine the walnuts, almonds, cinnamon, sesame seeds, and salt. Mix well. 4. Stuff each fig with 1 teaspoon of the filling, gently pressing the filling into the figs. Place the figs on the prepared baking sheet, and bake for 10 minutes. 5. While the figs are baking, add the honey to a small saucepan over medium heat. Heat the honey for 30 seconds or until it becomes thin and watery. 6. Transfer the roasted figs to a plate. Drizzle a few drops of the warm honey over each fig before serving. Store in an airtight container in the refrigerator for up to 2 weeks.

Per Serving:
calories: 114 | fat: 3g | protein: 2g | carbs: 22g | fiber: 4g | sodium: 2mg

Ultimate Nut Butter

Prep time: 5 minutes | Cook time: 30 minutes | Makes about 2 cups

1½ cups macadamia nuts
1 cup pecans
½ cup coconut butter
5 tablespoons light tahini

2 teaspoons cinnamon
1 teaspoon vanilla powder or 1 tablespoon unsweetened vanilla extract
¼ teaspoon salt

1. Preheat the oven to 285°F (140°C) fan assisted or 320°F (160°C) conventional. Line a baking tray with parchment. 2. Place the macadamias and pecans on the baking tray, transfer to the oven, and bake for about 30 minutes. Remove the nuts from the oven, let cool for about 10 minutes, and then transfer to a food processor while still warm. 3. Add the remaining ingredients. Blend until smooth and creamy, 2 to 3 minutes, scraping down the sides as needed with a spatula. Transfer to a jar and store at room temperature for up to 1 week or in the fridge for up to 1 month.

Per Serving:
¼ cup: calories: 374 | fat: 39g | protein: 3g | carbs: 6g | fiber: 4g | sodium: 76mg

Chapter 10 Vegetarian Mains

Cheese Stuffed Zucchini

Prep time: 20 minutes | Cook time: 8 minutes | Serves 4

1 large zucchini, cut into four pieces
2 tablespoons olive oil
1 cup Ricotta cheese, room temperature
2 tablespoons scallions, chopped
1 heaping tablespoon fresh

parsley, roughly chopped
1 heaping tablespoon coriander, minced
2 ounces (57 g) Cheddar cheese, preferably freshly grated
1 teaspoon celery seeds
½ teaspoon salt
½ teaspoon garlic pepper

1. Cook your zucchini in the air fryer basket for approximately 10 minutes at 350ºF (177ºC). Check for doneness and cook for 2-3 minutes longer if needed. 2. Meanwhile, make the stuffing by mixing the other items. 3. When your zucchini is thoroughly cooked, open them up. Divide the stuffing among all zucchini pieces and bake an additional 5 minutes.

Per Serving:
calories: 242 | fat: 20g | protein: 12g | carbs: 5g | fiber: 1g | sodium: 443mg

Beet and Carrot Fritters with Yogurt Sauce

Prep time: 15 minutes | Cook time: 15 minutes | Serves 2

For the Yogurt Sauce:
⅓ cup plain Greek yogurt
1 tablespoon freshly squeezed lemon juice
Zest of ½ lemon
¼ teaspoon garlic powder
¼ teaspoon salt
For the Fritters:
1 large carrot, peeled
1 small potato, peeled
1 medium golden or red beet, peeled

1 scallion, minced
2 tablespoons fresh minced parsley
¼ cup brown rice flour or unseasoned bread crumbs
¼ teaspoon garlic powder
¼ teaspoon salt
1 large egg, beaten
¼ cup feta cheese, crumbled
2 tablespoons olive oil (more if needed)

Make the Yogurt Sauce: In a small bowl, mix together the yogurt, lemon juice and zest, garlic powder, and salt. Set aside. Make the Fritters: 1. Shred the carrot, potato, and beet in a food processor with the shredding blade. You can also use a mandoline with a julienne shredding blade or a vegetable peeler. Squeeze out any moisture from the vegetables and place them in a large bowl. 2. Add the scallion, parsley, rice flour, garlic powder, salt, and egg. Stir the mixture well to combine. Add the feta cheese and stir briefly, leaving chunks of feta cheese throughout. 3. Heat a large nonstick sauté pan over medium-high heat and add 1 tablespoon of the olive oil. 4. Make the fritters by scooping about 3 tablespoons of the vegetable mixture into your hands and flattening it into a firm disc about 3 inches in diameter. 5. Place 2 fritters at a time in the pan and let them cook for about two minutes. Check to see if the underside is golden, and then flip and repeat on the other side. Remove from the heat, add the rest of the olive oil to the pan, and repeat with the remaining vegetable mixture. 6. To serve, spoon about 1 tablespoon of the yogurt sauce on top of each fritter.

Per Serving:
calories: 295 | fat: 14g | protein: 6g | carbs: 44g | fiber: 5g | sodium: 482mg

Stuffed Portobellos

Prep time: 10 minutes | Cook time: 8 minutes | Serves 4

3 ounces (85 g) cream cheese, softened
½ medium zucchini, trimmed and chopped
¼ cup seeded and chopped red bell pepper
1½ cups chopped fresh spinach

leaves
4 large portobello mushrooms, stems removed
2 tablespoons coconut oil, melted
½ teaspoon salt

1. In a medium bowl, mix cream cheese, zucchini, pepper, and spinach. 2. Drizzle mushrooms with coconut oil and sprinkle with salt. Scoop ¼ zucchini mixture into each mushroom. 3. Place mushrooms into ungreased air fryer basket. Adjust the temperature to 400ºF (204ºC) and air fry for 8 minutes. Portobellos will be tender and tops will be browned when done. Serve warm.

Per Serving:
calories: 151 | fat: 13g | protein: 4g | carbs: 6g | fiber: 2g | sodium: 427mg

Tortellini in Red Pepper Sauce

Prep time: 15 minutes | Cook time: 10 minutes | Serves 4

1 (16-ounce / 454-g) container fresh cheese tortellini (usually green and white pasta)
1 (16-ounce / 454-g) jar roasted red peppers, drained

1 teaspoon garlic powder
¼ cup tahini
1 tablespoon red pepper oil (optional)

1. Bring a large pot of water to a boil and cook the tortellini according to package directions. 2. In a blender, combine the red peppers with the garlic powder and process until smooth. Once blended, add the tahini until the sauce is thickened. If the sauce gets too thick, add up to 1 tablespoon red pepper oil (if using). 3. Once tortellini are cooked, drain and leave pasta in colander. Add the sauce to the bottom of the empty pot and heat for 2 minutes. Then, add the tortellini back into the pot and cook for 2 more minutes. Serve and enjoy!

Per Serving:
calories: 350 | fat: 11g | protein: 12g | carbs: 46g | fiber: 4g | sodium: 192mg

Mushroom Ragù with Parmesan Polenta

Prep time: 20 minutes | Cook time: 30 minutes | Serves 2

½ ounce (14 g) dried porcini mushrooms (optional but recommended)
2 tablespoons olive oil
1 pound (454 g) baby bella (cremini) mushrooms, quartered
1 large shallot, minced (about ⅓ cup)
1 garlic clove, minced
1 tablespoon flour
2 teaspoons tomato paste
½ cup red wine
1 cup mushroom stock (or reserved liquid from soaking the porcini mushrooms, if using)
½ teaspoon dried thyme
1 fresh rosemary sprig
1½ cups water
½ teaspoon salt
⅓ cup instant polenta
2 tablespoons grated Parmesan cheese

1. If using the dried porcini mushrooms, soak them in 1 cup of hot water for about 15 minutes to soften them. When they're softened, scoop them out of the water, reserving the soaking liquid. (I strain it through a coffee filter to remove any possible grit.) Mince the porcini mushrooms. 2. Heat the olive oil in a large sauté pan over medium-high heat. Add the mushrooms, shallot, and garlic, and sauté for 10 minutes, or until the vegetables are wilted and starting to caramelize. 3. Add the flour and tomato paste, and cook for another 30 seconds. Add the red wine, mushroom stock or porcini soaking liquid, thyme, and rosemary. Bring the mixture to a boil, stirring constantly until it thickens. Reduce the heat and let it simmer for 10 minutes. 4. While the mushrooms are simmering, bring the water to a boil in a saucepan and add salt. 5. Add the instant polenta and stir quickly while it thickens. Stir in the Parmesan cheese. Taste and add additional salt if needed.

Per Serving:
calories: 451 | fat: 16g | protein: 14g | carbs: 58g | fiber: 5g | sodium: 165mg

Crispy Tofu

Prep time: 30 minutes | Cook time: 15 to 20 minutes | Serves 4

1 (16-ounce / 454-g) block extra-firm tofu
2 tablespoons coconut aminos
1 tablespoon toasted sesame oil
1 tablespoon olive oil
1 tablespoon chili-garlic sauce
1½ teaspoons black sesame seeds
1 scallion, thinly sliced

1. Press the tofu for at least 15 minutes by wrapping it in paper towels and setting a heavy pan on top so that the moisture drains. 2. Slice the tofu into bite-size cubes and transfer to a bowl. Drizzle with the coconut aminos, sesame oil, olive oil, and chili-garlic sauce. Cover and refrigerate for 1 hour or up to overnight. 3. Preheat the air fryer to 400ºF (204ºC). 4. Arrange the tofu in a single layer in the air fryer basket. Pausing to shake the pan halfway through the cooking time, air fry for 15 to 20 minutes until crisp. Serve with any juices that accumulate in the bottom of the air fryer, sprinkled with the sesame seeds and sliced scallion.

Per Serving:
calories: 173 | fat: 14g | protein: 12g | carbs: 3g | fiber: 1g | sodium: 49mg

Sheet Pan Roasted Chickpeas and Vegetables with Harissa Yogurt

Prep time: 10 minutes | Cook time: 30 minutes | Serves 2

4 cups cauliflower florets (about ½ small head)
2 medium carrots, peeled, halved, and then sliced into quarters lengthwise
2 tablespoons olive oil, divided
½ teaspoon garlic powder, divided
½ teaspoon salt, divided
2 teaspoons za'atar spice mix, divided
1 (15-ounce / 425-g) can chickpeas, drained, rinsed, and patted dry
¾ cup plain Greek yogurt
1 teaspoon harissa spice paste

1. Preheat the oven to 400ºF (205ºC) and set the rack to the middle position. Line a sheet pan with foil or parchment paper. 2. Place the cauliflower and carrots in a large bowl. Drizzle with 1 tablespoon olive oil and sprinkle with ¼ teaspoon of garlic powder, ¼ teaspoon of salt, and 1 teaspoon of za'atar. Toss well to combine. 3. Spread the vegetables onto one half of the sheet pan in a single layer. 4. Place the chickpeas in the same bowl and season with the remaining 1 tablespoon of oil, ¼ teaspoon of garlic powder, and ¼ teaspoon of salt, and the remaining za'atar. Toss well to combine. 5. Spread the chickpeas onto the other half of the sheet pan. 6. Roast for 30 minutes, or until the vegetables are tender and the chickpeas start to turn golden. Flip the vegetables halfway through the cooking time, and give the chickpeas a stir so they cook evenly. 7. The chickpeas may need an extra few minutes if you like them crispy. If so, remove the vegetables and leave the chickpeas in until they're cooked to desired crispiness. 8. While the vegetables are roasting, combine the yogurt and harissa in a small bowl. Taste, and add additional harissa as desired.

Per Serving:
calories: 467 | fat: 23g | protein: 18g | carbs: 54g | fiber: 15g | sodium: 632mg

Three-Cheese Zucchini Boats

Prep time: 15 minutes | Cook time: 20 minutes | Serves 2

2 medium zucchini
1 tablespoon avocado oil
¼ cup low-carb, no-sugar-added pasta sauce
¼ cup full-fat ricotta cheese
¼ cup shredded Mozzarella
cheese
¼ teaspoon dried oregano
¼ teaspoon garlic powder
½ teaspoon dried parsley
2 tablespoons grated vegetarian Parmesan cheese

1. Cut off 1 inch from the top and bottom of each zucchini. Slice zucchini in half lengthwise and use a spoon to scoop out a bit of the inside, making room for filling. Brush with oil and spoon 2 tablespoons pasta sauce into each shell. 2. In a medium bowl, mix ricotta, Mozzarella, oregano, garlic powder, and parsley. Spoon the mixture into each zucchini shell. Place stuffed zucchini shells into the air fryer basket. 3. Adjust the temperature to 350ºF (177ºC) and air fry for 20 minutes. 4. To remove from the basket, use tongs or a spatula and carefully lift out. Top with Parmesan. Serve immediately.

Per Serving:
calories: 208 | fat: 14g | protein: 12g | carbs: 11g | fiber: 3g | sodium: 247mg

Mediterranean Baked Chickpeas

Prep time: 15 minutes | Cook time: 15 minutes | Serves 4

1 tablespoon extra-virgin olive oil
½ medium onion, chopped
3 garlic cloves, chopped
2 teaspoons smoked paprika
¼ teaspoon ground cumin
4 cups halved cherry tomatoes
2 (15-ounce / 425-g) cans chickpeas, drained and rinsed
½ cup plain, unsweetened, full-fat Greek yogurt, for serving
1 cup crumbled feta, for serving

1. Preheat the oven to 425°F (220°C). 2. In an oven-safe sauté pan or skillet, heat the oil over medium heat and sauté the onion and garlic. Cook for about 5 minutes, until softened and fragrant. Stir in the paprika and cumin and cook for 2 minutes. Stir in the tomatoes and chickpeas. 3. Bring to a simmer for 5 to 10 minutes before placing in the oven. 4. Roast in oven for 25 to 30 minutes, until bubbling and thickened. To serve, top with Greek yogurt and feta.

Per Serving:
calories: 412 | fat: 15g | protein: 20g | carbs: 51g | fiber: 13g | sodium: 444mg

Baked Mediterranean Tempeh with Tomatoes and Garlic

Prep time: 25 minutes | Cook time: 35 minutes | Serves 4

For the Tempeh:
12 ounces (340 g) tempeh
¼ cup white wine
2 tablespoons extra-virgin olive oil
2 tablespoons lemon juice
Zest of 1 lemon
¼ teaspoon kosher salt
¼ teaspoon freshly ground black pepper
For the Tomatoes and Garlic Sauce:
1 tablespoon extra-virgin olive
oil
1 onion, diced
3 garlic cloves, minced
1 (14½-ounce / 411-g) can no-salt-added crushed tomatoes
1 beefsteak tomato, diced
1 dried bay leaf
1 teaspoon white wine vinegar
1 teaspoon lemon juice
1 teaspoon dried oregano
1 teaspoon dried thyme
¾ teaspoon kosher salt
¼ cup basil, cut into ribbons

Make the Tempeh: 1. Place the tempeh in a medium saucepan. Add enough water to cover it by 1 to 2 inches. Bring to a boil over medium-high heat, cover, and lower heat to a simmer. Cook for 10 to 15 minutes. Remove the tempeh, pat dry, cool, and cut into 1-inch cubes. 2. In a large bowl, combine the white wine, olive oil, lemon juice, lemon zest, salt, and black pepper. Add the tempeh, cover the bowl, and put in the refrigerator for 4 hours, or up to overnight. 3. Preheat the oven to 375°F (190°C). Place the marinated tempeh and the marinade in a baking dish and cook for 15 minutes. Make the Tomatoes and Garlic Sauce: 4. Heat the olive oil in a large skillet over medium heat. Add the onion and sauté until transparent, 3 to 5 minutes. Add the garlic and sauté for 30 seconds. Add the crushed tomatoes, beefsteak tomato, bay leaf, vinegar, lemon juice, oregano, thyme, and salt. Mix well. Simmer for 15 minutes. 5. Add the baked tempeh to the tomato mixture and gently mix together. Garnish with the basil.

Per Serving:
calories: 330 | fat: 20g | protein: 18g | carbs: 22g | fiber: 4g | sodium: 305mg

Moroccan Vegetable Tagine

Prep time: 20 minutes | Cook time: 1 hour | Serves 6

½ cup extra-virgin olive oil
2 medium yellow onions, sliced
6 celery stalks, sliced into ¼-inch crescents
6 garlic cloves, minced
1 teaspoon ground cumin
1 teaspoon ginger powder
1 teaspoon salt
½ teaspoon paprika
½ teaspoon ground cinnamon
¼ teaspoon freshly ground black pepper
2 cups vegetable stock
1 medium eggplant, cut into 1-inch cubes
2 medium zucchini, cut into ½-inch-thick semicircles
2 cups cauliflower florets
1 (13¾-ounce / 390-g) can artichoke hearts, drained and quartered
1 cup halved and pitted green olives
½ cup chopped fresh flat-leaf parsley, for garnish
½ cup chopped fresh cilantro leaves, for garnish
Greek yogurt, for garnish (optional)

1. In a large, thick soup pot or Dutch oven, heat the olive oil over medium-high heat. Add the onion and celery and sauté until softened, 6 to 8 minutes. Add the garlic, cumin, ginger, salt, paprika, cinnamon, and pepper and sauté for another 2 minutes. 2. Add the stock and bring to a boil. Reduce the heat to low and add the eggplant, zucchini, and cauliflower. Simmer on low heat, covered, until the vegetables are tender, 30 to 35 minutes. Add the artichoke hearts and olives, cover, and simmer for another 15 minutes. 3. Serve garnished with parsley, cilantro, and Greek yogurt (if using).

Per Serving:
calories: 265 | fat: 21g | protein: 5g | carbs: 19g | fiber: 9g | sodium: 858mg

Cauliflower Steaks with Olive Citrus Sauce

Prep time: 15 minutes | Cook time: 30 minutes | Serves 4

1 or 2 large heads cauliflower (at least 2 pounds / 907 g, enough for 4 portions)
⅓ cup extra-virgin olive oil
¼ teaspoon kosher salt
⅛ teaspoon ground black pepper
Juice of 1 orange
Zest of 1 orange
¼ cup black olives, pitted and chopped
1 tablespoon Dijon or grainy mustard
1 tablespoon red wine vinegar
½ teaspoon ground coriander

1. Preheat the oven to 400°F (205°C). Line a baking sheet with parchment paper or foil. 2. Cut off the stem of the cauliflower so it will sit upright. Slice it vertically into four thick slabs. Place the cauliflower on the prepared baking sheet. Drizzle with the olive oil, salt, and black pepper. Bake for about 30 minutes, turning over once, until tender and golden brown. 3. In a medium bowl, combine the orange juice, orange zest, olives, mustard, vinegar, and coriander; mix well. 4. Serve the cauliflower warm or at room temperature with the sauce.

Per Serving:
calories: 265 | fat: 21g | protein: 5g | carbs: 19g | fiber: 4g | sodium: 310mg

Provençal Ratatouille with Herbed Breadcrumbs and Goat Cheese

Prep time: 10 minutes | Cook time: 1 hour 5 minutes | Serves 4

6 tablespoons olive oil, divided
2 medium onions, diced
2 cloves garlic, minced
2 medium eggplants, halved lengthwise and cut into ¾-inch thick half rounds
3 medium zucchini, halved lengthwise and cut into ¾-inch thick half rounds
2 red bell peppers, seeded and cut into 1½-inch pieces
1 green bell pepper, seeded and cut into 1½-inch pieces
1 (14-ounce / 397-g) can diced tomatoes, drained
1 teaspoon salt
½ teaspoon freshly ground black pepper
8 ounces (227 g) fresh breadcrumbs
1 tablespoon chopped fresh parsley
1 tablespoon chopped fresh basil
1 tablespoon chopped fresh chives
6 ounces (170 g) soft, fresh goat cheese

1. Preheat the oven to 375°F(190°C). 2. Heat 5 tablespoons of the olive oil in a large skillet over medium heat. Add the onions and garlic and cook, stirring frequently, until the onions are soft and beginning to turn golden, about 8 minutes. Add the eggplant, zucchini, and bell peppers and cook, turning the vegetables occasionally, for another 10 minutes. Stir in the tomatoes, salt, and pepper and let simmer for 15 minutes. 3. While the vegetables are simmering, stir together the breadcrumbs, the remaining tablespoon of olive oil, the parsley, basil, and chives. 4. Transfer the vegetable mixture to a large baking dish, spreading it out into an even layer. Crumble the goat cheese over the top, then sprinkle the breadcrumb mixture evenly over the top. Bake in the preheated oven for about 30 minutes, until the topping is golden brown and crisp. Serve hot.

Per Serving:
calories: 644 | fat: 37g | protein: 21g | carbs: 63g | fiber: 16g | sodium: 861mg

Parmesan Artichokes

Prep time: 10 minutes | Cook time: 10 minutes | Serves 4

2 medium artichokes, trimmed and quartered, center removed
2 tablespoons coconut oil
1 large egg, beaten
½ cup grated vegetarian Parmesan cheese
¼ cup blanched finely ground almond flour
½ teaspoon crushed red pepper flakes

1. In a large bowl, toss artichokes in coconut oil and then dip each piece into the egg. 2. Mix the Parmesan and almond flour in a large bowl. Add artichoke pieces and toss to cover as completely as possible, sprinkle with pepper flakes. Place into the air fryer basket. 3. Adjust the temperature to 400°F (204°C) and air fry for 10 minutes. 4. Toss the basket two times during cooking. Serve warm.

Per Serving:
calories: 207 | fat: 13g | protein: 10g | carbs: 15g | fiber: 5g | sodium: 211mg

Roasted Portobello Mushrooms with Kale and Red Onion

Prep time: 15 minutes | Cook time: 30 minutes | Serves 4

¼ cup white wine vinegar
3 tablespoons extra-virgin olive oil, divided
½ teaspoon honey
¾ teaspoon kosher salt, divided
¼ teaspoon freshly ground black pepper
4 large (4 to 5 ounces / 113 to 142 g each) portobello mushrooms, stems removed
1 red onion, julienned
2 garlic cloves, minced
1 (8-ounce / 227-g) bunch kale, stemmed and chopped small
¼ teaspoon red pepper flakes
¼ cup grated Parmesan or Romano cheese

1. Line a baking sheet with parchment paper or foil. In a medium bowl, whisk together the vinegar, 1½ tablespoons of the olive oil, honey, ¼ teaspoon of the salt, and the black pepper. Arrange the mushrooms on the baking sheet and pour the marinade over them. Marinate for 15 to 30 minutes. 2. Meanwhile, preheat the oven to 400°F (205°C). 3. Bake the mushrooms for 20 minutes, turning over halfway through. 4. Heat the remaining 1½ tablespoons olive oil in a large skillet or ovenproof sauté pan over medium-high heat. Add the onion and the remaining ½ teaspoon salt and sauté until golden brown, 5 to 6 minutes. Add the garlic and sauté for 30 seconds. Add the kale and red pepper flakes and sauté until the kale cooks down, about 5 minutes. 5. Remove the mushrooms from the oven and increase the temperature to broil. 6. Carefully pour the liquid from the baking sheet into the pan with the kale mixture; mix well. 7. Turn the mushrooms over so that the stem side is facing up. Spoon some of the kale mixture on top of each mushroom. Sprinkle 1 tablespoon Parmesan cheese on top of each. 8. Broil until golden brown, 3 to 4 minutes.

Per Serving:
calories: 200 | fat: 13g | protein: 8g | carbs: 16g | fiber: 4g | sodium: 365mg

Tangy Asparagus and Broccoli

Prep time: 25 minutes | Cook time: 22 minutes | Serves 4

½ pound (227 g) asparagus, cut into 1½-inch pieces
½ pound (227 g) broccoli, cut into 1½-inch pieces
2 tablespoons olive oil
Salt and white pepper, to taste
½ cup vegetable broth
2 tablespoons apple cider vinegar

1. Place the vegetables in a single layer in the lightly greased air fryer basket. Drizzle the olive oil over the vegetables. 2. Sprinkle with salt and white pepper. 3. Cook at 380°F (193°C) for 15 minutes, shaking the basket halfway through the cooking time. 4. Add ½ cup of vegetable broth to a saucepan; bring to a rapid boil and add the vinegar. Cook for 5 to 7 minutes or until the sauce has reduced by half. 5. Spoon the sauce over the warm vegetables and serve immediately. Bon appétit!

Per Serving:
calories: 93 | fat: 7g | protein: 3g | carbs: 6g | fiber: 3g | sodium: 89mg

Creamy Chickpea Sauce with Whole-Wheat Fusilli

Prep time: 15 minutes | Cook time: 20 minutes | Serves 4

¼ cup extra-virgin olive oil
½ large shallot, chopped
5 garlic cloves, thinly sliced
1 (15-ounce / 425-g) can chickpeas, drained and rinsed, reserving ½ cup canning liquid
Pinch red pepper flakes
1 cup whole-grain fusilli pasta
¼ teaspoon salt
⅛ teaspoon freshly ground black pepper
¼ cup shaved fresh Parmesan cheese
¼ cup chopped fresh basil
2 teaspoons dried parsley
1 teaspoon dried oregano
Red pepper flakes

1. In a medium pan, heat the oil over medium heat, and sauté the shallot and garlic for 3 to 5 minutes, until the garlic is golden. Add ¾ of the chickpeas plus 2 tablespoons of liquid from the can, and bring to a simmer. 2. Remove from the heat, transfer into a standard blender, and blend until smooth. At this point, add the remaining chickpeas. Add more reserved chickpea liquid if it becomes thick. 3. Bring a large pot of salted water to a boil and cook pasta until al dente, about 8 minutes. Reserve ½ cup of the pasta water, drain the pasta, and return it to the pot. 4. Add the chickpea sauce to the hot pasta and add up to ¼ cup of the pasta water. You may need to add more pasta water to reach your desired consistency. 5. Place the pasta pot over medium heat and mix occasionally until the sauce thickens. Season with salt and pepper. 6. Serve, garnished with Parmesan, basil, parsley, oregano, and red pepper flakes.

Per Serving:
1 cup pasta: calories: 310 | fat: 17g | protein: 10g | carbs: 33g | fiber: 7g | sodium: 243mg

Quinoa Lentil "Meatballs" with Quick Tomato Sauce

Prep time: 25 minutes | Cook time: 45 minutes | Serves 4

For the Meatballs:
Olive oil cooking spray
2 large eggs, beaten
1 tablespoon no-salt-added tomato paste
½ teaspoon kosher salt
½ cup grated Parmesan cheese
½ onion, roughly chopped
¼ cup fresh parsley
1 garlic clove, peeled
1½ cups cooked lentils
1 cup cooked quinoa
For the Tomato Sauce:
1 tablespoon extra-virgin olive oil
1 onion, minced
½ teaspoon dried oregano
½ teaspoon kosher salt
2 garlic cloves, minced
1 (28-ounce / 794-g) can no-salt-added crushed tomatoes
½ teaspoon honey
¼ cup fresh basil, chopped

Make the Meatballs: 1. Preheat the oven to 400ºF (205ºC). Lightly grease a 12-cup muffin pan with olive oil cooking spray. 2. In a large bowl, whisk together the eggs, tomato paste, and salt until fully combined. Mix in the Parmesan cheese. 3. In a food processor, add the onion, parsley, and garlic. Process until minced. Add to the egg mixture and stir together. Add the lentils to the food processor and process until puréed into a thick paste. Add to the large bowl and mix together. Add the quinoa and mix well. 4. Form balls, slightly larger than a golf ball, with ¼ cup of the quinoa mixture.

Place each ball in a muffin pan cup. Note: The mixture will be somewhat soft but should hold together. 5. Bake 25 to 30 minutes, until golden brown. Make the Tomato Sauce: 6. Heat the olive oil in a large saucepan over medium heat. Add the onion, oregano, and salt and sauté until light golden brown, about 5 minutes. Add the garlic and cook for 30 seconds. 7. Stir in the tomatoes and honey. Increase the heat to high and cook, stirring often, until simmering, then decrease the heat to medium-low and cook for 10 minutes. Remove from the heat and stir in the basil. Serve with the meatballs.

Per Serving:
3 meatballs: calories: 360 | fat: 10g | protein: 20g | carbs: 48g | fiber: 14g | sodium: 520mg

Crispy Eggplant Rounds

Prep time: 15 minutes | Cook time: 10 minutes | Serves 4

1 large eggplant, ends trimmed, cut into ½-inch slices
½ teaspoon salt
2 ounces (57 g) Parmesan 100%
cheese crisps, finely ground
½ teaspoon paprika
¼ teaspoon garlic powder
1 large egg

1. Sprinkle eggplant rounds with salt. Place rounds on a kitchen towel for 30 minutes to draw out excess water. Pat rounds dry. 2. In a medium bowl, mix cheese crisps, paprika, and garlic powder. In a separate medium bowl, whisk egg. Dip each eggplant round in egg, then gently press into cheese crisps to coat both sides. 3. Place eggplant rounds into ungreased air fryer basket. Adjust the temperature to 400ºF (204ºC) and air fry for 10 minutes, turning rounds halfway through cooking. Eggplant will be golden and crispy when done. Serve warm.

Per Serving:
calories: 113 | fat: 5g | protein: 7g | carbs: 10g | fiber: 4g | sodium: 567mg

Vegetable Burgers

Prep time: 10 minutes | Cook time: 12 minutes | Serves 4

8 ounces (227 g) cremini mushrooms
2 large egg yolks
½ medium zucchini, trimmed and chopped
¼ cup peeled and chopped
yellow onion
1 clove garlic, peeled and finely minced
½ teaspoon salt
¼ teaspoon ground black pepper

1. Place all ingredients into a food processor and pulse twenty times until finely chopped and combined. 2. Separate mixture into four equal sections and press each into a burger shape. Place burgers into ungreased air fryer basket. Adjust the temperature to 375ºF (191ºC) and air fry for 12 minutes, turning burgers halfway through cooking. Burgers will be browned and firm when done. 3. Place burgers on a large plate and let cool 5 minutes before serving.

Per Serving:
calories: 50 | fat: 3g | protein: 3g | carbs: 4g | fiber: 1g | sodium: 299mg

Crustless Spanakopita

Prep time: 15 minutes | Cook time: 45 minutes | Serves 6

12 tablespoons extra-virgin olive oil, divided
1 small yellow onion, diced
1 (32-ounce / 907-g) bag frozen chopped spinach, thawed, fully drained, and patted dry (about 4 cups)
4 garlic cloves, minced
½ teaspoon salt
½ teaspoon freshly ground black pepper
1 cup whole-milk ricotta cheese
4 large eggs
¾ cup crumbled traditional feta cheese
¼ cup pine nuts

1. Preheat the oven to 375°F (190°C). 2. In a large skillet, heat 4 tablespoons olive oil over medium-high heat. Add the onion and sauté until softened, 6 to 8 minutes. 3. Add the spinach, garlic, salt, and pepper and sauté another 5 minutes. Remove from the heat and allow to cool slightly. 4. In a medium bowl, whisk together the ricotta and eggs. Add to the cooled spinach and stir to combine. 5. Pour 4 tablespoons olive oil in the bottom of a 9-by-13-inch glass baking dish and swirl to coat the bottom and sides. Add the spinach-ricotta mixture and spread into an even layer. 6. Bake for 20 minutes or until the mixture begins to set. Remove from the oven and crumble the feta evenly across the top of the spinach. Add the pine nuts and drizzle with the remaining 4 tablespoons olive oil. Return to the oven and bake for an additional 15 to 20 minutes, or until the spinach is fully set and the top is starting to turn golden brown. Allow to cool slightly before cutting to serve.

Per Serving:
calories: 497 | fat: 44g | protein: 18g | carbs: 11g | fiber: 5g | sodium: 561mg

Asparagus and Mushroom Farrotto

Prep time: 20 minutes | Cook time: 45 minutes | Serves 2

1½ ounces (43 g) dried porcini mushrooms
1 cup hot water
3 cups low-sodium vegetable stock
2 tablespoons olive oil
½ large onion, minced (about 1 cup)
1 garlic clove
1 cup diced mushrooms (about
4 ounces / 113-g)
¾ cup farro
½ cup dry white wine
½ teaspoon dried thyme
4 ounces (113 g) asparagus, cut into ½-inch pieces (about 1 cup)
2 tablespoons grated Parmesan cheese
Salt

1. Soak the dried mushrooms in the hot water for about 15 minutes. When they're softened, drain the mushrooms, reserving the liquid. (I like to strain the liquid through a coffee filter in case there's any grit.) Mince the porcini mushrooms. 2. Add the mushroom liquid and vegetable stock to a medium saucepan and bring it to a boil. Reduce the heat to low just to keep it warm. 3. Heat the olive oil in a Dutch oven over high heat. Add the onion, garlic, and mushrooms, and sauté for 10 minutes. 4. Add the farro to the Dutch oven and sauté it for 3 minutes to toast. 5. Add the wine, thyme, and one ladleful of the hot mushroom and chicken stock. Bring it to a boil while stirring the farro. Do not cover the pot while the farro is cooking. 6. Reduce the heat to medium. When the liquid is absorbed, add another ladleful or two at a time to the pot, stirring occasionally, until the farro is cooked through. Keep an eye on the heat, to make sure it doesn't cook too quickly. 7. When the farro is al dente, add the asparagus and another ladleful of stock. Cook for another 3 to 5 minutes, or until the asparagus is softened. 8. Stir in Parmesan cheese and season with salt.

Per Serving:
calories: 341 | fat: 16g | protein: 13g | carbs: 26g | fiber: 5g | sodium: 259mg

Mozzarella and Sun-Dried Portobello Mushroom Pizza

Prep time: 10 minutes | Cook time: 10 minutes | Serves 4

4 large portobello mushroom caps
3 tablespoons extra-virgin olive oil
Salt
Freshly ground black pepper
4 sun-dried tomatoes
1 cup mozzarella cheese, divided
½ to ¾ cup low-sodium tomato sauce

1. Preheat the broiler on high. 2. On a baking sheet, drizzle the mushroom caps with the olive oil and season with salt and pepper. Broil the portobello mushrooms for 5 minutes on each side, flipping once, until tender. 3. Fill each mushroom cap with 1 sun-dried tomato, 2 tablespoons of cheese, and 2 to 3 tablespoons of sauce. Top each with 2 tablespoons of cheese. Place the caps back under the broiler for a final 2 to 3 minutes, then quarter the mushrooms and serve.

Per Serving:
calories: 218| fat: 16g | protein: 11g | carbs: 12g | fiber: 2g | sodium: 244mg

Ricotta, Basil, and Pistachio-Stuffed Zucchini

Prep time: 15 minutes | Cook time: 25 minutes | Serves 4

2 medium zucchini, halved lengthwise
1 tablespoon extra-virgin olive oil
1 onion, diced
1 teaspoon kosher salt
2 garlic cloves, minced
¾ cup ricotta cheese
¼ cup unsalted pistachios, shelled and chopped
¼ cup fresh basil, chopped
1 large egg, beaten
¼ teaspoon freshly ground black pepper

1. Preheat the oven to 425°F (220°C). Line a baking sheet with parchment paper or foil. 2. Scoop out the seeds/pulp from the zucchini, leaving ¼-inch flesh around the edges. Transfer the pulp to a cutting board and chop the pulp. 3. Heat the olive oil in a large skillet or sauté pan over medium heat. Add the onion, pulp, and salt and sauté about 5 minutes. Add the garlic and sauté 30 seconds. 4. In a medium bowl, combine the ricotta cheese, pistachios, basil, egg, and black pepper. Add the onion mixture and mix together well. 5. Place the 4 zucchini halves on the prepared baking sheet. Fill the zucchini halves with the ricotta mixture. Bake for 20 minutes, or until golden brown.

Per Serving:
calories: 200 | fat: 12g | protein: 11g | carbs: 14g | fiber: 3g | sodium: 360mg

Turkish Red Lentil and Bulgur Kofte

Prep time: 10 minutes | Cook time: 45 minutes | Serves 4

⅓ cup olive oil, plus 2 tablespoons, divided, plus more for brushing
1 cup red lentils
½ cup bulgur
1 teaspoon salt
1 medium onion, finely diced

2 tablespoons tomato paste
1 teaspoon ground cumin
¼ cup finely chopped flat-leaf parsley
3 scallions, thinly sliced
Juice of ½ lemon

1. Preheat the oven to 400°F(205°C). 2. Brush a large, rimmed baking sheet with olive oil. 3. In a medium saucepan, combine the lentils with 2 cups water and bring to a boil. Reduce the heat to low and cook, stirring occasionally, for about 15 minutes, until the lentils are tender and have soaked up most of the liquid. Remove from the heat, stir in the bulgur and salt, cover, and let sit for 15 minutes or so, until the bulgur is tender. 4. Meanwhile, heat ⅓ cup olive oil in a medium skillet over medium-high heat. Add the onion and cook, stirring frequently, until softened, about 5 minutes. Stir in the tomato paste and cook for 2 minutes more. Remove from the heat and stir in the cumin. 5. Add the cooked onion mixture to the lentil-bulgur mixture and stir to combine. Add the parsley, scallions, and lemon juice and stir to mix well. 6. Shape the mixture into walnut-sized balls and place them on the prepared baking sheet. Brush the balls with the remaining 2 tablespoons of olive oil and bake for 15 to 20 minutes, until golden brown. Serve hot.

Per Serving:
calories: 460 | fat: 25g | protein: 16g | carbs: 48g | fiber: 19g | sodium: 604mg

Eggplants Stuffed with Walnuts and Feta

Prep time: 10 minutes | Cook time: 55 minutes | Serves 6

3 medium eggplants, halved lengthwise
2 teaspoons salt, divided
¼ cup olive oil, plus 2 tablespoons, divided
2 medium onions, diced
1½ pints cherry or grape tomatoes, halved
¾ cup roughly chopped walnut

pieces
2¼ teaspoons ground cinnamon
1½ teaspoons dried oregano
½ teaspoon freshly ground black pepper
¼ cup whole-wheat breadcrumbs
⅔ cup (about 3 ounces / 85 g) crumbled feta cheese

1. Scoop out the flesh of the eggplants, leaving a ½-inch thick border of flesh in the skins. Dice the flesh that you removed and place it in a colander set over the sink. Sprinkle 1½ teaspoons of salt over the diced eggplant and inside the eggplant shells and let stand for 30 minutes. Rinse the shells and the pieces and pat dry with paper towels. 2. Heat ¼ cup of olive oil in a large skillet over medium heat. Add the eggplant shells, skin-side down, and cook for about 4 minutes, until browned and softened. Turn over and cook on the cut side until golden brown and soft, about 4 minutes more. Transfer to a plate lined with paper towel to drain. 3. Drain off all but about 1 to 2 tablespoons of the oil in the skillet and heat over medium-high heat. Add the onions and cook, stirring, until beginning to soften, about 3 minutes. Add the diced eggplant, tomatoes, walnuts, cinnamon, oregano, ¼ cup water, the remaining ½ teaspoon of salt, and the pepper. Cook, stirring occasionally, until the vegetables are golden brown and softened, about 8 minutes.

4. Preheat the broiler to high. 5. In a small bowl, toss together the breadcrumbs and 1 tablespoon olive oil. 6. Arrange the eggplant shells cut-side up on a large, rimmed baking sheet. Brush each shell with about ½ teaspoon of olive oil. Cook under the broiler until tender and just starting to turn golden brown, about 5 minutes. Remove the eggplants from the broiler and reduce the heat of the oven to 375°F (190°C). 7. Spoon the sautéed vegetable mixture into the eggplant shells, dividing equally. Sprinkle the breadcrumbs over the tops of the filled eggplants, dividing equally. Sprinkle the cheese on top, again dividing equally. Bake in the oven until the filling and shells are heated through and the topping is nicely browned and crisp, about 35 minutes.

Per Serving:
calories: 274 | fat: 15g | protein: 7g | carbs: 34g | fiber: 13g | sodium: 973mg

Roasted Veggie Bowl

Prep time: 10 minutes | Cook time: 15 minutes | Serves 2

1 cup broccoli florets
1 cup quartered Brussels sprouts
½ cup cauliflower florets
¼ medium white onion, peeled and sliced ¼ inch thick

½ medium green bell pepper, seeded and sliced ¼ inch thick
1 tablespoon coconut oil
2 teaspoons chili powder
½ teaspoon garlic powder
½ teaspoon cumin

1. Toss all ingredients together in a large bowl until vegetables are fully coated with oil and seasoning. 2. Pour vegetables into the air fryer basket. 3. Adjust the temperature to 360ºF (182ºC) and roast for 15 minutes. 4. Shake two or three times during cooking. Serve warm.

Per Serving:
calories: 112 | fat: 7.68g | protein: 3.64g | carbs: 10.67g | sugars: 3.08g | fiber: 4.6g | sodium: 106mg

Orzo-Stuffed Tomatoes

Prep time: 15 minutes | Cook time: 30 minutes | Serves 2

1 tablespoon olive oil
1 small zucchini, minced
½ medium onion, minced
1 garlic clove, minced
⅔ cup cooked orzo (from ¼ cup dry orzo, cooked according

to package instructions, or precooked)
½ teaspoon salt
2 teaspoons dried oregano
6 medium round tomatoes (not Roma)

1. Preheat the oven to 350ºF (180ºC). 2. Heat the olive oil in a large sauté pan over medium-high heat. Add the zucchini, onion, and garlic and sauté for 15 minutes, or until the vegetables turn golden. 3. Add the orzo, salt, and oregano and stir to heat through. Remove the pan from the heat and set aside. 4. Cut about ½ inch from the top of each tomato. With a paring knife, cut around the inner core of the tomato to remove about half of the flesh. Reserve for another recipe or a salad. 5. Stuff each tomato with the orzo mixture. 6. If serving hot, put the tomatoes in a baking dish, or, if they'll fit, a muffin tin. Roast the tomatoes for about 15 minutes, or until they're soft. Don't overcook them or they won't hold together. If desired, this can also be served without roasting the tomatoes.

Per Serving:
calories: 241 | fat: 8g | protein: 7g | carbs: 38g | fiber: 6g | sodium: 301mg

Caprese Eggplant Stacks

Prep time: 5 minutes | Cook time: 12 minutes | Serves 4

1 medium eggplant, cut into ¼-inch slices	Mozzarella, cut into ½-ounce / 14-g slices
2 large tomatoes, cut into ¼-inch slices	2 tablespoons olive oil
4 ounces (113 g) fresh	¼ cup fresh basil, sliced

1. In a baking dish, place four slices of eggplant on the bottom. Place a slice of tomato on top of each eggplant round, then Mozzarella, then eggplant. Repeat as necessary. 2. Drizzle with olive oil. Cover dish with foil and place dish into the air fryer basket. 3. Adjust the temperature to 350°F (177°C) and bake for 12 minutes. 4. When done, eggplant will be tender. Garnish with fresh basil to serve.

Per Serving:
calories: 97 | fat: 7g | protein: 2g | carbs: 8g | fiber: 4g | sodium: 11mg

Cheesy Cauliflower Pizza Crust

Prep time: 15 minutes | Cook time: 11 minutes | Serves 2

1 (12-ounce / 340-g) steamer bag cauliflower	2 tablespoons blanched finely ground almond flour
½ cup shredded sharp Cheddar cheese	1 teaspoon Italian blend seasoning
1 large egg	

1. Cook cauliflower according to package instructions. Remove from bag and place into cheesecloth or paper towel to remove excess water. Place cauliflower into a large bowl. 2. Add cheese, egg, almond flour, and Italian seasoning to the bowl and mix well. 3. Cut a piece of parchment to fit your air fryer basket. Press cauliflower into 6-inch round circle. Place into the air fryer basket. 4. Adjust the temperature to 360°F (182°C) and air fry for 11 minutes. 5. After 7 minutes, flip the pizza crust. 6. Add preferred toppings to pizza. Place back into air fryer basket and cook an additional 4 minutes or until fully cooked and golden. Serve immediately.

Per Serving:
calories: 251 | fat: 17g | protein: 15g | carbs: 12g | fiber: 5g | sodium: 375mg

Spinach-Artichoke Stuffed Mushrooms

Prep time: 10 minutes | Cook time: 10 to 14 minutes | Serves 4

2 tablespoons olive oil	crumbled
4 large portobello mushrooms, stems removed and gills scraped out	½ cup chopped marinated artichoke hearts
½ teaspoon salt	1 cup frozen spinach, thawed and squeezed dry
¼ teaspoon freshly ground pepper	½ cup grated Parmesan cheese
4 ounces (113 g) goat cheese,	2 tablespoons chopped fresh parsley

1. Preheat the air fryer to 400°F (204°C). 2. Rub the olive oil over the portobello mushrooms until thoroughly coated. Sprinkle both sides with the salt and black pepper. Place top-side down on a clean work surface. 3. In a small bowl, combine the goat cheese, artichoke hearts, and spinach. Mash with the back of a fork until thoroughly combined. Divide the cheese mixture among the mushrooms and sprinkle with the Parmesan cheese. 4. Air fry for 10 to 14 minutes until the mushrooms are tender and the cheese has begun to brown. Top with the fresh parsley just before serving.

Per Serving:
calories: 284 | fat: 21g | protein: 16g | carbs: 10g | fiber: 4g | sodium: 686mg

Broccoli-Cheese Fritters

Prep time: 5 minutes | Cook time: 20 to 25 minutes | Serves 4

1 cup broccoli florets	1 teaspoon garlic powder
1 cup shredded Mozzarella cheese	Salt and freshly ground black pepper, to taste
¾ cup almond flour	2 eggs, lightly beaten
½ cup flaxseed meal, divided	½ cup ranch dressing
2 teaspoons baking powder	

1. Preheat the air fryer to 400°F (204°C). 2. In a food processor fitted with a metal blade, pulse the broccoli until very finely chopped. 3. Transfer the broccoli to a large bowl and add the Mozzarella, almond flour, ¼ cup of the flaxseed meal, baking powder, and garlic powder. Stir until thoroughly combined. Season to taste with salt and black pepper. Add the eggs and stir again to form a sticky dough. Shape the dough into 1¼-inch fritters. 4. Place the remaining ¼ cup flaxseed meal in a shallow bowl and roll the fritters in the meal to form an even coating. 5. Working in batches if necessary, arrange the fritters in a single layer in the basket of the air fryer and spray generously with olive oil. Pausing halfway through the cooking time to shake the basket, air fry for 20 to 25 minutes until the fritters are golden brown and crispy. Serve with the ranch dressing for dipping.

Per Serving:
calories: 388 | fat: 30g | protein: 19g | carbs: 14g | fiber: 7g | sodium: 526mg

Quinoa with Almonds and Cranberries

Prep time: 15 minutes | Cook time: 0 minutes | Serves 4

2 cups cooked quinoa	½ teaspoon ground cumin
⅓ teaspoon cranberries or currants	½ teaspoon turmeric
¼ cup sliced almonds	¼ teaspoon ground cinnamon
2 garlic cloves, minced	¼ teaspoon freshly ground black pepper
1¼ teaspoons salt	

1. In a large bowl, toss the quinoa, cranberries, almonds, garlic, salt, cumin, turmeric, cinnamon, and pepper and stir to combine. Enjoy alone or with roasted cauliflower.

Per Serving:
calories: 194 | fat: 6g | protein: 7g | carbs: 31g | fiber: 4g | sodium: 727mg

Pesto Spinach Flatbread

Prep time: 10 minutes | Cook time: 8 minutes | Serves 4

1 cup blanched finely ground almond flour
2 ounces (57 g) cream cheese
2 cups shredded Mozzarella cheese
1 cup chopped fresh spinach leaves
2 tablespoons basil pesto

1. Place flour, cream cheese, and Mozzarella in a large microwave-safe bowl and microwave on high 45 seconds, then stir. 2. Fold in spinach and microwave an additional 15 seconds. Stir until a soft dough ball forms. 3. Cut two pieces of parchment paper to fit air fryer basket. Separate dough into two sections and press each out on ungreased parchment to create 6-inch rounds. 4. Spread 1 tablespoon pesto over each flatbread and place rounds on parchment into ungreased air fryer basket. Adjust the temperature to 350ºF (177ºC) and air fry for 8 minutes, turning crusts halfway through cooking. Flatbread will be golden when done. 5. Let cool 5 minutes before slicing and serving.

Per Serving:
calories: 387 | fat: 28g | protein: 28g | carbs: 10g | fiber: 5g | sodium: 556mg

Broccoli Crust Pizza

Prep time: 15 minutes | Cook time: 12 minutes | Serves 4

3 cups riced broccoli, steamed and drained well
1 large egg
½ cup grated vegetarian Parmesan cheese
3 tablespoons low-carb Alfredo sauce
½ cup shredded Mozzarella cheese

1. In a large bowl, mix broccoli, egg, and Parmesan. 2. Cut a piece of parchment to fit your air fryer basket. Press out the pizza mixture to fit on the parchment, working in two batches if necessary. Place into the air fryer basket. 3. Adjust the temperature to 370ºF (188ºC) and air fry for 5 minutes. 4. The crust should be firm enough to flip. If not, add 2 additional minutes. Flip crust. 5. Top with Alfredo sauce and Mozzarella. Return to the air fryer basket and cook an additional 7 minutes or until cheese is golden and bubbling. Serve warm.

Per Serving:
calories: 87 | fat: 2g | protein: 11g | carbs: 5g | fiber: 1g | sodium: 253mg

Kate's Warm Mediterranean Farro Bowl

Prep time: 15 minutes | Cook time: 10 minutes | Serves 4 to 6

⅓ cup extra-virgin olive oil
½ cup chopped red bell pepper
⅓ cup chopped red onions
2 garlic cloves, minced
1 cup zucchini, cut in ½-inch slices
½ cup canned chickpeas, drained and rinsed
½ cup coarsely chopped artichokes
3 cups cooked farro
Salt
Freshly ground black pepper
¼ cup sliced olives, for serving (optional)
½ cup crumbled feta cheese, for serving (optional)
2 tablespoons fresh basil, chiffonade, for serving
(optional)
3 tablespoons balsamic reduction, for serving (optional)

1. In a large sauté pan or skillet, heat the oil over medium heat and sauté the pepper, onions, and garlic for about 5 minutes, until tender. 2. Add the zucchini, chickpeas, and artichokes, then stir and continue to sauté vegetables, approximately 5 more minutes, until just soft. 3. Stir in the cooked farro, tossing to combine and cooking enough to heat through. Season with salt and pepper and remove from the heat. 4. Transfer the contents of the pan into the serving vessels or bowls. 5. Top with olives, feta, and basil (if using). Drizzle with balsamic reduction (if using) to finish.

Per Serving:
calories: 367 | fat: 20g | protein: 9g | carbs: 51g | fiber: 9g | sodium: 87mg

Cauliflower Rice-Stuffed Peppers

Prep time: 10 minutes | Cook time: 15 minutes | Serves 4

2 cups uncooked cauliflower rice
¾ cup drained canned petite diced tomatoes
2 tablespoons olive oil
1 cup shredded Mozzarella cheese
¼ teaspoon salt
¼ teaspoon ground black pepper
4 medium green bell peppers, tops removed, seeded

1. In a large bowl, mix all ingredients except bell peppers. Scoop mixture evenly into peppers. 2. Place peppers into ungreased air fryer basket. Adjust the temperature to 350ºF (177ºC) and air fry for 15 minutes. Peppers will be tender and cheese will be melted when done. Serve warm.

Per Serving:
calories: 144 | fat: 7g | protein: 11g | carbs: 11g | fiber: 5g | sodium: 380mg

Pesto Vegetable Skewers

Prep time: 30 minutes | Cook time: 8 minutes | Makes 8 skewers

1 medium zucchini, trimmed and cut into ½-inch slices
½ medium yellow onion, peeled and cut into 1-inch squares
1 medium red bell pepper, seeded and cut into 1-inch squares
16 whole cremini mushrooms
⅓ cup basil pesto
½ teaspoon salt
¼ teaspoon ground black pepper

1. Divide zucchini slices, onion, and bell pepper into eight even portions. Place on 6-inch skewers for a total of eight kebabs. Add 2 mushrooms to each skewer and brush kebabs generously with pesto. 2. Sprinkle each kebab with salt and black pepper on all sides, then place into ungreased air fryer basket. Adjust the temperature to 375ºF (191ºC) and air fry for 8 minutes, turning kebabs halfway through cooking. Vegetables will be browned at the edges and tender-crisp when done. Serve warm.

Per Serving:
calories: 75 | fat: 6g | protein: 3g | carbs: 4g | fiber: 1g | sodium: 243mg

Root Vegetable Soup with Garlic Aioli

Prep time: 10 minutes | Cook time 25 minutes | Serves 4

For the Soup:
8 cups vegetable broth
½ teaspoon salt
1 medium leek, cut into thick rounds
1 pound (454 g) carrots, peeled and diced
1 pound (454 g) potatoes, peeled and diced
1 pound (454 g) turnips, peeled and cut into 1-inch cubes

1 red bell pepper, cut into strips
2 tablespoons fresh oregano
For the Aioli:
5 garlic cloves, minced
¼ teaspoon salt
⅔ cup olive oil
1 drop lemon juice

1. Bring the broth and salt to a boil and add the vegetables one at a time, letting the water return to a boil after each addition. Add the carrots first, then the leeks, potatoes, turnips, and finally the red bell peppers. Let the vegetables cook for about 3 minutes after adding the green beans and bringing to a boil. The process will take about 20 minutes in total. 2. Meanwhile, make the aioli. In a mortar and pestle, grind the garlic to a paste with the salt. Using a whisk and whisking constantly, add the olive oil in a thin stream. Continue whisking until the mixture thickens to the consistency of mayonnaise. Add the lemon juice. 3. Serve the vegetables in the broth, dolloped with the aioli and garnished with the fresh oregano.

Per Serving:
calories: 538 | fat: 37g | protein: 5g | carbs: 50g | fiber: 9g | sodium: 773mg

Crustless Spinach Cheese Pie

Prep time: 10 minutes | Cook time: 20 minutes | Serves 4

6 large eggs
¼ cup heavy whipping cream
1 cup frozen chopped spinach, drained

1 cup shredded sharp Cheddar cheese
¼ cup diced yellow onion

1. In a medium bowl, whisk eggs and add cream. Add remaining ingredients to bowl. 2. Pour into a round baking dish. Place into the air fryer basket. 3. Adjust the temperature to 320ºF (160ºC) and bake for 20 minutes. 4. Eggs will be firm and slightly browned when cooked. Serve immediately.

Per Serving:
calories: 263 | fat: 20g | protein: 18g | carbs: 4g | fiber: 1g | sodium: 321mg

Chapter 11 Vegetables and Sides

Coriander-Cumin Roasted Carrots

Prep time: 10 minutes | Cook time: 20 minutes | Serves 2

½ pound (227 g) rainbow carrots (about 4)
2 tablespoons fresh orange juice

1 tablespoon honey
½ teaspoon coriander
Pinch salt

1. Preheat oven to 400°F(205°C) and set the oven rack to the middle position. 2. Peel the carrots and cut them lengthwise into slices of even thickness. Place them in a large bowl. 3. In a small bowl, mix together the orange juice, honey, coriander, and salt. 4. Pour the orange juice mixture over the carrots and toss well to coat. 5. Spread carrots onto a baking dish in a single layer. 6. Roast for 15 to 20 minutes, or until fork-tender.

Per Serving:
calories: 85 | fat: 0g | protein: 1g | carbs: 21g | fiber: 3g | sodium: 156mg

Spinach and Paneer Cheese

Prep time: 15 minutes | Cook time: 2 to 4 hours |
Serves 6

2 pounds (907 g) fresh spinach
1½-inch piece fresh ginger, roughly chopped
5 garlic cloves, whole
2 fresh green chiles, roughly chopped
1 onion, roughly chopped
1 teaspoon salt
½ teaspoon turmeric
4 tomatoes, finely chopped

1 to 2 tablespoons cornstarch to thicken (if required)
4 tablespoons butter
1 teaspoon cumin seeds
3 garlic cloves, minced
1 tablespoon dried fenugreek leaves
2 tablespoons rapeseed oil
12 ounces (340 g) paneer, cut into cubes

1. Heat the slow cooker to high and add the spinach, ginger, garlic, chiles, onion, salt, turmeric, and tomatoes. 2. Cover and cook on high for 3 hours, or on low for 6 hours. 3. Using your immersion blender or a food processor, purée the greens to a fine, glossy consistency. The aim is to have a thick and bright-green purée. If it's a little watery you may need to reduce it on the stove to thicken, or if your slow cooker has a boil function, use it to boil off a little of the liquid. You can also thicken it up by sprinkling with some cornstarch. 4. Heat the butter in a pan and add the cumin seeds until they sizzle. Then add the minced garlic and stir until it just browns. Remove from the heat. Add the dried fenugreek leaves and pour everything into the saag that's in the slow cooker. Whisk through. 5. Fry the cubes of paneer in a little oil in the same pan, until they are golden brown. Stir into the saag. Replace the lid and let everything sit for another 10 minutes before serving.

Per Serving:
calories: 252 | fat: 17g | protein: 10g | carbs: 20g | net carbs: 14g | sugars: 5g | fiber: 6g | sodium: 682mg | cholesterol: 24mg

Crispy Garlic Oven Potatoes

Prep time: 30 minutes | Cook time: 30 minutes | Serves 2

10 ounces (283 g) golden mini potatoes, halved
4 tablespoons extra-virgin olive oil
2 teaspoons dried, minced garlic

1 teaspoon onion salt
½ teaspoon paprika
¼ teaspoon freshly ground black pepper
¼ teaspoon red pepper flakes
¼ teaspoon dried dill

1. Preheat the oven to 400°F(205°C). 2. Soak the potatoes and put in a bowl of ice water for 30 minutes. Change the water if you return and the water is milky. 3. Rinse and dry the potatoes, then put them on a baking sheet. 4. Drizzle the potatoes with oil and sprinkle with the garlic, onion salt, paprika, pepper, red pepper flakes, and dill. Using tongs or your hands, toss well to coat. 5. Lower the heat to 375°F(190°C), add potatoes to the oven, and bake for 20 minutes. 6. At 20 minutes, check and flip potatoes. Bake for another 10 minutes, or until the potatoes are fork-tender.

Per Serving:
½ cup: calories: 344 | fat: 28g | protein: 3g | carbs: 24g | fiber: 4g | sodium: 723mg

Green Beans with Tomatoes and Potatoes

Prep time: 15 minutes | Cook time: 5 minutes | Serves 8

1 pound (454 g) small new potatoes
1 cup water
1 teaspoon salt
2 pounds (907 g) fresh green beans, trimmed
2 medium tomatoes, seeded and diced

2 tablespoons olive oil
1 tablespoon red wine vinegar
1 clove garlic, peeled and minced
½ teaspoon dry mustard powder
¼ teaspoon smoked paprika
¼ teaspoon ground black pepper

1. Place potatoes in a steamer basket. Place the rack in the Instant Pot®, add water, and then top with the steamer basket. Close lid, set steam release to Sealing, press the Manual button, and set time to 4 minutes. When the timer beeps, quick-release the pressure until the float valve drops. Press the Cancel button and open lid. 2. Add salt, green beans, and tomatoes to the Instant Pot®. Close lid, set steam release to Sealing, press the Manual button, and set time to 1 minute. When the timer beeps, quick-release the pressure until the float valve drops, press the Cancel button, and open lid. Transfer mixture to a serving platter or large bowl. 3. In a small bowl, whisk oil, vinegar, garlic, mustard, paprika, and pepper. Pour dressing over vegetables and gently toss to coat. Serve hot.

Per Serving:
calories: 112 | fat: 4g | protein: 2g | carbs: 20g | fiber: 5g | sodium: 368mg

Roasted Radishes with Sea Salt

Prep time: 5 minutes | Cook time: 18 minutes | Serves 4

1 pound (454 g) radishes, ends trimmed if needed

2 tablespoons olive oil
½ teaspoon sea salt

1. Preheat the air fryer to 360°F(182°C). 2. In a large bowl, combine the radishes with olive oil and sea salt. 3. Pour the radishes into the air fryer and roast for 10 minutes. Stir or turn the radishes over and roast for 8 minutes more, then serve.

Per Serving:
calories: 80 | fat: 7g | protein: 1g | carbs: 5g | fiber: 2g | sodium: 315mg

Parmesan-Thyme Butternut Squash

Prep time: 15 minutes | Cook time: 20 minutes | Serves 4

2½ cups butternut squash, cubed into 1-inch pieces (approximately 1 medium)
2 tablespoons olive oil
¼ teaspoon salt

¼ teaspoon garlic powder
¼ teaspoon black pepper
1 tablespoon fresh thyme
¼ cup grated Parmesan

1. Preheat the air fryer to 360°F(182°C). 2. In a large bowl, combine the cubed squash with the olive oil, salt, garlic powder, pepper, and thyme until the squash is well coated. 3. Pour this mixture into the air fryer basket, and roast for 10 minutes. Stir and roast another 8 to 10 minutes more. 4. Remove the squash from the air fryer and toss with freshly grated Parmesan before serving.

Per Serving:
calories: 127 | fat: 9g | protein: 3g | carbs: 12g | fiber: 2g | sodium: 262mg

Asparagus Fries

Prep time: 15 minutes | Cook time: 5 to 7 minutes per batch | Serves 4

12 ounces (340 g) fresh asparagus spears with tough ends trimmed off
2 egg whites
¼ cup water

¾ cup panko bread crumbs
¼ cup grated Parmesan cheese, plus 2 tablespoons
¼ teaspoon salt
Oil for misting or cooking spray

1. Preheat the air fryer to 390°F (199°C). 2. In a shallow dish, beat egg whites and water until slightly foamy. 3. In another shallow dish, combine panko, Parmesan, and salt. 4. Dip asparagus spears in egg, then roll in crumbs. Spray with oil or cooking spray. 5. Place a layer of asparagus in air fryer basket, leaving just a little space in between each spear. Stack another layer on top, crosswise. Air fry at 390°F (199°C) for 5 to 7 minutes, until crispy and golden brown. 6. Repeat to cook remaining asparagus.

Per Serving:
calories: 132 | fat: 3g | protein: 8g | carbs: 19g | fiber: 3g | sodium: 436mg

Citrus-Roasted Broccoli Florets

Prep time: 5 minutes | Cook time: 12 minutes | Serves 6

4 cups broccoli florets (approximately 1 large head)
2 tablespoons olive oil
½ teaspoon salt

½ cup orange juice
1 tablespoon raw honey
Orange wedges, for serving (optional)

1. Preheat the air fryer to 360°F(182°C). 2. In a large bowl, combine the broccoli, olive oil, salt, orange juice, and honey. Toss the broccoli in the liquid until well coated. 3. Pour the broccoli mixture into the air fryer basket and roast for 6 minutes. Stir and roast for 6 minutes more. 4. Serve alone or with orange wedges for additional citrus flavor, if desired.

Per Serving:
calories: 73 | fat: 5g | protein: 2g | carbs: 8g | fiber: 0g | sodium: 207mg

Cauliflower with Lime Juice

Prep time: 10 minutes | Cook time: 7 minutes | Serves 4

2 cups chopped cauliflower florets
2 tablespoons coconut oil, melted

2 teaspoons chili powder
½ teaspoon garlic powder
1 medium lime
2 tablespoons chopped cilantro

1. In a large bowl, toss cauliflower with coconut oil. Sprinkle with chili powder and garlic powder. Place seasoned cauliflower into the air fryer basket. 2. Adjust the temperature to 350°F (177°C) and set the timer for 7 minutes. 3. Cauliflower will be tender and begin to turn golden at the edges. Place into a serving bowl. 4. Cut the lime into quarters and squeeze juice over cauliflower. Garnish with cilantro.

Per Serving:
calories: 80 | fat: 7g | protein: 1g | carbs: 5g | fiber: 2g | sodium: 55mg

Roasted Beets with Oranges and Onions

Prep time: 10 minutes | Cook time: 40 minutes | Serves 6

4 medium beets, trimmed and scrubbed
Juice and zest of 2 oranges
1 red onion, thinly sliced
2 tablespoons olive oil

1 tablespoon red wine vinegar
Juice of 1 lemon
Sea salt and freshly ground pepper, to taste

1. Preheat oven to 400°F (205°C). 2. Wrap the beets in a foil pack and close tightly. Place them on a baking sheet and roast 40 minutes until tender enough to be pierced easily with a knife. 3. Cool until easy to handle. 4. Combine the beets with the orange juice and zest, red onion, olive oil, vinegar, and lemon juice. 5. Season with sea salt and freshly ground pepper to taste, and toss lightly. Allow to sit for about 15 minutes for the flavors to meld before serving.

Per Serving:
calories: 86 | fat: 5g | protein: 1g | carbs: 10g | fiber: 2g | sodium: 44mg

Polenta with Mushroom Bolognese

Prep time: 5 minutes |Cook time: 25 minutes| Serves: 4

2 (8-ounce / 227-g) packages white button mushrooms	polenta, cut into 8 slices
3 tablespoons extra-virgin olive oil, divided	¼ cup tomato paste
	1 tablespoon dried oregano, crushed between your fingers
1½ cups finely chopped onion (about ¾ medium onion)	¼ teaspoon ground nutmeg
½ cup finely chopped carrot (about 1 medium carrot)	¼ teaspoon kosher or sea salt
	¼ teaspoon freshly ground black pepper
4 garlic cloves, minced (about 2 teaspoons)	½ cup dry red wine
	½ cup whole milk
1 (18-ounce / 510-g) tube plain	½ teaspoon sugar

1. Put half the mushrooms in a food processor bowl and pulse about 15 times until finely chopped but not puréed, similar to the texture of ground meat. Repeat with the remaining mushrooms and set aside. (You can also use the food processor to chop the onion, carrot, and garlic, instead of chopping with a knife.) 2. In a large stockpot over medium-high heat, heat 2 tablespoons of oil. Add the onion and carrot and cook for 5 minutes, stirring occasionally. Add the mushrooms and garlic and cook for 5 minutes, stirring frequently. 3. While the vegetables are cooking, add the remaining 1 tablespoon of oil to a large skillet and heat over medium-high heat. Add 4 slices of polenta to the skillet and cook for 3 to 4 minutes, until golden; flip and cook for 3 to 4 minutes more. Remove the polenta from the skillet, place it on a shallow serving dish, and cover with aluminum foil to keep warm. Repeat with the remaining 4 slices of polenta. 4. To the mushroom mixture in the stockpot, add the tomato paste, oregano, nutmeg, salt, and pepper and stir. Continue cooking for another 2 to 3 minutes, until the vegetables have softened and begun to brown. Add the wine and cook for 1 to 2 minutes, scraping up any bits from the bottom of the pan while stirring with a wooden spoon. Cook until the wine is nearly all evaporated. Lower the heat to medium. 5. Meanwhile, in a small, microwave-safe bowl, mix the milk and sugar together and microwave on high for 30 to 45 seconds, until very hot. Slowly stir the milk into the mushroom mixture and simmer for 4 more minutes, until the milk is absorbed. To serve, pour the mushroom veggie sauce over the warm polenta slices.

Per Serving:
calories: 313 | fat: 12g | protein: 7g | carbs: 41g | fiber: 4g | sodium: 467mg

Cheesy Cauliflower Tots

Prep time: 15 minutes | Cook time: 12 minutes |
Makes 16 tots

1 large head cauliflower	1 large egg
1 cup shredded Mozzarella cheese	¼ teaspoon garlic powder
	¼ teaspoon dried parsley
½ cup grated Parmesan cheese	⅛ teaspoon onion powder

1. On the stovetop, fill a large pot with 2 cups water and place a steamer in the pan. Bring water to a boil. Cut the cauliflower into florets and place on steamer basket. Cover pot with lid. 2. Allow cauliflower to steam 7 minutes until fork tender. Remove from steamer basket and place into cheesecloth or clean kitchen towel and let cool. Squeeze over sink to remove as much excess moisture as possible. The mixture will be too soft to form into tots if not all the moisture is removed. Mash with a fork to a smooth consistency. 3. Put the cauliflower into a large mixing bowl and add Mozzarella, Parmesan, egg, garlic powder, parsley, and onion powder. Stir until fully combined. The mixture should be wet but easy to mold. 4. Take 2 tablespoons of the mixture and roll into tot shape. Repeat with remaining mixture. Place into the air fryer basket. 5. Adjust the temperature to 320ºF (160ºC) and set the timer for 12 minutes. 6. Turn tots halfway through the cooking time. Cauliflower tots should be golden when fully cooked. Serve warm.

Per Serving:
2 tots: calories: 82 | fat: 3g | protein: 9g | carbs: 7g | fiber: 2g | sodium: 258mg

One-Pan Herb-Roasted Tomatoes, Green Beans, and Baby Potatoes

Prep time: 10 minutes | Cook time: 30 minutes | Serves 6

¼ cup chopped mixed fresh herbs, such as flat-leaf parsley, oregano, mint, and dill	1 pound (454 g) baby potatoes, halved
3 tablespoons olive oil	1 pound (454 g) green beans, trimmed and halved
½ teaspoon kosher salt	2 large shallots, cut into wedges
½ teaspoon ground black pepper	2 pints cherry tomatoes

1. Preheat the oven to 400ºF (205ºC). 2. In a small bowl, whisk together the herbs, oil, salt, and pepper. Place the potatoes, string beans, and shallots on a large rimmed baking sheet. Drizzle the herb mixture over the vegetables and toss thoroughly to coat. 3. Roast the vegetables until the potatoes are just tender, about 15 minutes. Remove from the oven and toss in the tomatoes. Roast until the tomatoes blister and the potatoes are completely tender, about 15 minutes.

Per Serving:
calories: 173 | fat: 8g | protein: 5g | carbs: 26g | fiber: 5g | sodium: 185mg

Zucchini Casserole

Prep time: 20 minutes | Cook time: 3 hours | Serves 4

1 medium red onion, sliced	1 teaspoon sea salt
1 green bell pepper, cut into thin strips	½ teaspoon black pepper
	½ teaspoon basil
4 medium zucchini, sliced	1 tablespoon extra-virgin olive oil
1 (15-ounce / 425-g) can diced tomatoes, with the juice	¼ cup grated Parmesan cheese

1. Combine the onion slices, bell pepper strips, zucchini slices, and tomatoes in the slow cooker. Sprinkle with the salt, pepper, and basil. 2. Cover and cook on low for 3 hours. 3. Drizzle the olive oil over the casserole and sprinkle with the Parmesan. Cover and cook on low for 1½ hours more. Serve hot.

Per Serving:
calories: 124 | fat: 6g | protein: 6g | carbs: 15g | fiber: 5g | sodium: 723mg

Parmesan and Herb Sweet Potatoes

Prep time: 10 minutes | Cook time: 18 minutes | Serves 4

2 large sweet potatoes, peeled
and cubed
¼ cup olive oil
1 teaspoon dried rosemary

½ teaspoon salt
2 tablespoons shredded
Parmesan

1. Preheat the air fryer to 360°F(182ºC). 2. In a large bowl, toss the sweet potatoes with the olive oil, rosemary, and salt. 3. Pour the potatoes into the air fryer basket and roast for 10 minutes, then stir the potatoes and sprinkle the Parmesan over the top. Continue roasting for 8 minutes more. 4. Serve hot and enjoy.

Per Serving:
calories: 186 | fat: 14g | protein: 2g | carbs: 13g | fiber: 2g | sodium: 369mg

Mini Moroccan Pumpkin Cakes

Prep time: 10 minutes | Cook time: 10 minutes | Serves 6

2 cups cooked brown rice
1 cup pumpkin purée
½ cup finely chopped walnuts
3 tablespoons olive oil, divided
½ medium onion, diced
½ red bell pepper, diced

1 teaspoon ground cumin
Sea salt and freshly ground
pepper, to taste
1 teaspoon hot paprika or a
pinch of cayenne

1. Combine the rice, pumpkin, and walnuts in a large bowl; set aside. 2. In a medium skillet, heat the olive oil over medium heat, add the onion and bell pepper, and cook until soft, about 5 minutes. 3. Add the cumin to the onions and bell peppers. Add onion mixture to the rice mixture. 4. Mix thoroughly and season with sea salt, freshly ground pepper, and paprika or cayenne. 5. In a large skillet, heat 2 tablespoons of olive oil over medium heat. 6. Form the rice mixture into 1-inch patties and add them to the skillet. Cook until both sides are browned and crispy. 7. Serve with Greek yogurt or tzatziki on the side.

Per Serving:
calories: 193 | fat: 12g | protein: 3g | carbs: 20g | fiber: 3g | sodium: 6mg

Zucchini Pomodoro

Prep time: 15 minutes | Cook time: 12 minutes | Serves 4

1 tablespoon vegetable oil
1 large onion, peeled and diced
3 cloves garlic, peeled and
minced
1 (28-ounce / 794-g) can diced
tomatoes, including juice
½ cup water

1 tablespoon Italian seasoning
½ teaspoon salt
½ teaspoon ground black
pepper
2 medium zucchini, trimmed
and spiralized

1. Press the Sauté button on the Instant Pot® and heat oil. Add onion and cook until translucent, about 5 minutes. Add garlic and cook for an additional 30 seconds. Add tomatoes, water, Italian seasoning, salt, and pepper. Add zucchini and toss to combine. Press the Cancel button. 2. Close lid, set steam release to Sealing, press the Manual button, and set time to 1 minute. When the timer beeps,

let pressure release naturally for 5 minutes. Quick-release any remaining pressure until the float valve drops and open lid. Press the Cancel button. 3. Transfer zucchini to four bowls. Press the Sauté button, then press the Adjust button to change the temperature to Less, and simmer sauce in the Instant Pot® uncovered for 5 minutes. Ladle over zucchini and serve immediately.

Per Serving:
calories: 72 | fat: 4g | protein: 2g | carbs: 9g | fiber: 2g | sodium: 476mg

Roasted Cauliflower and Tomatoes

Prep time: 5 minutes | Cook time: 25 minutes | Serves 4

4 cups cauliflower, cut into
1-inch pieces
6 tablespoons extra-virgin olive
oil, divided
1 teaspoon salt, divided

4 cups cherry tomatoes
½ teaspoon freshly ground
black pepper
½ cup grated Parmesan cheese

1. Preheat the oven to 425°F(220ºC). 2. Add the cauliflower, 3 tablespoons of olive oil, and ½ teaspoon of salt to a large bowl and toss to evenly coat. Pour onto a baking sheet and spread the cauliflower out in an even layer. 3. In another large bowl, add the tomatoes, remaining 3 tablespoons of olive oil, and ½ teaspoon of salt, and toss to coat evenly. Pour onto a different baking sheet. 4. Put the sheet of cauliflower and the sheet of tomatoes in the oven to roast for 17 to 20 minutes until the cauliflower is lightly browned and tomatoes are plump. 5. Using a spatula, spoon the cauliflower into a serving dish, and top with tomatoes, black pepper, and Parmesan cheese. Serve warm.

Per Serving:
calories: 294 | fat: 26g | protein: 9g | carbs: 13g | fiber: 4g | sodium: 858mg

Puff Pastry Turnover with Roasted Vegetables

Prep time: 10 minutes | Cook time: 35 minutes | Serves 4 to 6

Nonstick cooking spray
1 zucchini, cut in ¼-inch-thick
slices
½ bunch asparagus, cut into
quarters

1 package (6-inch) whole-
grain pastry discs, in the freezer
section (Goya brand preferred),
at room temperature
1 large egg, beaten

1. Preheat the oven to 350°F(180ºC). 2. Spray a baking sheet with cooking spray and arrange the zucchini and asparagus on it in a single layer. Roast for 15 to 20 minutes, until tender. Set aside to cool. 3. Allow the pastry dough to warm to room temperature. Place the discs on a floured surface. 4. Place a roasted zucchini slice on one half of each disc, then top with asparagus. Fold the empty side over the full side and pinch the turnover closed with a fork. 5. Once all discs are full and closed, brush the turnovers with the beaten egg and put them onto a baking sheet. Bake for 10 to 15 minutes, until golden brown. Let cool completely before eating.

Per Serving:
calories: 334 | fat: 15g | protein: 9g | carbs: 42g | fiber: 4g | sodium: 741mg

Grilled Vegetables

Prep time: 15 minutes | Cook time: 8 minutes | Serves 4

4 carrots, peeled and cut in half
2 onions, quartered
1 zucchini, cut into ½-inch rounds
1 red bell pepper, seeded and cut into cubes
¼ cup olive oil
Sea salt and freshly ground pepper, to taste
Balsamic vinegar

1. Heat the grill to medium-high. 2. Brush the vegetables lightly with olive oil, and season with sea salt and freshly ground pepper. 3. Place the carrots and onions on the grill first because they take the longest. Cook the vegetables for 3–4 minutes on each side. 4. Transfer to a serving dish, and drizzle with olive oil and balsamic vinegar.

Per Serving:
calories: 209 | fat: 14g | protein: 3g | carbs: 20g | fiber: 6g | sodium: 92mg

Heirloom Tomato Basil Soup

Prep time: 15 minutes | Cook time: 15 minutes | Serves 4

1 tablespoon olive oil
1 small onion, peeled and diced
1 stalk celery, sliced
8 medium heirloom tomatoes, seeded and quartered
¼ cup julienned fresh basil
½ teaspoon salt
3 cups low-sodium chicken broth
1 cup heavy cream
1 teaspoon ground black pepper

1. Press the Sauté button on the Instant Pot® and heat oil. Add onion and celery and cook until translucent, about 5 minutes. Add tomatoes and cook for 3 minutes, or until tomatoes are tender and start to break down. Add basil, salt, and broth. Press the Cancel button. 2. Close lid, set steam release to Sealing, press the Manual button, and set time to 7 minutes. When the timer beeps, quick-release the pressure until the float valve drops and then open lid. 3. Add cream and pepper. Purée soup with an immersion blender, or purée in batches in a blender. Ladle into bowls and serve warm.

Per Serving:
calories: 282 | fat: 24g | protein: 4g | carbs: 9g | fiber: 1g | sodium: 466mg

Mediterranean Cauliflower Tabbouleh

Prep time: 15 minutes | Cook time: 5 minutes | Serves 6

6 tablespoons extra-virgin olive oil, divided
4 cups riced cauliflower
3 garlic cloves, finely minced
1½ teaspoons salt
½ teaspoon freshly ground black pepper
½ large cucumber, peeled, seeded, and chopped
½ cup chopped mint leaves
½ cup chopped Italian parsley
½ cup chopped pitted Kalamata olives
2 tablespoons minced red onion
Juice of 1 lemon (about 2 tablespoons)
2 cups baby arugula or spinach leaves
2 medium avocados, peeled, pitted, and diced
1 cup quartered cherry tomatoes

1. In a large skillet, heat 2 tablespoons of olive oil over medium-high heat. Add the riced cauliflower, garlic, salt, and pepper and sauté until just tender but not mushy, 3 to 4 minutes. Remove from the heat and place in a large bowl. 2. Add the cucumber, mint, parsley, olives, red onion, lemon juice, and remaining 4 tablespoons olive oil and toss well. Place in the refrigerator, uncovered, and refrigerate for at least 30 minutes, or up to 2 hours. 3. Before serving, add the arugula, avocado, and tomatoes and toss to combine well. Season to taste with salt and pepper and serve cold or at room temperature.

Per Serving:
calories: 273 | fat: 25g | protein: 4g | carbs: 13g | fiber: 7g | sodium: 697mg

Greek Bean Soup

Prep time: 10 minutes | Cook time: 45 minutes | Serves 4

2 tablespoons olive oil
1 large onion, chopped
1 (15-ounce / 425-g) can diced tomatoes
1 (15-ounce / 425-g) can great northern beans, drained and rinsed
2 celery stalks, chopped
2 carrots, cut into long ribbons
⅓ teaspoon chopped fresh thyme
¼ cup chopped fresh Italian parsley
1 bay leaf
Sea salt
Freshly ground black pepper

1. In a Dutch oven, heat the olive oil over medium-high heat. Add the onion and sauté for 4 minutes, or until softened. Add the tomatoes, beans, celery, carrots, thyme, parsley, and bay leaf, then add water to cover by about 2 inches. 2. Bring the soup to a boil, reduce the heat to low, cover, and simmer for 30 minutes, or until the vegetables are tender. 3. Remove the bay leaf, season with salt and pepper, and serve.

Per Serving:
calories: 185 | fat: 7g | protein: 7g | carbs: 25g | fiber: 8g | sodium: 155mg

Roasted Fennel with Parmesan

Prep time: 5 minutes | Cook time: 30 minutes | Serves 4

2 fennel bulbs (about 2 pounds / 907 g), cored and cut into 8 wedges each (reserve fronds for garnish)
¼ cup olive oil
Salt
Freshly ground black pepper
1¼ teaspoons red pepper flakes
½ cup freshly grated Parmesan cheese

1. Preheat the oven to 350°F (180°C). 2. Arrange the fennel wedges on a large, rimmed baking sheet and drizzle the oil over the top. 3. Sprinkle each wedge with a pinch each of salt, black pepper, and red pepper flakes. Sprinkle the cheese over the top. 4. Bake in the preheated oven for about 30 minutes, until the fennel is tender and the cheese is golden brown. Remove from the oven and let cool in the oil until just warm. Using a slotted metal spatula, transfer the fennel to plates and garnish with the reserved fennel fronds.

Per Serving:
calories: 237 | fat: 19g | protein: 11g | carbs: 10g | fiber: 4g | sodium: 363mg

Garlic and Thyme Tomatoes

Prep time: 10 minutes | Cook time: 15 minutes |
Serves 2 to 4

4 Roma tomatoes
1 tablespoon olive oil
Salt and freshly ground black

pepper, to taste
1 clove garlic, minced
½ teaspoon dried thyme

1. Preheat the air fryer to 390ºF (199ºC). 2. Cut the tomatoes in half and scoop out the seeds and any pithy parts with your fingers. Place the tomatoes in a bowl and toss with the olive oil, salt, pepper, garlic and thyme. 3. Transfer the tomatoes to the air fryer, cut side up. Air fry for 15 minutes. The edges should just start to brown. Let the tomatoes cool to an edible temperature for a few minutes and then use in pastas, on top of crostini, or as an accompaniment to any poultry, meat or fish.

Per Serving:
calories: 56 | fat: 5g | protein: 1g | carbs: 4g | fiber: 1g | sodium: 4mg

Rosemary New Potatoes

Prep time: 10 minutes | Cook time: 5 to 6 minutes |
Serves 4

3 large red potatoes (enough to make 3 cups sliced)
¼ teaspoon ground rosemary
¼ teaspoon ground thyme

⅛ teaspoon salt
⅛ teaspoon ground black pepper
2 teaspoons extra-light olive oil

1. Preheat the air fryer to 330ºF (166ºC). 2. Place potatoes in large bowl and sprinkle with rosemary, thyme, salt, and pepper. 3. Stir with a spoon to distribute seasonings evenly. 4. Add oil to potatoes and stir again to coat well. 5. Air fry at 330ºF (166ºC) for 4 minutes. Stir and break apart any that have stuck together. 6. Cook an additional 1 to 2 minutes or until fork-tender.

Per Serving:
calories: 214 | fat: 3g | protein: 5g | carbs: 44g | fiber: 5g | sodium: 127mg

Green Bean Casserole

Prep time: 10 minutes | Cook time: 20 minutes | Serves 4

1 pound (454 g) fresh green beans, ends trimmed, strings removed, and chopped into 2-inch pieces
1 (8-ounce / 227-g) package sliced brown mushrooms
½ onion, sliced
1 clove garlic, minced

1 tablespoon olive oil
½ teaspoon salt
¼ teaspoon freshly ground black pepper
4 ounces (113 g) cream cheese
½ cup chicken stock
¼ teaspoon ground nutmeg
½ cup grated Cheddar cheese

1. Preheat the air fryer to 400ºF (204ºC). Coat a casserole dish with olive oil and set aside. 2. In a large bowl, combine the green beans, mushrooms, onion, garlic, olive oil, salt, and pepper. Toss until the vegetables are thoroughly coated with the oil and seasonings. 3. Transfer the mixture to the air fryer basket. Pausing halfway through the cooking time to shake the basket, air fry for 10 minutes until tender. 4. While the vegetables are cooking, in a 2-cup glass measuring cup, warm the cream cheese and chicken stock in the microwave on high for 1 to 2 minutes until the cream cheese is melted. Add the nutmeg and whisk until smooth. 5. Transfer the vegetables to the prepared casserole dish and pour the cream cheese mixture over the top. Top with the Cheddar cheese. Air fry for another 10 minutes until the cheese is melted and beginning to brown.

Per Serving:
calories: 230 | fat: 18g | protein: 8g | carbs: 11g | fiber: 3g | sodium: 502mg

Greek Fasolakia (Green Beans)

Prep time: 10 minutes | Cook time: 6 to 8 hours |
Serves 6

2 pounds (907 g) green beans, trimmed
1 (15-ounce / 425-g) can no-salt-added diced tomatoes, with juice
1 large onion, chopped
4 garlic cloves, chopped
Juice of 1 lemon

1 teaspoon dried dill
1 teaspoon ground cumin
1 teaspoon dried oregano
1 teaspoon sea salt
½ teaspoon freshly ground black pepper
¼ cup feta cheese, crumbled

1. In a slow cooker, combine the green beans, tomatoes and their juice, onion, garlic, lemon juice, dill, cumin, oregano, salt, and pepper. Stir to mix well. 2. Cover the cooker and cook for 6 to 8 hours on Low heat. 3. Top with feta cheese for serving.

Per Serving:
calories: 94 | fat: 2g | protein: 5g | carbs: 18g | fiber: 7g | sodium: 497mg

Mashed Sweet Potato Tots

Prep time: 10 minutes | Cook time: 12 to 13 minutes
per batch | Makes 18 to 24 tots

1 cup cooked mashed sweet potatoes
1 egg white, beaten
⅛ teaspoon ground cinnamon
1 dash nutmeg

2 tablespoons chopped pecans
1½ teaspoons honey
Salt, to taste
½ cup panko bread crumbs
Oil for misting or cooking spray

1. Preheat the air fryer to 390ºF (199ºC). 2. In a large bowl, mix together the potatoes, egg white, cinnamon, nutmeg, pecans, honey, and salt to taste. 3. Place panko crumbs on a sheet of wax paper. 4. For each tot, use about 2 teaspoons of sweet potato mixture. To shape, drop the measure of potato mixture onto panko crumbs and push crumbs up and around potatoes to coat edges. Then turn tot over to coat other side with crumbs. 5. Mist tots with oil or cooking spray and place in air fryer basket in single layer. 6. Air fry at 390ºF (199ºC) for 12 to 13 minutes, until browned and crispy. 7. Repeat steps 5 and 6 to cook remaining tots.

Per Serving:
calories: 51 | fat: 1g | protein: 1g | carbs: 9g | fiber: 1g | sodium: 45mg

Spanish Green Beans

Prep time: 10 minutes | Cook time: 20 minutes | Serves 4

¼ cup extra-virgin olive oil
1 large onion, chopped
4 cloves garlic, finely chopped
1 pound (454 g) green beans, fresh or frozen, trimmed

1½ teaspoons salt, divided
1 (15-ounce / 425-g) can diced tomatoes
½ teaspoon freshly ground black pepper

1. In a large pot over medium heat, heat the olive oil, onion, and garlic; cook for 1 minute. 2. Cut the green beans into 2-inch pieces. 3. Add the green beans and 1 teaspoon of salt to the pot and toss everything together; cook for 3 minutes. 4. Add the diced tomatoes, remaining ½ teaspoon of salt, and black pepper to the pot; continue to cook for another 12 minutes, stirring occasionally. 5. Serve warm.

Per Serving:
calories: 200 | fat: 14g | protein: 4g | carbs: 18g | fiber: 6g | sodium: 844mg

Indian Eggplant Bharta

Prep time: 15 minutes | Cook time: 20 minutes | Serves 4

1 medium eggplant
2 tablespoons vegetable oil
½ cup finely minced onion
½ cup finely chopped fresh tomato

2 tablespoons fresh lemon juice
2 tablespoons chopped fresh cilantro
½ teaspoon kosher salt
⅛ teaspoon cayenne pepper

1. Rub the eggplant all over with the vegetable oil. Place the eggplant in the air fryer basket. Set the air fryer to 400ºF (204ºC) for 20 minutes, or until the eggplant skin is blistered and charred. 2. Transfer the eggplant to a resealable plastic bag, seal, and set aside for 15 to 20 minutes (the eggplant will finish cooking in the residual heat trapped in the bag). 3. Transfer the eggplant to a large bowl. Peel off and discard the charred skin. Roughly mash the eggplant flesh. Add the onion, tomato, lemon juice, cilantro, salt, and cayenne. Stir to combine.

Per Serving:
calories: 105 | fat: 7g | protein: 2g | carbs: 11g | fiber: 5g | sodium: 295mg

Citrus Asparagus with Pistachios

Prep time: 10 minutes | Cook time: 15 minutes | Serves 4

5 tablespoons extra-virgin olive oil, divided
Zest and juice of 2 clementines or 1 orange (about ¼ cup juice and 1 tablespoon zest)
Zest and juice of 1 lemon
1 tablespoon red wine vinegar

1 teaspoon salt, divided
¼ teaspoon freshly ground black pepper
½ cup shelled pistachios
1 pound (454 g) fresh asparagus
1 tablespoon water

1. In a small bowl, whisk together 4 tablespoons olive oil, the clementine and lemon juices and zests, vinegar, ½ teaspoon salt, and pepper. Set aside. 2. In a medium dry skillet, toast the pistachios over medium-high heat until lightly browned, 2 to 3 minutes, being careful not to let them burn. Transfer to a cutting board and coarsely chop. Set aside. 3. Trim the rough ends off the asparagus, usually the last 1 to 2 inches of each spear. In a skillet, heat the remaining 1 tablespoon olive oil over medium-high heat. Add the asparagus and sauté for 2 to 3 minutes. Sprinkle with the remaining ½ teaspoon salt and add the water. Reduce the heat to medium-low, cover, and cook until tender, another 2 to 4 minutes, depending on the thickness of the spears. 4. Transfer the cooked asparagus to a serving dish. Add the pistachios to the dressing and whisk to combine. Pour the dressing over the warm asparagus and toss to coat.

Per Serving:
calories: 271 | fat: 24g | protein: 6g | carbs: 12g | fiber: 4g | sodium: 585mg

Toasted Pita Wedges

Prep time: 5 minutes | Cook time: 12 minutes |
Makes 32 wedges

4 whole-wheat pita rounds
1 tablespoon olive oil
1 teaspoon garlic powder

¼ teaspoon paprika
Sea salt and freshly ground pepper, to taste

1. Preheat oven to 400ºF (205ºC). 2. Cut the pita rounds into 8 wedges each, and lay on a parchment-lined baking sheet in an even layer. 3. Drizzle with olive oil, and sprinkle with garlic powder and paprika. Season with sea salt and freshly ground pepper. 4. Bake for 10–12 minutes, until wedges are lightly browned and crisp. Allow to cool completely before serving for crisper wedges.

Per Serving:
4 wedges: calories: 102 | fat: 3g | protein: 3g | carbs: 18g | fiber: 2g | sodium: 142mg

Stuffed Artichokes

Prep time: 20 minutes | Cook time: 5 to 7 hours |
Serves 4 to 6

4 to 6 fresh large artichokes
½ cup bread crumbs
½ cup grated Parmesan cheese or Romano cheese
4 garlic cloves, minced
½ teaspoon sea salt
½ teaspoon freshly ground

black pepper
¼ cup water
2 tablespoons extra-virgin olive oil
2 tablespoons chopped fresh parsley for garnish (optional)

1. To trim and prepare the artichokes, cut off the bottom along with 1 inch from the top of each artichoke. Pull off and discard the lowest leaves nearest the stem end. Trim off any pointy tips of artichoke leaves that are poking out. Set aside. 2. In a small bowl, stir together the bread crumbs, Parmesan cheese, garlic, salt, and pepper. 3. Spread apart the artichoke leaves and stuff the bread-crumb mixture into the spaces, down to the base. 4. Pour the water into a slow cooker. 5. Place the artichokes in the slow cooker in a single layer. Drizzle the olive oil over the artichokes. 6. Cover the cooker and cook for 5 to 7 hours on Low heat, or until the artichokes are tender. 7. Garnish with fresh parsley if desired.

Per Serving:
calories: 224 | fat: 12g | protein: 12g | carbs: 23g | fiber: 8g | sodium: 883mg

Greek Stewed Zucchini

Prep time: 5 minutes | Cook time: 40 minutes | Serves 4 to 6

¼ cup extra-virgin olive oil
1 small yellow onion, peeled and slivered
4 medium zucchini squash, cut into ½-inch-thick rounds
4 small garlic cloves, minced
1 to 2 teaspoons dried oregano

2 cups chopped tomatoes
½ cup halved and pitted Kalamata olives
¾ cup crumbled feta cheese
¼ cup chopped fresh flat-leaf Italian parsley, for garnish (optional)

1. In a large skillet, heat the oil over medium-high heat. Add the slivered onion and sauté until just tender, 6 to 8 minutes. Add the zucchini, garlic, and oregano and sauté another 6 to 8 minutes, or until zucchini is just tender. 2. Add the tomatoes and bring to a boil. Reduce the heat to low and add the olives. Cover and simmer on low heat for 20 minutes, or until the flavors have developed and the zucchini is very tender. 3. Serve warm topped with feta and parsley (if using).

Per Serving:
calories: 183 | fat: 15g | protein: 5g | carbs: 10g | fiber: 3g | sodium: 269mg

Cucumbers with Feta, Mint, and Sumac

Prep time: 15 minutes | Cook time: 0 minutes | Serves 4

1 tablespoon extra-virgin olive oil
1 tablespoon lemon juice
2 teaspoons ground sumac
½ teaspoon kosher salt
2 hothouse or English cucumbers, diced

¼ cup crumbled feta cheese
1 tablespoon fresh mint, chopped
1 tablespoon fresh parsley, chopped
⅛ teaspoon red pepper flakes

1. In a large bowl, whisk together the olive oil, lemon juice, sumac, and salt. Add the cucumber and feta cheese and toss well. 2. Transfer to a serving dish and sprinkle with the mint, parsley, and red pepper flakes.

Per Serving:
calories: 85 | fat: 6g | protein: 3g | carbs: 8g | fiber: 1g | sodium: 230mg

Brussels Sprouts with Pecans and Gorgonzola

Prep time: 10 minutes | Cook time: 25 minutes | Serves 4

½ cup pecans
1½ pounds (680 g) fresh Brussels sprouts, trimmed and quartered
2 tablespoons olive oil

Salt and freshly ground black pepper, to taste
¼ cup crumbled Gorgonzola cheese

1. Spread the pecans in a single layer of the air fryer and set the heat to 350°F (177°C). Air fry for 3 to 5 minutes until the pecans are lightly browned and fragrant. Transfer the pecans to a plate and continue preheating the air fryer, increasing the heat to 400°F (204°C). 2. In a large bowl, toss the Brussels sprouts with the olive oil and season with salt and black pepper to taste. 3. Working in batches if necessary, arrange the Brussels sprouts in a single layer in the air fryer basket. Pausing halfway through the baking time to shake the basket, air fry for 20 to 25 minutes until the sprouts are tender and starting to brown on the edges. 4. Transfer the sprouts to a serving bowl and top with the toasted pecans and Gorgonzola. Serve warm or at room temperature.

Per Serving:
calories: 253 | fat: 18g | protein: 9g | carbs: 17g | fiber: 8g | sodium: 96mg

Brown Rice and Vegetable Pilaf

Prep time: 20 minutes | Cook time: 5 hours | Makes 9 (¾-cup) servings

1 onion, minced
1 cup sliced cremini mushrooms
2 carrots, sliced
2 garlic cloves, minced
1½ cups long-grain brown rice
2½ cups vegetable broth

½ teaspoon salt
½ teaspoon dried marjoram leaves
⅛ teaspoon freshly ground black pepper
⅓ cup grated Parmesan cheese

1. In the slow cooker, combine the onion, mushrooms, carrots, garlic, and rice. 2. Add the broth, salt, marjoram, and pepper, and stir. 3. Cover and cook on low for 5 hours, or until the rice is tender and the liquid is absorbed. 4. Stir in the cheese and serve.

Per Serving:
calories: 68 | fat: 1g | protein: 2g | carbs: 12g | net carbs: 11g | sugars: 2g | fiber: 1g | sodium: 207mg | cholesterol: 3mg

Hearty Minestrone Soup

Prep time: 20 minutes | Cook time: 20 minutes | Serves 8

2 cups dried Great Northern beans, soaked overnight and drained
1 cup orzo
2 large carrots, peeled and diced
1 bunch Swiss chard, ribs removed and roughly chopped
1 medium zucchini, trimmed and diced
2 stalks celery, diced
1 medium onion, peeled and

diced
1 teaspoon minced garlic
1 tablespoon Italian seasoning
1 teaspoon salt
½ teaspoon ground black pepper
2 bay leaves
1 (14½-ounce / 411-g) can diced tomatoes, including juice
4 cups vegetable broth
1 cup tomato juice

1. Place all ingredients in the Instant Pot® and stir to combine. Close lid, set steam release to Sealing, press the Soup button, and cook for the default time of 20 minutes. 2. When the timer beeps, let pressure release naturally for 10 minutes. Quick-release any remaining pressure until the float valve drops and open lid. Remove and discard bay leaves. 3. Ladle into bowls and serve warm.

Per Serving:
calories: 207 | fat: 1g | protein: 12g | carbs: 47g | fiber: 10g | sodium: 814mg

Dill-and-Garlic Beets

Prep time: 10 minutes | Cook time: 30 minutes | Serves 4

4 beets, cleaned, peeled, and sliced
1 garlic clove, minced
2 tablespoons chopped fresh
dill
¼ teaspoon salt
¼ teaspoon black pepper
3 tablespoons olive oil

1. Preheat the air fryer to 380°F(193°C). 2. In a large bowl, mix together all of the ingredients so the beets are well coated with the oil. 3. Pour the beet mixture into the air fryer basket, and roast for 15 minutes before stirring, then continue roasting for 15 minutes more.

Per Serving:
calories: 136 | fat: 2g | protein: 2g | carbs: 10g | fiber: 3g | sodium: 210mg

Spicy Creamer Potatoes

Prep time: 10 minutes | Cook time: 8 hours | Makes 7 (1-cup) servings

2 pounds (907 g) creamer potatoes
1 onion, chopped
3 garlic cloves, minced
1 chipotle chile in adobo sauce, minced
2 tablespoons freshly squeezed
lemon juice
2 tablespoons water
1 tablespoon chili powder
½ teaspoon ground cumin
½ teaspoon salt
⅛ teaspoon freshly ground black pepper

1. In the slow cooker, combine all the ingredients and stir. 2. Cover and cook on low for 7 to 8 hours, or until the potatoes are tender, and serve.

Per Serving:
calories: 113 | fat: 0g | protein: 3g | carbs: 25g | net carbs: 21g | sugars: 2g | fiber: 4g | sodium: 208mg | cholesterol: 0mg

Individual Asparagus and Goat Cheese Frittatas

Prep time: 15 minutes | Cook time: 15 minutes | Serves 4

1 tablespoon extra-virgin olive oil
8 ounces (227 g) asparagus, trimmed and sliced ¼ inch thick
1 red bell pepper, stemmed, seeded, and chopped
2 shallots, minced
2 ounces (57 g) goat cheese, crumbled (½ cup)
1 tablespoon minced fresh tarragon
1 teaspoon grated lemon zest
8 large eggs
½ teaspoon table salt

1. Using highest sauté function, heat oil in Instant Pot until shimmering. Add asparagus, bell pepper, and shallots; cook until softened, about 5 minutes. Turn off Instant Pot and transfer vegetables to bowl. Stir in goat cheese, tarragon, and lemon zest. 2. Arrange trivet included with Instant Pot in base of now-empty insert and add 1 cup water. Spray four 6-ounce ramekins with vegetable oil spray. Beat eggs, ¼ cup water, and salt in large bowl until thoroughly combined. Divide vegetable mixture between prepared ramekins, then pour egg mixture over top (you may have some left over). Set ramekins on trivet. Lock lid in place and close pressure release valve. Select high pressure cook function and cook for 10 minutes. 3. Turn off Instant Pot and quick-release pressure. Carefully remove lid, allowing steam to escape away from you. Using tongs, transfer ramekins to wire rack and let cool slightly. Run paring knife around inside edge of ramekins to loosen frittatas, then invert onto individual serving plates. Serve.

Per Serving:
calories: 240 | fat: 16g | protein: 17g | carbs: 6g | fiber: 2g | sodium: 500mg

Caramelized Root Vegetables

Prep time: 20 minutes | Cook time: 40 minutes | Serves 6

2 medium carrots, peeled and cut into chunks
2 medium red or gold beets, cut into chunks
2 turnips, peeled and cut into chunks
2 tablespoons olive oil
1 teaspoon cumin
1 teaspoon sweet paprika
Sea salt and freshly ground pepper, to taste
Juice of 1 lemon
1 small bunch flat-leaf parsley, chopped

1. Preheat oven to 400°F (205°C). 2. Toss the vegetables with the olive oil and seasonings. 3. Lay in a single layer on a sheet pan, cover with lemon juice, and roast for 30–40 minutes, until veggies are slightly browned and crisp. 4. Serve warm, topped with the chopped parsley.

Per Serving:
calories: 79 | fat: 5g | protein: 1g | carbs: 9g | fiber: 3g | sodium: 69mg

Herb Vinaigrette Potato Salad

Prep time: 10 minutes | Cook time: 4 minutes | Serves 10

¼ cup olive oil
3 tablespoons red wine vinegar
¼ cup chopped fresh flat-leaf parsley
2 tablespoons chopped fresh dill
2 tablespoons chopped fresh chives
1 clove garlic, peeled and
minced
½ teaspoon dry mustard powder
¼ teaspoon ground black pepper
2 pounds (907 g) baby Yukon Gold potatoes
1 cup water
1 teaspoon salt

1. Whisk together oil, vinegar, parsley, dill, chives, garlic, mustard, and pepper in a small bowl. Set aside. 2. Place potatoes in a steamer basket. Place the rack in the Instant Pot®, add water and salt, then top with the steamer basket. Close lid, set steam release to Sealing, press the Manual button, and set time to 4 minutes. When the timer beeps, quick-release the pressure until the float valve drops. Press the Cancel button and open lid. 3. Transfer hot potatoes to a serving bowl. Pour dressing over potatoes and gently toss to coat. Serve warm or at room temperature.

Per Serving:
calories: 116 | fat: 6g | protein: 2g | carbs: 16g | fiber: 1g | sodium: 239mg

Spicy Wilted Greens with Garlic

Prep time: 10 minutes | Cook time: 5 minutes | Serves 2

1 tablespoon olive oil
2 garlic cloves, minced
3 cups sliced greens (kale, spinach, chard, beet greens, dandelion greens, or a

combination)
Pinch salt
Pinch red pepper flakes (or more to taste)

1. Heat the olive oil in a sauté pan over medium-high heat. Add garlic and sauté for 30 seconds, or just until it's fragrant. 2. Add the greens, salt, and pepper flakes and stir to combine. Let the greens wilt, but do not overcook. Remove the pan from the heat and serve.

Per Serving:
calories: 91 | fat: 7g | protein: 1g | carbs: 7g | fiber: 3g | sodium: 111mg

Roasted Eggplant

Prep time: 15 minutes | Cook time: 15 minutes | Serves 4

1 large eggplant
2 tablespoons olive oil

¼ teaspoon salt
½ teaspoon garlic powder

1. Remove top and bottom from eggplant. Slice eggplant into ¼-inch-thick round slices. 2. Brush slices with olive oil. Sprinkle with salt and garlic powder. Place eggplant slices into the air fryer basket. 3. Adjust the temperature to 390ºF (199ºC) and set the timer for 15 minutes. 4. Serve immediately.

Per Serving:
calories: 95| fat: 7g | protein: 1g | carbs: 8g | net carbs: 4g | fiber: 4g

Balsamic Beets

Prep time: 15 minutes | Cook time: 3 to 4 hours |
Serves 8

Cooking spray or 1 tablespoon extra-virgin olive oil
3 pounds (1.4 kg) beets, scrubbed, peeled, and cut into wedges
2 garlic cloves, minced
1 cup white grape or apple juice
½ cup balsamic vinegar
1 tablespoon honey

2 fresh thyme sprigs
1 teaspoon kosher salt, plus more for seasoning
½ teaspoon freshly ground black pepper, plus more for seasoning
1 tablespoon cold water
1 tablespoon cornstarch

1. Use the cooking spray or olive oil to coat the inside (bottom and sides) of the slow cooker. Add the beets, garlic, juice, vinegar, honey, thyme, salt, and pepper. Stir to combine. Cover and cook on high for 3 to 4 hours. 2. About 10 minutes before serving, combine the water and cornstarch in a small bowl, stirring until no lumps remain. Add to the slow cooker and continue to cook for 10 minutes, or until the sauce thickens. 3. Discard the thyme. Season with additional salt and pepper, as needed. Serve.

Per Serving:
calories: 129 | fat: 2g | protein: 3g | carbs: 26g | net carbs: 21g | sugars: 19g | fiber: 5g | sodium: 429mg | cholesterol: 0mg

Wild Mushroom Soup

Prep time: 30 minutes | Cook time: 16 minutes | Serves 8

3 tablespoons olive oil
1 stalk celery, diced
1 medium carrot, peeled and diced
½ medium yellow onion, peeled and diced
1 clove garlic, peeled and minced
1 (8-ounce / 227-g) container hen of the woods mushrooms, sliced
1 (8-ounce / 227-g) container

porcini or chanterelle mushrooms, sliced
2 cups sliced shiitake mushrooms
2 tablespoons dry sherry
4 cups vegetable broth
2 cups water
1 tablespoon chopped fresh tarragon
½ teaspoon salt
½ teaspoon ground black pepper

1. Press the Sauté button on the Instant Pot® and heat oil. Add celery, carrot, and onion. Cook, stirring often, until softened, about 5 minutes. Add garlic and cook 30 seconds until fragrant, then add mushrooms and cook until beginning to soften, about 5 minutes. 2. Add sherry, broth, water, tarragon, salt, and pepper to pot, and stir well. Press the Cancel button. Close lid, set steam release to Sealing, press the Manual button, and set time to 5 minutes. 3. When the timer beeps, let pressure release naturally, about 15 minutes. Press the Cancel button, open lid, and stir well. Serve hot.

Per Serving:
calories: 98 | fat: 6g | protein: 1g | carbs: 11g | fiber: 2g | sodium: 759mg

Melitzanes Yiahni (Braised Eggplant)

Prep time: 15 minutes | Cook time: 30 minutes | Serves 6

2 large eggplants, cut into 1" pieces
1¾ teaspoons salt, divided
3 tablespoons extra-virgin olive oil, divided
1 medium yellow onion, peeled and diced
3 cloves garlic, peeled and

minced
2 cups diced fresh tomatoes
1 cup water
1 tablespoon dried oregano
½ teaspoon ground black pepper
2 tablespoons minced fresh basil

1. Place eggplant in a colander and sprinkle with 1½ teaspoons salt. Place colander over a plate. Let stand 30 minutes to drain. 2. Press the Sauté button on the Instant Pot® and heat 2 tablespoons oil. Add onion and cook until soft, about 5 minutes. Add garlic and cook until fragrant, about 30 seconds. Add tomatoes and water. Press the Cancel button. 3. Rinse eggplant well and drain. Add to pot. Close lid, set steam release to Sealing, press the Manual button, and set time to 8 minutes. Once timer beeps, quick-release the pressure until the float valve drops, press the Cancel button, and open lid. Add oregano, pepper, and remaining ¼ teaspoon salt. 4. Add remaining 1 tablespoon oil to pot and stir well. Press the Sauté button and simmer for 15 minutes to thicken. Add basil and serve hot.

Per Serving:
calories: 121 | fat: 7g | protein: 2g | carbs: 14g | fiber: 7g | sodium: 107mg

Zesty Cabbage Soup

Prep time: 25 minutes | Cook time: 30 minutes | Serves 8

2 tablespoons extra-virgin olive oil
3 medium onions, peeled and chopped
1 large carrot, peeled, quartered, and sliced
1 stalk celery, chopped
3 bay leaves
1 teaspoon smoked paprika
3 cups sliced white cabbage
1 teaspoon fresh thyme leaves
3 cloves garlic, peeled and minced
½ cup chopped roasted red

pepper
1 (15-ounce / 425-g) can white navy beans, drained and rinsed
1½ cups low-sodium vegetable cocktail beverage
7 cups low-sodium vegetable stock
1 dried chili pepper
2 medium zucchini, trimmed, halved lengthwise, and thinly sliced
1 teaspoon salt
½ teaspoon ground black pepper

1. Press the Sauté button on the Instant Pot® and heat oil. Add onions, carrot, celery, and bay leaves. Cook for 7–10 minutes or until vegetables are soft. 2. Add paprika, cabbage, thyme, garlic, roasted red pepper, and beans. Stir to combine and cook for 2 minutes. Add vegetable cocktail beverage, stock, and chili pepper. Press the Cancel button. 3. Close lid, set steam release to Sealing, press the Soup button, and cook for default time of 20 minutes. When the timer beeps, quick-release the pressure until the float valve drops and open lid. 4. Remove and discard bay leaves. Add zucchini, close lid, and let stand on the Keep Warm setting for 15 minutes. Season with salt and pepper. Serve hot.

Per Serving:
calories: 157 | fat: 4g | protein: 7g | carbs: 25g | fiber: 8g | sodium: 360mg

Mediterranean Lentil Sloppy Joes

Prep time: 5 minutes |Cook time: 15 minutes| Serves: 4

1 tablespoon extra-virgin olive oil
1 cup chopped onion (about ½ medium onion)
1 cup chopped bell pepper, any color (about 1 medium bell pepper)
2 garlic cloves, minced (about 1 teaspoon)
1 (15-ounce / 425-g) can lentils, drained and rinsed
1 (14½-ounce / 411-g) can low-

sodium or no-salt-added diced tomatoes, undrained
1 teaspoon ground cumin
1 teaspoon dried thyme
¼ teaspoon kosher or sea salt
4 whole-wheat pita breads, split open
1½ cups chopped seedless cucumber (1 medium cucumber)
1 cup chopped romaine lettuce

1. In a medium saucepan over medium-high heat, heat the oil. Add the onion and bell pepper and cook for 4 minutes, stirring frequently. Add the garlic and cook for 1 minute, stirring frequently. Add the lentils, tomatoes (with their liquid), cumin, thyme, and salt. Turn the heat to medium and cook, stirring occasionally, for 10 minutes, or until most of the liquid has evaporated. 2. Stuff the lentil mixture inside each pita. Lay the cucumbers and lettuce on top of the lentil mixture and serve.

Per Serving:
calories: 530 | fat: 6g | protein: 31g | carbs: 93g | fiber: 17g | sodium: 292mg

Crispy Green Beans

Prep time: 5 minutes | Cook time: 8 minutes | Serves 4

2 teaspoons olive oil
½ pound (227 g) fresh green beans, ends trimmed
¼ teaspoon salt
¼ teaspoon ground black pepper

1. In a large bowl, drizzle olive oil over green beans and sprinkle with salt and pepper. 2. Place green beans into ungreased air fryer basket. Adjust the temperature to 350°F (177°C) and set the timer for 8 minutes, shaking the basket two times during cooking. Green beans will be dark golden and crispy at the edges when done. Serve warm.

Per Serving:
calories: 33 | fat: 3g | protein: 1g | carbs: 3g | fiber: 1g | sodium: 147mg

Roasted Asparagus and Fingerling Potatoes with Thyme

Prep time: 5 minutes | Cook time: 20 minutes | Serves 4

1 pound (454 g) asparagus, trimmed
1 pound (454 g) fingerling potatoes, cut into thin rounds
2 scallions, thinly sliced
3 tablespoons olive oil
¾ teaspoon salt
¼ teaspoon freshly ground black pepper
1 tablespoon fresh thyme leaves

1. Preheat the oven to 450°F (235°C). 2. In a large baking dish, combine the asparagus, potatoes, and scallions and toss to mix. Add the olive oil, salt, and pepper and toss again to coat all of the vegetables in the oil. Spread the vegetables out in as thin a layer as possible and roast in the preheated oven, stirring once, until the vegetables are tender and nicely browned, about 20 minutes. Just before serving, sprinkle with the thyme leaves. Serve hot.

Per Serving:
calories: 197 | fat: 11g | protein: 5g | carbs: 24g | fiber: 5g | sodium: 449mg

Sweet and Crispy Roasted Pearl Onions

Prep time: 5 minutes | Cook time: 18 minutes | Serves 3

1 (14½-ounce / 411-g) package frozen pearl onions (do not thaw)
2 tablespoons extra-virgin olive oil
2 tablespoons balsamic vinegar
2 teaspoons finely chopped fresh rosemary
½ teaspoon kosher salt
¼ teaspoon black pepper

1. In a medium bowl, combine the onions, olive oil, vinegar, rosemary, salt, and pepper until well coated. 2. Transfer the onions to the air fryer basket. Set the air fryer to 400°F (204°C) for 18 minutes, or until the onions are tender and lightly charred, stirring once or twice during the cooking time.

Per Serving:
calories: 145 | fat: 9g | protein: 2g | carbs: 15g | fiber: 2g | sodium: 396mg

Corn Croquettes

Prep time: 10 minutes | Cook time: 12 to 14 minutes | Serves 4

½ cup leftover mashed potatoes
2 cups corn kernels (if frozen, thawed, and well drained)
¼ teaspoon onion powder
⅛ teaspoon ground black

pepper
¼ teaspoon salt
½ cup panko bread crumbs
Oil for misting or cooking spray

1. Place the potatoes and half the corn in food processor and pulse until corn is well chopped. 2. Transfer mixture to large bowl and stir in remaining corn, onion powder, pepper and salt. 3. Shape mixture into 16 balls. 4. Roll balls in panko crumbs, mist with oil or cooking spray, and place in air fryer basket. 5. Air fry at 360°F (182°C) for 12 to 14 minutes, until golden brown and crispy.

Per Serving:
calories: 149 | fat: 1g | protein: 5g | carbs: 33g | fiber: 3g | sodium: 250mg

Broccoli Salad

Prep time: 5 minutes | Cook time: 7 minutes | Serves 4

2 cups fresh broccoli florets, chopped
1 tablespoon olive oil
¼ teaspoon salt
⅛ teaspoon ground black

pepper
¼ cup lemon juice, divided
¼ cup shredded Parmesan cheese
¼ cup sliced roasted almonds

1. In a large bowl, toss broccoli and olive oil together. Sprinkle with salt and pepper, then drizzle with 2 tablespoons lemon juice. 2. Place broccoli into ungreased air fryer basket. Adjust the temperature to 350°F (177°C) and set the timer for 7 minutes, shaking the basket halfway through cooking. Broccoli will be golden on the edges when done. 3. Place broccoli into a large serving bowl and drizzle with remaining lemon juice. Sprinkle with Parmesan and almonds. Serve warm.

Per Serving:
calories: 76 | fat: 5g | protein: 3g | carbs: 5g | fiber: 1g | sodium: 273mg

Turkish Stuffed Eggplant

Prep time: 10 minutes | Cook time: 2 hours 10 minutes | Serves 6

½ cup extra-virgin olive oil
3 small eggplants
1 teaspoon sea salt
½ teaspoon black pepper
1 large yellow onion, finely chopped
4 garlic cloves, minced

1 (15-ounce / 425-g) can diced tomatoes, with the juice
¼ cup finely chopped fresh flat-leaf parsley
6 (8-inch) round pita breads, quartered and toasted
1 cup plain Greek yogurt

1. Pour ¼ cup of the olive oil into the slow cooker, and generously coat the interior of the crock. 2. Cut each eggplant in half lengthwise. You can leave the stem on. Score the cut side of each half every ¼ inch, being careful not to cut through the skin. 3.

Arrange the eggplant halves, skin-side down, in the slow cooker. Sprinkle with 1 teaspoon salt and ½ teaspoon pepper. 4. In a large skillet, heat the remaining ¼ cup olive oil over medium-high heat. Sauté the onion and garlic for 3 minutes, or until the onion begins to soften. 5. Add the tomatoes and parsley to the skillet. Season with salt and pepper. Sauté for another 5 minutes, until the liquid has almost evaporated. 6. Using a large spoon, spoon the tomato mixture over the eggplants, covering each half with some of the mixture. 7. Cover and cook on high for 2 hours or on low for 4 hours. When the dish is finished, the eggplant should feel very tender when you insert the tip of a sharp knife into the thickest part. 8. Uncover the slow cooker, and let the eggplant rest for 10 minutes. Then transfer the eggplant to a serving dish. If there is any juice in the bottom of the cooker, spoon it over the eggplant. Serve hot with toasted pita wedges and yogurt on the side.

Per Serving:
calories: 449 | fat: 22g | protein: 11g | carbs: 59g | fiber: 15g | sodium: 706mg

Caramelized Eggplant with Harissa Yogurt

Prep time: 10 minutes | Cook time: 15 minutes | Serves 2

1 medium eggplant (about ¾ pound / 340 g), cut crosswise into ½-inch-thick slices and quartered
2 tablespoons vegetable oil
Kosher salt and freshly ground

black pepper, to taste
½ cup plain yogurt (not Greek)
2 tablespoons harissa paste
1 garlic clove, grated
2 teaspoons honey

1. In a bowl, toss together the eggplant and oil, season with salt and pepper, and toss to coat evenly. Transfer to the air fryer and air fry at 400°F (204°C), shaking the basket every 5 minutes, until the eggplant is caramelized and tender, about 15 minutes. 2. Meanwhile, in a small bowl, whisk together the yogurt, harissa, and garlic, then spread onto a serving plate. 3. Pile the warm eggplant over the yogurt and drizzle with the honey just before serving.

Per Serving:
calories: 247 | fat: 16g | protein: 5g | carbs: 25g | fiber: 8g | sodium: 34mg

Rustic Cauliflower and Carrot Hash

Prep time: 10 minutes | Cook time: 10 minutes | Serves 4

3 tablespoons extra-virgin olive oil
1 large onion, chopped
1 tablespoon garlic, minced
2 cups carrots, diced

4 cups cauliflower pieces, washed
1 teaspoon salt
½ teaspoon ground cumin

1. In a large skillet over medium heat, cook the olive oil, onion, garlic, and carrots for 3 minutes. 2. Cut the cauliflower into 1-inch or bite-size pieces. Add the cauliflower, salt, and cumin to the skillet and toss to combine with the carrots and onions. 3. Cover and cook for 3 minutes. 4. Toss the vegetables and continue to cook uncovered for an additional 3 to 4 minutes. 5. Serve warm.

Per Serving:
calories: 159 | fat: 11g | protein: 3g | carbs: 15g | fiber: 5g | sodium: 657mg

Garlic Zucchini and Red Peppers

Prep time: 5 minutes | Cook time: 15 minutes | Serves 6

2 medium zucchini, cubed
1 red bell pepper, diced
2 garlic cloves, sliced

2 tablespoons olive oil
½ teaspoon salt

1. Preheat the air fryer to 380°F(193°C). 2. In a large bowl, mix together the zucchini, bell pepper, and garlic with the olive oil and salt. 3. Pour the mixture into the air fryer basket, and roast for 7 minutes. Shake or stir, then roast for 7 to 8 minutes more.
Per Serving:
calories: 59 | fat: 5g | protein: 1g | carbs: 4g | fiber: 1g | sodium: 200mg

Cauliflower Steaks with Creamy Tahini Sauce

Prep time: 10 minutes | Cook time: 45 minutes | Serves 4

¼ cup olive oil
4 garlic cloves, minced
1 teaspoon sea salt
1 teaspoon freshly ground black pepper
2 large heads cauliflower, stem end trimmed (core left intact)

and cut from top to bottom into thick slabs
½ cup tahini
Juice of 1 lemon
¼ cup chopped fresh Italian parsley

1. Preheat the oven to 400ºF (205ºC). Line a baking sheet with parchment paper. 2. In a small bowl, combine the olive oil, garlic, salt, and pepper. Brush this mixture on both sides of the cauliflower steaks and place them in a single layer on the baking sheet. Drizzle any remaining oil mixture over the cauliflower steaks. Bake for 45 minutes, or until the cauliflower is soft. 3. While the steaks are baking, in a small bowl, stir together the tahini and lemon juice. Season with salt and pepper. 4. Remove the cauliflower steaks from the oven and transfer them to four plates. Drizzle the lemon tahini sauce evenly over the cauliflower and garnish with the parsley. Serve.
Per Serving:
calories: 339 | fat: 30g | protein: 8g | carbs: 15g | fiber: 6g | sodium: 368mg

Garlic and Herb Roasted Grape Tomatoes

Prep time: 10 minutes | Cook time: 45 minutes | Serves 2

1 pint grape tomatoes
10 whole garlic cloves, skins removed
¼ cup olive oil

½ teaspoon salt
1 fresh rosemary sprig
1 fresh thyme sprig

1. Preheat oven to 350°F(180ºC). 2. Toss tomatoes, garlic cloves, oil, salt, and herb sprigs in a baking dish. 3. Roast tomatoes until they are soft and begin to caramelize, about 45 minutes. 4. Remove herbs before serving.
Per Serving:
calories: 271 | fat: 26g | protein: 3g | carbs: 12g | fiber: 3g | sodium: 593mg

Beet and Watercress Salad with Orange and Dill

Prep time: 20 minutes | Cook time: 8 minutes | Serves 4

2 pounds (907 g) beets, scrubbed, trimmed, and cut into ¾-inch pieces
½ cup water
1 teaspoon caraway seeds
½ teaspoon table salt
1 cup plain Greek yogurt
1 small garlic clove, minced to paste
5 ounces (142 g) watercress, torn into bite-size pieces
1 tablespoon extra-virgin olive

oil, divided, plus extra for drizzling
1 tablespoon white wine vinegar, divided
1 teaspoon grated orange zest plus 2 tablespoons juice
¼ cup hazelnuts, toasted, skinned, and chopped
¼ cup coarsely chopped fresh dill
Coarse sea salt

1. Combine beets, water, caraway seeds, and table salt in Instant Pot. Lock lid in place and close pressure release valve. Select high pressure cook function and cook for 8 minutes. Turn off Instant Pot and quick-release pressure. Carefully remove lid, allowing steam to escape away from you. 2. Using slotted spoon, transfer beets to plate; set aside to cool slightly. Combine yogurt, garlic, and 3 tablespoons beet cooking liquid in bowl; discard remaining cooking liquid. In large bowl toss watercress with 2 teaspoons oil and 1 teaspoon vinegar. Season with table salt and pepper to taste. 3. Spread yogurt mixture over surface of serving dish. Arrange watercress on top of yogurt mixture, leaving 1-inch border of yogurt mixture. Add beets to now-empty large bowl and toss with orange zest and juice, remaining 2 teaspoons vinegar, and remaining 1 teaspoon oil. Season with table salt and pepper to taste. Arrange beets on top of watercress mixture. Drizzle with extra oil and sprinkle with hazelnuts, dill, and sea salt. Serve.
Per Serving:
calories: 240 | fat: 15g | protein: 9g | carbs: 19g | fiber: 5g | sodium: 440mg

Roasted Broccolini with Garlic and Romano

Prep time: 5 minutes | Cook time: 10 minutes | Serves 2

1 bunch broccolini (about 5 ounces / 142 g)
1 tablespoon olive oil
½ teaspoon garlic powder

¼ teaspoon salt
2 tablespoons grated Romano cheese

1. Preheat the oven to 400°F(205ºC) and set the oven rack to the middle position. Line a sheet pan with parchment paper or foil. 2. Slice the tough ends off the broccolini and place in a medium bowl. Add the olive oil, garlic powder, and salt and toss to combine. Arrange broccolini on the lined sheet pan. 3. Roast for 7 minutes, flipping pieces over halfway through the roasting time. 4. Remove the pan from the oven and sprinkle the cheese over the broccolini. With a pair of tongs, carefully flip the pieces over to coat all sides. Return to the oven for another 2 to 3 minutes, or until the cheese melts and starts to turn golden.
Per Serving:
calories: 114 | fat: 9g | protein: 4g | carbs: 5g | fiber: 2g | sodium: 400mg

Green Beans with Pine Nuts and Garlic

Prep time: 10 minutes | Cook time: 20 minutes |
Serves 4 to 6

1 pound (454 g) green beans, trimmed	½ teaspoon kosher salt
1 head garlic (10 to 12 cloves), smashed	¼ teaspoon red pepper flakes
2 tablespoons extra-virgin olive oil	1 tablespoon white wine vinegar
	¼ cup pine nuts, toasted

1. Preheat the oven to 425ºF (220ºC). Line a baking sheet with parchment paper or foil. 2. In a large bowl, combine the green beans, garlic, olive oil, salt, and red pepper flakes and mix together. Arrange in a single layer on the baking sheet. Roast for 10 minutes, stir, and roast for another 10 minutes, or until golden brown. 3. Mix the cooked green beans with the vinegar and top with the pine nuts.
Per Serving:
calories: 165 | fat: 13g | protein: 4g | carbs: 12g | fiber: 4g | sodium: 150mg

Root Vegetable Hash

Prep time: 20 minutes | Cook time: 8 hours | Makes
9 (¾-cup) servings

4 carrots, peeled and cut into 1-inch cubes	⅛ teaspoon freshly ground black pepper
3 large russet potatoes, peeled and cut into 1-inch cubes	½ teaspoon dried thyme leaves
1 onion, diced	1 sprig rosemary
3 garlic cloves, minced	½ cup vegetable broth
½ teaspoon salt	3 plums, cut into 1-inch pieces

1. In the slow cooker, combine the carrots, potatoes, onion, and garlic. Sprinkle with the salt, pepper, and thyme, and stir. 2. Imbed the rosemary sprig in the vegetables. 3. Pour the broth over everything. 4. Cover and cook on low for 7½ hours, or until the vegetables are tender. 5. Stir in the plums, cover, and cook on low for 30 minutes, until tender. 6. Remove and discard the rosemary sprig, and serve.
Per Serving:
calories: 137 | fat: 0g | protein: 3g | carbs: 32g | net carbs: 28g | sugars: 6g | fiber: 4g | sodium: 204mg | cholesterol: 0mg

Herbed Shiitake Mushrooms

Prep time: 10 minutes | Cook time: 5 minutes | Serves 4

8 ounces (227 g) shiitake mushrooms, stems removed and caps roughly chopped	1 teaspoon chopped fresh thyme leaves
1 tablespoon olive oil	1 teaspoon chopped fresh oregano
½ teaspoon salt	1 tablespoon chopped fresh parsley
Freshly ground black pepper, to taste	

1. Preheat the air fryer to 400ºF (204ºC). 2. Toss the mushrooms with the olive oil, salt, pepper, thyme and oregano. Air fry for 5 minutes, shaking the basket once or twice during the cooking process. The mushrooms will still be somewhat chewy with a meaty texture. If you'd like them a little more tender, add a couple of minutes to this cooking time. 3. Once cooked, add the parsley to the mushrooms and toss. Season again to taste and serve.
Per Serving:
calories: 50 | fat: 4g | protein: 1g | carbs: 4g | fiber: 2g | sodium: 296mg

Stuffed Red Peppers with Herbed Ricotta and Tomatoes

Prep time: 10 minutes | Cook time: 20 minutes | Serves 4

2 red bell peppers	3 tablespoons fresh basil, chopped
1 cup cooked brown rice	3 tablespoons fresh oregano, chopped
2 Roma tomatoes, diced	
1 garlic clove, minced	¼ cup shredded Parmesan, for topping
¼ teaspoon salt	
¼ teaspoon black pepper	
4 ounces (113 g) ricotta	

1. Preheat the air fryer to 360°F(182ºC). 2. Cut the bell peppers in half and remove the seeds and stem. 3. In a medium bowl, combine the brown rice, tomatoes, garlic, salt, and pepper. 4. Distribute the rice filling evenly among the four bell pepper halves. 5. In a small bowl, combine the ricotta, basil, and oregano. Put the herbed cheese over the top of the rice mixture in each bell pepper. 6. Place the bell peppers into the air fryer and roast for 20 minutes. 7. Remove and serve with shredded Parmesan on top.
Per Serving:
calories: 152 | fat: 6g | protein: 7g | carbs: 18g | fiber: 3g | sodium: 261mg

Baba Ghanoush

Prep time: 15 minutes | Cook time: 2 to 4 hours |
Serves 6

1 large eggplant (2 to 4 pounds / 907 g to 1.8 kg), peeled and diced	oil, plus more as needed
¼ cup freshly squeezed lemon juice	¼ teaspoon sea salt, plus more as needed
2 garlic cloves, minced	⅛ teaspoon freshly ground black pepper, plus more as needed
2 tablespoons tahini	
1 teaspoon extra-virgin olive	2 tablespoons chopped fresh parsley

1. In a slow cooker, combine the eggplant, lemon juice, garlic, tahini, olive oil, salt, and pepper. Stir to mix well. 2. Cover the cooker and cook for 2 to 4 hours on Low heat. 3. Using a spoon or potato masher, mash the mixture. If you prefer a smoother texture, transfer it to a food processor and blend to your desired consistency. Taste and season with olive oil, salt, and pepper as needed. 4. Garnish with fresh parsley for serving.
Per Serving:
calories: 81 | fat: 4g | protein: 3g | carbs: 12g | fiber: 4g | sodium: 108mg

Green Veg & Macadamia Smash

Prep time: 25 minutes | Cook time: 15 minutes | Serves 6

⅔ cup macadamia nuts
Enough water to cover and soak the macadamias
7 ounces (198 g) cavolo nero or kale, stalks removed and chopped
1 medium head broccoli, cut into florets, or broccolini
2 cloves garlic, crushed

¼ cup extra-virgin olive oil
2 tablespoons fresh lemon juice
4 medium spring onions, sliced
¼ cup chopped fresh herbs, such as parsley, dill, basil, or mint
Salt and black pepper, to taste

1. Place the macadamias in a small bowl and add enough water to cover them. Soak for about 2 hours, then drain. Discard the water. 2. Fill a large pot with about 1½ cups (360 ml) of water, then insert a steamer colander. Bring to a boil over high heat, then reduce to medium-high. Add the cavolo nero and cook for 6 minutes. Add the broccoli and cook for 8 minutes or until fork-tender. Remove the lid, let the steam escape, and let cool slightly. 3. Place the cooked vegetables in a blender or a food processor. Add the soaked macadamias, garlic, olive oil, lemon juice, spring onions, and fresh herbs (you can reserve some for topping). 4. Process to the desired consistency (smooth or chunky). Season with salt and pepper to taste and serve. To store, let cool completely and store in a sealed container in the fridge for up to 5 days.

Per Serving:
calories: 250 | fat: 22g | protein: 5g | carbs: 12g | fiber: 5g | sodium: 44mg

Chapter 12 Salads

Greek Salad with Lemon-Oregano Vinaigrette

Prep time: 15 minutes | Cook time: 15 minutes | Serves 8

½ red onion, thinly sliced
¼ cup extra-virgin olive oil
3 tablespoons fresh lemon juice or red wine vinegar
1 clove garlic, minced
1 teaspoon chopped fresh oregano or ½ teaspoon dried
½ teaspoon ground black pepper
¼ teaspoon kosher salt
4 tomatoes, cut into large chunks

1 large English cucumber, peeled, seeded (if desired), and diced
1 large yellow or red bell pepper, chopped
½ cup pitted kalamata or Niçoise olives, halved
¼ cup chopped fresh flat-leaf parsley
4 ounces (113 g) Halloumi or feta cheese, cut into ½' cubes

1. In a medium bowl, soak the onion in enough water to cover for 10 minutes. 2. In a small bowl, combine the oil, lemon juice or vinegar, garlic, oregano, black pepper, and salt. 3. Drain the onion and add to a large bowl with the tomatoes, cucumber, bell pepper, olives, and parsley. Gently toss to mix the vegetables. 4. Pour the vinaigrette over the salad. Add the cheese and toss again to distribute. 5. Serve immediately, or chill for up to 30 minutes.

Per Serving:
calories: 190 | fat: 16g | protein: 5g | carbs: 8g | fiber: 2g | sodium: 554mg

Tossed Green Mediterranean Salad

Prep time: 15 minutes | Cook time: 0 minutes | Serves 4

1 medium head romaine lettuce, washed, dried, and chopped into bite-sized pieces
2 medium cucumbers, peeled and sliced
3 spring onions (white parts only), sliced

½ cup finely chopped fresh dill
⅓ cup extra virgin olive oil
2 tablespoons fresh lemon juice
¼ teaspoon fine sea salt
4 ounces (113 g) crumbled feta
7 Kalamata olives, pitted

1. Add the lettuce, cucumber, spring onions, and dill to a large bowl. Toss to combine. 2. In a small bowl, whisk together the olive oil and lemon juice. Pour the dressing over the salad, toss, then sprinkle the sea salt over the top. 3. Sprinkle the feta and olives over the top and then gently toss the salad one more time. Serve promptly. (This recipe is best served fresh.)

Per Serving:
calories: 284 | fat: 25g | protein: 7g | carbs: 10g | fiber: 5g | sodium: 496mg

Citrusy Spinach Salad

Prep time: 10 minutes | Cook time: 5 minutes | Serves 4

1 large ripe tomato
1 medium red onion
½ teaspoon fresh lemon zest
3 tablespoons balsamic vinegar

¼ cup extra-virgin olive oil
½ teaspoon salt
1 pound (454 g) baby spinach, washed, stems removed

1. Dice the tomato into ¼-inch pieces and slice the onion into long slivers. 2. In a small bowl, whisk together the lemon zest, balsamic vinegar, olive oil, and salt. 3. Put the spinach, tomatoes, and onions in a large bowl. Pour the dressing over the salad and lightly toss to coat.

Per Serving:
calories: 172 | fat: 14g | protein: 4g | carbs: 10g | fiber: 4g | sodium: 389mg

Chopped Greek Antipasto Salad

Prep time: 20 minutes |Cook time: 0 minutes| Serves: 6

For the Salad:
1 head Bibb lettuce or ½ head romaine lettuce, chopped (about 2½ cups)
¼ cup loosely packed chopped basil leaves
1 (15-ounce / 425-g) can chickpeas, drained and rinsed
1 (14-ounce / 397-g) can artichoke hearts, drained and halved
1 pint grape tomatoes, halved (about 1½ cups)
1 seedless cucumber, peeled and chopped (about 1½ cups)
½ cup cubed feta cheese (about

2 ounces / 57 g)
1 (2¼-ounce / 35-g) can sliced black olives (about ½ cup)
For the Dressing:
3 tablespoons extra-virgin olive oil
1 tablespoon red wine vinegar
1 tablespoon freshly squeezed lemon juice (from about ½ small lemon)
1 tablespoon chopped fresh oregano or ½ teaspoon dried oregano
1 teaspoon honey
¼ teaspoon freshly ground black pepper

1. In a medium bowl, toss the lettuce and basil together. Spread out on a large serving platter or in a large salad bowl. Arrange the chickpeas, artichoke hearts, tomatoes, cucumber, feta, and olives in piles next to each other on top of the lettuce layer. 2. In a small pitcher or bowl, whisk together the oil, vinegar, lemon juice, oregano, honey, and pepper. Serve on the side with the salad, or drizzle over all the ingredients right before serving.

Per Serving:
calories: 267 | fat: 13g | protein: 11g | carbs: 31g | fiber: 11g | sodium: 417mg

Orange-Tarragon Chicken Salad Wrap

Prep time: 15 minutes | Cook time: 0 minutes | Serves 4

½ cup plain whole-milk Greek yogurt
2 tablespoons Dijon mustard
2 tablespoons extra-virgin olive oil
2 tablespoons chopped fresh tarragon or 1 teaspoon dried tarragon
½ teaspoon salt
¼ teaspoon freshly ground

black pepper
2 cups cooked shredded chicken
½ cup slivered almonds
4 to 8 large Bibb lettuce leaves, tough stem removed
2 small ripe avocados, peeled and thinly sliced
Zest of 1 clementine, or ½ small orange (about 1 tablespoon)

1. In a medium bowl, combine the yogurt, mustard, olive oil, tarragon, orange zest, salt, and pepper and whisk until creamy. 2. Add the shredded chicken and almonds and stir to coat. 3. To assemble the wraps, place about ½ cup chicken salad mixture in the center of each lettuce leaf and top with sliced avocados.
Per Serving:
calories: 491 | fat: 38g | protein: 28g | carbs: 14g | fiber: 9g | sodium: 454mg

Arugula and Fennel Salad with Fresh Basil

Prep time: 5 minutes | Cook time: 0 minutes | Serves 4

3 tablespoons olive oil
3 tablespoons lemon juice
1 teaspoon honey
½ teaspoon salt
1 medium bulb fennel, very thinly sliced
1 small cucumber, very thinly

sliced
2 cups arugula
¼ cup toasted pine nuts
½ cup crumbled feta cheese
¼ cup julienned fresh basil leaves

1. In a medium bowl, whisk together the olive oil, lemon juice, honey, and salt. Add the fennel and cucumber and toss to coat and let sit for 10 minutes or so. 2. Put the arugula in a large salad bowl. Add the marinated cucumber and fennel, along with the dressing, to the bowl and toss well. Serve immediately, sprinkled with pine nuts, feta cheese, and basil.
Per Serving:
calories: 237 | fat: 21g | protein: 6g | carbs: 11g | fiber: 3g | sodium: 537mg

Asparagus Salad

Prep time: 10 minutes | Cook time: 0 minutes | Serves 4

1 pound (454 g) asparagus
Sea salt and freshly ground pepper, to taste

4 tablespoons olive oil
1 tablespoon balsamic vinegar
1 tablespoon lemon zest

1. Either roast the asparagus or, with a vegetable peeler, shave it into thin strips. 2. Season to taste. 3. Toss with the olive oil and vinegar, garnish with a sprinkle of lemon zest, and serve.
Per Serving:
calories: 146 | fat: 14g | protein: 3g | carbs: 5g | fiber: 3g | sodium: 4mg

Italian Summer Vegetable Barley Salad

Prep time: 1 minutes | Cook time: 25 to 45 minutes | Serves 4

1 cup uncooked barley (hulled or pearl)
3 cups water
¾ teaspoon fine sea salt, divided
1 teaspoon plus 3 tablespoons extra virgin olive oil, divided
3 tablespoons fresh lemon juice
2 medium zucchini, washed and

chopped
15 Kalamata olives, pitted and sliced or chopped
¼ cup chopped fresh parsley
¼ cup chopped fresh basil
1 cup cherry tomatoes, halved
½ teaspoon freshly ground black pepper

1. Place the barley in a medium pot and add 3 cups of water and ¼ teaspoon of the sea salt. Bring to a boil over high heat, then reduce the heat to low. Simmer for 25–40 minutes, depending on the type of barley you're using, adding small amounts of hot water if the barley appears to be drying out. Cook until the barley is soft but still chewy, then transfer to a mesh strainer and rinse with cold water. 2. Empty the rinsed barley into a large bowl, drizzle 1 teaspoon of the olive oil over the top, fluff with a fork, and then set aside. 3. In a small bowl, combine the remaining 3 tablespoons of olive oil and the lemon juice. Whisk until the dressing thickens. 4. In a large bowl, combine the barley, zucchini, olives, parsley, and basil. Toss and then add the cherry tomatoes, remaining ½ teaspoon of sea salt, and black pepper. Toss gently, drizzle the dressing over the top, and continue tossing until the ingredients are coated with the dressing. Serve promptly. Store covered in the refrigerator for up to 3 days.
Per Serving:
calories: 308 | fat: 13g | protein: 7g | carbs: 45g | fiber: 10g | sodium: 614mg

Dakos (Cretan Salad)

Prep time: 7 minutes | Cook time: 00 minutes | Serves 1

1 medium ripe tomato (any variety)
2 whole-grain crispbreads or rusks (or 1 slice toasted whole-grain, wheat, or barley bread)
1 tablespoon plus 1 teaspoon

extra virgin olive oil
Pinch of kosher salt
1½ ounces (43 g) crumbled feta
2 teaspoons capers, drained
2 Kalamata olives, pitted
Pinch of dried oregano

1. Slice a thin round off the bottom of the tomato. Hold the tomato from the stem side and begin grating the tomato over a plate, using the largest holes of the grater. Grate until only the skin of the tomato remains, then discard the skin. Use a fine mesh strainer to drain the liquid from the grated tomato. 2. Place the crisps on a plate, one next to the other, and sprinkle with a few drops of water. Drizzle 1 tablespoon of the olive oil over the crisps and then top the crisps with the grated tomato, ensuring the crisps are thoroughly covered with the tomato. 3. Sprinkle the kosher salt over the tomato, then layer the crumbled feta over the top. Top with the capers and olives, and sprinkle the oregano over the top and drizzle with the remaining 1 teaspoon of olive oil. Serve promptly. (This salad is best served fresh.)
Per Serving:
calories: 346 | fat: 24g | protein: 12g | carbs: 21g | fiber: 4g | sodium: 626mg

Greek Potato Salad

Prep time: 15 minutes | Cook time: 15 to 18 minutes | Serves 6

1½ pounds (680 g) small red or new potatoes
½ cup olive oil
⅓ cup red wine vinegar
1 teaspoon fresh Greek oregano
4 ounces (113 g) feta cheese, crumbled, if desired, or 4 ounces (113 g) grated Swiss

cheese (for a less salty option)
1 green bell pepper, seeded and chopped (1¼ cups)
1 small red onion, halved and thinly sliced (generous 1 cup)
½ cup Kalamata olives, pitted and halved

1. Put the potatoes in a large saucepan and add water to cover. Bring the water to a boil and cook until tender, 15 to 18 minutes. Drain and set aside until cool enough to handle. 2. Meanwhile, in a large bowl, whisk together the olive oil, vinegar, and oregano. 3. When the potatoes are just cool enough to handle, cut them into 1-inch pieces and add them to the bowl with the dressing. Toss to combine. Add the cheese, bell pepper, onion, and olives and toss gently. Let stand for 30 minutes before serving.

Per Serving:
calories: 315 | fat: 23g | protein: 5g | carbs: 21g | fiber: 3g | sodium: 360mg

Pear-Fennel Salad with Pomegranate

Prep time: 15 minutes | Cook time: 5 minutes | Serves 6

Dressing:
2 tablespoons red wine vinegar
1½ tablespoons pomegranate molasses
2 teaspoons finely chopped shallot
½ teaspoon Dijon mustard
½ teaspoon kosher salt
¼ teaspoon ground black pepper
¼ cup extra-virgin olive oil
Salad:
¼ cup walnuts, coarsely

chopped, or pine nuts
2 red pears, halved, cored, and very thinly sliced
1 bulb fennel, halved, cored, and very thinly sliced, fronds reserved
1 tablespoon fresh lemon juice
4 cups baby arugula
½ cup pomegranate seeds
⅓ cup crumbled feta cheese or shaved Parmigiano-Reggiano cheese

1. Make the Dressing: In a small bowl or jar with a lid, combine the vinegar, pomegranate molasses, shallot, mustard, salt, and pepper. Add the oil and whisk until emulsified (or cap the jar and shake vigorously). Set aside. 2. Make the Salad: In a small skillet over medium heat, toast the nuts until golden and fragrant, 4 to 5 minutes. Remove from the skillet to cool. 3. In a large bowl, combine the pears and fennel. Sprinkle with the lemon juice and toss gently. 4. Add the arugula and toss again to evenly distribute. Pour over 3 to 4 tablespoons of the dressing, just enough to moisten the arugula, and toss. Add the pomegranate seeds, cheese, and nuts and toss again. Add more dressing, if necessary, or store remainder in the refrigerator for up to 1 week. Serve the salad topped with the reserved fennel fronds.

Per Serving:
calories: 165 | fat: 10g | protein:31g | carbs: 18g | fiber: 4g | sodium: 215mg

Mediterranean No-Mayo Potato Salad

Prep time: 5 minutes | Cook time: 15 minutes | Serves 4

2 pounds (907 g) potatoes (white or Yukon Gold varieties), peeled and cut into 1½-inch chunks
¼ cup extra virgin olive oil

3 tablespoons red wine vinegar
½ medium red onion, chopped
2 tablespoons dried oregano
½ teaspoon fine sea salt

1. Fill a medium pot with water and place it over high heat. When the water comes to a boil, carefully place the potatoes in the water, reduce the heat to medium, and simmer for 12–15 minutes or until the potatoes can be pierced with a fork but are not falling apart. Use a slotted spoon to transfer the potatoes to a colander, rinse briefly with cold water, then set aside to drain. 2. In a small bowl, whisk the olive oil and red wine vinegar. 3. Transfer the potatoes to a large bowl. Add the olive oil and vinegar mixture to the potatoes and toss gently and then add the onions. Rub the oregano between your fingers to release the aroma, then sprinkle it over the potatoes and toss again. Add the sea salt and toss once more. Store in an airtight container in the refrigerator for up to 3 days.

Per Serving:
calories: 347 | fat: 14g | protein: 5g | carbs: 50g | fiber: 6g | sodium: 309mg

Wild Greens Salad with Fresh Herbs

Prep time: 10 minutes | Cook time: 20 minutes | Serves 6 to 8

¼ cup olive oil
2 pounds (907 g) dandelion greens, tough stems removed and coarsely chopped
1 small bunch chicory, trimmed and coarsely chopped
1 cup chopped fresh flat-leaf parsley, divided
1 cup chopped fresh mint, divided
½ cup water
2 tablespoons red wine vinegar

or apple cider vinegar
1 tablespoon fresh thyme, chopped
2 cloves garlic, minced
½ teaspoon kosher salt
½ teaspoon ground black pepper
¼ cup almonds or walnuts, coarsely chopped
2 tablespoons chopped fresh chives or scallion greens
1 tablespoon chopped fresh dill

1. In a large pot over medium heat, warm the oil. Add the greens, half of the parsley, half of the mint, the water, vinegar, thyme, garlic, salt, and pepper. Reduce the heat to a simmer and cook until the greens are very tender, about 20 minutes. 2. Meanwhile, in a small skillet over medium heat, toast the nuts until golden and fragrant, 5 to 8 minutes. Remove from the heat. 3. If serving immediately, stir the chives or scallion greens, dill, and the remaining parsley and mint into the pot. If serving as a cool or cold salad, allow to come to room temperature or refrigerate until cold before stirring in the fresh herbs. Top with the toasted nuts before serving.

Per Serving:
calories: 190 | fat: 13g | protein: 6g | carbs: 17g | fiber: 7g | sodium: 279mg

Panzanella (Tuscan Tomato and Bread Salad)

Prep time: 1 hour 5 minutes | Cook time: 0 minutes | Serves 2

3 tablespoons white wine vinegar, divided
1 small red onion, thinly sliced
4 ounces (113 g) stale, dense bread, such as French baguette or Italian (Vienna-style)
1 large tomato (any variety), chopped into bite-sized pieces
1 large Persian (or mini) cucumber, sliced
¼ cup chopped fresh basil
2 tablespoons extra virgin olive oil, divided
Pinch of kosher salt
⅛ teaspoon freshly ground black pepper

1. Add 2 tablespoons of the vinegar to a small bowl filled with water. Add the onion and then set aside. 2. In a medium bowl, combine the remaining tablespoon of vinegar and 2 cups of water. Add the bread to the bowl and soak for 2–3 minutes (depending on how hard the bread is) until the bread has softened on the outside but is not falling apart. Place the bread in a colander and gently squeeze out any excess water and then chop into bite-sized pieces. Arrange the bread pieces on a large plate. 3. Drain the onion and add it to plate with the bread. Add the tomato, cucumber, basil, 1 tablespoon of the olive oil, kosher salt, and black pepper. Toss the ingredients carefully, then cover and transfer to the refrigerator to chill for a minimum of 1 hour. 4. When ready to serve, drizzle the remaining 1 tablespoon of olive oil over the top of the salad and serve promptly. This salad can be stored in the refrigerator for up to 5 hours, but should be consumed on the same day it is prepared.

Per Serving:
calories: 325 | fat: 16g | protein: 7g | carbs: 38g | fiber: 4g | sodium: 358mg

Arugula Spinach Salad with Shaved Parmesan

Prep time: 10 minutes | Cook time: 2 minutes | Serves 3

3 tablespoons raw pine nuts
3 cups arugula
3 cups baby leaf spinach
5 dried figs, pitted and chopped
2½ ounces (71 g) shaved Parmesan cheese
For the Dressing:
4 teaspoons balsamic vinegar
1 teaspoon Dijon mustard
1 teaspoon honey
5 tablespoons extra virgin olive oil

1. In a small pan over low heat, toast the pine nuts for 2 minutes or until they begin to brown. Promptly remove them from the heat and transfer to a small bowl. 2. Make the dressing by combining the balsamic vinegar, Dijon mustard, and honey in a small bowl. Using a fork to whisk, gradually add the olive oil while continuously mixing. 3. In a large bowl, toss the arugula and baby spinach and then top with the figs, Parmesan cheese, and toasted pine nuts. Drizzle the dressing over the top and toss until the ingredients are thoroughly coated with the dressing. Serve promptly. (This salad is best served fresh.)

Per Serving:
calories: 416 | fat: 35g | protein: 10g | carbs: 18g | fiber: 3g | sodium: 478mg

Citrus Avocado Salad

Prep time: 5 minutes | Cook time: 0 minutes | Serves 2

½ medium orange (any variety), peeled and cut into bite-sized chunks
1 medium tangerine, peeled and sectioned
½ medium white grapefruit, peeled and cut into bite-sized chunks
2 thin slices red onion
1 medium avocado, peeled, pitted, and sliced
Pinch of freshly ground black pepper
For the Dressing:
3 tablespoons extra virgin olive oil
1 tablespoon fresh lemon juice
½ teaspoon ground cumin
½ teaspoon coarse sea salt
Pinch of freshly ground black pepper

1. Make the dressing by combining the olive oil, lemon juice, cumin, sea salt, and black pepper in a small jar or bowl. Whisk or shake to combine. 2. Toss the orange, tangerine, and grapefruit in a medium bowl, then place the sliced onion on top. Drizzle half the dressing over the salad. 3. Fan the avocado slices over the top of the salad. Drizzle the remaining dressing over the salad and then sprinkle a pinch of black pepper over the top. 4. Toss gently before serving. (This salad is best eaten fresh, but can be stored in the refrigerator for up to 1 day.)

Per Serving:
calories: 448 | fat: 36g | protein: 4g | carbs: 35g | fiber: 11g | sodium: 595mg

Roasted Golden Beet, Avocado, and Watercress Salad

Prep time: 15 minutes | Cook time: 1 hour | Serves 4

1 bunch (about 1½ pounds / 680 g) golden beets
1 tablespoon extra-virgin olive oil
1 tablespoon white wine vinegar
½ teaspoon kosher salt
¼ teaspoon freshly ground black pepper
1 bunch (about 4 ounces / 113 g) watercress
1 avocado, peeled, pitted, and diced
¼ cup crumbled feta cheese
¼ cup walnuts, toasted
1 tablespoon fresh chives, chopped

1. Preheat the oven to 425ºF (220ºC). Wash and trim the beets (cut an inch above the beet root, leaving the long tail if desired), then wrap each beet individually in foil. Place the beets on a baking sheet and roast until fully cooked, 45 to 60 minutes depending on the size of each beet. Start checking at 45 minutes; if easily pierced with a fork, the beets are cooked. 2. Remove the beets from the oven and allow them to cool. Under cold running water, slough off the skin. Cut the beets into bite-size cubes or wedges. 3. In a large bowl, whisk together the olive oil, vinegar, salt, and black pepper. Add the watercress and beets and toss well. Add the avocado, feta, walnuts, and chives and mix gently.

Per Serving:
calories: 235 | fat: 16g | protein: 6g | carbs: 21g | fiber: 8g | sodium: 365mg

Peachy Tomato Salad

Prep time: 15 minutes | Cook time: 0 minutes | Serves 2

2 ripe peaches, pitted and sliced into wedges
2 ripe tomatoes, cut into wedges
½ red onion, thinly sliced
Sea salt and freshly ground pepper, to taste
3 tablespoons olive oil
1 tablespoon lemon juice

1. Toss the peaches, tomatoes, and red onion in a large bowl. Season to taste. 2. Add the olive oil and lemon juice, and gently toss. Serve at room temperature.

Per Serving:
calories: 272 | fat: 21g | protein: 3g | carbs: 22g | fiber: 4g | sodium: 8mg

Easy Greek Salad

Prep time: 10 minutes | Cook time: 0 minutes |
Serves 4 to 6

1 head iceberg lettuce
1 pint (2 cups) cherry tomatoes
1 large cucumber
1 medium onion
½ cup extra-virgin olive oil
¼ cup lemon juice
1 teaspoon salt
1 clove garlic, minced
1 cup Kalamata olives, pitted
1 (6-ounce / 170-g) package feta cheese, crumbled

1. Cut the lettuce into 1-inch pieces and put them in a large salad bowl. 2. Cut the tomatoes in half and add them to the salad bowl. 3. Slice the cucumber into bite-size pieces and add them to the salad bowl. 4. Thinly slice the onion and add it to the salad bowl. 5. In another small bowl, whisk together the olive oil, lemon juice, salt, and garlic. Pour the dressing over the salad and gently toss to evenly coat. 6. Top the salad with the Kalamata olives and feta cheese and serve.

Per Serving:
calories: 297 | fat: 27g | protein: 6g | carbs: 11g | fiber: 3g | sodium: 661mg

Zucchini and Ricotta Salad

Prep time: 5 minutes | Cook time: 2 minutes | Serves 1

2 teaspoons raw pine nuts
5 ounces (142 g) whole-milk ricotta cheese
1 tablespoon chopped fresh mint
1 teaspoon chopped fresh basil
1 tablespoon chopped fresh parsley
Pinch of fine sea salt
1 medium zucchini, very thinly sliced horizontally with a
mandoline slicer
Pinch of freshly ground black pepper
For the Dressing:
1½ tablespoons extra virgin olive oil
1 tablespoon fresh lemon juice
Pinch of fine sea salt
Pinch of freshly ground black pepper

1. Add the pine nuts to a small pan placed over medium heat. Toast the nuts, turning them frequently, for 2 minutes or until golden. Set aside. 2. In a food processor, combine the ricotta, mint, basil, parsley, and a pinch of sea salt. Process until smooth and then set aside. 3. Make the dressing by combining the olive oil and lemon juice in a small bowl. Use a fork to stir rapidly until the mixture thickens, then add a pinch of sea salt and a pinch of black pepper. Stir again. 4. Place the sliced zucchini in a medium bowl. Add half of the dressing, and toss to coat the zucchini. 5. To serve, place half of the ricotta mixture in the center of a serving plate, then layer the zucchini in a circle, covering the cheese. Add the rest of the cheese in the center and on top of the zucchini, then sprinkle the toasted pine nuts over the top. Drizzle the remaining dressing over the top, and finish with a pinch of black pepper. Store covered in the refrigerator for up to 1 day.

Per Serving:
calories: 504 | fat: 43g | protein: 19g | carbs: 13g | fiber: 3g | sodium: 136mg

Tuscan Kale Salad with Anchovies

Prep time: 15 minutes | Cook time: 0 minutes | Serves 4

1 large bunch lacinato or dinosaur kale
¼ cup toasted pine nuts
1 cup shaved or coarsely shredded fresh Parmesan cheese
¼ cup extra-virgin olive oil
8 anchovy fillets, roughly
chopped
2 to 3 tablespoons freshly squeezed lemon juice (from 1 large lemon)
2 teaspoons red pepper flakes (optional)

1. Remove the rough center stems from the kale leaves and roughly tear each leaf into about 4-by-1-inch strips. Place the torn kale in a large bowl and add the pine nuts and cheese. 2. In a small bowl, whisk together the olive oil, anchovies, lemon juice, and red pepper flakes (if using). Drizzle over the salad and toss to coat well. Let sit at room temperature 30 minutes before serving, tossing again just prior to serving.

Per Serving:
calories: 333 | fat: 27g | protein: 16g | carbs: 12g | fiber: 4g | sodium: 676mg

Italian Tuna and Olive Salad

Prep time : 5 minutes | Cook time: 0 minutes | Serves 4

¼ cup olive oil
3 tablespoons white wine vinegar
1 teaspoon salt
1 cup pitted green olives
1 medium red bell pepper,
seeded and diced
1 small clove garlic, minced
2 (6-ounce / 170-g) cans or jars tuna in olive oil, well drained
Several leaves curly green or red lettuce

1. In a large bowl, whisk together the olive oil, vinegar, and salt. 2. Add the olives, bell pepper, and garlic to the dressing and toss to coat. Stir in the tuna, cover, and chill in the refrigerator for at least 1 hour to let the flavors meld. 3. To serve, line a serving bowl with the lettuce leaves and spoon the salad on top. Serve chilled.

Per Serving:
calories: 339 | fat: 24g | protein: 25g | carbs: 4g | fiber: 2g | sodium: 626mg

Sicilian Salad

Prep time: 5 minutes | Cook time: 0 minutes | Serves 2

2 tablespoons extra virgin olive oil
1 tablespoon red wine vinegar
2 medium tomatoes (preferably beefsteak variety), sliced
½ medium red onion, thinly sliced
2 tablespoons capers, drained
6 green olives, halved
1 teaspoon dried oregano
Pinch of fine sea salt

1. Make the dressing by combining the olive oil and vinegar in a small bowl. Use a fork to whisk until the mixture thickens slightly. Set aside. 2. Arrange the sliced tomatoes on a large plate and then scatter the onions, capers, and olives over the tomatoes. 3. Sprinkle the oregano and sea salt over the top, then drizzle the dressing over the salad. Serve promptly. (This salad is best served fresh, but can be stored covered in the refrigerator for up to 1 day.)

Per Serving:
calories: 169 | fat: 15g | protein: 2g | carbs: 8g | fiber: 3g | sodium: 336mg

Pistachio-Parmesan Kale-Arugula Salad

Prep time: 20 minutes |Cook time: 0 minutes| Serves: 6

6 cups raw kale, center ribs removed and discarded, leaves coarsely chopped
¼ cup extra-virgin olive oil
2 tablespoons freshly squeezed lemon juice (from about 1 small lemon)
½ teaspoon smoked paprika
2 cups arugula
⅓ cup unsalted shelled pistachios
6 tablespoons grated Parmesan or Pecorino Romano cheese

1. In a large salad bowl, combine the kale, oil, lemon juice, and smoked paprika. With your hands, gently massage the leaves for about 15 seconds or so, until all are thoroughly coated. Let the kale sit for 10 minutes. 2. When you're ready to serve, gently mix in the arugula and pistachios. Divide the salad among six serving bowls, sprinkle 1 tablespoon of grated cheese over each, and serve.

Per Serving:
calories: 150 | fat: 14g | protein: 4g | carbs: 5g | fiber: 1g | sodium: 99mg

French Lentil Salad with Parsley and Mint

Prep time: 20 minutes | Cook time:25 minutes | Serves 6

For the Lentils:
1 cup French lentils
1 garlic clove, smashed
1 dried bay leaf
For the Salad:
2 tablespoons extra-virgin olive oil
2 tablespoons red wine vinegar
½ teaspoon ground cumin
½ teaspoon kosher salt
¼ teaspoon freshly ground black pepper
2 celery stalks, diced small
1 bell pepper, diced small
½ red onion, diced small
¼ cup fresh parsley, chopped
¼ cup fresh mint, chopped

Make the Lentils: 1. Put the lentils, garlic, and bay leaf in a large saucepan. Cover with water by about 3 inches and bring to a boil. Reduce the heat, cover, and simmer until tender, 20 to 30 minutes.

2. Drain the lentils to remove any remaining water after cooking. Remove the garlic and bay leaf. Make the Salad: 3. In a large bowl, whisk together the olive oil, vinegar, cumin, salt, and black pepper. Add the celery, bell pepper, onion, parsley, and mint and toss to combine. 4. Add the lentils and mix well.

Per Serving:
calories: 200 | fat: 8g | protein: 10g | carbs: 26g | fiber: 10g | sodium: 165mg

Panzanella (Tuscan Bread and Tomatoes Salad)

Prep time: 10 minutes | Cook time: 20 minutes | Serves 6

4 ounces (113 g) sourdough bread, cut into 1' slices
3 tablespoons extra-virgin olive oil, divided
2 tablespoons red wine vinegar
2 cloves garlic, mashed to a paste
1 teaspoon finely chopped fresh oregano or ½ teaspoon dried
1 teaspoon fresh thyme leaves
½ teaspoon Dijon mustard
Pinch of kosher salt
Few grinds of ground black pepper
2 pounds (907 g) ripe tomatoes (mixed colors)
6 ounces (170 g) fresh mozzarella pearls
1 cucumber, cut into ½'-thick half-moons
1 small red onion, thinly sliced
1 cup baby arugula
½ cup torn fresh basil

1. Coat a grill rack or grill pan with olive oil and prepare to medium-high heat. 2. Brush 1 tablespoon of the oil all over the bread slices. Grill the bread on both sides until grill marks appear, about 2 minutes per side. Cut the bread into 1' cubes. 3. In a large bowl, whisk together the vinegar, garlic, oregano, thyme, mustard, salt, pepper, and the remaining 2 tablespoons oil until emulsified. 4. Add the bread, tomatoes, mozzarella, cucumber, onion, arugula, and basil. Toss to combine and let sit for 10 minutes to soak up the flavors.

Per Serving:
calories: 219 | fat: 12g | protein: 10g | carbs: 19g | fiber: 3g | sodium: 222mg

Four-Bean Salad

Prep time: 20 minutes | Cook time: 0 minutes | Serves 4

½ cup white beans, cooked
½ cup black-eyed peas, cooked
½ cup fava beans, cooked
½ cup lima beans, cooked
1 red bell pepper, diced
1 small bunch flat-leaf parsley,
chopped
2 tablespoons olive oil
1 teaspoon ground cumin
Juice of 1 lemon
Sea salt and freshly ground pepper, to taste

1. You can cook the beans a day or two in advance to speed up the preparation of this dish. 2. Combine all ingredients in a large bowl and mix well. Season to taste. 3. Allow to sit for 30 minutes, so the flavors can come together before serving.

Per Serving:
calories: 189 | fat: 7g | protein: 8g | carbs: 24g | fiber: 7g | sodium: 14mg

Traditional Greek Salad

Prep time: 10 minutes | Cook time: 0 minutes | Serves 4

2 large English cucumbers	lemon juice
4 Roma tomatoes, quartered	1 tablespoon red wine vinegar
1 green bell pepper, cut into 1- to 1½-inch chunks	1 tablespoon chopped fresh oregano or 1 teaspoon dried oregano
¼ small red onion, thinly sliced	
4 ounces (113 g) pitted Kalamata olives	¼ teaspoon freshly ground black pepper
¼ cup extra-virgin olive oil	4 ounces (113 g) crumbled
2 tablespoons freshly squeezed	traditional feta cheese

1. Cut the cucumbers in half lengthwise and then into ½-inch-thick half-moons. Place in a large bowl. 2. Add the quartered tomatoes, bell pepper, red onion, and olives. 3. In a small bowl, whisk together the olive oil, lemon juice, vinegar, oregano, and pepper. Drizzle over the vegetables and toss to coat. 4. Divide between salad plates and top each with 1 ounce (28 g) of feta.

Per Serving:
calories: 256 | fat: 22g | protein: 6g | carbs: 11g | fiber: 3g | sodium: 476mg

Grain-Free Kale Tabbouleh

Prep time: 15 minutes | Cook time: 0 minutes | Serves 8

2 plum tomatoes, seeded and chopped	1 cup finely chopped fresh mint
½ cup finely chopped fresh parsley	1 small Persian cucumber, peeled, seeded, and diced
4 scallions (green onions), finely chopped	3 tablespoons extra-virgin olive oil
1 head kale, finely chopped (about 2 cups)	2 tablespoons fresh lemon juice
	Coarsely ground black pepper (optional)

1. Place the tomatoes in a strainer set over a bowl and set aside to drain as much liquid as possible. 2. In a large bowl, stir to combine the parsley, scallions, kale, and mint. 3. Shake any remaining liquid from the tomatoes and add them to the kale mixture. Add the cucumber. 4. Add the olive oil and lemon juice and toss to combine. Season with pepper, if desired.

Per Serving:
1 cup: calories: 65 | fat: 5g | protein: 1g | carbs: 4g | fiber: 1g | sodium: 21mg

Mediterranean Quinoa and Garbanzo Salad

Prep time: 10 minutes | Cook time: 30 minutes | Serves 8

4 cups water	garbanzo beans, rinsed and drained
2 cups red or yellow quinoa	
2 teaspoons salt, divided	⅓ cup extra-virgin olive oil
1 cup thinly sliced onions (red or white)	¼ cup lemon juice
1 (16-ounce / 454-g) can	1 teaspoon freshly ground black pepper

1. In a 3-quart pot over medium heat, bring the water to a boil. 2. Add the quinoa and 1 teaspoon of salt to the pot. Stir, cover, and let cook over low heat for 15 to 20 minutes. 3. Turn off the heat, fluff the quinoa with a fork, cover again, and let stand for 5 to 10 more minutes. 4. Put the cooked quinoa, onions, and garbanzo beans in a large bowl. 5. In a separate small bowl, whisk together the olive oil, lemon juice, remaining 1 teaspoon of salt, and black pepper. 6. Add the dressing to the quinoa mixture and gently toss everything together. Serve warm or cold.

Per Serving:
calories: 318 | fat: 13g | protein: 9g | carbs: 43g | fiber: 6g | sodium: 585mg

Pipirrana (Spanish Summer Salad)

Prep time: 15 minutes | Cook time: 0 minutes | Serves 2

1 medium red onion, diced	Pinch of ground cumin
2 large tomatoes, cut into small cubes	½ teaspoon salt plus a pinch for the garlic paste
1 large Persian or mini cucumber, cut into small cubes	3 tablespoons extra virgin olive oil plus a few drops for the garlic paste
1 large green bell pepper, seeded and diced	
2 garlic cloves, minced	2 tablespoons red wine vinegar

1. Place the onions in a small bowl filled with water. Set aside to soak. 2. Place the tomatoes, cucumber, and bell pepper in a medium bowl. Drain the onions and then combine them with the rest of the vegetables. Mix well. 3. In a mortar or small bowl, combine the garlic, cumin, a pinch of salt, and a few drops of olive oil, then roll or mash the ingredients until a paste is formed. 4. In another small bowl, combine 3 tablespoons of the olive oil, vinegar, and ½ teaspoon of the salt. Add the garlic paste and mix well. 5. Add the dressing to the salad and mix well. 6. Cover and refrigerate for 30 minutes before serving. Store in the refrigerator for up to 2 days.

Per Serving:
calories: 274 | fat: 21g | protein: 4g | carbs: 20g | fiber: 6g | sodium: 600mg

Flank Steak Spinach Salad

Prep time: 15 minutes | Cook time: 10 minutes | Serves 4

1 pound (454 g) flank steak	4 cups baby spinach leaves
1 teaspoon extra-virgin olive oil	10 cherry tomatoes, halved
1 tablespoon garlic powder	10 cremini or white mushrooms, sliced
½ teaspoon salt	
½ teaspoon freshly ground black pepper	1 small red onion, thinly sliced
	½ red bell pepper, thinly sliced

1. Preheat the broiler. Line a baking sheet with aluminum foil. 2. Rub the top of the flank steak with the olive oil, garlic powder, salt, and pepper and let sit for 10 minutes before placing under the broiler. Broil for 5 minutes on each side for medium rare. Allow the meat to rest on a cutting board for 10 minutes. 3. Meanwhile, in a large bowl, combine the spinach, tomatoes, mushrooms, onion, and bell pepper and toss well. 4. To serve, divide the salad among 4 dinner plates. Slice the steak on the diagonal and place 4 to 5 slices on top of each salad. Serve with your favorite vinaigrette.

Per Serving:
calories: 211 | fat: 7g | protein: 28g | carbs: 9g | fiber: 2g | sodium: 382mg

Citrus Fennel Salad

Prep time: 15 minutes | Cook time: 0 minutes | Serves 2

For the Dressing:
2 tablespoons fresh orange juice
3 tablespoons olive oil
1 tablespoon blood orange vinegar, other orange vinegar, or cider vinegar
1 tablespoon honey
Salt
Freshly ground black pepper
For the Salad:

2 cups packed baby kale
1 medium navel or blood orange, segmented
½ small fennel bulb, stems and leaves removed, sliced into matchsticks
3 tablespoons toasted pecans, chopped
2 ounces (57 g) goat cheese, crumbled

Make the Dressing: Combine the orange juice, olive oil, vinegar, and honey in a small bowl and whisk to combine. Season with salt and pepper. Set the dressing aside. Make the Salad: 1. Divide the baby kale, orange segments, fennel, pecans, and goat cheese evenly between two plates. 2. Drizzle half of the dressing over each salad.

Per Serving:
calories: 502 | fat: 39g | protein: 13g | carbs: 31g | fiber: 6g | sodium: 158mg

Warm Fennel, Cherry Tomato, and Spinach Salad

Prep time: 15 minutes | Cook time: 0 minutes | Serves 2

4 tablespoons chicken broth
4 cups baby spinach leaves
10 cherry tomatoes, halved
Sea salt and freshly ground

pepper, to taste
1 fennel bulb, sliced
¼ cup olive oil
Juice of 2 lemons

1. In a large sauté pan, heat the chicken broth over medium heat. Add the spinach and tomatoes and cook until spinach is wilted. Season with sea salt and freshly ground pepper to taste. 2. Remove from heat and toss fennel slices in with the spinach and tomatoes. Let the fennel warm in the pan, then transfer to a large bowl. 3. Drizzle with the olive oil and lemon juice, and serve immediately.

Per Serving:
calories: 319 | fat: 28g | protein: 5g | carbs: 18g | fiber: 6g | sodium: 123mg

No-Mayo Florence Tuna Salad

Prep time: 10 minutes | Cook time: 0 minutes | Serves 4

4 cups spring mix greens
1 (15-ounce / 425-g) can cannellini beans, drained
2 (5-ounce / 142-g) cans water-packed, white albacore tuna, drained (I prefer Wild Planet brand)
⅔ cup crumbled feta cheese
½ cup thinly sliced sun-dried tomatoes
¼ cup sliced pitted kalamata

olives
¼ cup thinly sliced scallions, both green and white parts
3 tablespoons extra-virgin olive oil
½ teaspoon dried cilantro
2 or 3 leaves thinly chopped fresh sweet basil
1 lime, zested and juiced
Kosher salt
Freshly ground black pepper

1. In a large bowl, combine greens, beans, tuna, feta, tomatoes, olives, scallions, olive oil, cilantro, basil, and lime juice and zest. Season with salt and pepper, mix, and enjoy!

Per Serving:
1 cup: calories: 355 | fat: 19g | protein: 22g | carbs: 25g | fiber: 8g | sodium: 744mg

Toasted Pita Bread Salad

Prep time: 10 minutes | Cook time: 0 minutes | Serves 4

For the Dressing:
½ cup lemon juice
½ cup olive oil
1 small clove garlic, minced
1 teaspoon salt
½ teaspoon ground sumac
¼ teaspoon freshly ground black pepper
For the Salad:
2 cups shredded romaine lettuce
1 large or 2 small cucumbers, seeded and diced

2 medium tomatoes, diced
½ cup chopped fresh flat-leaf parsley leaves
¼ cup chopped fresh mint leaves
1 small green bell pepper, diced
1 bunch scallions, thinly sliced
2 whole-wheat pita bread rounds, toasted and broken into quarter-sized pieces
Ground sumac for garnish

1. To make the dressing, whisk together the lemon juice, olive oil, garlic, salt, sumac, and pepper in a small bowl. 2. To make the salad, in a large bowl, combine the lettuce, cucumber, tomatoes, parsley, mint, bell pepper, scallions, and pita bread. Toss to combine. Add the dressing and toss again to coat well. 3. Serve immediately sprinkled with sumac.

Per Serving:
calories: 359 | fat: 27g | protein: 6g | carbs: 29g | fiber: 6g | sodium: 777mg

Arugula Salad with Grapes, Goat Cheese, and Za'atar Croutons

Prep time: 10 minutes | Cook time: 10 minutes | Serves 4

Croutons:
2 slices whole wheat bread, cubed
2 teaspoons olive oil, divided
1 teaspoon za'atar
Vinaigrette:
2 tablespoons olive oil
1 tablespoon red wine vinegar
½ teaspoon chopped fresh rosemary

¼ teaspoon kosher salt
⅛ teaspoon ground black pepper
Salad:
4 cups baby arugula
1 cup grapes, halved
½ red onion, thinly sliced
2 ounces (57 g) goat cheese, crumbled

1. Make the Croutons: Toss the bread cubes with 1 teaspoon of the oil and the za'atar. In a medium skillet over medium heat, warm the remaining 1 teaspoon oil. Cook the bread cubes, stirring frequently, until browned and crispy, 8 to 10 minutes. 2. Make the Vinaigrette: In a small bowl, whisk together the oil, vinegar, rosemary, salt, and pepper. 3. Make the Salad: In a large bowl, toss the arugula, grapes, and onion with the vinaigrette. Top with the cheese and croutons.

Per Serving:
calories: 204 | fat: 14g | protein: 6g | carbs: 15g | fiber: 2g | sodium: 283mg

Taverna-Style Greek Salad

Prep time: 20 minutes | Cook time: 0 minutes | Serves 4

4 to 5 medium tomatoes, roughly chopped
1 large cucumber, peeled and roughly chopped
1 medium green bell pepper, sliced
1 small red onion, sliced
16 pitted Kalamata olives
¼ cup capers, or more olives

1 teaspoon dried oregano or fresh herbs of your choice, such as parsley, cilantro, chives, or basil, divided
½ cup extra-virgin olive oil, divided
1 pack feta cheese
Optional: salt, pepper, and fresh oregano, for garnish

1. Place the vegetables in a large serving bowl. Add the olives, capers, feta, half of the dried oregano and half of the olive oil. Mix to combine. Place the whole piece of feta cheese on top, sprinkle with the remaining dried oregano, and drizzle with the remaining olive oil. Season to taste and serve immediately, or store in the fridge for up to 1 day.

Per Serving:
calories: 320 | fat: 31g | protein: 3g | carbs: 11g | fiber: 4g | sodium: 445mg

Turkish Shepherd'S Salad

Prep time: 15 minutes | Cook time: 0 minutes | Serves 6

¼ cup extra-virgin olive oil
2 tablespoons apple cider vinegar
2 tablespoons lemon juice
½ teaspoon kosher salt
¼ teaspoon ground black pepper
3 plum tomatoes, seeded and chopped
2 cucumbers, seeded and chopped
1 red bell pepper, seeded and chopped

1 green bell pepper, seeded and chopped
1 small red onion, chopped
⅓ cup pitted black olives (such as kalamata), halved
½ cup chopped fresh flat-leaf parsley
¼ cup chopped fresh mint
¼ cup chopped fresh dill
6 ounces (170 g) feta cheese, cubed

1. In a small bowl, whisk together the oil, vinegar, lemon juice, salt, and black pepper. 2. In a large serving bowl, combine the tomatoes, cucumber, bell peppers, onion, olives, parsley, mint, and dill. Pour the dressing over the salad, toss gently, and sprinkle with the cheese.

Per Serving:
calories: 238 | fat: 20g | protein: 6g | carbs: 10g | fiber: 2g | sodium: 806mg

Tricolor Tomato Summer Salad

Prep time: 10 minutes | Cook time: 0 minutes | Serves 3 to 4

¼ cup while balsamic vinegar
2 tablespoons Dijon mustard
1 tablespoon sugar
½ teaspoon freshly ground black pepper
½ teaspoon garlic salt

¼ cup extra-virgin olive oil
1½ cups chopped orange, yellow, and red tomatoes
½ cucumber, peeled and diced
1 small red onion, thinly sliced
¼ cup crumbled feta (optional)

1. In a small bowl, whisk the vinegar, mustard, sugar, pepper, and garlic salt. Next, slowly whisk in the olive oil. 2. In a large bowl, add the tomatoes, cucumber, and red onion. Add the dressing. Toss once or twice, and serve with feta crumbles (if using) on top.

Per Serving:
calories: 246 | fat: 18g | protein: 1g | carbs: 19g | fiber: 2g | sodium: 483mg

Chapter 13 Desserts

Slow-Cooked Fruit Medley

Prep time: 10 minutes | Cook time: 3 to 5 hours | Serves 4 to 6

Nonstick cooking spray
1 pound (454 g) fresh or frozen fruit of your choice, stemmed and chopped as needed
⅓ cup almond milk or low-sugar fruit juice of your choice
½ cup honey

1. Generously coat a slow cooker with cooking spray, or line the bottom and sides with parchment paper or aluminum foil. 2. In a slow cooker, combine the fruit and milk. Gently stir to mix. 3. Drizzle the fruit with the honey. 4. Cover the cooker and cook for 3 to 5 hours on Low heat.
Per Serving:
calories: 192 | fat: 0g | protein: 1g | carbs: 50g | fiber: 3g | sodium: 27mg

Date and Honey Almond Milk Ice Cream

Prep time: 10 minutes | Cook time: 5 minutes | Serves 4

¾ cup (about 4 ounces/ 113 g) pitted dates
¼ cup honey
½ cup water
2 cups cold unsweetened almond milk
2 teaspoons vanilla extract

1. Combine the dates and water in a small saucepan and bring to a boil over high heat. Remove the pan from the heat, cover, and let stand for 15 minutes. 2. In a blender, combine the almond milk, dates, the date soaking water, honey, and the vanilla and process until very smooth. 3. Cover the blender jar and refrigerate the mixture until cold, at least 1 hour. 4. Transfer the mixture to an electric ice cream maker and freeze according to the manufacturer's instructions. 5. Serve immediately or transfer to a freezer-safe storage container and freeze for 4 hours (or longer). Serve frozen.
Per Serving:
calories: 106 | fat: 2g | protein: 1g | carbs: 23g | fiber: 3g | sodium: 92mg

Baklava and Honey

Prep time: 40 minutes | Cook time: 1 hour | Serves 6 to 8

2 cups very finely chopped walnuts or pecans
1 teaspoon cinnamon
1 cup (2 sticks) of unsalted
butter, melted
1 (16-ounce / 454-g) package phyllo dough, thawed
1 (12-ounce / 340-g) jar honey

1. Preheat the oven to 350°F(180°C). 2. In a bowl, combine the chopped nuts and cinnamon. 3. Using a brush, butter the sides and bottom of a 9-by-13-inch inch baking dish. 4. Remove the phyllo dough from the package and cut it to the size of the baking dish using a sharp knife. 5. Place one sheet of phyllo dough on the bottom of the dish, brush with butter, and repeat until you have 8 layers. 6. Sprinkle ⅓ cup of the nut mixture over the phyllo layers. Top with a sheet of phyllo dough, butter that sheet, and repeat until you have 4 sheets of buttered phyllo dough. 7. Sprinkle ⅓ cup of the nut mixture for another layer of nuts. Repeat the layering of nuts and 4 sheets of buttered phyllo until all the nut mixture is gone. The last layer should be 8 buttered sheets of phyllo. 8. Before you bake, cut the baklava into desired shapes; traditionally this is diamonds, triangles, or squares. 9. Bake the baklava for 1 hour or until the top layer is golden brown. 10. While the baklava is baking, heat the honey in a pan just until it is warm and easy to pour. 11. Once the baklava is done baking, immediately pour the honey evenly over the baklava and let it absorb it, about 20 minutes. Serve warm or at room temperature.
Per Serving:
calories: 1235 | fat: 89g | protein: 18g | carbs: 109g | fiber: 7g | sodium: 588mg

Cretan Cheese Pancakes

Prep time: 15 minutes | Cook time: 25 minutes | Serves 4

2 cups all-purpose flour, plus extra for kneading
½ cup water
2 tablespoons olive oil, plus extra for frying
1 tablespoon freshly squeezed lemon juice
1 tablespoon brandy
1 teaspoon sea salt
5 tablespoons crumbled feta cheese
2 tablespoons olive oil
½ cup chopped nuts of your choice
⅛ to ¼ teaspoon ground cinnamon, for topping
1 tablespoon honey, for drizzling

1. In a large bowl, stir together the flour, water, olive oil, lemon juice, brandy, and salt until a ball of dough forms. Turn the dough out onto a lightly floured surface and knead for 10 minutes. If the dough is too wet, add a little more flour. If it's too dry, add some water. 2. Divide the dough into 5 equal pieces and roll each piece into a ball. Place a dough ball on a lightly floured surface and roll it out into a 6-inch-wide circle about ¼ inch thick. Place 1 tablespoon of the feta in the center, fold the dough over, and knead the dough and cheese together. Once the cheese is well incorporated, roll the dough out flat to the same size. Repeat with the remaining balls of dough. 3. In a large skillet, heat the oil over medium-high heat. Place one round of dough in the skillet and cook for 5 to 6 minutes on each side, until golden brown. Transfer the cooked pancake to a paper towel–lined plate to drain. Repeat to cook the remaining dough pancakes. 4. Sprinkle the pancakes evenly with the nuts and cinnamon, drizzle with the honey, and serve.
Per Serving:
calories: 480 | fat: 24g | protein: 11g | carbs: 57g | fiber: 3g | sodium: 396mg

Chocolate Pudding

Prep time: 10 minutes | Cook time: 0 minutes | Serves 4

2 ripe avocados, halved and pitted
¼ cup unsweetened cocoa powder
¼ cup heavy whipping cream, plus more if needed
2 teaspoons vanilla extract

1 to 2 teaspoons liquid stevia or monk fruit extract (optional)
½ teaspoon ground cinnamon (optional)
¼ teaspoon salt
Whipped cream, for serving (optional)

1. Using a spoon, scoop out the ripe avocado into a blender or large bowl, if using an immersion blender. Mash well with a fork. 2. Add the cocoa powder, heavy whipping cream, vanilla, sweetener (if using), cinnamon (if using), and salt. Blend well until smooth and creamy, adding additional cream, 1 tablespoon at a time, if the mixture is too thick. 3. Cover and refrigerate for at least 1 hour before serving. Serve chilled with additional whipped cream, if desired.

Per Serving:
calories: 205 | fat: 18g | protein: 3g | carbs: 12g | fiber: 9g | sodium: 156mg

Fresh Figs with Chocolate Sauce

Prep time: 5 minutes | Cook time: 0 minutes | Serves 4

¼ cup honey
2 tablespoons cocoa powder

8 fresh figs

1. Combine the honey and cocoa powder in a small bowl, and mix well to form a syrup. 2. Cut the figs in half and place cut side up. Drizzle with the syrup and serve.

Per Serving:
calories: 112 | fat: 1g | protein: 1g | carbs: 30g | fiber: 3g | sodium: 3mg

Tahini Baklava Cups

Prep time: 10 minutes | Cook time: 25 minutes | Serves 8

1 box (about 16) mini phyllo dough cups, thawed
⅓ cup tahini
¼ cup shelled pistachios or walnuts, chopped, plus more for

garnish
4 tablespoons honey, divided
1 teaspoon ground cinnamon
Pinch of kosher salt
½ teaspoon rosewater (optional)

1. Preheat the oven to 350°F(180°C). Remove the phyllo cups from the packaging and place on a large rimmed baking sheet. 2. In a small bowl, stir together the tahini, nuts, 1 tablespoon of the honey, the cinnamon, and salt. Divide this mixture among the phyllo cups and top each with a few more nuts. Bake until golden and warmed through, 10 minutes. Remove from the oven and cool for 5 minutes. 3. Meanwhile, in a small saucepan or in a microwaveable bowl, stir together the remaining 3 tablespoons honey and the rosewater, if using, and heat until warmed, about 5 minutes over medium heat o

Per Serving:
calories: 227 | fat: 9g | protein: 5g | carbs: 32g | fiber: 2g | sodium: 195mg

Spiced Baked Pears with Mascarpone

Prep time: 10 minutes | Cook time: 20 minutes | Serves 2

2 ripe pears, peeled
1 tablespoon plus 2 teaspoons honey, divided
1 teaspoon vanilla, divided
¼ teaspoon ginger

¼ teaspoon ground coriander
¼ cup minced walnuts
¼ cup mascarpone cheese
Pinch salt

1. Preheat the oven to 350°F(180°C) and set the rack to the middle position. Grease a small baking dish. 2. Cut the pears in half lengthwise. Using a spoon, scoop out the core from each piece. Place the pears with the cut side up in the baking dish. 3. Combine 1 tablespoon of honey, ½ teaspoon of vanilla, ginger, and coriander in a small bowl. Pour this mixture evenly over the pear halves. 4. Sprinkle walnuts over the pear halves. 5. Bake for 20 minutes, or until the pears are golden and you're able to pierce them easily with a knife. 6. While the pears are baking, mix the mascarpone cheese with the remaining 2 teaspoons honey, ½ teaspoon of vanilla, and a pinch of salt. Stir well to combine. 7. Divide the mascarpone among the warm pear halves and serve.

Per Serving:
calories: 307 | fat: 16g | protein: 4g | carbs: 43g | fiber: 6g | sodium: 89mg

Steamed Dessert Bread

Prep time: 5 minutes | Cook time: 1 hour | Serves 8

½ cup all-purpose flour
½ cup stone-ground cornmeal
½ cup whole-wheat flour
½ teaspoon baking powder
¼ teaspoon salt

¼ teaspoon baking soda
½ cup maple syrup
½ cup buttermilk
1 large egg
1 cup water

1. Grease the inside of a 6-cup heatproof pudding mold or baking pan. 2. Add flour, cornmeal, whole-wheat flour, baking powder, salt, and baking soda to a medium mixing bowl. Stir to combine. Add maple syrup, buttermilk, and egg to another mixing bowl or measuring cup. Whisk to mix and then pour into the flour mixture. Mix until a thick batter is formed. 3. Pour enough batter into prepared baking pan to fill it three-quarters full. 4. Butter one side of a piece of heavy-duty aluminum foil large enough to cover the top of the baking dish. Place the foil butter side down over the pan and crimp the edges to seal. 5. Add water to the Instant Pot® and place the rack inside. Fold a long piece of aluminum foil in half lengthwise. Lay foil over rack to form a sling. Place pan on rack so it rests on the sling. 6. Close lid, set steam release to Sealing, press the Manual button, set time to 1 hour, and press the Adjust button and set pressure to Low. When the timer beeps, let pressure release naturally, about 25 minutes. 7. Open lid, lift pan from Instant Pot® using the sling, and place on a cooling rack. Remove foil. Test bread with a toothpick. If the toothpick comes out wet, place the foil over the pan and return it to the Instant Pot® to cook for 10 additional minutes. If the bread is done, use a knife to loosen it and invert it onto the cooling rack. Serve warm.

Per Serving:
calories: 175 | fat: 1g | protein: 4g | carbs: 37g | fiber: 2g | sodium: 102mg

Dark Chocolate Bark with Fruit and Nuts

Prep time: 15 minutes | Cook time: 0 minutes | Serves 2

2 tablespoons chopped nuts (almonds, pecans, walnuts, hazelnuts, pistachios, or any combination of those)
3 ounces (85 g) good-quality dark chocolate chips (about ⅔ cup)
¼ cup chopped dried fruit (apricots, blueberries, figs, prunes, or any combination of those)

1. Line a sheet pan with parchment paper. 2. Place the nuts in a skillet over medium-high heat and toast them for 60 seconds, or just until they're fragrant. 3. Place the chocolate in a microwave-safe glass bowl or measuring cup and microwave on high for 1 minute. Stir the chocolate and allow any unmelted chips to warm and melt. If necessary, heat for another 20 to 30 seconds, but keep a close eye on it to make sure it doesn't burn. 4. Pour the chocolate onto the sheet pan. Sprinkle the dried fruit and nuts over the chocolate evenly and gently pat in so they stick. 5. Transfer the sheet pan to the refrigerator for at least 1 hour to let the chocolate harden. 6. When solid, break into pieces. Store any leftover chocolate in the refrigerator or freezer.

Per Serving:
calories: 284 | fat: 16g | protein: 4g | carbs: 39g | fiber: 2g | sodium: 2mg

Grilled Pineapple and Melon

Prep time: 10 minutes | Cook time: 7 minutes | Serves 4

8 fresh pineapple rings, rind removed
8 watermelon triangles, with rind
1 tablespoon honey
½ teaspoon freshly ground black pepper

1. Preheat an outdoor grill or a grill pan over high heat. 2. Drizzle the fruit slices with honey and sprinkle one side of each piece with pepper. Grill for 5 minutes, turn, and grill for another 2 minutes. Serve.

Per Serving:
calories: 244 | fat: 1g | protein: 4g | carbs: 62g | fiber: 4g | sodium: 7mg

Crispy Apple Phyllo Tart

Prep time: 15 minutes | Cook time: 30 minutes | Serves 4

5 teaspoons extra virgin olive oil
2 teaspoons fresh lemon juice
¼ teaspoon ground cinnamon
1½ teaspoons granulated sugar, divided
1 large apple (any variety), peeled and cut into ⅛-inch thick slices
5 phyllo sheets, defrosted
1 teaspoon all-purpose flour
1½ teaspoons apricot jam

1. Preheat the oven to 350°F (180°C). Line a baking sheet with parchment paper, and pour the olive oil into a small dish. Set aside. 2. In a separate small bowl, combine the lemon juice, cinnamon, 1 teaspoon of the sugar, and the apple slices. Mix well to ensure the apple slices are coated in the seasonings. Set aside. 3. On a clean working surface, stack the phyllo sheets one on top of the other. Place a large bowl with an approximate diameter of 15 inches on top of the sheets, then draw a sharp knife around the edge of the bowl to cut out a circle through all 5 sheets. Discard the remaining phyllo. 4. Working quickly, place the first sheet on the lined baking sheet and then brush with the olive oil. Repeat the process by placing a second sheet on top of the first sheet, then brushing the second sheet with olive oil. Repeat until all the phyllo sheets are in a single stack. 5. Sprinkle the flour and remaining sugar over the top of the sheets. Arrange the apples in overlapping circles 4 inches from the edge of the phyllo. 6. Fold the edges of the phyllo in and then twist them all around the apple filling to form a crust edge. Brush the edge with the remaining olive oil. Bake for 30 minutes or until the crust is golden and the apples are browned on the edges. 7. While the tart is baking, heat the apricot jam in a small sauce pan over low heat until it's melted. 8. When the tart is done baking, brush the apples with the jam sauce. Slice the tart into 4 equal servings and serve warm. Store at room temperature, covered in plastic wrap, for up to 2 days.

Per Serving:
calories: 165 | fat: 7g | protein: 2g | carbs: 24g | fiber: 2g | sodium: 116mg

Ricotta Cheesecake

Prep time: 2 minutes | Cook time: 45 to 50 minutes | Serves 12

2 cups skim or fat-free ricotta cheese (one 15-ounce / 425-g container)
1¼ cups sugar
1 teaspoon vanilla extract
6 eggs
Zest of 1 orange

1. Preheat the oven to 375ºF (190ºC). Grease an 8-inch square baking pan with butter or cooking spray. 2. In a medium bowl, stir together the ricotta and sugar. Add the eggs one at a time until well incorporated. Stir in the vanilla and orange zest. 3. Pour the batter into the prepared pan. Bake for 45 to 50 minutes, until set. Let cool in the pan for 20 minutes. Serve warm.

Per Serving:
calories: 160 | fat: 5g | protein: 12g | carbs: 15g | fiber: 0g | sodium: 388mg

Crunchy Sesame Cookies

Prep time: 10 minutes | Cook time: 15 minutes | Yield 14 to 16

1 cup sesame seeds, hulled
1 cup sugar
8 tablespoons (1 stick) salted
butter, softened
2 large eggs
1¼ cups flour

1. Preheat the oven to 350°F(180°C). Toast the sesame seeds on a baking sheet for 3 minutes. Set aside and let cool. 2. Using a mixer, cream together the sugar and butter. 3. Add the eggs one at a time until well-blended. 4. Add the flour and toasted sesame seeds and mix until well-blended. 5. Drop spoonfuls of cookie dough onto a baking sheet and form them into round balls, about 1-inch in diameter, similar to a walnut. 6. Put in the oven and bake for 5 to 7 minutes or until golden brown. 7. Let the cookies cool and enjoy.

Per Serving:
calories: 218 | fat: 12g | protein: 4g | carbs: 25g | fiber: 2g | sodium: 58mg

Spanish Cream

Prep time: 5 minutes | Cook time: 0 minutes | Serves 6

3 large eggs
1¼ cups unsweetened almond milk, divided
1 tablespoon gelatin powder
1¼ cups goat's cream, heavy whipping cream, or coconut cream
1 teaspoon vanilla powder or 1

tablespoon unsweetened vanilla extract
1 teaspoon cinnamon, plus more for dusting
½ ounce (14 g) grated 100% chocolate, for topping
Optional: low-carb sweetener, to taste

1. Separate the egg whites from the egg yolks. Place ½ cup (120 ml) of the almond milk in a small bowl, then add the gelatin and let it bloom. 2. Place the yolks, cream, and the remaining ¾ cup (180 ml) almond milk in a heatproof bowl placed over a small saucepan filled with 1 cup (240 ml) of water, placed over medium heat, ensuring that the bottom of the bowl doesn't touch the water. Whisk while heating until the mixture is smooth and thickened. 3. Stir in the vanilla, cinnamon, sweetener (if using), and the bloomed gelatin. Cover with plastic wrap pressed to the surface, and chill for 30 minutes. At this point the mixture will look runny. Don't panic! This is absolutely normal. It will firm up. 4. In a bowl with a hand mixer, or in a stand mixer, whisk the egg whites until stiff, then fold them through the cooled custard. Divide among six serving glasses and chill until fully set, 3 to 4 hours. Sprinkle with the grated chocolate and, optionally, add the sweetener and a dusting of cinnamon. Store covered in the refrigerator for up to 5 days.

Per Serving:
calories: 172 | fat: 13g | protein: 5g | carbs: 7g | fiber: 1g | sodium: 83mg

Banana Cream Pie Parfaits

Prep time: 10 minutes | Cook time: 0 minutes | Serves 2

1 cup nonfat vanilla pudding
2 low-sugar graham crackers, crushed

1 banana, peeled and sliced
¼ cup walnuts, chopped
Honey for drizzling

1. In small parfait dishes or glasses, layer the ingredients, starting with the pudding and ending with chopped walnuts. 2. You can repeat the layers, depending on the size of the glass and your preferences. 3. Drizzle with the honey. Serve chilled.

Per Serving:
calories: 312 | fat: 11g | protein: 7g | carbs: 50g | fiber: 3g | sodium: 273mg

Almond Rice Pudding

Prep time: 5 minutes | Cook time: 45 minutes | Serves 8

1 cup Arborio rice
¼ teaspoon kosher salt
5 cups unsweetened almond milk
2 tablespoons chopped preserved lemon or dried

lemons
½ cup sugar
2 teaspoons vanilla extract
2 tablespoons slivered almonds, toasted (optional)

1. In a medium saucepan, combine the rice, salt, and 2 cups water.

Bring to a boil. Reduce the heat to low-medium, cover the pan with the lid ajar, and cook until the water has been almost completely absorbed, 6 to 8 minutes, stirring occasionally. 2. Stir in the almond milk, sugar, dried or preserved lemon, and vanilla. Bring the mixture to a simmer, stirring occasionally, and cook until the rice is tender and the mixture has thickened, 30 to 35 minutes. Let cool slightly before serving. 3. Serve warm, topped with toasted almonds, if desired.

Per Serving:
calories: 203 | fat: 10g | protein: 9g | carbs: 23g | fiber: 4g | sodium: 146mg

Fruit Compote

Prep time: 15 minutes | Cook time: 11 minutes | Serves 6

1 cup apple juice
1 cup dry white wine
2 tablespoons honey
1 cinnamon stick
¼ teaspoon ground nutmeg
1 tablespoon grated lemon zest
1½ tablespoons grated orange

zest
3 large apples, peeled, cored, and chopped
3 large pears, peeled, cored, and chopped
½ cup dried cherries

1. Place all ingredients in the Instant Pot® and stir well. Close lid, set steam release to Sealing, press the Manual button, and set time to 1 minute. When the timer beeps, quick-release the pressure until the float valve drops. Press the Cancel button and open lid. 2. Use a slotted spoon to transfer fruit to a serving bowl. Remove and discard cinnamon stick. Press the Sauté button and bring juice in the pot to a boil. Cook, stirring constantly, until reduced to a syrup that will coat the back of a spoon, about 10 minutes. 3. Stir syrup into fruit mixture. Allow to cool slightly, then cover with plastic wrap and refrigerate overnight.

Per Serving:
calories: 211 | fat: 1g | protein: 2g | carbs: 44g | fiber: 5g | sodium: 7mg

Almond Cookies

Prep time: 5 minutes | Cook time: 10 minutes |
Serves 4 to 6

½ cup sugar
8 tablespoons (1 stick) room temperature salted butter
1 large egg

1½ cups all-purpose flour
1 cup ground almonds or almond flour

1. Preheat the oven to 375°F(190°C). 2. Using a mixer, cream together the sugar and butter. 3. Add the egg and mix until combined. 4. Alternately add the flour and ground almonds, ½ cup at a time, while the mixer is on slow. 5. Once everything is combined, line a baking sheet with parchment paper. Drop a tablespoon of dough on the baking sheet, keeping the cookies at least 2 inches apart. 6. Put the baking sheet in the oven and bake just until the cookies start to turn brown around the edges, about 5 to 7 minutes.

Per Serving:
calories: 604 | fat: 36g | protein: 11g | carbs: 63g | fiber: 4g | sodium: 181mg

Cocoa and Coconut Banana Slices

Prep time: 10 minutes | Cook time: 0 minutes | Serves 1

1 banana, peeled and sliced
2 tablespoons unsweetened, shredded coconut

1 tablespoon unsweetened cocoa powder
1 teaspoon honey

1. Lay the banana slices on a parchment-lined baking sheet in a single layer. Put in the freezer for about 10 minutes, until firm but not frozen solid. Mix the coconut with the cocoa powder in a small bowl. 2. Roll the banana slices in honey, followed by the coconut mixture. 3. You can either eat immediately or put back in the freezer for a frozen, sweet treat.

Per Serving:
calories: 187 | fat: 4g | protein: 3g | carbs: 41g | fiber: 6g | sodium: 33mg

Golden Coconut Cream Pops

Prep time: 5 minutes | Cook time: 0 minutes | Makes 8 cream pops

1½ cups coconut cream
½ cup coconut milk
4 egg yolks
2 teaspoons ground turmeric
1 teaspoon ground ginger
1 teaspoon cinnamon
1 teaspoon vanilla powder or 1

tablespoon unsweetened vanilla extract
¼ teaspoon ground black pepper
Optional: low-carb sweetener, to taste

1. Place all of the ingredients in a blender (including the optional sweetener) and process until well combined. Pour into eight ⅓-cup (80 ml) ice pop molds. Freeze until solid for 3 hours, or until set. 2. To easily remove the ice pops from the molds, fill a pot as tall as the ice pops with warm (not hot) water and dip the ice pop molds in for 15 to 20 seconds. Remove the ice pops from the molds and then freeze again. Store in the freezer in a resealable bag for up to 3 months.

Per Serving:
calories: 219 | fat: 21g | protein: 3g | carbs: 5g | fiber: 2g | sodium: 9mg

Figs with Mascarpone and Honey

Prep time: 5 minutes | Cook time: 5 minutes | Serves 4

⅓ cup walnuts, chopped
8 fresh figs, halved
¼ cup mascarpone cheese

1 tablespoon honey
¼ teaspoon flaked sea salt

1. In a skillet over medium heat, toast the walnuts, stirring often, 3 to 5 minutes. 2. Arrange the figs cut-side up on a plate or platter. Using your finger, make a small depression in the cut side of each fig and fill with mascarpone cheese. Sprinkle with a bit of the walnuts, drizzle with the honey, and add a tiny pinch of sea salt.

Per Serving:
calories: 200 | fat: 13g | protein: 3g | carbs: 24g | fiber: 3g | sodium: 105mg

Loukoumades (Honey Dumplings)

Prep time: 10 minutes | Cook time: 35 minutes | Serves 24

4 cups olive oil or vegetable oil
1 cup all-purpose flour
¾ cup whole wheat flour
½ cup sugar
1 teaspoon baking powder
½ teaspoon table salt
½ teaspoon ground cardamom
¼ teaspoon baking soda
⅓ cup buttermilk

⅓ cup fresh orange juice
1 egg
2 tablespoons olive oil
½ cup honey
3 tablespoons fresh lemon juice
1 teaspoon ground cinnamon
2 tablespoons finely ground walnuts or pistachios, or sesame seeds

1. In a 4-quart heavy-bottom pot fitted with an oil thermometer over medium heat, warm the 4 cups oil until it reaches 375ºF. (This will take about 15 minutes.) Line a baking sheet with paper towels. 2. In a large bowl, whisk together the flours, sugar, baking powder, salt, cardamom, and baking soda. 3. In a separate medium bowl, whisk together the buttermilk, orange juice, egg, and the 2 tablespoons oil. Add the buttermilk mixture to the flour mixture and stir until just combined. The dough will be sticky. 4. Turn the dough out onto a well-floured work surface and with floured hands, pat down into a square ½' thick. With a floured pastry cutter, cut the dough into 1' squares. 5. With floured hands, gently roll 8 of the dough squares into balls and carefully lower them into the oil. Fry until deeply golden, about 50 seconds on each side. (They should turn over all on their own.) Constantly monitor the heat to maintain oil temperature. 6. Remove the dumplings with a slotted spoon to the baking sheet to drain. Repeat with the remaining dough. 7. Meanwhile, in a small saucepan over medium heat, warm the honey, lemon juice, and cinnamon, stirring until combined, about 5 minutes. 8. Transfer the dumplings to a serving platter and drizzle with the warm honey mixture. Top with the nuts or sesame seeds. Alternatively, serve 2 loukoumades per person, drizzled with 1 teaspoon of the honey syrup and a pinch of nuts or sesame seeds.

Per Serving:
calories: 170 | fat: 11g | protein: 2g | carbs: 18g | fiber: 1g | sodium: 90mg

Strawberry Ricotta Parfaits

Prep time: 10 minutes | Cook time: 0 minutes | Serves 4

2 cups ricotta cheese
¼ cup honey
2 cups sliced strawberries
1 teaspoon sugar

Toppings such as sliced almonds, fresh mint, and lemon zest (optional)

1. In a medium bowl, whisk together the ricotta and honey until well blended. Place the bowl in the refrigerator for a few minutes to firm up the mixture. 2. In a medium bowl, toss together the strawberries and sugar. 3. In each of four small glasses, layer 1 tablespoon of the ricotta mixture, then top with a layer of the strawberries and finally another layer of the ricotta. 4. Finish with your preferred toppings, if desired, then serve.

Per Serving:
calories: 311 | fat: 16g | protein: 14g | carbs: 29g | fiber: 2g | sodium: 106mg

Toasted Almonds with Honey

Prep time: 15 minutes | Cook time: 5 minutes | Serves 4

½ cup raw almonds
3 tablespoons good-quality

honey, plus more if desired

1. Fill a medium saucepan three-quarters full with water and bring to a boil over high heat. Add the almonds and cook for 1 minute. Drain the almonds in a fine-mesh sieve and rinse them under cold water to cool and stop the cooking. Remove the skins from the almonds by rubbing them in a clean kitchen towel. Place the almonds on a paper towel to dry. 2. In the same saucepan, combine the almonds and honey and cook over medium heat until the almonds get a little golden, 4 to 5 minutes. Remove from the heat and let cool completely, about 15 minutes, before serving or storing.

Per Serving:
calories: 151 | fat: 9g | protein: 4g | carbs: 17g | fiber: 2g | sodium: 1mg

Fruit with Mint and Crème Fraîche

Prep time: 10 minutes | Cook time: 0 minutes | Serves 4

4 cups chopped fresh fruit (such as strawberries, honeydew, cantaloupe, watermelon, and blueberries)
1 cup crème fraîche

1 teaspoon sugar (optional)
¼ cup chopped fresh mint leaves, plus mint sprigs for garnish

1. Evenly divide the fruit among four bowls. 2. In a small bowl, mix the crème fraîche and sugar, if desired. Top the fruit with a generous spoonful or two of the crème fraîche. 3. Sprinkle the mint over each bowl, garnish with 1 to 2 whole sprigs of mint, and serve.

Per Serving:
calories: 164 | fat: 12g | protein: 2g | carbs: 14g | fiber: 3g | sodium: 29mg

Almond Pistachio Biscotti

Prep time: 5 minutes | Cook time: 1 hour 20 minutes | Serves 12

2 cups almond flour or hazelnut flour
½ packed cup flax meal
½ teaspoon baking soda
½ teaspoon ground nutmeg
½ teaspoon vanilla powder or 1½ teaspoons unsweetened vanilla extract
¼ teaspoon salt
1 tablespoon fresh lemon zest

2 large eggs
2 tablespoons extra-virgin olive oil
1 tablespoon unsweetened almond extract
1 teaspoon apple cider vinegar or fresh lemon juice
Optional: low-carb sweetener, to taste
⅔ cup unsalted pistachio nuts

1. Preheat the oven to 285°F (140°C) fan assisted or 320°F (160°C) conventional. Line one or two baking trays with parchment paper. 2. In a bowl, mix the almond flour, flax meal, baking soda, nutmeg, vanilla, salt, and lemon zest. Add the eggs, olive oil, almond extract, vinegar, and optional sweetener. Mix well until a dough forms, then mix in the pistachio nuts. 3. Form the dough into a low, wide log shape, about 8 × 5 inches (20 × 13 cm). Place in the oven and bake for about 45 minutes. Remove from oven and let cool for 15 to 20 minutes. Using a sharp knife, cut into 12 slices. 4. Reduce the oven temperature to 250°F (120°C) fan assisted or 285°F (140°C) conventional. Lay the slices very carefully in a flat layer on the lined trays. Bake for 15 to 20 minutes, flip over, and bake for 15 to 20 minutes. 5. Remove from the oven and let the biscotti cool down completely to fully crisp up. Store in a sealed jar for up to 2 weeks.

Per Serving:
calories: 196 | fat: 17g | protein: 7g | carbs: 7g | fiber: 4g | sodium: 138mg

Ricotta-Lemon Cheesecake

Prep time: 5 minutes | Cook time: 1 hour | Serves 8 to 10

2 (8-ounce / 227-g) packages full-fat cream cheese
1 (16-ounce / 454-g) container full-fat ricotta cheese

1½ cups granulated sugar
1 tablespoon lemon zest
5 large eggs
Nonstick cooking spray

1. Preheat the oven to 350°F (180°C) . 2. Using a mixer, blend together the cream cheese and ricotta cheese. 3. Blend in the sugar and lemon zest. 4. Blend in the eggs; drop in 1 egg at a time, blend for 10 seconds, and repeat. 5. Line a 9-inch springform pan with parchment paper and nonstick spray. Wrap the bottom of the pan with foil. Pour the cheesecake batter into the pan. 6. To make a water bath, get a baking or roasting pan larger than the cheesecake pan. Fill the roasting pan about ⅓ of the way up with warm water. Put the cheesecake pan into the water bath. Put the whole thing in the oven and let the cheesecake bake for 1 hour. 7. After baking is complete, remove the cheesecake pan from the water bath and remove the foil. Let the cheesecake cool for 1 hour on the countertop. Then put it in the fridge to cool for at least 3 hours before serving.

Per Serving:
calories: 489 | fat: 31g | protein: 15g | carbs: 42g | fiber: 0g | sodium: 264mg

Minty Watermelon Salad

Prep time: 10 minutes | Cook time: 0 minutes | Serves 6 to 8

1 medium watermelon
1 cup fresh blueberries
2 tablespoons fresh mint leaves

2 tablespoons lemon juice
⅓ cup honey

1. Cut the watermelon into 1-inch cubes. Put them in a bowl. 2. Evenly distribute the blueberries over the watermelon. 3. Finely chop the mint leaves and put them into a separate bowl. 4. Add the lemon juice and honey to the mint and whisk together. 5. Drizzle the mint dressing over the watermelon and blueberries. Serve cold.

Per Serving:
calories: 238 | fat: 1g | protein: 4g | carbs: 61g | fiber: 3g | sodium: 11mg

Grilled Stone Fruit

Prep time: 15 minutes | Cook time: 6 minutes | Serves 2

2 peaches, halved and pitted
2 plums, halved and pitted
3 apricots, halved and pitted
½ cup low-fat ricotta cheese
2 tablespoons honey

1. Heat grill to medium heat. 2. Oil the grates or spray with cooking spray. 3. Place the fruit cut side down on the grill, and grill for 2–3 minutes per side, until lightly charred and soft. 4. Serve warm with the ricotta and drizzle with honey.

Per Serving:
calories: 263 | fat: 6g | protein: 10g | carbs: 48g | fiber: 4g | sodium: 63mg

Greek Yogurt Ricotta Mousse

**Prep time: 1 hour 5 minutes | Cook time: 0 minutes |
Serves 4**

9 ounces (255 g) full-fat ricotta cheese
4½ ounces (128 g) 2% Greek yogurt
3 teaspoons fresh lemon juice
½ teaspoon pure vanilla extract
2 tablespoons granulated sugar

1. Combine all of the ingredients in a food processor. Blend until smooth, about 1 minute. 2. Divide the mousse between 4 serving glasses. Cover and transfer to the refrigerator to chill for 1 hour before serving. Store covered in the refrigerator for up to 4 days.

Per Serving:
calories: 156 | fat: 8g | protein: 10g | carbs: 10g | fiber: 0g | sodium: 65mg

Mediterranean Orange Yogurt Cake

**Prep time: 10 minutes | Cook time: 3 to 5 hours |
Serves 4 to 6**

Nonstick cooking spray
¾ cup all-purpose flour
¾ cup whole-wheat flour
2 teaspoons baking powder
¼ teaspoon salt
1 cup coconut palm sugar
½ cup plain Greek yogurt
½ cup mild-flavored, extra-virgin olive oil
3 large eggs
2 teaspoons vanilla extract
Grated zest of 1 orange
Juice of 1 orange

1. Generously coat a slow cooker with cooking spray, or line the bottom and sides with parchment paper or aluminum foil. 2. In a large bowl, whisk together the all-purpose and whole-wheat flours, baking powder, and salt. 3. In another large bowl, whisk together the sugar, yogurt, olive oil, eggs, vanilla, orange zest, and orange juice until smooth. 4. Add the dry ingredients to the wet ingredients and mix together until well-blended. Pour the batter into the prepared slow cooker. 5. Cover the cooker and cook for 3 to 5 hours on Low heat, or until the middle has set and a knife inserted into it comes out clean.

Per Serving:
calories: 544 | fat: 33g | protein: 11g | carbs: 53g | fiber: 4g | sodium: 482mg

Blueberry Panna Cotta

Prep time: 5 minutes | Cook time: 0 minutes | Serves 6

1 tablespoon gelatin powder
2 tablespoons water
2 cups goat's cream, coconut cream, or heavy whipping cream
2 cups wild blueberries, fresh
or frozen, divided
½ teaspoon vanilla powder or
1½ teaspoons unsweetened vanilla extract
Optional: low-carb sweetener, to taste

1. In a bowl, sprinkle the gelatin powder over the cold water. Set aside to let it bloom. 2. Place the goat's cream, half of the blueberries, and the vanilla in a blender and process until smooth and creamy. Alternatively, use an immersion blender. 3. Pour the blueberry cream into a saucepan. Gently heat; do not boil. Scrape the gelatin into the hot cream mixture together with the sweetener, if using. Mix well until all the gelatin has dissolved. 4. Divide among 6 (4-ounce / 113-g) jars or serving glasses and fill them about two-thirds full, leaving enough space for the remaining blueberries. Place in the fridge for 3 to 4 hours, or until set. 5. When the panna cotta has set, evenly distribute the remaining blueberries among the jars. Serve immediately or store in the fridge for up to 4 days.

Per Serving:
calories: 172 | fat: 15g | protein: 2g | carbs: 8g | fiber: 2g | sodium: 19mg

Pomegranate-Quinoa Dark Chocolate Bark

Prep time: 10 minutes |Cook time: 10 minutes| Serves: 6

Nonstick cooking spray
½ cup uncooked tricolor or regular quinoa
½ teaspoon kosher or sea salt
8 ounces (227 g) dark chocolate
or 1 cup dark chocolate chips
½ cup fresh pomegranate seeds

1. In a medium saucepan coated with nonstick cooking spray over medium heat, toast the uncooked quinoa for 2 to 3 minutes, stirring frequently. Do not let the quinoa burn. Remove the pan from the stove, and mix in the salt. Set aside 2 tablespoons of the toasted quinoa to use for the topping. 2. Break the chocolate into large pieces, and put it in a gallon-size zip-top plastic bag. Using a metal ladle or a meat pounder, pound the chocolate until broken into smaller pieces. (If using chocolate chips, you can skip this step.) Dump the chocolate out of the bag into a medium, microwave-safe bowl and heat for 1 minute on high in the microwave. Stir until the chocolate is completely melted. Mix the toasted quinoa (except the topping you set aside) into the melted chocolate. 3. Line a large, rimmed baking sheet with parchment paper. Pour the chocolate mixture onto the sheet and spread it evenly until the entire pan is covered. Sprinkle the remaining 2 tablespoons of quinoa and the pomegranate seeds on top. Using a spatula or the back of a spoon, press the quinoa and the pomegranate seeds into the chocolate. 4. Freeze the mixture for 10 to 15 minutes, or until set. Remove the bark from the freezer, and break it into about 2-inch jagged pieces. Store in a sealed container or zip-top plastic bag in the refrigerator until ready to serve.

Per Serving:
calories: 290 | fat: 17g | protein: 5g | carbs: 29g | fiber: 6g | sodium: 202mg

Tortilla Fried Pies

Prep time: 10 minutes | Cook time: 5 minutes per batch | Makes 12 pies

12 small flour tortillas (4-inch diameter)
½ cup fig preserves
¼ cup sliced almonds

2 tablespoons shredded, unsweetened coconut
Oil for misting or cooking spray

1. Wrap refrigerated tortillas in damp paper towels and heat in microwave 30 seconds to warm. 2. Working with one tortilla at a time, place 2 teaspoons fig preserves, 1 teaspoon sliced almonds, and ½ teaspoon coconut in the center of each. 3. Moisten outer edges of tortilla all around. 4. Fold one side of tortilla over filling to make a half-moon shape and press down lightly on center. Using the tines of a fork, press down firmly on edges of tortilla to seal in filling. 5. Mist both sides with oil or cooking spray. 6. Place hand pies in air fryer basket close but not overlapping. It's fine to lean some against the sides and corners of the basket. You may need to cook in 2 batches. 7. Air fry at 390ºF (199ºC) for 5 minutes or until lightly browned. Serve hot. 8. Refrigerate any leftover pies in a closed container. To serve later, toss them back in the air fryer basket and cook for 2 or 3 minutes to reheat.

Per Serving:
1 pie: calories: 137 | fat: 4g | protein: 4g | carbs: 22g | fiber: 2g | sodium: 279mg

Chocolate Hazelnut "Powerhouse" Truffles

Prep time: 5 minutes | Cook time: 50 minutes | Makes 12 truffles

Filling:
1¾ cups blanched hazelnuts, divided
½ cup coconut butter
4 tablespoons butter or ¼ cup virgin coconut oil
¼ cup collagen powder
¼ cup raw cacao powder
1 teaspoon vanilla powder or

cinnamon
Optional: low-carb sweetener, to taste
Chocolate Coating:
2½ ounces (71 g) 100% dark chocolate
1 ounce (28 g) cacao butter
Pinch of salt

1. Preheat the oven to 285°F (140°C) fan assisted or 320°F (160°C) conventional. 2. To make the filling: Spread the hazelnuts on a baking tray and roast for 40 to 50 minutes, until lightly golden. Remove from the oven and let cool for a few minutes. 3. Place 1 cup of the roasted hazelnuts in a food processor. Process for 1 to 2 minutes, until chunky. Add the coconut butter, butter, collagen powder, cacao powder, vanilla, and sweetener, if using. Process again until well combined. Place the dough in the fridge to set for 1 hour. 4. Reserve 12 hazelnuts for filling and crumble the remaining hazelnuts unto small pieces. 5. To make the chocolate coating: Line a baking tray with parchment. Melt the dark chocolate and cacao butter in a double boiler, or use a heatproof bowl placed over a small saucepan filled with 1 cup of water, placed over medium heat. Remove from the heat and let cool to room temperature before using for coating. Alternatively, use a microwave and melt in short 10- to 15-second bursts until melted, stirring in between. 6. Remove the dough from the fridge and use a spoon to scoop about 1 ounce (28 g) of the dough. Press one whole hazelnut into the center and use your hands to wrap the dough around to create a truffle. Place in the freezer for about 15 minutes. 7. Gently pierce each very cold truffle with a toothpick or a fork. Working one at a time, hold the truffle over the melted chocolate and spoon the chocolate over it to coat completely. Turn the toothpick as you work until the coating is solidified. Place the coated truffles on the lined tray and drizzle any remaining coating over them. Before they become completely solid, roll them in the chopped nuts. Refrigerate the coated truffles for at least 15 minutes to harden. 8. Keep refrigerated for up to 1 week or freeze for up to 3 months.

Per Serving:
calories: 231 | fat: 22g | protein: 4g | carbs: 8g | fiber: 4g | sodium: 3mg

Red Grapefruit Granita

Prep time: 5 minutes | Cook time: 0 minutes | Serves 4 to 6

3 cups red grapefruit sections
1 cup freshly squeezed red grapefruit juice
¼ cup honey

1 tablespoon freshly squeezed lime juice
Fresh basil leaves for garnish

1. Remove as much pith (white part) and membrane as possible from the grapefruit segments. 2. Combine all ingredients except the basil in a blender or food processor and pulse just until smooth. 3. Pour the mixture into a shallow glass baking dish and place in the freezer for 1 hour. Stir with a fork and freeze for another 30 minutes, then repeat. To serve, scoop into small dessert glasses and garnish with fresh basil leaves.

Per Serving:
calories: 94 | fat: 0g | protein: 1g | carbs: 24g | fiber: 1g | sodium: 1mg

Red Wine–Poached Figs with Ricotta and Almond

Prep time: 5 minutes | Cook time: 1 minute | Serves 4

2 cups water
2 cups red wine
¼ cup honey
1 cinnamon stick
1 star anise
1 teaspoon vanilla bean paste

12 dried mission figs
1 cup ricotta cheese
1 tablespoon confectioners' sugar
¼ teaspoon almond extract
1 cup toasted sliced almonds

1. Add water, wine, honey, cinnamon, star anise, and vanilla to the Instant Pot® and whisk well. Add figs, close lid, set steam release to Sealing, press the Manual button, and set time to 1 minute. 2. When the timer beeps, quick-release the pressure until the float valve drops. Press the Cancel button and open lid. With a slotted spoon, transfer figs to a plate and set aside to cool for 5 minutes. 3. In a small bowl, mix together ricotta, sugar, and almond extract. Serve figs with a dollop of sweetened ricotta and a sprinkling of almonds.

Per Serving:
calories: 597 | fat: 21g | protein: 13g | carbs: 56g | fiber: 9g | sodium: 255mg

Creamy Spiced Almond Milk

Prep time: 5 minutes | Cook time: 1 minute | Serves 6

1 cup raw almonds	1 teaspoon vanilla bean paste
5 cups filtered water, divided	½ teaspoon pumpkin pie spice

1. Add almonds and 1 cup water to the Instant Pot®. Close lid, set steam release to Sealing, press the Manual button, and set time to 1 minute. 2. When the timer beeps, quick-release the pressure until the float valve drops. Press the Cancel button and open lid. Strain almonds and rinse under cool water. Transfer to a high-powered blender with remaining 3.cups water. Purée for 2 minutes on high speed. 4. Pour mixture into a nut milk bag set over a large bowl. Squeeze bag to extract all liquid. Stir in vanilla and pumpkin pie spice. Transfer to a Mason jar or sealed jug and refrigerate for 8 hours. Stir or shake gently before serving.

Per Serving:
calories: 86 | fat: 8g | protein: 3g | carbs: 3g | fiber: 2g | sodium: 0mg

Roasted Plums with Nut Crumble

Prep time: 5 minutes | Cook time: 25 minutes | Serves 4

¼ cup honey	1 tablespoon nuts, coarsely
¼ cup freshly squeezed orange juice	chopped (your choice; I like almonds, pecans, and walnuts)
4 large plums, halved and pitted	1½ teaspoons canola oil
¼ cup whole-wheat pastry flour	½ cup plain Greek yogurt
1 tablespoon pure maple sugar	

1. Preheat the oven to 400°F (205°C). Combine the honey and orange juice in a square baking dish. Place the plums, cut-side down, in the dish. Roast about 15 minutes, and then turn the plums over and roast an additional 10 minutes, or until tender and juicy. 2. In a medium bowl, combine the flour, maple sugar, nuts, and canola oil and mix well. Spread on a small baking sheet and bake alongside the plums, tossing once, until golden brown, about 5 minutes. Set aside until the plums have finished cooking. 3. Serve the plums drizzled with pan juices and topped with the nut crumble and a dollop of yogurt.

Per Serving:
calories: 175 | fat: 3g | protein: 4g | carbs: 36g | fiber: 2g | sodium: 10mg

Cranberry-Orange Cheesecake Pears

Prep time: 10 minutes | Cook time: 30 minutes | Serves 5

5 firm pears	½ cup low-fat cream cheese,
1 cup unsweetened cranberry juice	softened
1 cup freshly squeezed orange juice	¼ teaspoon ground ginger
	¼ teaspoon almond extract
1 tablespoon pure vanilla extract	¼ cup dried, unsweetened cranberries
½ teaspoon ground cinnamon	¼ cup sliced almonds, toasted

1. Peel the pears and slice off the bottoms so they sit upright. Remove the inside cores, and put the pears in a wide saucepan.

2. Add the cranberry and orange juice, as well as the vanilla and cinnamon extract. 3. Bring to a boil, and reduce to a simmer. 4. Cover and simmer on low heat for 25–30 minutes, until pears are soft but not falling apart. 5. Beat the cream cheese with the ginger and almond extract. 6. Stir the cranberries and almonds into the cream cheese mixture. 7. Once the pears have cooled, spoon the cream cheese into them. 8. Boil the remaining juices down to a syrup, and drizzle over the top of the filled pears.

Per Serving:
calories: 187 | fat: 6g | protein: 4g | carbs: 29g | fiber: 6g | sodium: 88mg

Creamy Rice Pudding

Prep time: 5 minutes | Cook time: 45 minutes | Serves 6

1¼ cups long-grain rice	1 tablespoon rose water or
5 cups whole milk	orange blossom water
1 cup sugar	1 teaspoon cinnamon

1. Rinse the rice under cold water for 30 seconds. 2. Put the rice, milk, and sugar in a large pot. Bring to a gentle boil while continually stirring. 3. Turn the heat down to low and let simmer for 40 to 45 minutes, stirring every 3 to 4 minutes so that the rice does not stick to the bottom of the pot. 4. Add the rose water at the end and simmer for 5 minutes. 5. Divide the pudding into 6 bowls. Sprinkle the top with cinnamon. Cool for at least 1 hour before serving. Store in the fridge.

Per Serving:
calories: 394 | fat: 7g | protein: 9g | carbs: 75g | fiber: 1g | sodium: 102mg

Olive Oil Ice Cream

Prep time: 5 minutes | Cook time: 25 minutes | Serves 8

4 large egg yolks	cup whole milk
⅓ cup powdered sugar-free sweetener (such as stevia or monk fruit extract)	1 teaspoon vanilla extract
	⅛ teaspoon salt
2 cups half-and-half or 1 cup heavy whipping cream and 1	¼ cup light fruity extra-virgin olive oil

1. Freeze the bowl of an ice cream maker for at least 12 hours or overnight. 2. In a large bowl, whisk together the egg yolks and sugar-free sweetener. 3. In a small saucepan, heat the half-and-half over medium heat until just below a boil. Remove from the heat and allow to cool slightly. 4. Slowly pour the warm half-and-half into the egg mixture, whisking constantly to avoid cooking the eggs. Return the eggs and cream to the saucepan over low heat. 5. Whisking constantly, cook over low heat until thickened, 15 to 20 minutes. Remove from the heat and stir in the vanilla extract and salt. Whisk in the olive oil and transfer to a glass bowl. Allow to cool, cover, and refrigerate for at least 6 hours. 6. Freeze custard in an ice cream maker according to manufacturer's directions.

Per Serving:
calories: 168 | fat: 15g | protein: 2g | carbs: 8g | fiber: 0g | sodium: 49mg

Blueberry Pomegranate Granita

Prep time: 5 minutes | Cook time: 10 minutes | Serves 2

1 cup frozen wild blueberries
1 cup pomegranate or pomegranate blueberry juice
¼ cup sugar
¼ cup water

1. Combine the frozen blueberries and pomegranate juice in a saucepan and bring to a boil. Reduce the heat and simmer for 5 minutes, or until the blueberries start to break down. 2. While the juice and berries are cooking, combine the sugar and water in a small microwave-safe bowl. Microwave for 60 seconds, or until it comes to a rolling boil. Stir to make sure all of the sugar is dissolved and set the syrup aside. 3. Combine the blueberry mixture and the sugar syrup in a blender and blend for 1 minute, or until the fruit is completely puréed. 4. Pour the mixture into an 8-by-8-inch baking pan or a similar-sized bowl. The liquid should come about ½ inch up the sides. Let the mixture cool for 30 minutes, and then put it into the freezer. 5. Every 30 minutes for the next 2 hours, scrape the granita with a fork to keep it from freezing solid. 6. Serve it after 2 hours, or store it in a covered container in the freezer.

Per Serving:
calories: 214 | fat: 0g | protein: 1g | carbs: 54g | fiber: 2g | sodium: 15mg

Apple and Brown Rice Pudding

Prep time: 10 minutes | Cook time: 20 minutes | Serves 6

2 cups almond milk
1 cup long-grain brown rice
½ cup golden raisins
1 Granny Smith apple, peeled,
cored, and chopped
¼ cup honey
1 teaspoon vanilla extract
½ teaspoon ground cinnamon

1. Place all ingredients in the Instant Pot®. Stir to combine. Close lid, set steam release to Sealing, press the Manual button, and set time to 20 minutes. 2. When the timer beeps, let pressure release naturally for 15 minutes, then quick-release the remaining pressure. Press the Cancel button and open lid. Serve warm or at room temperature.

Per Serving:
calories: 218 | fat: 2g | protein: 3g | carbs: 51g | fiber: 4g | sodium: 54mg

Poached Apricots and Pistachios with Greek Yogurt

Prep time: 2 minutes | Cook time: 18 minutes | Serves 4

½ cup orange juice
2 tablespoons brandy
2 tablespoons honey
¾ cup water
1 cinnamon stick
12 dried apricots
⅓ cup 2% Greek yogurt
2 tablespoons mascarpone cheese
2 tablespoons shelled pistachios

1. Place a saucepan over medium heat and add the orange juice, brandy, honey, and water. Stir to combine, then add the cinnamon stick. 2. Once the honey has dissolved, add the apricots. Bring the mixture to a boil, then cover, reduce the heat to low, and simmer for 15 minutes. 3. While the apricots are simmering, combine the Greek yogurt and mascarpone cheese in a small serving bowl. Stir until smooth, then set aside. 4. When the cooking time for the apricots is complete, uncover, add the pistachios, and continue simmering for 3 more minutes. Remove the pan from the heat. 5. To serve, divide the Greek yogurt–mascarpone cheese mixture into 4 serving bowls and top each serving with 3 apricots, a few pistachios, and 1 teaspoon of the syrup. The apricots and syrup can be stored in a jar at room temperature for up to 1 month.

Per Serving:
calories: 146 | fat: 3g | protein: 4g | carbs: 28g | fiber: 4g | sodium: 62mg

Strawberry Panna Cotta

Prep time: 10 minutes | Cook time: 10 minutes | Serves 4

2 tablespoons warm water
2 teaspoons gelatin powder
2 cups heavy cream
1 cup sliced strawberries, plus more for garnish
1 to 2 tablespoons sugar-free
sweetener of choice (optional)
1½ teaspoons pure vanilla extract
4 to 6 fresh mint leaves, for garnish (optional)

1. Pour the warm water into a small bowl. Sprinkle the gelatin over the water and stir well to dissolve. Allow the mixture to sit for 10 minutes. 2. In a blender or a large bowl, if using an immersion blender, combine the cream, strawberries, sweetener (if using), and vanilla. Blend until the mixture is smooth and the strawberries are well puréed. 3. Transfer the mixture to a saucepan and heat over medium-low heat until just below a simmer. Remove from the heat and cool for 5 minutes. 4. Whisking constantly, add in the gelatin mixture until smooth. Divide the custard between ramekins or small glass bowls, cover and refrigerate until set, 4 to 6 hours. 5. Serve chilled, garnishing with additional sliced strawberries or mint leaves (if using).

Per Serving:
calories: 229 | fat: 22g | protein: 3g | carbs: 5g | fiber: 1g | sodium: 26mg

Dark Chocolate Lava Cake

Prep time: 5 minutes | Cook time: 10 minutes | Serves 4

Olive oil cooking spray
¼ cup whole wheat flour
1 tablespoon unsweetened dark chocolate cocoa powder
⅛ teaspoon salt
½ teaspoon baking powder
¼ cup raw honey
1 egg
2 tablespoons olive oil

1. Preheat the air fryer to 380°F(193°C). Lightly coat the insides of four ramekins with olive oil cooking spray. 2. In a medium bowl, combine the flour, cocoa powder, salt, baking powder, honey, egg, and olive oil. 3. Divide the batter evenly among the ramekins. 4. Place the filled ramekins inside the air fryer and bake for 10 minutes. 5. Remove the lava cakes from the air fryer and slide a knife around the outside edge of each cake. Turn each ramekin upside down on a saucer and serve.

Per Serving:
calories: 179 | fat: 8g | protein: 3g | carbs: 26g | fiber: 1g | sodium: 95mg

Peaches Poached in Rose Water

Prep time: 15 minutes | Cook time: 1 minute | Serves 6

1 cup water
1 cup rose water
¼ cup wildflower honey
8 green cardamom pods, lightly crushed

1 teaspoon vanilla bean paste
6 large yellow peaches, pitted and quartered
½ cup chopped unsalted roasted pistachio meats

1. Add water, rose water, honey, cardamom, and vanilla to the Instant Pot®. Whisk well, then add peaches. Close lid, set steam release to Sealing, press the Manual button, and set time to 1 minute. 2. When the timer beeps, quick-release the pressure until the float valve drops. Press the Cancel button and open lid. Allow peaches to stand for 10 minutes. Carefully remove peaches from poaching liquid with a slotted spoon. 3. Slip skins from peach slices. Arrange slices on a plate and garnish with pistachios. Serve warm or at room temperature.

Per Serving:
calories: 145 | fat: 3g | protein: 2g | carbs: 28g | fiber: 2g | sodium: 8mg

Chocolate-Dipped Fruit Bites

Prep time: 10 minutes | Cook time: 0 minutes | Serves 4 to 6

½ cup semisweet chocolate chips
¼ cup low-fat milk
½ teaspoon pure vanilla extract
½ teaspoon ground nutmeg

¼ teaspoon salt
2 kiwis, peeled and sliced
1 cup honeydew melon chunks (about 2-inch chunks)
1 pound (454 g) whole strawberries

1. Place the chocolate chips in a small bowl. 2. In another small bowl, microwave the milk until hot, about 30 seconds. Pour the milk over the chocolate chips and let sit for 1 minute, then whisk until the chocolate is melted and smooth. Stir in the vanilla, nutmeg, and salt and allow to cool for 5 minutes. 3. Line a baking sheet with wax paper. Dip each piece of fruit halfway into the chocolate, tap gently to remove excess chocolate, and place the fruit on the baking sheet. 4. Once all the fruit has been dipped, allow it to sit until dry, about 30 minutes. Arrange on a platter and serve.

Per Serving:
calories: 125 | fat: 5g | protein: 2g | carbs: 21g | fiber: 3g | sodium: 110mg

Chapter 14 Staples, Sauces, Dips, and Dressings

Sofrito

Prep time: 10 minutes | Cook time: 10 minutes | Serves 8 to 10

4 tablespoons olive oil
1 small onion, chopped
1 medium green bell pepper, seeded and chopped
¼ teaspoon salt
6 garlic cloves, minced
½ teaspoon red pepper flakes

¼ teaspoon freshly ground black pepper
1 cup finely chopped fresh cilantro
2 tablespoons red wine vinegar or sherry vinegar

1. In a 10-inch skillet, heat 2 tablespoons of the olive oil over medium-high heat. Add the onion, bell pepper, and salt. Cook, stirring occasionally, for 6 to 8 minutes, until softened. 2. Add the garlic, red pepper flakes, and black pepper; cook for 1 minute. 3. Transfer the vegetables to a blender or food processor and add the remaining 2 tablespoons olive oil, the cilantro, and the vinegar. Blend until smooth.

Per Serving:
calories: 63 | fat: 6g | protein: 0g | carbs: 2g | fiber: 0g | sodium: 67mg

Classic Basil Pesto

Prep time: 5 minutes | Cook time: 13 minutes | Makes about 1½ cups

6 garlic cloves, unpeeled
½ cup pine nuts
4 cups fresh basil leaves
¼ cup fresh parsley leaves

1 cup extra-virgin olive oil
1 ounce (28 g) Parmesan cheese, grated fine (½ cup)

1. Toast garlic in 8-inch skillet over medium heat, shaking skillet occasionally, until softened and spotty brown, about 8 minutes. When garlic is cool enough to handle, remove and discard skins and chop coarsely. Meanwhile, toast pine nuts in now-empty skillet over medium heat, stirring often, until golden and fragrant, 4 to 5 minutes. 2. Place basil and parsley in 1-gallon zipper-lock bag. Pound bag with flat side of meat pounder or with rolling pin until all leaves are bruised. 3. Process garlic, pine nuts, and herbs in food processor until finely chopped, about 1 minute, scraping down sides of bowl as needed. With processor running, slowly add oil until incorporated. Transfer pesto to bowl, stir in Parmesan, and season with salt and pepper to taste. (Pesto can be refrigerated for up to 3 days or frozen for up to 3 months. To prevent browning, press plastic wrap flush to surface or top with thin layer of olive oil.

Bring to room temperature before using.)
Per Serving:
¼ cup: calories: 423 | fat: 45g | protein: 4g | carbs: 4g | fiber: 1g | sodium: 89mg

Chermoula

Prep time: 10 minutes | Cook time: 0 minutes | Makes about 1½ cups

2¼ cups fresh cilantro leaves
8 garlic cloves, minced
1½ teaspoons ground cumin
1½ teaspoons paprika
½ teaspoon cayenne pepper

½ teaspoon table salt
6 tablespoons lemon juice (2 lemons)
¾ cup extra-virgin olive oil

1. Pulse cilantro, garlic, cumin, paprika, cayenne, and salt in food processor until cilantro is coarsely chopped, about 10 pulses. Add lemon juice and pulse briefly to combine. Transfer mixture to medium bowl and slowly whisk in oil until incorporated and mixture is emulsified. Cover and let sit at room temperature for at least 30 minutes to allow flavors to meld. (Sauce can be refrigerated for up to 2 days; bring to room temperature before serving.)

Per Serving:
¼ cup: calories: 253 | fat: 27g | protein: 1g | carbs: 3g | fiber: 1g | sodium: 199mg

Crunchy Yogurt Dip

Prep time: 5 minutes | Cook time: 0 minutes | Serves 2 to 3

1 cup plain, unsweetened, full-fat Greek yogurt
½ cup cucumber, peeled, seeded, and diced
1 tablespoon freshly squeezed lemon juice

1 tablespoon chopped fresh mint
1 small garlic clove, minced
Salt
Freshly ground black pepper

1. In a food processor, combine the yogurt, cucumber, lemon juice, mint, and garlic. Pulse several times to combine, leaving noticeable cucumber chunks. 2. Taste and season with salt and pepper.
Per Serving:
calories: 128 | fat: 6g | protein: 11g | carbs: 7g | fiber: 0g | sodium: 47mg

Cider Yogurt Dressing

Prep time: 5 minutes | Cook time: 0 minutes | Serves 2

1 cup plain, unsweetened, full-fat Greek yogurt
½ cup extra-virgin olive oil
1 tablespoon apple cider vinegar
½ lemon, juiced
1 tablespoon chopped fresh

oregano
½ teaspoon dried parsley
½ teaspoon kosher salt
¼ teaspoon garlic powder
¼ teaspoon freshly ground black pepper

1. In a large bowl, combine the yogurt, olive oil, vinegar, lemon juice, oregano, parsley, salt, garlic powder, and pepper and whisk well.

Per Serving:
calories: 402 | fat: 40g | protein: 8g | carbs: 4g | fiber: 1g | sodium: 417mg

Pepper Sauce

Prep time: 10 minutes | Cook time: 20 minutes | Makes 4 cups

2 red hot fresh chiles, seeded
2 dried chiles
½ small yellow onion, roughly chopped

2 garlic cloves, peeled
2 cups water
2 cups white vinegar

1. In a medium saucepan, combine the fresh and dried chiles, onion, garlic, and water. Bring to a simmer and cook for 20 minutes, or until tender. Transfer to a food processor or blender. 2. Add the vinegar and blend until smooth.

Per Serving:
1 cup: calories: 41 | fat: 0g | protein: 1g | carbs: 5g | fiber: 1g | sodium: 11mg

Marinated Artichokes

Prep time: 10 minutes | Cook time: 0 minutes | Makes 2 cups

2 (13¾-ounce / 390-g) cans artichoke hearts, drained and quartered
¾ cup extra-virgin olive oil
4 small garlic cloves, crushed with the back of a knife
1 tablespoon fresh rosemary

leaves
2 teaspoons chopped fresh oregano or 1 teaspoon dried oregano
1 teaspoon red pepper flakes (optional)
1 teaspoon salt

1. In a medium bowl, combine the artichoke hearts, olive oil, garlic, rosemary, oregano, red pepper flakes (if using), and salt. Toss to combine well. 2. Store in an airtight glass container in the refrigerator and marinate for at least 24 hours before using. Store in the refrigerator for up to 2 weeks.

Per Serving:
¼ cup: calories: 228 | fat: 20g | protein: 3g | carbs: 11g | fiber: 5g | sodium: 381mg

Cucumber Yogurt Dip

Prep time: 5 minutes | Cook time: 0 minutes | Serves 2 to 3

1 cup plain, unsweetened, full-fat Greek yogurt
½ cup cucumber, peeled, seeded, and diced
1 tablespoon freshly squeezed lemon juice

1 tablespoon chopped fresh mint
1 small garlic clove, minced
Salt and freshly ground black pepper, to taste

1. In a food processor, combine the yogurt, cucumber, lemon juice, mint, and garlic. Pulse several times to combine, leaving noticeable cucumber chunks. 2. Taste and season with salt and pepper.

Per Serving:
calories: 55 | fat: 3g | protein: 3g | carbs: 5g | fiber: 0g | sodium: 38mg

Peanut Sauce

Prep time: 5 minutes | Cook time: 0 minutes | Serves 4

⅓ cup peanut butter
¼ cup hot water
2 tablespoons soy sauce
2 tablespoons rice vinegar

Juice of 1 lime
1 teaspoon minced fresh ginger
1 teaspoon minced garlic
1 teaspoon black pepper

1. In a blender container, combine the peanut butter, hot water, soy sauce, vinegar, lime juice, ginger, garlic, and pepper. Blend until smooth. 2. Use immediately or store in an airtight container in the refrigerator for a week or more.

Per Serving:
calories: 408 | fat: 33g | protein: 16g | carbs: 18g | fiber: 5g | sodium: 2525mg

Arugula and Walnut Pesto

Prep time: 5 minutes | Cook time: 0 minutes | Serves 8 to 10

6 cups packed arugula
1 cup chopped walnuts
½ cup shredded Parmesan cheese

2 garlic cloves, peeled
½ teaspoon salt
1 cup extra-virgin olive oil

1. In a food processor, combine the arugula, walnuts, cheese, and garlic and process until very finely chopped. Add the salt. With the processor running, stream in the olive oil until well blended. 2. If the mixture seems too thick, add warm water, 1 tablespoon at a time, until smooth and creamy. Store in a sealed container in the refrigerator.

Per Serving:
calories: 292 | fat: 31g | protein: 4g | carbs: 3g | fiber: 1g | sodium: 210mg

Pickled Onions

Prep time: 5 minutes | Cook time: 0 minutes | Serves 8 to 10

3 red onions, finely chopped
½ cup warm water
¼ cup granulated sugar

¼ cup red wine vinegar
1 teaspoon dried oregano

1. In a jar, combine the onions, water, sugar, vinegar, and oregano, then shake well and put it in the refrigerator. The onions will be pickled after 1 hour.

Per Serving:
calories: 40 | fat: 0g | protein: 1g | carbs: 10g | fiber: 1g | sodium: 1mg

Zucchini Noodles

Prep time: 5 minutes | Cook time: 0 minutes | Serves 4

2 medium to large zucchini

1. Cut off and discard the ends of each zucchini and, using a spiralizer set to the smallest setting, spiralize the zucchini to create zoodles. 2. To serve, simply place a ½ cup or so of spiralized zucchini into the bottom of each bowl and spoon a hot sauce over top to "cook" the zoodles to al dente consistency. Use with any of your favorite sauces, or just toss with warmed pesto for a simple and quick meal.

Per Serving:
calories: 27 | fat: 1g | protein: 2g | carbs: 5g | fiber: 2g | sodium: 13mg

Whole-Wheat Pizza Dough

Prep time: 10 minutes | Cook time: 10 to 12 minutes | Makes 1 pound (454 g)

¾ cup hot tap water
½ teaspoon honey
1 envelope quick-rising yeast, (2¼ teaspoons)
1 tablespoon olive oil, plus

more for oiling the bowl
1 cup whole-wheat flour
1 cup all-purpose flour
1 teaspoon salt

1. Preheat the oven to 500°F (260°C). 2. In a non-reactive bowl, stir together the hot water and honey. Sprinkle the yeast over the top, stir to mix, and let sit for about 10 minutes, until foamy. Add 1 tablespoon of olive oil. 3. In a food processor or the bowl of a stand mixer fitted with a dough hook, combine the whole-wheat and all-purpose flours, and the salt. With the food processor or mixer running, slowly add the yeast and water mixture until the dough comes together in a ball. The dough should be quite soft and tacky, but not overly sticky. If it is too dry, you can add warm water 1 tablespoon at a time, mixing after each addition, until the right consistency is achieved. Likewise, if it seems too wet, you can add all-purpose flour, 1 tablespoon at a time, until the desired consistency is achieved. Process for about 1 more minute to knead the dough. 4. Oil a large bowl lightly with olive oil. Put the dough in the bowl and turn to coat with oil. Cover the bowl with a clean dish towel and set it in a warm place (like on your stovetop or in a sunny spot on the kitchen counter) and let rise for 1 hour, during which time it should double in size. 5. Using your hands or a rolling pin, shape the dough into whatever shape you like. Top as desired and bake in a preheated oven for 10 to 12 minutes, until crisp and lightly browned.

Per Serving:
2 ounces / 57 g: calories: 135 | fat: 2g | protein: 5g | carbs: 24g | fiber: 3g | sodium: 294mg

Vinaigrette

Prep time: 5 minutes | Cook time: 0 minutes | Serves 4

2 tablespoons balsamic vinegar
2 large garlic cloves, minced
1 teaspoon dried rosemary, crushed

¼ teaspoon freshly ground black pepper
¼ cup olive oil

1. In a small bowl, whisk together the vinegar, garlic, rosemary, and pepper. While whisking, slowly stream in the olive oil and whisk until emulsified. Store in an airtight container in the refrigerator for up to 3 days.

Per Serving:
1 cup: calories: 129 | fat: 1g | protein: 3g | carbs: 0g | fiber: 0g | sodium: 2mg

Versatile Sandwich Round

Prep time: 5 minutes | Cook time: 2 minutes | Serves 1

3 tablespoons almond flour
1 tablespoon extra-virgin olive oil
1 large egg
½ teaspoon dried rosemary,

oregano, basil, thyme, or garlic powder (optional)
¼ teaspoon baking powder
⅛ teaspoon salt

1. In a microwave-safe ramekin, combine the almond flour, olive oil, egg, rosemary (if using), baking powder, and salt. Mix well with a fork. 2. Microwave for 90 seconds on high. 3. Slide a knife around the edges of ramekin and flip to remove the bread. 4. Slice in half with a serrated knife if you want to use it to make a sandwich.

Per Serving:
calories: 354 | fat: 33g | protein: 12g | carbs: 6g | fiber: 3g | sodium: 388mg

Apple Cider Dressing

Prep time: 5 minutes | Cook time: 0 minutes | Serves 2

2 tablespoons apple cider vinegar
⅓ lemon, juiced

⅓ lemon, zested
Salt and freshly ground black pepper, to taste

1. In a jar, combine the vinegar, lemon juice, and zest. Season with salt and pepper, cover, and shake well.

Per Serving:
calories: 7 | fat: 0g | protein: 0g | carbs: 1g | fiber: 0g | sodium: 1mg

Lemon Tahini Dressing

Prep time: 5 minutes | Cook time: 0 minutes | Makes ½ cup

¼ cup tahini
3 tablespoons lemon juice
3 tablespoons warm water
¼ teaspoon kosher salt

¼ teaspoon pure maple syrup
¼ teaspoon ground cumin
⅛ teaspoon cayenne pepper

1. In a medium bowl, whisk together the tahini, lemon juice, water, salt, maple syrup, cumin, and cayenne pepper until smooth. Place in the refrigerator until ready to serve. Store any leftovers in the refrigerator in an airtight container up to 5 days.

Per Serving:
2 tablespoons: calories: 90 | fat: 7g | protein: 3g | carbs: 5g | fiber: 1g | sodium: 80mg

Harissa Spice Mix

Prep time: 5 minutes | Cook time: 0 minutes | Makes about 7 tablespoons

2 tablespoons ground cumin
4 teaspoons paprika
4 teaspoons ground turmeric
2 teaspoons ground coriander

2 teaspoons chili powder
1 teaspoon garlic powder
1 teaspoon ground caraway seeds
½ teaspoon cayenne powder

1. Place all of the ingredients in a jar. Seal and shake well to combine. Store in a sealed jar at room temperature for up to 6 months.

Per Serving:
1 tablespoon: calories: 21 | fat: 1g | protein: 1g | carbs: 4g | fiber: 2g | sodium: 27mg

White Bean Dip with Garlic and Herbs

Prep time: 10 minutes | Cook time: 30 minutes | Serves 16

1 cup dried white beans, rinsed and drained
3 cloves garlic, peeled and crushed
8 cups water
¼ cup extra-virgin olive oil
¼ cup chopped fresh flat-leaf parsley
1 tablespoon chopped fresh oregano

1 tablespoon chopped fresh tarragon
1 teaspoon chopped fresh thyme leaves
1 teaspoon grated lemon zest
¼ teaspoon salt
¼ teaspoon ground black pepper

1. Place beans and garlic in the Instant Pot® and stir well. Add water, close lid, set steam release to Sealing, press the Manual button, and set time to 30 minutes. 2. When the timer beeps, let pressure release naturally, about 20 minutes. Open lid and check that beans are tender. Press the Cancel button, drain off excess water, and transfer beans and garlic to a food processor with olive oil. Pulse until mixture is smooth with some small chunks. Add parsley, oregano, tarragon, thyme, lemon zest, salt, and pepper, and pulse 3–5 times to mix. Transfer to a storage container and refrigerate for 4.hours or overnight. Serve cold or at room temperature.

Per Serving:
calories: 47 | fat: 3g | protein: 1g | carbs: 3g | fiber: 1g | sodium: 38mg

Olive Tapenade

Prep time: 10 minutes | Cook time: 0 minutes | Makes about 1 cup

¾ cup pitted brine-cured green or black olives, chopped fine
1 small shallot, minced
2 tablespoons extra-virgin olive oil

1 tablespoon capers, rinsed and minced
1½ teaspoons red wine vinegar
1 teaspoon minced fresh oregano

1. Combine all ingredients in bowl. (Tapenade can be refrigerated for up to 1 week.)

Per Serving:
¼ cup: calories: 92 | fat: 9g | protein: 0g | carbs: 2g | fiber: 1g | sodium: 236mg

Appendix 1: Measurement Conversion Chart

MEASUREMENT CONVERSION CHART

VOLUME EQUIVALENTS(DRY)

US STANDARD	METRIC (APPROXIMATE)
1/8 teaspoon	0.5 mL
1/4 teaspoon	1 mL
1/2 teaspoon	2 mL
3/4 teaspoon	4 mL
1 teaspoon	5 mL
1 tablespoon	15 mL
1/4 cup	59 mL
1/2 cup	118 mL
3/4 cup	177 mL
1 cup	235 mL
2 cups	475 mL
3 cups	700 mL
4 cups	1 L

WEIGHT EQUIVALENTS

US STANDARD	METRIC (APPROXIMATE)
1 ounce	28 g
2 ounces	57 g
5 ounces	142 g
10 ounces	284 g
15 ounces	425 g
16 ounces (1 pound)	455 g
1.5 pounds	680 g
2 pounds	907 g

VOLUME EQUIVALENTS(LIQUID)

US STANDARD	US STANDARD (OUNCES)	METRIC (APPROXIMATE)
2 tablespoons	1 fl.oz.	30 mL
1/4 cup	2 fl.oz.	60 mL
1/2 cup	4 fl.oz.	120 mL
1 cup	8 fl.oz.	240 mL
1 1/2 cup	12 fl.oz.	355 mL
2 cups or 1 pint	16 fl.oz.	475 mL
4 cups or 1 quart	32 fl.oz.	1 L
1 gallon	128 fl.oz.	4 L

TEMPERATURES EQUIVALENTS

FAHRENHEIT(F)	CELSIUS(C) (APPROXIMATE)
225 °F	107 °C
250 °F	120 °C
275 °F	135 °C
300 °F	150 °C
325 °F	160 °C
350 °F	180 °C
375 °F	190 °C
400 °F	205 °C
425 °F	220 °C
450 °F	235 °C
475 °F	245 °C
500 °F	260 °C

Appendix 2: The Dirty Dozen and Clean Fifteen

The Dirty Dozen and Clean Fifteen

The Environmental Working Group (EWG) is a nonprofit, nonpartisan organization dedicated to protecting human health and the environment Its mission is to empower people to live healthier lives in a healthier environment. This organization publishes an annual list of the twelve kinds of produce, in sequence, that have the highest amount of pesticide residue-the Dirty Dozen-as well as a list of the fifteen kinds ofproduce that have the least amount of pesticide residue-the Clean Fifteen.

THE DIRTY DOZEN	THE CLEAN FIFTEEN
• The 2016 Dirty Dozen includes the following produce. These are considered among the year's most important produce to buy organic:	• The least critical to buy organically are the Clean Fifteen list. The following are on the 2016 list:

Strawberries	Spinach	Avocados	Papayas
Apples	Tomatoes	Corn	Kiw
Nectarines	Bell peppers	Pineapples	Eggplant
Peaches	Cherry tomatoes	Cabbage	Honeydew
Celery	Cucumbers	Sweet peas	Grapefruit
Grapes	Kale/collard greens	Onions	Cantaloupe
Cherries	Hot peppers	Asparagus	Cauliflower
		Mangos	

• *The Dirty Dozen list contains two additional itemskale/collard greens and hot peppers-because they tend to contain trace levels of highly hazardous pesticides.*

• *Some of the sweet corn sold in the United States are made from genetically engineered (GE) seedstock. Buy organic varieties of these crops to avoid GE produce.*

Appendix 3 Recipes Index

U

V

W

Z